Yamagata Aritomo in the Rise of Modern Japan, 1838–1922

Harvard East Asian Series 60

The East Asian Research Center at Harvard University administers research projects designed to further scholarly understanding of China, Japan, Korea, Vietnam, and adjacent areas.

Field Marshal Prince Yamagata Aritomo

Yamagata Aritomo
in the
Rise of Modern Japan,
1838–1922

Roger F. Hackett

Harvard University Press
Cambridge, Massachusetts
1971

Distributed in Great Britain by Oxford University Press, London

Preparation of this volume has been aided by a grant from the
Ford Foundation.

Library of Congress Catalog Card Number 74–139719

SBN 674–96301–6

Printed in the United States of America

To Carol

Acknowledgments

With no intention of shifting to others the responsibility for the short-comings of this book, for which I am alone accountable, it is my pleasant obligation to acknowledge the many debts I have accumulated in the course of its completion. I have long awaited an opportunity to express my gratitude to two former teachers and advisers: to Edwin O. Reischauer for his judicious guidance at an early stage of the evolution of this work and to John K. Fairbank for his unflagging encouragement. My thanks also go to Professors Oka Yoshitake, Hayashi Shigeru, and Okubo Toshi-aki, who gave freely of their time and knowledge when I began this study at Tokyo University under a grant generously provided by the Social Science Research Council. A long and rewarding friendship with Professor Umetani Noboru of Osaka University has provided me with valuable insights into modern Japanese history and a constant source of kind assistance. For assistance in translating Yamagata's poetry I wish to thank Mrs. Ueno Tazuko and Professor Saeki Shōichi of Tokyo Metropolitan University.

At various stages I have received financial assistance to carry out the research for this study. I wish to express my appreciation to the East Asian Institute of Columbia University for a research fellowship and to the Carnegie Corporation of New York City for financial aid.

Acknowledgment is made to the University of Nebraska Press for permission to use portions of my article "Yamagata and the Taishō Crisis, 1912–1913," which appeared in *Studies on Asia,* ed. Sidney D. Brown (Lincoln, Nebraska, 1962). I am also indebted to Princeton University Press for permission to use the substance of my chapter "The Meiji Leaders and Modernization: The Case of Yamagata Aritomo," in Marius B. Jansen, ed., *Changing Japanese Attitudes toward Modernization.*

Finally, my heaviest obligation is to my wife, Carol, for her help and understanding at every stage.

Contents

The Appointment of Hara Kei
Hara and Yamagata
The Disengagement from Siberia
The Sad Affair

Yamagata Aritomo

in the

Rise of Modern Japan,

1838–1922

1

The Making of a

Revolutionary Loyalist

How Japan withstood the acute internal strains and surmounted the grave external dangers to which she was exposed in the middle of the nineteenth century and then transformed herself into a modern nation by the end of the century is still the most dramatic episode of Japanese history. Of the many explanations for this rapid transition of Japan from an isolated, backward country to an advanced international power, the least contestable is the brilliant leadership provided by a group of able young men. The commanding guidance they gave to their nation in perilous times is undeniably a major reason for Japan's successful adjustment to the modern world. So a study of this vigorous group that shaped a new nation is a natural and important approach to the history of modern Japan. The careful examination of their careers, the analysis of their motives and aims, affords one of the most useful approaches to the understanding of Japan.

No one figure better represents the leadership of modern Japan than Yamagata Aritomo. He was born in 1838 and lived eighty-four years until 1922, so his life spanned the entire rise of Japan as a modern state. After participating in the movement to restore the emperor to power, he served for over half a century in high positions of authority. Throughout his long career his influence increased steadily so that during this period of Japan's history there were few nationally significant political, military, and administrative developments with which he was not associated. Therefore his career gives us a continuous intimate view of the country from before the Meiji Restoration in 1868 to after the end of World War I.

Yamagata's career was typical of the Meiji oligarchs. He rose from modest beginnings to enter and eventually dominate the small ruling group which led the Restoration and redirected the course of the nation.

Within this oligarchy a careful balance of power was maintained between the representatives of the two western fiefs of Chōshū and Satsuma. Despite this balancing of power and despite the fact that authority tended to rest in a ruling group rather than an individual, it is still possible to discern at different times the dominance of one or two of its members. By the turn of the century there is little doubt that Yamagata occupied a commanding position within the oligarchy. He has been compared to Tokugawa Ieyasu in Japan[1] and to Wellington and Bismarck in the West. Such comparisons are misleading, yet he did hold more power for a longer period than any other individual in modern Japanese history.

How is one to explain this achievement? What were the qualities he possessed and the character of the historical circumstances he encountered that distinguish his rise to the pinnacle of political power? These and other questions about his career must first be approached through the events of his youth and the early experiences which transformed him from an obscure, lowly samurai to a revolutionary activist in the movement to overthrow the political system into which he was born.

Early Years in Hagi

Yamagata Aritomo was born on June 14, 1838, in a small house nestled in a grove of camellia trees along the bank of the Abu River that flowed through the castle town of Hagi. Located at the southwestern tip of the main island of Japan on the coast facing Korea, Hagi was built around the castle headquarters of the prominent Mōri house which governed the domain of Chōshū. Within the shadows of this castle were born many of the outstanding leaders of modern Japanese history: Yoshida Shōin, an intellectual forerunner of the Restoration of 1868; Kusaka Genzui and Takasugi Shinsaku, military leaders in the revolutionary activities culminating in the Restoration; Kido Takayoshi, a key figure in the transition of Japan to a new order; Inoue Kaoru, Itō Hirobumi, and Yamagata Aritomo, leading statesmen of Meiji Japan (1868–1912).

Within the confines of this "cradle of the Restoration," Yamagata spent his youth. Tatsunosuke,[2] as he was first named, was born into a family

1. The title Ōgosho (literally, the Imperial Palace), an honorific title used to refer to Tokugawa Ieyasu, was popularly used in referring to Yamagata in his later years.
2. As was the custom, Yamagata's given name was changed several times in his early years. He was known successively by the names Shōsuke and Kyōsuke before finally assuming, in 1872, the name Aritomo by which he is recognized today. He also used

which, according to genealogical tables, traced its ancestry to one of the Minamoto clans descended from an emperor of the ninth century. But while the genealogy curiously includes impressive details on his remote ancestors, it devotes little space to the eight generations of the Tokugawa period. The names of Minamoto forebears of the tenth and eleventh centuries are carefully listed, but his own great-grandfather and great-great-grandfather are left unidentified.[3] However respectable the lineage may have been, the family's fortunes had gradually declined. Yamagata's father had inherited the rank of *chūgen,* the lowest of twenty-three ranks among the lower category of direct vassals of the daimyo.[4] The *chūgen* rank was organized into six or more groups and attached to branches of the han administration or assigned other specific duties. Yamagata's father was one of 289 *chūgen* attached to the han warehouse and treasury.[5] Although in the military organization of the han to which all ranks and duties were theoretically geared the *chūgen* were trained to bear arms and serve as common soldiers, generations of unbroken peace had accorded them the role of handymen, minor clerks, or even janitors in the various offices of the han government.

The annual stipends of the lowest category of the samurai class were not recorded by the han but, inasmuch as the stipends of the upper samurai varied widely from as high as 16,000 *koku* awarded to the wealthiest Elder (*karō*) house to under fifteen *koku,* the much lower ranking soldiers received far less — probably one to five *koku.*[6] Economically then members of the *chūgen* rank were poor, often poorer than land-owning peasants, although there is no evidence that Yamagata's family was poverty stricken. This low economic status was compensated for, however, by their enjoyment of some of the privileges of

two pen names, Sokyō and Gansetsu, and in signing letters he frequently adopted the name he had given to the residence from where he was writing.

3. The genealogical tables of Yamagata's family appear in Tokutomi Iichirō, *Kōshaku Yamagata Aritomo den* (Tokyo, 1933), I, 1–26 (hereafter cited as *Yamagata den*).

4. The samurai of Chōshū were divided into direct retainers — those with the privilege of approaching the daimyo — and rear vassals. In turn, the upper (*shi,* or knights) and lower (*sotsu,* or soldiers) samurai were separated into seventeen and twenty-three ranks respectively. Together they numbered nearly 11,000 families, or roughly 50,000 persons, out of a total han population of approximately 550,000. A general discussion of the ranks and income differences is found in Suematsu Kenchō, *Bōchō kaiten shi* (Tokyo, 1921), I, 35–68. An excellent analysis of the composition of the Chōshū samurai class is given by Albert M. Craig, *Chōshū in the Meiji Restoration* (Cambridge, Mass., 1961), pp. 98–102.

5. *Yamagata den,* I, 89–90.

6. Suematsu, *Bōchō kaiten shi,* I, 41. A *koku* was equivalent to 4.96 bushels, and in theory was sufficient to feed one person for a year.

CHAPTER ONE

the whole samurai class. They were permitted to carry two swords, dress as samurai, with the exception of the white belt, and use the family surname, except on official documents.[7] Thus while the *chūgen* represented the lowest possible level in the ranks of the retainers of the daimyo, their duties and remuneration were hardly distinguishable from those of the common people. So, however tenuously, Yamagata was born into the advantages reserved for the small ruling class of Tokugawa Japan.

Information is lacking that would permit any detailed reconstruction of Yamagata's childhood experiences. Legends have grown, as for all heroes, to embellish and distort the stories of his early years. It is known that there were four others in the household into which he was born: his parents, an older sister, and a grandmother. His mother died when he was five years old and his grandmother assumed the responsibility for raising him; she has been pictured as a devoted, self-sacrificing woman, dedicated to developing in him the ideals of the samurai. An account in a children's book published by a patriotic organization illustrates his grandmother's character. One day, the story goes, Yamagata was insulted by the neighborhood children's remarks about his father's low rank and started a fight. When he returned, his grandmother admonished him, saying, "The Way of the samurai is to be patient no matter what is said. Samurai must die for loyalty but for other things you should not inflict even a scratch."[8] The stories of her devotion are climaxed by the tale of her suicidal plunge into the Abu River in 1865 when Yamagata was away from home. The reasons prompting this fatal act are explained in a message she allegedly left behind: "If an old woman like me leans upon you, your resolution will become enervated. I, therefore, go to the other world, so that you may concentrate your mind and devote your life to the clan service."[9] To some authors[10] this is an apocryphal tale, but Yamagata himself is quoted as saying, "She committed suicide that I might not be fettered by family ties."[11] The truth of these stories will probably never be known, yet they perhaps reflect accurately the stern and devoted care under which Yamagata was raised.

His father, Yamagata Arinori, had some literary talent and scholarly interests which earned a modest local reputation. In particular, his abil-

7. *Yamagata den,* I, 49.
8. Dai Nihon Yūben Kōdansha, pub., *Yoshida Shōin* (Tokyo, 1941), p. 72.
9. Quoted by Tadashige Matsumoto, *Stories of Fifty Japanese Heroes* (Tokyo, 1929), p. 353.
10. Abe Shinnosuke, "Yamagata Aritomo," *Bungei shunjū* 30.1:224–235 (January 1952).
11. "Prince Yamagata," *America-Japan* 11.2:18 (February 1922).

4

ity to write attractive poems drew favorable attention. These interests
were inherited by Yamagata who, under his father's tutelage and through
private instruction, was schooled in the classical literature of China and
Japan, and at an early age showed that he had acquired his father's
talent for writing poetry. The first evidence of a life-long habit of writing
verse is a thirty-one-syllable poem he wrote at the age of thirteen:

> The sound of falling snow
> fades on the bamboo.
> Near the window
> the moon's shadow pales
> with the dawn of snow.[12]

Yamagata's father died in 1860, five years before his grandmother's suicide and during his twenty-second year. In later years, he acknowledged
his father's encouragement and inspiration by always displaying promi-
nently in his home a scroll on which his father had written a motto
exhorting him to build a strong character.[13]

Yamagata's youth is depicted with the stereotyped attributes of a good
samurai boy: quiet, taciturn, a diligent and able student. But he seems
to have enjoyed the usual games of childhood: throwing stones into the
nearby river, playing tag in the narrow streets of his neighborhood. After
the Russo-Japanese War, when he was the preeminent political figure
of the nation, he learned that the Itsukushima shrine in Hagi which
housed the family tutelary deity was to be combined with another shrine
and nostalgically recalled his youth:

> I yearn for the time
> when we played
> hobbyhorse
> in the shade of the pines
> of the tutelary shrine.[14]

Yamagata's early schooling must have made him keenly aware of how
each samurai family had its proper place in the graded hierarchy of
Chōshū society. The sons of the upper-class as well as the higher ranks
of the lower-class samurai families were educated in the han school,
while the sons of the lowest-ranking samurai were taught at home and
by special instructors. This gave them a less formal and sometimes only
a part-time education, but those of Yamagata's rank read many of the

---

12. *Yamagata den,* I, 52.
13. *Ibid.,* I, 48.
14. *Ibid.,* I, 75.

same basic Confucian treatises learned at the han school and received the same type of intellectual and moral training imparted to all samurai. For all, stress was placed on inculcating the virtues of discipline and loyalty and on instilling the duty to help govern and protect the existing society. Furthermore, all sons of samurai were taught the military arts. From private instructors Yamagata learned to fence, to fight with a spear, and to defend himself with jujitsu. He was an apt pupil of literary texts, and at sixteen his proficiency in fencing and jujitsu was rewarded with a certificate of accomplishment.

This education was pursued while he was employed in a variety of tasks. At the age of thirteen, he was made an errand boy in the treasury office — the first of several jobs in various han administrative offices. Three years later he moved into the han school building as a servant and helper. Next, after successfully passing a short oral examination, he was given a minor position in the local district office, one of sixteen district administrative offices of Chōshū.[15] When he was seventeen, he became an informer in the han police organization. In each of these posts Yamagata appears to have served faithfully and well, a fact which did not escape the notice of his superiors and led in time to his selection for more important duties. However modest his duties, these experiences gave him some familiarity with the administrative organization of the han, and he was made aware that the alert performance of his assignments led to duties of slightly greater responsibility.

That Yamagata was brought up in Hagi to serve the daimyo Mōri as a loyal retainer was itself a major if accidental factor in his life. For despite its changing fortunes, the Mōri house had by the 1830's succeeded in revitalizing its han of Chōshū. Before the Tokugawa shogunate was created, Mōri Terumoto, the most powerful warlord in western Japan, ruled from his castle at Hiroshima over a vast domain with an income of over one million *koku* of rice. For his assistance in unifying Japan at the end of the sixteenth century, Toyotomi Hideyoshi, the great unifier, selected him as one of five daimyo to form a regency during the minority of Hideyoshi's son. When a conflict broke out among the regents, however, Mōri Terumoto was defeated. In the crucial battle of Sekigahara in 1600, he opposed Ieyasu, the commander of the Tokugawa forces. During the battle he was responsible for the defense of Osaka castle, but when he heard of the reversal of other anti-Tokugawa armies at Sekigahara he surrendered to Ieyasu. This move did not produce the leniency he hoped for, and Ieyasu reduced the domain of the Mōri

15. *Ibid.,* I, 102.

family to the two provinces of Nagato and Suō, the westernmost of its possessions, with an officially listed rice production of 396,411 *koku*. Although Chōshū was to be one of the largest and wealthiest among the approximately 270 han of Tokugawa Japan, the drastic reduction in size was a humiliation which was never assuaged. Mortified, Terumoto became a priest and turned over his shrunken domain to his son.

Deprived of its castle at Hiroshima, the Mōri house was forced to build a new castle at Hagi. The Tokugawa bakufu, the newly formed central government, purposely selected this geographically remote locality to place the han at a disadvantage. In the course of time, however, the geographic isolation of Hagi proved to be of great advantage. Surrounded by mountains on three sides, with access by land limited to four narrow mountain passes, Hagi enjoyed a strong defensive position. Within these protected surroundings, beneath a hill at the outer point of a diamond-shaped delta formed by the Abu River, Hagi castle, headquarters of the Chōshū han, was constructed in 1604.[16]

The system of feudal states established in 1600 was controlled by the Tokugawa house government, or bakufu, under the head of the house, the shogun. Hegemony was maintained through the bakufu's dual system of control: by domination of the Tokugawa domains, which constituted about one-quarter of the wealth of the country, and by the checks placed on the external affairs of the 260-odd han. All daimyo were required permanently to keep their families in Edo and spend every other year there themselves; they were prohibited from conducting relations with other daimyo and the imperial court at Kyoto; and they were periodically forced to submit to financial levies. Within this framework, however, each daimyo was allowed considerable latitude in governing his fief. This relative autonomy was of particular advantage to naturally rich fiefs located farthest from the center of Tokugawa power in Edo. If fiefs used their freedom wisely — which normally meant if the daimyo's councillors were wise — they might increase their economic position even while the bakufu's economic strength waned. Chōshū, Satsuma, and Tosa were all examples of such rich fiefs, located far from the center of Tokugawa political power; they produced able administrators who reversed in their fiefs the progressive economic decline which generally characterized Tokugawa Japan in the nineteenth century.

When Mōri Takachika became daimyo of Chōshū in 1837, one year before Yamagata was born, he inherited an unhealthy financial con-

16. Sawada Hisao, ed., *Nihon chimei daijiten* (Tokyo, 1935), V, 4706.

dition. The fief was in debt 80,000 *kan*,[17] an amount almost equal to the monetary value of the annual official rice income of the fief. The situation was further aggravated by floods which reduced the han's annual rice output by almost half. The resulting famine and the sharp rise in the price of available rice triggered a peasant rebellion.[18] It was clear to the han authorities that reforms were needed to improve conditions.

Mōri Takachika encouraged reforms. In 1838, for example, he decreed that luxurious and extravagant living should be given up by all samurai and that plain cotton overcoats should be substituted for the splendid garments to which the upper samurai were accustomed. Nevertheless the effort to balance the fief's budget failed in 1840 by almost 3,500 *kan*, even though the actual income of the fief (895,000 *koku*) far exceeded the nominal official income. Then, in the early 1840's, under the skilled leadership of Murata Seifū, a leading han councillor, a series of drastic reforms were instituted which dramatically revived economic conditions. The key reforms included a reorganization of the land, based upon a new survey, and the use of an office for savings and loans (*buikukyoku*)[19] in which the income from rice grown on reclaimed land was held. With the latter special fund, kept separate from the regular accounts, the han improved its precarious financial state, gave relief to its people, and entered into profitable enterprises such as financing shipping interests operating between north Japan and Osaka. As a result of these and other reforms, Chōshū was able to build up savings of 5,000 *ryō*[20] by 1850 in spite of its continuing debt. Tax laws were revised to lighten the load of the people and the samurai were given thirty-seven years for repayment of their debts. The significance of these reforms of the 1840's was that the han's economy was strengthened. Expansion in production and consequent increase in the han's tax income, relief of the economic strain on the lower samurai, and other han-instituted economic reforms provided the financial strength that enabled Chōshū to develop her military power. And ultimately it was military strength and the presence of competent leaders which were to prove decisive in determining Chōshū's role in the national crises.

17. Watanabe Yōsuke, "Ishin no henkaku to Chōshū han," in *Meiji ishinshi kenkyū* (Tokyo, 1929), p. 626. In 1837 a *koku* of rice was valued at about 250 *momme* (2.07 lbs.) of sliver. Thus 80,000 *kan* (1 *kan* = 1000 *momme*) was roughly equal to the value of 320,000 *koku* of rice. Hugh Borton, "Peasant Uprisings in Japan of the Tokugawa Period," *Transactions of the Asiatic Society of Japan*, 2nd ser., 16:209 (May 1938).

18. Watanabe, p. 626.

19. On the *buikukyoku* see Craig, *Chōshū in the Meiji Restoration*, pp. 45–49.

20. Watanabe, "Ishin no henkaku to Chōshū han," p. 628.

Accompanying the economic reforms were a variety of other measures which stimulated the social and intellectual life of Chōshū. Advice was widely sought from the wisest in the land and scholars from other fiefs were invited to teach in a reorganized educational system. Schools were opened in local districts. The han school in Hagi was revitalized and expanded to include the teaching of civil as well as military matters, and national literature was emphasized. Foreign learning was also encouraged, both in a new medical school and through a new bureau for the translation of foreign works. Students were encouraged to study outside the han and given expenses regardless of their rank. Some of these students went to Nagasaki where they studied the art of gunnery and learned about modern developments such as electricity and photography. Some Chōshū students joined the bakufu center for Western studies in Edo, and one was aboard the Tokugawa vessel which crossed the Pacific to America in 1860. A gun-casting plant was built and a reverberatory furnace was begun but never completed at Hagi.[21] Although the growth of Western studies in Chōshū lagged behind similar developments in the bakufu and in other han, they were well advanced before the Restoration.[22]

It is not recorded what effect these changes in han policy had on Yamagata, but it is difficult to believe that as an alert samurai, however junior his rank, who worked in different offices in the han bureaucracy, however lowly his task, he was unaffected by the political shifts and economic changes taking place. It was a time of change and innovation, when young men from Hagi were venturing forth to seek new knowledge to benefit the han, a time when bold reforms were being instituted to strengthen the economic sinews of the han and thus its political welfare. Conscious of the new approaches taken by his superiors to the problems besetting the house of Mōri, surely Yamagata must have been infected by this atmosphere of change and made aware of the desirability and advantages of innovative actions to improve the welfare of his han and the position of ambitious samurai. In any case, the changing internal conditions of the han must be included as a factor in influencing the rise of Chōshū revolutionary activists.

In addition to these internal changes, national political currents deeply affected the life of Hagi at this time. The Mōri family, free from

21. Thomas C. Smith, "The Introduction of Western Industry to Japan During the Last Years of the Tokugawa Period," *Harvard Journal of Asiatic Studies* 11.1:130–152 (June 1948).

22. Horie Yasuzō, "Yamaguchi han ni okeru bakumatsu no yōshiki kōgyō," *Keizai ronsō* 40:153–165 (January 1935).

marriage ties with the Tokugawa family, had kept alive in Chōshū an anti-Tokugawa attitude and a strong feeling of loyalty toward the emperor. In time, Hagi was to become one of the centers of growing national dissatisfaction with the Tokugawa government and of sentiment favoring the restoration of real authority to the emperor in Kyoto. The shift from primary concern with han affairs to a growing involvement in national politics was a consequence of dramatic events in the late 1850's far removed from Hagi.

When Commodore Perry arrived in Japanese waters in the summer of 1853 and in the following spring caused the bakufu to open ports to foreign intercourse in violation of the long-standing policy of seclusion, an important link was forged in the chain of events which culminated in the Restoration of 1868. The internal play of forces — the balance between the bakufu and the powerful han, the inactivity of the court in national affairs, and the seclusion of Japan from foreign interference — was upset by the impact of Western power. In 1854 the bakufu's acquiescence in foreign demands in the face of that power was opposed by the majority of the han as well as by the court, which for the first time in two centuries was consulted on an important policy decision. When in July of 1858 the bakufu again yielded to foreign pressure and without waiting for endorsement of its action from the court signed the Treaty of Commerce with the United States, it caused an open split between the court and the bakufu. Although official Chōshū policy in that year called for "loyalty to the Court, trust to the Bakufu, and filial duty to the ancestors [of the house of Mōri]," [23] the han supported the imperial position in denouncing the Treaty of Commerce.

The significant point is that in the split between the court and the bakufu Chōshū and other major han were drawn into asserting a line of action in national affairs. The commitment to support the court did not mean that Chōshū was then prepared to overthrow the bakufu, but it did imply that the han had decided to atempt to influence a national policy which would reflect the imperial will.

Kyoto and Yoshida Shōin

The events of 1858 and Chōshū's involvement in national affairs moved Yamagata, shortly after he reached the age of twenty, from the relative calm of his youthful training and experience into the turbulent stream of national political activities. In June of that year, he and five

23. Quoted by Craig, *Chōshū*, p. 120.

other young Chōshū samurai made their way up through the Inland Sea to Kyoto where they were instructed to serve as the "eyes and ears" of the han as part of a policy of keeping abreast of the changing situation. In selecting young samurai to send to Kyoto, the han authorities were influenced by the recommendations of Yoshida Shōin. Yoshida Shōin was requested to recommend from among his pupils those who might accompany han representatives being sent to Kyoto to keep the han informed of the rapidly changing situation in the capital. Although Yoshida had not yet met Yamagata, some of his pupils were acquainted with him and considered him a promising young man who could contribute to the han's political activities. Specifically, Irie Kūichi, one of Shōin's students who had already been selected to go to Kyoto, was impressed by his zeal and ability, and it was through his recommendation that Yoshida Shōin included Yamagata among the six assigned to the intelligence mission in Kyoto.[24]

As the group, which included Itō Hirobumi, left Hagi they were given a letter of encouragement from Yoshida Shōin in which he suggested that they attempt to establish the accuracy of a rumor that Ii Naosuke, the senior official of the bakufu, planned to reduce court opposition by removing the emperor to Hikone on Lake Biwa, Naosuke's own fief. If the rumor were true, Yoshida warned, they must be prepared to thwart the plot and rescue the emperor.[25]

Activities in Kyoto had taken on new meaning with the foreign crisis, and samurai and *rōnin* (masterless samurai) from many areas of Japan concentrated there to lend support to the court in its opposition to the foreign policy of the bakufu. Supporting this opposition was the intellectual movement dating from the middle of the Tokugawa period which claimed that political power had been improperly usurped by the Tokugawa family and should be restored to the emperor. Among the *kuge* (nobles) living in Kyoto were influential scholars, philosophers, and priests, subsisting by delivering lectures or serving regularly as teachers in the aristocratic families. These men carried on the anti-bakufu intellectual tradition and opposed the Confucian doctrine officially approved by the Tokugawa government, a stand which precluded their employment by the bakufu and many of the fiefs. Rejected by the Tokugawa government, they welcomed opportunities to embarrass its officials and further the cause of imperial rule.

The most prominent of these scholars often provided the key link be-

24. Suematsu, *Bōchō kaiten shi*, II, 237.
25. Yoshida Shōin's message is quoted in *Yamagata den*, I, 127–129.

tween sympathetic factions among the court aristocracy and samurai of the western han. Among these, Yanagawa Seigan (1789–1858), who has been called the "father of the Sonnō (Revere the Emperor) party," [26] was one of the most influential in determining the attitude of the Kyoto court. An outstanding Confucian scholar from the province of Mino, he had studied and taught in Edo, until his strong pro-emperor, antiforeign views brought him into disfavor and forced him to seek the protection of friendly *kuge* in Kyoto. Although periodically placed under house arrest for inflammatory writings, he nevertheless continued to increase his influence through a wide following. Both Yoshida Shōin and Saigō Takamori, the latter from Satsuma and one of the key figures in the Restoration movement, visited Yanagawa at Kyoto and were influenced by his antiforeign and anti-bakufu ideas. He not only encouraged resolution in the face of the foreign threat and determination in restoring imperial rule, he also helped to coordinate the efforts of certain court groups with particular factions within the western han which shared his objectives.

Umeda Umpin (1826–1859) was another leading scholar residing in Kyoto who enjoyed widespread influence. Born in the Obama fief in north central Japan, he had gone to Kyoto after establishing himself as a leading Confucian scholar and poet in Edo. Like Yanagawa, he was an untiring supporter of the imperial cause and an advocate of bold measures to turn back the threat of foreign encroachment. Umeda has been called "the leader of the most active loyalist group in Kyoto" [27] because of his association with the extremist faction of Chōshū. It was through Umeda that the Chōshū samurai in Kyoto were able to ally themselves with sympathetic factions at court. In 1857 Umeda had traveled to Hagi to persuade Chōshū to assume the leadership in a movement to support the court. Although his stand was too extreme for the Chōshū daimyo's councillors, it met a favorable response from some of the younger samurai who, under the influence of Yoshida Shōin, were already sympathetic toward his views.

It was only natural then that Yamagata and his companions should be welcomed to Kyoto in 1858 by these scholars. Kusaka Genzui, a prominent student of Yoshida Shōin whom Yamagata met in Kyoto, introduced the young samurai to Yanagawa and Umeda.[28] Through conversations Yanagawa enlisted their sympathy and Umeda informed them about the

26. *Ibid.*, I, 138.
27. *Ibid.*, I, 144. See also James Murdoch, *A History of Japan* (London, 1926), III, 688–689.
28. Asahina Chisen, *Meiji kōshinroku* (Tokyo, 1924), p. 373.

complex activities of the various factions in Kyoto and thus assisted the young samurai in their intelligence function. In addition, they delivered lectures on the state of the nation and presented their convictions on the course that should be followed. This is the manner in which their ideas were disseminated to sympathetic samurai in Kyoto.

There is every reason to believe that Yamagata already sympathized with the anti-Tokugawa, antiforeign ideas of the other Chōshū men with whom he was now associated, but these meetings in Kyoto were his first recorded contact with prominent scholars committed to reviving the authority of the court. The arguments of these scholars were powerfully strengthened by political developments that Yamagata witnessed, for it was during his stay in Kyoto that the bakufu defied the position of the court and signed the commercial treaty with the United States. In August, the bakufu, in an attempt to reassert the power of the shogun, began to suppress all opposition. As a result of this policy, Umeda and others were shortly to be arrested. Whatever his attitude before this time, under the influence of these men and the events of the day, Yamagata was brought face to face with the acute political problems of the time. His first visit to Kyoto must have persuaded him that drastic measures would be required both to restore imperial rule over the nation and to reverse the bakufu policy of yielding to the demands of the foreigners. This first step in his political education was soon to be reinforced.

Yamagata returned to Hagi in October 1858, carrying with him a letter of introduction to Yoshida Shōin written by Kusaka Genzui. The letter was to persuade Shōin to accept Yamagata as a student, a step which presumably was not difficult because Shōin had already expressed his approval of Yamagata by recommending him to the han for the assignment in Kyoto before becoming acquainted with him. For almost six months Yamagata received instruction at Shōin's school, known as Shōka sonjuku (lit., "the school beneath the pines"), and was inspired by the celebrated teacher to dedicate himself to action to achieve the ideals of the "honor the emperor, expel the barbarians" (sonnō jōi) movement.

We have seen how the sentiment of loyalty to the emperor (sonnō), nurtured in Chōshū by traditional hostility to the Tokugawa house, was combined with opposition to the bakufu's decision to sign the 1858 Treaty of Commerce without imperial sanction. It was this development which caused the han to intrude into national politics and led to Yamagata's first encounter with the major political conflict of the day. No one in Chōshū contributed more to the emergence of the political movements to express loyalty to the emperor by opposing the foreigners than Yoshida Shōin. Who was this samurai whose recommendations had been sought by the han government in selecting young men to go to Kyoto? Who was this man who awakened the minds of many young Hagi samurai to the crisis confronting Japan and who seemed so successful in arousing them to political action?

Born in 1830, near Hagi, the son of middle-ranking samurai, Yoshida Shōin was adopted into the Yoshida family which provided professional instructors at the han school in the art of military science as taught by Yamaga Sokō, a Confucian scholar of the seventeenth century. At an early age he succeeded his adoptive father as head of the Yamaga school of military science. A studious, precocious boy, he mastered his subject and at the age of eleven gained a wide reputation for the lectures on military science he delivered before the Chōshū daimyo. He rapidly increased his knowledge and broadened his interests by assiduous study and by travel, first to Nagasaki, where he learned some Dutch and observed the foreigners, then to Edo, where he came under the influence of Sakuma Shōzan, a leading critic of the Tokugawa government and exponent of a plan to build up the nation's defense against Western countries, and finally to Mito where he adopted many of the views of the influential school of nationalistic thought centered there. In Hagi, he became the chief spokesman of a doctrine of loyalty to the throne and the need for measures to contain the external threat. The many visionary schemes he proposed to the han for reforming the political situation exerted little actual influence and almost all of his personal activities met with failure, but the radical nature of his teachings got him in trouble. In 1852, he was deprived of his samurai title and his hereditary income for disobeying han orders; in 1854 he was arrested for his attempt to go abroad on one of Commodore Perry's ships. Although he was imprisoned by his han for this reckless act, he was soon released to domiciliary confinement. In 1855, he was permitted to open a school in his residence. He continued to enjoy the respect of the daimyo, but the pressure of the bakufu and the opinion of the han councillors, who disapproved of the extreme actions he called for, forced him to remain under house arrest in Hagi. While his movements were restrained, his teachings exerted an ever increasing influence through the activities of his followers. It is not known how many students studied with him (one estimate is eighty during the three years the school was open),[29] but he was remarkably

29. Kimura Toshio, *Yoshida Shōin* (Tokyo, 1938), p. 266.

successful in attracting a group of young samurai who became prominent in han national affairs.[30]

In Hagi there were several private schools, which, unlike the han school, were not restricted to those of upper samurai rank. These private schools concentrated on literature and the Chinese classics with the exception of Shōin's private school. Yoshida's teachings, on the other hand, combined the ideas of Confucianism[31] and the ideals of the samurai, with a concern for the practical application of his ideas. He built a system of thought based on Confucianism and its Five Relationships, with Yamaga Sokō's *bushidō* teachings as the ideal standard of personal character, the Mito school's reverence for the imperial institution and the national past, and Sakuma Shōzan's advocacy of adopting Western techniques and science while rejecting Western ideas. But within this complex philosophy the central notion was loyalty — to family, to the han, to the emperor, and to the divine nation. His was a nationalistic, patriotic philosophy enjoining all samurai to fulfill their obligations of duty and loyalty. Under the motto, "The lord-vassal relationship is man's first principle, and preserving independence from the barbarians is the nation's main task," [32] he taught his pupils that the virtues of loyalty and self-sacrifice must be the foundations for strengthening the nation and opposing the foreigners.

In all his instructions the momentous issues of the day were discussed and lines of action suggested. The han school presumably had this task as one of its aims, but it was the training school for future han officials and as such bore the conservative stamp of the more conservative han authorities. Shōin's school seemed to satisfy demands which the han school could not, and thus it attracted the young and vigorous (including sons of upper samurai, such as Kido Takayoshi, who could have gone to the han school) who sought answers and approaches to the problems then gripping the nation. His reputation as a brilliant scholar and a fearless samurai caught the admiration of young, ambitious men; and he was able to relate their ambitions to a line of political action for the era in which they lived.

30. Among Yoshida Shōin's students who became leaders in the Restoration in later years were: Takasugi Shinsaku, Irie Kūichi, Kusaka Genzui, Kido Takayoshi, Inoue Kaoru, Itō Hirobumi, Yamada Akiyoshi, Shinagawa Yajirō.

31. One of the principles Yoshida taught was that "man differs from animals because of the Five Relationships. Among these the most important are the ruler-subject and the father-son relationships; therefore, loyalty and filial piety are the essence of man." Quoted in Sawada, ed., *Nihon chimei daijiten*, V, 4709–4710.

32. *Yamagata den*, I, 160.

Yoshida's thought constantly evolved during his short life; his concept of *sonnō* did not originally mean a rejection of the bakufu or the Tokugawa political system, and his concept of *jōi* never meant a rejection of all Western things. He accepted the necessity of learning the technology of the West but preached against allowing the barbarians to weaken the nation as he felt the treaties would. Originally he advocated an agreement between the Tokugawa government and the factions at the Kyoto court as the best means of strengthening the nation against the Western powers. He felt that loyalty to the bakufu was based upon the assumption that the shogun was loyal to the emperor, as all daimyo were assumed to be, but the weak stand of the bakufu in the face of foreign threats aroused his doubts. By 1858, when the bakufu proceeded to sign the commercial treaties without receiving the approval of either the court or the daimyo, and when it became clear that the bakufu was attempting to reassert its power by checking the influence of the western han at court, Shōin's doubts were confirmed. He ceased to believe that anything short of the total destruction of the bakufu could restore imperial prestige and achieve a strong united nation, and he began to conceive of schemes and plots to weaken and destroy the power of the Tokugawa government.[33]

Yamagata asked to join the school at a time when Yoshida's efforts were devoted to plotting the downfall of the bakufu. This may explain why Shōin, when he approved of Yamagata as his pupil, asked him, "Are you ready to die?" To this Yamagata answered, "If it is for my han, I am prepared to die at any time." [34] When he entered the school, Yamagata's rank was so low that he could sit only in the hallway and not in the lecture room to hear his new teacher. For nearly six months he listened daily to lectures on military science, the thought of Mencius, the proper code of behavior for all samurai,[35] and the solutions to contemporary problems. Perhaps of more importance than the philosophic content of the lectures was the fiery passion of young Shōin that seems to have evoked in his pupil a spirit of devotion and loyalty to a great national cause.

It is easy to exaggerate the impact of Yoshida Shōin on the political movement which restored the emperor in 1868. Many years preceding his

---

33. For a concise account of Yoshida's thought and activities, see Naramoto Tatsuya, *Yoshida Shōin* (Tokyo, 1951), p. 168. In English, a study of his thought is to be found in David Earl's *Emperor and Nation in Japan* (Seattle, 1964), Part II.

34. *Yamagata den*, I, 158.

35. Translated in Henri Van Straelen, *Yoshida Shōin, Forerunner of the Meiji Restoration* (Leiden, 1952), pp. 83–84.

activity there were other scholars in Chōshū and elsewhere who had stressed the importance of loyalty to the emperor; and his own han advocated policies in fulfillment of that sentiment. Furthermore, few of Shōin's suggestions for practical action found favor with han authorities; even some of his students rejected his radical plans. His views did not guide the han. Nevertheless, his doctrines exerted telling effect on many Hagi samurai who were either too young or too low in rank to influence policy.

In the summer of 1859, after han officials disclosed to the bakufu a plot that he had conceived to kill a Tokugawa official in Kyoto, Yoshida Shōin was delivered into the hands of the Edo government and executed; he was a victim, along with Umeda Umpin and other outspoken advocates of imperial Restoration, of a new policy of the bakufu to suppress all opposition to its authority. His death, Yamagata recalled in later years, was "an ineradicable tragedy, causing great sadness to all loyalists and ineffable sorrow to me." [36]

For Yamagata, as for the other students of the Shōka sonjuku, the encounter with Yoshida Shōin was crucially important. By his teaching, by his example, and by the force of his personality Yoshida succeeded in arousing in them the spirit of the samurai and prepared them to sacrifice themselves in a cause. More important, however, was his success in transmuting loyalty to the han with patriotism for a national cause. By giving his students a convincing definition of the existing political situation and a philosophy which suited their samurai status and fit the Chōshū tradition of reverence for the throne and hostility to the Tokugawa house, he lifted local political loyalty to a national sacred cause. In this way they were able to integrate their personalities with the social demands of the time, to gain new bearings that permitted them to identify revolutionary acts with national patriotism. The audacious actions upon which they were to embark were, in this sense, committed in memory of his inspiration. Yamagata spoke for his fellow students when he celebrated Shōin's school in this poem:

> May the school under the pines
> be prosperous
> for a thousand years
> showing the way [to recover]
> the great reigns of the past.[37]

36. *Gansetsu Yamagata kō ikō* (Tokyo, 1926), Part I, p. 4.
37. *Yamagata den,* I, 174.

The experiences of 1858 were therefore a turning point in Yamagata's career. He had moved on to the national stage by his appointment as a han agent in Kyoto. He had been made aware of the national crisis and the need for action through his encounter with Yanagawa Seigan and Umeda Umpin in Kyoto, and Yoshida Shōin had provided the inspiration which directed his activities on behalf of a national cause. In short, he was launched on his career as a revolutionary loyalist.

Activities as a Revolutionary Loyalist

For the next decade, in company with a zealous clique of radical Chōshū samurai, Yamagata engaged in activities against the "barbarians" and conspired to advance the political role of the court in national politics and weaken the authority of the Tokugawa government. These aims of the *sonnō jōi* faction, however, met the resistance of han authorities who rejected demands for extreme measures and, instead, adhered to a three-fold policy of respect for the court, trust in the bakufu, and loyalty to the house of Mōri. Behind these aims was a growing anti-foreign sentiment which the radicals wanted to express in direct action against the "barbarians."

This desire is illustrated in Yamagata's bitter reaction to an incident in the summer of 1860. A British vessel had touched at a Chōshū village along the coast of the Shimonoseki straits, landed a crew, and demanded fuel and food. When refused, they coerced a local official into supplying their needs and forced a guard to accompany the vessel to Nagasaki. Hagi officials protested this action to the bakufu through the han representative in Edo. In turn, the bakufu complained to the British consul in Nagasaki. The consul conceded the violation and secured the release of the Japanese held aboard the ship. When this story reached the ears of the Hagi loyalists, they sought permission to proceed to Shimonoseki to demonstrate forcefully against the foreigners. The request was denied but Yamagata expressed the anger of the group in verse.

> Although there are many countries,
> the country of abundant rice has
> been governed by the gods
> for thousands of years, and
> is rich and sufficient in what
> grows in the mountains and in the sea.
> That being so,

the ugly English barbarians,
who come from a distance as far as the
white cloud, felt envious, and came forth
to get the good things, and
to exchange the sullied things of England
for the precious things
of the divine country,
so that their home
country would prosper.
With spirit and vigor,
a large ship with oars,
like wild, overgrown summer grasses,
sailed from port to port
where the waves are rough, and
anchored near the Toyama Sea.
The ugly English barbarians
behaved with extreme
disorder and uncontrollable uncouthness.
To measure the depth of the sea
they rowed their boats to the shore over the white waves,
and in violation of the order of the emperor
disgraced the soil of our mighty country
created benevolently by the god of the emperor.
And, furthermore, they frightened
with loud thunder-like sounds of cannon
the people, who became as fearful as
one confronted by the tiger who has found his grain.
With many warriors with their bows and arrows
we will defeat
the impudent, ugly barbarians.
When we unsheath our swords and kill them
they will suffer the force
of the divine wind from Isuzu shrine
and will be thrown into the deep sea
like bits of seaweed.[38]

The denial of permission to take direct action reflected the controlling position of moderates in the councils of the han. In 1862 the Chōshū administration embarked on a policy of mediation between the bakufu and the court. Nagai Uta, a ranking han official, had successfully per-suaded the daimyo to increase Chōshū's influence by fostering a reconcili-

38. *Ibid.*, I, 280–282.

ation between Edo and Kyoto and by encouraging the opening of the country.[39] The assassination of the leading bakufu minister in 1860 had abruptly ended the attempt to reassert the traditional Tokugawa dominance over national affairs. There followed a period of uncertain leadership under which concessions were made to the growing opposition. One such concession was to revise the regulation requiring all daimyo to live in Edo every other year to only 100 days in three years. Under these circumstances Nagai's efforts to draw Edo and Kyoto together initially met with success. Even the court seemed pleased to accept the mediation despite its opposition to the opening of the country. But two stumbling blocks caused the plan to fail. The first was the jealousy of the powerful han of Satsuma at seeing Chōshū expand its influence at the court and among Tokugawa officials. It led the daimyo of Satsuma, Shimazu Hisamitsu, to propose alternative plans to achieve the same objective of mediation. His plan called for the shogun to visit Kyoto, for the appointment of bakufu officials supporting cooperation with the court, and for a stronger voice for the lords of the strong western han. Unlike Chōshū's recommendations, it did not advocate the bakufu's policy of opening the country. This difference and the skill of Satsuma authorities in insinuating their influence contributed to Satsuma's success.

The second reason for the failure of Chōshū's mediation policy was the opposition of the loyalist clique within the han. Yoshida Shōin's radical policy of openly challenging the authority of the bakufu for its defiance of the court's wishes had been rejected by Chōshū leaders. The bakufu's retaliating measures which extremism provoked encouraged the han bureaucrats to pursue a conciliatory program. But the students of Shōin, who formed the core of the loyalist clique, continued their *sonnō jōi* activities and opposed Nagai Uta's plans. In the end, their agitation succeeded in winning away some of the han officials from Nagai's position. This weakened the Chōshū policy so that when Satsuma plunged into the struggle for power at Kyoto the han's efforts were doomed. Nagai was disgraced, removed from office, and ordered to commit suicide.

Angered by their han's policy of mediation, Yamagata and such fellow loyalists as Kido Takayoshi, Kusaka Genzui, and Takasugi Shinsaku agitated for their *sonnō jōi* views and sought support from like-minded samurai in other han. In February 1862, for example, the followers of Yoshida Shōin pledged in a blood oath that they would exert every effort to establish relations with sympathetic parties in other han and weld together a national *sonnō jōi* movement. Illness prevented Yama-

39. Nagai Uta's proposal is summarized in Craig, *Chōshū,* pp. 169–170.

gata from participating in this blood oath, but he associated himself wholeheartedly with its aims.[40]

This was a significant development and the extremists enjoyed a number of advantages in pursuing the objective. As lesser samurai without the responsibility for forming han policy they were free to move about and establish associations with samurai of other han; that is, they could violate more easily the Tokugawa policy restricting relations between han. In 1862, for example, under han instructions to gather information on the attitude toward national events of the han in Kyushu, Yamagata traveled around the southern island, avoiding bakufu police by disguising himself and assuming the name of Hagiwara, and established contact with local samurai groups favoring the *sonnō jōi* policy.[41] Later in the same year, he accompanied a han official to Edo where he met Kido Takayoshi, who was residing at the Chōshū quarters in Edo, and disclosed information he had gathered in Kyushu and in Kyoto en route. Through such activities an information network was developing which often made the loyalist cliques far better informed on the swiftly changing situation than their superior officials. Moreover, such activity helped to break down the walls separating the han and to build up a united political force.

Yet the *sonnō* cliques were limited in what they could accomplish. They did not as yet have the power to determine han policy, although they clearly were gaining in influence. They had no base of power and could not opearte as an autonomous political force. Also, they still regarded themselves as virtuous samurai and loyal vassals of their daimyo. In Chōshū, however, the failure of Nagai's mediation policy expanded their opportunities and the han authorities, stung by the success of Satsuma's plan in Edo and Kyoto, moved close to the *sonnō jōi* program.

By the end of 1862 Kyoto had become the center of national politics. The court and the Kyoto nobles moved to the center of the political arena. This was symbolized by the visit of the shogun to Kyoto, early in 1863, for the first time in over 200 years. But in Kyoto two groups were locked in a struggle for competing policies: on the one hand were the *sonnō jōi* factions made up of the extremist nobles and loyalists from Chōshū and several other han; on the other hand there were the forces maneuvering to bring together the court and the bakufu composed of some of the nobles, leading bakufu officials, the Satsuma daimyo, and han loyal to the Tokugawa house. The first group employed terrorism

40. *Yamagata den*, I, 189–191.
41. *Ibid.*, I, 201–202.

and assassination to put into effect its policy of loyalty to the emperor in order to unite against the foreigners; the second tried to control extremism, resist action against the foreign nations, and increase the cooperation between the emperor and the shogun. Conditions in 1863 first favored the extremists. The court officially committed itself to a policy of expelling the foreigners and the bakufu reluctantly agreed to June 25 as the expulsion date.

The order gave the loyalists new life. Few of them believed that they could literally "expel the barbarians," but they were prepared, as Tōyama Shigeki has suggested, to change the policy of "revering the emperor" for the sake of "expelling the foreigners" to one of "expelling the barbarians" for the sake of "revering the emperor" and oppressing the bakufu.[42]

Yamagata and many other Chōshū loyalists who were in Kyoto when the announcement to oust the foreigners went into effect immediately departed for home. They were still en route when, on June 25, 1863, in fulfillment of the imperial order, two of the han's three foreign-style war vessels, which Chōshū had recently purchased at Nagasaki, suddenly opened fire on the *Pembroke*, an American steamer owned by Russell and Company, which was passing through the straits of Shimonoseki. A land battery from one of the many forts the han had built along its southern coast joined in the shelling, but the *Pembroke* was able to escape into the darkness.[43] Chōshū had prepared for action by shifting government headquarters from Hagi to Yamaguchi city near the center of the han. On July 8, the coastal guns opened fire on a French ship, and three days later a Dutch corvette was forced to fight its way through the straits against the combined fire of the Chōshū warships and seven batteries.[44] These actions, aimed at closing the straits to foreign vessels, were reported to Kyoto and Edo and were promptly commended.

Yamagata was not on the scene during these Chōshū attacks but arrived in time to experience the retaliation these actions provoked. On July 26, the U.S. warship *Wyoming* arrived in the Shimonoseki straits from Yokohama and there sank two of Chōshū's foreign vessels and crippled the third, but it was forced to retire because its four 32 pounders

---

42. Tōyama Shigeki, *Meiji ishin* (Tokyo, 1951), p. 94.

43. The British embassy reported to London that in 1863 Chōshū had purchased "The steamer 'Lancefield' and brig 'Lemrick' the former for 125,000 dollars and the latter for about 25,000 dollars." British Sessional Papers, *Accounts and Papers*, LXVI (1864), 265.

44. Mayahara Jirō, *Bōchō jūgonen shi* (Tokyo, 1915), p. 453.

could not oppose the thirty-four guns of the shore batteries.[45] Four days later French warships arrived, bombarded the Chōshū forts, which curiously remained silent, and then landed a party of marines who assaulted and captured the main forts located at the villages of Dannoura and Maeda. The defenders were helpless. Yamagata, in command of one of the forts, withdrew his small group to a wooded area farther inland and sniped at the invaders with little effect. The French marines spiked the guns, threw powder and ammunition into the sea, confiscated the rifles and swords they found in the forts, and burned down the camp used by the defenders as well as scores of houses in the nearby village.[46]

This frustration of the first Chōshū effort to carry out the imperial order to "expel the barbarians" was soon followed by the defeat of Chōshū in Kyoto. Chōshū's voice in Kyoto, as we have seen, had grown strong when the court first accepted Nagai Uta's mediation offer. This influence was expressed concretely by entrusting to Chōshū samurai the protection of one of the nine palace gates. But the official policy of Chōshū, which implied approval of relations with the Western nations, was not acceptable to the han radicals, and it had evoked a strong Satsuma action to counter Chōshū influence. With the sudden increase in the number of violent acts of Chōshū samurai in Kyoto, the court became alarmed and with the encouragement of the Satsuma daimyo was persuaded to replace Chōshū as the intermediary between the court and the bakufu. Chōshū leaders suddenly discovered that they were forbidden to enter the court and, in September 1863, Satsuma troops seized the gate entrusted to Chōshū forces and a major clash seemed imminent. But it was too late. An imperial edict ordered the far more numerous Satsuma and Aizu troops to guard the palace. Outmaneuvered by the combined forces of Satsuma and Aizu, the Chōshū extremists in Kyoto intensified their plotting with friendly nobles and conspired to reverse the unfavorable situation which had developed. Some of these compromising schemes were discovered and Lord Mōri was accused of complicity. All Chōshū men were ordered out of the palace precincts, and seven nobles were banished from Kyoto and fled to Chōshū.[47]

45. An eyewitness recorded that all the Chōshū "vessels were flying the Japanese flag at the peak, and the private colours of the Prince of Nagato at the main." The latter was described as a "blue flag with three balls in a triangle and a white stripe above." *Accounts and Papers*, LXVI (1864), 266.

46. Mr. Bleckman, an interpreter attached to the French admiralty, gave an account of the retaliatory measures in the Yokohama newspaper, the *Japan Herald*, which is quoted in *Accounts and Papers*, LXVI (1864), 263–264.

47. Murdoch, *History of Japan*, III, 736–738.

The debacle at Kyoto seriously impaired the influence of Chōshū on national decisions, and the successful actions of the Satsuma–Aizu samurai aroused the bitter enmity of Chōshū loyalists. Defeat at Shimonoseki and disgrace at Kyoto, within a period of two months, slowed Chōshū's *sonnō jōi* movement. But it did not dissuade the han from further antiforeign action. When the bakufu sent a message to Chōshū demanding an end to the attacks on foreign ships, the han refused to accept the order and on his departure the emissary was assassinated by loyalists. Yamagata was surely voicing the antiforeign animus of the extremists in a verse he composed in the summer of 1863:

> Even if I should
> die in the water
> I will spit
> on the ugly barbarians.[48]

Nevertheless, the marked superiority of the Western fire power and the landing of the French marines convinced the han authorities of the necessity for sweeping military reforms. New methods and new leaders were needed and the han adopted bold plans. One of the most significant reforms, and one with which Yamagata was closely associated, was to organize effective military units which included both commoners and samurai to reinforce the regular han army. Plans for the creation of irregular military forces that might include commoners had been proposed before but had never been acted upon. The jaring events of 1863, especially the bombardment of Shimonoseki, stimulated their organization.

The daimyo summoned Takasugi Shinsaku, pardoned him for an offense for which he had been confined to his residence in Hagi, and ordered him to organize a military force to bear responsibility for the defense of Shimonoseki. Takasugi, then twenty-five years old, was an able student of Yoshida Shōin who had acquired a reputation for his daring defiance of the han authorities. He shared the radical views of the other students of Yoshida Shōin and was outspoken in his criticism of many samurai whom he accused of having lost their courage and fighting ability, but he was also distinguished for his specialized knowledge of Western military science. Within two days after his appointment, Takasugi proceeded to Shimonoseki and set about organizing a new military unit. The result was a force of some 300 men centering around a group of loyalist *rōnin* and samurai who had been attracted to Shimonoseki by the possibility of participating in antiforeign action and who had already

48. *Yamagata den,* I, 299.

organized themselves into a volunteer unit under the leadership of Ku-saka Gensui.[49] Yamagata, a close friend of Takasugi, had joined these irregulars in the attack on the foreign vessels and now he was appointed an officer in the new organization.

The new unit was named the Kiheitai (lit., "strange" or "surprise" troops) to indicate that it was an irregular unit formed outside of the eight units which constituted the regular han army, or Seiheitai. A sig-nificant feature of the Kiheitai as a military body was its unique organ-ization. Takasugi's first report to the han government indicated he would welcome all volunteers on the basis of their courage and resolution re-gardless of their social position. "It is the purpose of the Kiheitai," he wrote, "to gather together volunteers who are resolute regardless of whether they be samurai, lesser vassals, or foot soldiers, and to form a strong force." [50] Both Japanese and Western arms were to be used in fighting, with the emphasis on the latter. The organization of the Kiheitai cut across feudal lines of social distinction — merchants and farmers were also permitted to join — and used funds supplied by merchants for part of its expenses.[51] It brought together from various classes a deter-mined group of young men who favored the radical loyalist stand taken by Takasugi, Yamagata, and the other Kiheitai leaders. Assembling the Kiheitai at Shimonoseki, Takasugi set the new force to repairing the forts, studying the tactics of the foreigners, training in the Western style of fighting, and in general strengthening the han's southern defenses. The vigorous activity of the Kiheitai did much to restore the confidence and regenerate the strength of Chōshū.

But the long-range importance of the Kiheitai overshadowed, in time, the immediate stimulus it gave the revival of the han's confidence. In the first place, a leading young loyalist had been given an official appoint-ment by the han government. In the second place, it gave the extremist elements a strong, cohesive military force set apart from the regular han troops who were under the influence of more conservative leaders. It also gave the extremists a base of operation, for Shimonoseki became a

49. The size of this group varied from 200 to 400 between 1864 and 1869. See Ume-tani Noboru, "Meiji ishin shi ni okeru kiheitai no mondai," *Jimbun gakuhō* 3:33 (Mar. 1953).

50. *Yamagata den,* I, 312.

51. In a message to the han authorities, Takasugi mentioned a wealthy merchant, Yamashita Shishinojō of Gofuku village, as a possible source of financial support. For mention of other merchants who supported the Kiheitai, see E. Herbert Norman, *Japan's Emergence as a Modern State* (New York, 1940), p. 66, footnote 48. However, it needs to be emphasized that the Kiheitai was always dependent upon han finances and supplies. See Umetani, "Meiji ishin shi ni okeru kiheitai no mondai," p. 39.

center for the organization and activities of those who were dissatisfied with the compromising position taken by the han councillors toward the bakufu. In addition, of course, the revolutionary policy of making merit rather than social position the basis of selection for fighting men had profound and long-lasting consequences. Furthermore, its leaders were samurai whose ranks were lower than those of the samurai of who led the regular han army. Yet the Kiheitai did not, as is sometimes suggested, represent a revolt of the peasantry controlled from above.[52] The military unit was indeed controlled from above by the han, but the peasants were probably never a majority in the Kiheitai.[53] Furthermore, within the unit the commoners dressed differently and received different treatment, although they were expected to accept samurai standards of behavior, based on the Confucian texts read while in camp, and were permitted to take surnames and wear swords. If anything, the adoption of the samurai mentality and privileges would weaken the desire of peasants to revolt against the feudal system. This does not deny its unusual organization.

The radically different nature of the Kiheitai and the esprit de corps and even swashbuckling arrogance of its members were resented by the regular han troops, some of whom were also stationed in Shimonoseki. When members of the Kiheitai openly criticized the han troops for their poor showing against the French, a sharp fight was provoked. Because of this incident conservative han leaders were later to demand the dissolution of the Kiheitai. But for the present, to avoid any recurrence of intra-han hostilities, the Kiheitai was ordered away from Shimonoseki for a short period, and Takasugi was forced to resign from its command. Yamagata, who had fallen ill soon after the formation of the Kiheitai and had gone to Hagi to recuperate, was away when this fracas occurred; but by December 1863 he had returned to Shimonoseki where the unit was again stationed, assumed command of the Dannoura fort, and for a short period became the commanding officer of the Kiheitai.

The formation of the Kiheitai and the continuation of unsettled conditions led to the organization of many other small semiprivate military forces. Within a few years Chōshū had no less than 156 auxiliary militia

52. This is the thesis of E. Herbert Norman in *Soldier and Peasant in Japan* (New York, 1943), p. 32. Tōyama has challenged this interpretation in his *Meiji ishin,* p. 153.
53. In April 1864, 53 percent of the 292 members of the Kiheitai were samurai, 33 percent were commoners (i.e., peasants and merchants), and 24 percent were unknown. Even if all the unknown were commoners, 40 percent of the members would still be samurai which makes it difficult to call the Kiheitai a peasant unit. Umetani, "Meiji ishin shi ni okeru kiheitai no mondai," p. 34.

units known as *shotai,* many of them led by loyalist sympathizers.[54] With the exception of the Kiheitai, however, each unit was made up of members of one occupation or social group. There were, for example, units of peasants, Buddhist monks, sumo wrestlers, Shinto priests, and even landlords. One of the most interesting groups was that formed by outcasts from the pariah district of Yamaguchi, the second city of Chōshū. To make up this unit five hardy men were selected from each hundred households and permitted to wear the two swords of the samurai, thus ridding themselves of the stigma attached to the outcast class.[55]

By 1864 the han military reforms had made considerable progress. With renewed confidence the extremists continued to encourage bold acts against the bakufu and revenge against the foreigners, while the han authorities counseled moderation. To extend their strength, Yamagata submitted a memorial to the han government pressing for cooperation with the loyalists within neighboring han and an alliance of anti-bakufu forces, but it met with no response.[56] It became clear that such an alliance could not be accomplished until the loyalist faction could gain a commanding position within Chōshū. This possibility had to await further disasters.

The 1863 pattern of defeat at the hands of the foreigners at Shimonoseki and failure at Kyoto was repeated in 1864. Chōshū authorities were split over the question of how to reestablish the han's influence in Kyoto, where a year before it had had a controlling hand, and how to carry out the policy of expelling the foreigners. The failures of 1863 had caused a shift in han ministers, and those who came to power favored reviving the policy of working for an accommodation between Edo and Kyoto. This threatened shift in han policy stimulated the young extremists to rededicate themselves to direct action against both the bakufu and the foreigners. The dedication was underlined by a blood oath taken by Yamagata and twenty-five others who formed the hard core of the Kiheitai, which declared that the threat to the nation had dangerously increased since the death of Yoshida Shōin. At the risk of dire consequences they pledged their lives, "regardless of the dangers involved and no matter what changes may occur, to joint effort, fearless of death." [57]

Yamagata did not always agree with the plans of action advocated by

54. For a table of some of the *shotai,* see Tōyama, *Meiji ishin,* pp. 150–151, and the discussion by Craig, *Chōshū,* pp. 271–285.

55. Tōyama, *Meiji ishin,* p. 154, note 5.

56. Quoted in *Yamagata den,* I, 295.

57. The oath appears in *ibid.,* I, 315–316.

some of his own radical colleagues. One plan advanced to regain power in Kyoto called for the Kiheitai to cross the narrow Shimonoseki straits and gain control of the northern Kyushu han of Bungo and Bizen, both friendly to the Edo government. With Chōshū's southern border thus protected, it was argued, the adopted son of Lord Mōri, who took an active part in the han government, and the nobles who had taken refuge in Chōshū could lead a strong Chōshū contingent in an attack on Kyoto.[58] Yamagata considered this plan unrealistic and suggested other means to gain the same end. He argued:

> With the present domestic and foreign problems, an audacious attack on Kyoto would have some merit, no doubt, but it cannot be called a sound policy. I advocate an alliance with the clans of Aki and Bizen and winning the inhabitants of those ten provinces, which were in the past under the Mōri clan, to our point of view. Then an impressive advance, displaying great power, could be made by land and sea. Any who oppose and obstruct this advance should be met decisively. What we must consider is that if we undertake a long sea expedition we will be advancing like a wild boar losing our maneuverability and leaving our rear vulnerable. So, rather than occupy Hikeyama [in Bungo], we should advance along the northern coast, occupying the important points and establishing advanced bases as we go.[59]

Yamagata's views were submitted after those calling for a direct assault on Kyoto had already gained their point, thereby committing the han to an anti-Tokugawa policy. They are worth recording, however, because they were an early indication of his tendency to take a more cautious and realistic stand than many of his comrades. Despite his disagreement, he desired to accompany the Chōshū force of 500 warriors which set out to attack Kyoto in January 1864, but he was instructed to prepare for the defense of Shimonoseki.

The plan inspired by the Hagi extremists to regain by force of arms a controlling voice for Chōshū in the councils of the court at Kyoto was ill-fated. Early on the morning of August 20, 1864, Chōshū troops assembled on the hills outside of Kyoto and advanced into the city. In the short, sharp struggle that ensued large sections of the city were put to fire and the population was thrown into a panic.[60] At the height of

58. *Ibid.*, I, 349–350.
59. Quoted in *ibid.*, I, 359–360.
60. It is interesting to note that Alcock, the British minister to Japan, received an

their attack Chōshū samurai captured two gates of the palace, but the troops of Aizu and Satsuma, led by Saigō Takamori, the future military hero of the imperial Restoration, gained the upper hand and finally routed the Chōshū forces completely. Only a small group survived and two able Chōshū leaders, Kusaka Genzui and Irie Kūichi, were killed. The daring assault thus ended in disaster. Accused of disregarding court orders and disobeying the bakufu mandate forbidding his troops from entering Kyoto, Lord Mōri and his heir were declared rebels and ordered to be arrested and brought for trial in Edo. The shogun also ordered a punitive expedition to chastise the unruly han.

Yamagata did not engage in the attack on Kyoto, but less than three weeks later he participated in a second disaster at Shimonoseki. The forts along the coast had continued to harass foreign shipping passing through the narrow straits and caused Western emissaries to lodge complaints with the bakufu. On the day after Chōshū forces came to grief in Kyoto, the British minister in Edo delivered a memorandum declaring that "The hostile position taken by the Prince of Chōshū is one which cannot be long endured." [61] Warning that Chōshū could not hope to stand up against any of the Western powers and that armies might be sent to Kyoto — "as similar conduct led the armies of Great Britain and France victoriously to Pekin not 5 years ago" — the memorandum demanded an end to Chōshū hindrances and concluded, "Trade never yet, in the history of the world, impoverished a nation." [62] This assertion was coupled with the notice that "The treaty powers will not consent to a policy of restrictions and exclusion — not only because it is contrary to the best interest of commerce but because it is a policy tending to perpetrate itself in wrong and mischief." [63] The Western powers held the bakufu accountable for Chōshū's actions, but when it became clear that the Tokugawa government was unable to control the willful anti-foreign acts they decided to take direct military measures. The folly of engaging the foreign powers in military action had become clear to a few Chōshū samurai. Itō Hirobumi and Inoue Kaoru, for example, who had made their way to London, had discovered that forceful exclusion of vastly stronger Western nations would be impossible and hastened

---

eyewitness report of the engagement only three days after it occurred. *Accounts and Papers*, LXIII (1865), 639.

61. British Government Publications, *British and Foreign State Papers, 1872–1873*, LXIII, 867. The memorandum was written on July 21, 1864.

62. *Ibid.*, p. 869.

63. *Ibid.*, p. 869.

home to dissuade their han from foolhardy actions. But the majority in Chōshū, and indeed in the nation, still favored action against the foreigners.[64] Yamagata in later years recalled: "I was at Yuda when I met Itō and heard from him about the situation in Europe and their superior military forces and arms. Nevertheless, I opposed Itō contending that conditions had become very serious and even if Shimonoseki were demolished we must carry out the aim of expelling the barbarians."[65]

Receiving no satisfaction either in Edo or in negotiations with Chōshū representatives, the treaty powers with "an entire identity of views and unity of action"[66] decided to take joint action to compel Chōshū's submission. Many of the han gun emplacements along the northern coast of the straits were manned by the *shotai*. The Kiheitai occupied two of these positions; the main force was stationed at Maeda fort and a smaller group under Yamagata's command was at the fort of Dannoura. On the afternoon of September 4, 1864, after all mediation efforts had failed, an allied fleet of eighteen French, Dutch, British, and American warships began a bombardment of the Chōshū forts strung out along the coast. "It was a beautiful show," wrote Ernest Satow, who accompanied the British task force as interpreter, "as the allied squadrons steamed in the consciousness of irresistible strength across the unruffled waters of the Inland Sea."[67] The allied bombardment was devastating in its accuracy and counterfire from the forts fell short. Yamagata left his own account of the first day's fighting:

> During the fighting the four ships which made up the enemy's left flank fired continuously on the Dannoura fort so I was unable to give any assistance to Fort Maeda [which was also under heavy attack]. In return we fired on the enemy ships from Dannoura and the sky was filled with shells which made it sound like a typhoon. However, the enemy's fire was far more severe, shells landing on the side embankment throwing earth and rocks skyward and causing much suffering. Shells landed in the hill behind the fort crushing and splintering the trees. Others exploded after sinking into the soft rice

64. Sir Ernest Satow, who participated in the mediation attempts, commented in a report on his efforts that the daimyo of Chōshū "was conscious of his own inability to cope with the forces of Western nations" but felt obliged to carry out imperial orders. Satow was also informed of efforts to involve the British in the domestic struggles: "They suggested it as a good measure that the foreign Representatives should throw the Tycoon overboard and going to Osaka, demand an interview with the Mikado's Ministers, and conclude a treaty with him." "Correspondence Respecting Affairs in Japan," *Accounts and Papers*, LVII (1865), 620.
65. *Gansetsu*, Part I, p. 64.
66. *Accounts and Papers*, LVII (1865), 609.
67. Ernest M. Satow, *A Diplomat in Japan* (London, 1921), p. 104.

fields in front sending forth earth and debris producing an amazing and dramatic spectacle.[68]

"Early the following morning," recounts Satow, "one of the Maeda batteries re-opened fire on the squadron anchored off Tanoura." According to Yamagata's account, as commander of the Dannoura fort he was responsible for this exchange which was accurate enough to cause some damage to the foreign vessels anchored close to shore.[69] The reply of the foreign guns was swift and accurate and Yamagata's guns were knocked out of action. The resistance made to the landings which followed the bombardment on September 5 was no obstacle to the superior foreign troops. The Kiheitai and other defending troops were thrown into confusion and could do little to prevent the capture and dismantling of all the forts. During the engagement on land Yamagata suffered a slight wound on his forearm, a mark which reminded him throughout his life of the helpless efforts of Chōshū to expel the vastly superior Western forces.[70]

During the heat of battle the leader of the Kiheitai had fled and Yamagata assumed overall command. The resolute way in which he took charge and fought during the battle won for him a commendation from his daimyo and a reward of an annual stipend of twenty-five *koku* of rice.[71] After the fighting Yamagata led the defeated Kiheitai inland where they encamped to regroup. This defeat, unlike the previous one at Shimonoseki in 1863, was followed by little talk of continuing the struggle against the foreigners. Yamagata was impressed as never before by the overwhelming power of the Westerners, the accuracy of their weapons, and the effectiveness of their open ranks in the attack. The bravery of the defending foot soldiers, more than equal to the courage of the samurai, justified the principle on which the Kiheitai was built, but inadequate and antiquated military training pointed to the need for drastic changes.[72]

It is difficult to understand what Chōshū hoped to gain by challenging the overwhelming power of the allied fleet. In view of the similar defeat the previous year and the warnings of Itō and Inoue and the disinclination of others, the action can be explained only by the fanaticism of the

68. *Gansetsu*, Part I, pp. 46–47.
69. *Ibid.*, Part I, p. 47.
70. This action is well described in Ishin shiryō hensan jimukyoku, comp., *Ishinshi* (Tokyo, 1939–1941), III, 483–486.
71. *Yamagata den*, I, 394.
72. Yamagata gave his reflections on the need for changes years later to a close acquaintance, Takahashi Yoshio, and the latter included them in his *San kō iretsu* (Tokyo, 1925), p. 80.

antiforeign sentiment determined to carry out imperial orders. This sentiment had been strengthened by the events suffered in 1863, and with a new fighting unit born out of former defeat a reasoned solution could gain little headway. But the second Shimonoseki battle was a defeat of far greater magnitude; the strength of the foreign powers was many times as large and the fact that they had joined forces with skill multiplied the disaster. In 1863 the French forces landed to destroy the forts in order to give Chōshū a lesson; in 1864 the allies demanded guarantees that the forts would never again obstruct commerce. On September 10, Chōshū was forced to agree to the allied demands. In the negotiations conducted aboard the British flagship *Euryalus,* Chōshū promised to allow foreign ships safe passage through the straits and, when necessary, to take on provisions and coal. No coastal batteries were to be allowed along the straits and an indemnity was exacted, which in time the bakufu undertook to pay.

The bombardment of Shimonoseki which forced Chōshū to capitulate to foreign demands, combined with the British devastation of the Satsuma capital the pevious year, represented a turning point in the movement to "expel the barbarians." In Yamagata it occasioned a sudden shift in attitude. The antiforeign policy was patently impossible of fulfillment in view of the great military inequality. Some months later two unidentified Chōshū retainers wrote the British chargé d'affaires a letter in which they declared:

> Hitherto there had been a great number of stupid and ignorant persons in our provinces, who still adhered to the foolish old arguments. They were unaware of the daily progress of the Western nations in the arts, being like the frog at the bottom of the well. But lately they have learnt in battle (though small) the accuracy of the foreign mechanical contrivances; the ease with which these are transported from place to place. The eyes and ears of the stupid having thus been opened, the question of opening the country to foreigners, or shutting ourselves up again, has become clear of itself, and there is very little difference of opinion on the subject.[73]

The experience emphasized the need to continue the reform of the Chōshū military system by incorporating more Western arms and tactics. As in the case of the defeat in 1863, both the Kyoto and Shimonoseki incidents pointed to the need for far more drastic measures. Greater military strength was required, not to face the foreigners with whom a

73. The letter, quite probably written by Inoue and Itō, was dated April 5, 1865, and sent to Mr. Winchester. Reprinted in *Accounts and Papers,* LXXVI (1866), 457.

new relationship had been established,[74] but to face the threat of the bakufu forces gathering to force the han's submission.

The "Chōshū Restoration"

Only a fortnight had separated the Chōshū attack on Kyoto and the foreign naval bombardment of Shimonoseki. The loyalist samurai had been humiliated and subdued, and the han faced military reprisal from the bakufu. It seemed that the gloomiest predictions of conservative Hagi bureaucrats on the probable consequence of adventurous action had been borne out. That Chōshū could recover again to lead the pro-court forces throughout the nation did not appear a reasonable possibility. However, peace had been made with the foreigners and the han undertook swift steps to meet the challenge of the bakufu.

Ever since the Chōshū troops had been vanquished in Kyoto in 1864, the bakufu had regained some of its former confidence in its ability to control national affairs. With the firm support of Satsuma and Aizu han, as well as the backing of other domains traditionally loyal to the Tokugawa house, the bakufu drew from the court an order to punish Chōshū. This was to be carried out by an "Army of Chastisement" before the end of the year. Assembling forces from several han at Hiroshima under the command of the daimyo of a Tokugawa cadet family, the bakufu gave every indication of ordering an invasion of Chōshū territory to force its submission. However, there was some opposition to this plan of action and, in any case, leaders of the operation, including Saigō Takamori of Satsuma, were convinced that the threat of invasion was all that would be needed to produce Chōshū obedience. This belief was not misplaced.

Although the loyalists in Chōshū were not prepared to defer to bakufu power, the pressure of imminent invasion had produced a change in the Chōshū government which did lead to the meek submission of the han.[75] Moderate leaders, who had been carried along by the rash policy advo-

---

74. In August 1865, soon after Harry Parkes had taken over as British minister in Edo, the foreign secretary informed him that "Both Prince Satsuma and Prince Choshiu immediately after the destruction of Kagoshima and Shimonoseki, sent agents with friendly overtures to the European Representatives in Japan. They declared that in attacking foreigners and resisting all intercourse with them, they were acting under the orders of the Tycoon, and that they were not opposed to such intercourse; but that, on the contrary, they were ready to open their ports to foreigners, and were only prevented doing so by the Tycoon who desired to have the monopoly of foreign trade, and to exclude the rival daimios from any share in it." Quoted from "Correspondence Respecting Affairs in Japan," *Accounts and Papers*, LXXVI (1866), 469.

75. For a description of these developments, I have relied on *Ishinshi*, IV, 155–187.

cated by extremists, fell from power and conservative bureaucrats established their dominance within the han councils. They quickly took control of all influential posts and prepared to accept all the demands of the bakufu.

The conservatives, known to the radicals as the *zokurontō* (vulgar party), acknowledged Chōshū's guilt and adopted measures to demonstrate the han's submission. The daimyo and his heir were moved to Hagi, where the seat of the government was now returned, and on December 24 they shaved their heads and went into domiciliary confinement in a temple outside Hagi castle. The fortifications in the city of Yamaguchi, which had served as han headquarters for over a year, were demolished. The asylum offered the court nobles was withdrawn and they were ordered out of Chōshū territory. Even certain changes in dress and manner were decreed to prove the han's peaceful intentions: blue *tabi* (socks) ordinarily worn during combat were forbidden, and feminine forms of the language, a sure sign of nonbelligerence, were ordered adopted. The most dramatic evidence of submission was the punishment of high han officials who were charged with the responsibility for the attack on Kyoto. Many were forced to quit their posts; four were sentenced to death; and the three leaders of the attack were ordered to commit suicide and their severed heads were taken to Hiroshima where they were duly identified by bakufu officials.

These measures satisfied the Tokugawa authorities charged with the duty of punishing Chōshū, so in January 1865 the army gathered in Hiroshima was disbanded and the contingents assembled from various areas returned to their han. The pressure from the bakufu was thus reduced by the conservatives who came to power, but they were unable to consolidate their strength within Chōshū. The loyalists and their military units, the *shotai*, openly resisted the efforts to suppress them and organized themselves to oppose the humiliating submission to bakufu demands. This loyalist faction, sometimes identified as the *seigitō* (virtuous party), had agreed that provocative acts against the bakufu should be avoided, but it stoutly rejected the policy of nonresistance. After Lord Mōri had been forced into semiretirement, this faction resolved that the conservative leadership of the han must be defeated. The *seigitō* based its strength on the auxiliary militia units which had been organized in 1863, of which the Kiheitai was the best known; these units were led by the same lesser samurai who had sparked the pro-court and antiforeign acts of the past. But through the lessons of ignominious defeat they had acquired a new sense of political strategy and discipline. For

Yamagata and other *shotai* leaders, such as Takasugi, Itō, and Inoue, the notion of "expelling the barbarians" was now rejected. They had all become aware of the power of the West and now the political situation which faced Chōshū caused them to direct their attention to new plans. They were no less committed than before to enhancing the power of the court and to bringing glory to the house of Mōri, but the strength of the bakufu, now supported by the emperor' approval of its punitive action, had caused the downfall of han authorities sympathetic to their goals and had brought dishonor to the Mōri daimyo.

Therefore, they were now determined to use the military strength of the *shotai* they commanded, first to regain control of the han government and restore the daimyo, and then to defeat the bakufu and restore the emperor to his rightful place.

In a general way, developments which took place in Chōshū at the end of 1864 were to resemble later events in the nation at large. Elements roughly similar to those which made up the complex political pattern of Japan could be found in Chōshū. The anti-Chōshū pressure of an unfriendly Tokugawa government and the han which responded to its orders might be considered analogous to the persistent pressure of the Western powers against Japan. Both pressures accelerated active internal movements for political reform. To gain power, radical loyalists of the nation clustered about the court in Kyoto and schemed to restore the authority of the emperor. In both situations court nobles, and in the case of Sanjō Sanetomi the same person, played an important role. The *zokurontō* in Hagi, like the bakufu in Edo, attempted not only to temporize external military pressure, which threatened to undermine its position, but to consolidate its local political control. Takasugi Shinsaku, one of the leaders of the anti-*zokurontō* group, was forced to flee from Chōshū just as the Chōshū extremists had been forced to withdraw from Kyoto. Military action finally gave victory to the *seigitō* and destroyed the *zokurontō* just as, a few years later, the bakufu was brought to an end by the combined military strength of the loyalists of the western han. Significantly it was the leaders of the "Chōshū restoration" who went on to become leaders in the imperial Restoration.

The actions of Yamagata during the waning months of 1864 are known only in outline. He led the defeated Kiheitai to Mitajiri, east of Shimonoseki on the southern coast, where a camp and a temporary hospital were established for the wounded. Before the conservatives swept aside all opposing sentiment from official positions, he succeeded in securing from a sympathetic official sufficient funds to cover the expenses of the

Kiheitai for a year. To improve the strength and discipline of the Kiheitai he met with some of the other *shotai* leaders to draw up regulations for their troops while continuing to submit petitions to the han government against the policy of submission.

The regulations adopted were designed to win the sympathy of the people as well as to improve troop discipline. Simple dress was ordered. The troops were ordered to use polite language, cultivate friends, and not to alienate the people of the countryside among whom they were forced to camp. Troops were not permitted to stay in farmers' homes or enter their fields; they were specifically warned against cutting down trees and stealing fruit and grain owned by the farmers.[76]

It is estimated that the forces of the *shotai* around Yamaguchi in late 1864 numbered 2,000 men.[77] With the growing strength of the *zokurontō* forces, these troops were forced to shift their location to a town on the southern coast where the headman was sympathetic to their cause. Here the irregulars waited for an opportune moment to strike against the han government.

As part of the unconditional surrender to the bakufu the *zokurontō* attempted to disband the irregular military units. To avoid any suspicion on the part of Tokugawa officials and to consolidate its own control in Chōshū, the *zokurontō* summoned the commanders of the various *shotai* to Hagi and instructed them to discharge their men. Instead of obeying this order, the *shotai* leaders, encouraged by Sanjō Sanetomi, held a joint meeting in Yamaguchi and drew up a statement condemning the *zokurontō* leaders for their execution of rival han officials and their appeasement of the bakufu.

It was Takasugi Shinsaku, who had fled to a neighboring han to escape death, who initiated the first act in the "Chōshū restoration." Upon hearing of the severe measures ordered by the "vulgar party," he secretly returned to Chōshū and with Yamagata's aid alerted the *shotai* for action. On January 13, 1865, he led two militia units, one of which was under the command of Itō Hirobumi, in a raid to seize money and supplies in Shimonoseki — the former base of the *shotai* which the "vulgar party" now held with regular han troops. Two weeks later the Shimonoseki garrison was defeated, the city was brought under the control of the *shotai,* and shortly thereafter they successfully repulsed a larger force of han troops sent to dislodge them.[78]

76. *Gansetsu,* Part II, p. 224.
77. *Ishinshi,* IV, 187.
78. In his correspondence with the foreign secretary, chargé d'affaires Winchester

Regrouping their forces, Takasugi, Yamagata, and other *shotai* leaders prepared for an attack on the han strongholds. Advancing north and east, they engaged the "vulgar party" forces, in February 1865, in a crucial battle at the towns of Edo and Ota, west of the city of Yamaguchi. Victory in this battle enabled the "virtuous party" to gain control of Yamaguchi and the *shotai* marched northward for an attack on Hagi. Hagi soon fell and the "virtuous party" put to death the han officials responsible for Chōshū's surrender to the bakufu, released Lord Mōri and his son from confinement, and kept them away from the conservative senior retainers. The older "vulgar party" officials were rapidly replaced by young, vigorous officials in full sympathy with the radical *shotai* leaders.

Yamagata led a force of some 200 men in the crucial battle of Edo–Ota. Edo–Ota was the decisive military engagement preceding the "Chōshū restoration," much as the battle of Toba Fushimi, near Kyoto, was to be the decisive engagement in the Meiji Restoration. In his own account Yamagata indicated the far-reaching consequences of this engagement: "The final victory which we were able to achieve through this fierce and bitterly contested battle caused great joy not only in our unit but in the two provinces of Nagato and Suō [i.e., Chōshū] and was to be the source of great rejoicing in the nation. From any point of view, if this battle had been lost, the han of Chōshū, the main element in the Restoration, would have lost its chance for revival."[79]

Reforms and the Alliance with Satsuma

By March 1865 the civil war in Chōshū was over and the conservative officials who had bowed to bakufu pressure were swept out of office. In their place, the daimyo selected ministers of moderate views who were sympathetic to the demands of the *shotai* leaders. A few extremists, notably Kido and Takasugi, were given official posts, and from these positions they were able to advance the aims of the radical samurai. The leaders of the new Chōshū government were fully aware that the outcome of the civil war would provoke countermeasures by the bakufu so

---

reported on March 30, 1865, that, after their final victory, Chōshū samurai who went to Nagasaki to purchase arms told a Mr. Siebold with satisfaction that in their action they were "imitating the tactics of the Admirals of September last, first bombarded the stockade from the ships, then landed men and took the enclosure by a flank attack." *Accounts and Papers*, LXXVI (1866), 444.

79. *Gansetsu*, Part III, p. 29.

their main task was to strengthen the power of the han to withstand the anticipated counteraction.

The bakufu was indeed alarmed by the sudden change. The triumph of the anti-bakufu faction in Chōshū posed a threat to its plan, which had made considerable progress, to regain its former authority in Kyoto and throughout the nation. As a consequence, the shogun ordered the Mōri daimyo to Edo and warned that a failure to agree to the summons would invite military punishment. The daimyo refused to obey and the shogun was left no alternative but to carry out his warning. Moving to Osaka, the shogun set about preparing for an expedition against Chōshū. Preparations required gaining support from powerful han and the sanction of the court. The latter was obtained but disagreements over the wisdom of subjugating Chōshū arose among the han generally supporting the bakufu. For almost a year, until mid-1866, the bakufu conducted negotiations, held conferences, and coped with the shifting positions of the han; only then could it complete the organization of the army of the second expedition against Chōshū. By the time the attack was finally launched, in the summer of 1866, the bakufu had lost so much time and had aroused so much hostility among previously friendly han that success was precluded from the start.

Time and the bakufu's inability to forge a strong military alliance gave Chōshū two critical advantages. First, it enabled it to mobilize for war; second, it permitted it to develop a military alliance with Satsuma. In the development of the first of these advantages, the threat of extinction provided the stimulus for military reforms. Learning the lessons of the *shotai* victory in the han civil war, han officials called upon those who had gained experience in the organization and development of the mixed samurai-commoner irregular units to carry out a complete military reorganization. The mobilization of all classes for the defense of the han was a conspicuous feature of these reforms. Yamagata and the other revolutionary loyalists participated in these reforms with enthusiasm.

In this undertaking the han was blessed by the presence of a remarkable student of military affairs, Ōmura Masujirō.[80] Ōmura, whose towering statue still dominates the main approach to the Yasukuni shrine in Tokyo, was a sedulous student of "Western learning." Born in 1824, in Suō, one of the Chōshū provinces, he had traveled to Nagasaki, where

80. A good brief account of Ōmura's career appears in Murata Minejirō, *Ōmura Masujirō sensei jiseki* (Tokyo, 1919).

he became acquainted with the distinguished scholar-physician Philip Franz von Siebold. Later he carried on his study of foreign things in Edo under the tutelage of the eminent Presbyterian medical missionary Dr. J. C. Hepburn. At first his talents went unrecognized in his own han but he gained a solid reputation in Edo for his knowledge in a wide variety of fields. In 1864, his own han belatedly sought his services and, with an annual stipend of 100 *koku*, appointed him instructor in military affairs at the han school. After the civil war in Chōshū, he was charged with the task of military reorganization and it was his suggestions which formed the basis for Chōshū's military reforms. His knowledge of military affairs came from his work of translating foreign books on military theory and practice. This knowledge was put to effect not only in his lectures on tactics and plans for military reforms but in the strategic plan he drew up to meet the threat of bakufu military action.[81]

The main feature of the reorganization was the Westernization of all military forces of the han. Prior to this, foreign weapons and tactics had filtered into Chōshū, but now a concerted effort was made to secure Western weapons on a large scale and to introduce all han troops to Western fighting methods and training. Instructors in the Western art of warfare who had learned from the foreigners at Nagasaki were invited to assist in the training and organization of the new military units. In April 1865, a han decision was made to replace as rapidly as possible all old-style weapons with modern rifles. Samurai with stipends of from 160 to 1,500 *koku* were formed into rifle units as were the *ashigaru*. The lower vassals of the six Mōri families in Chōshū and the two hereditary *karō*, or Elder, families were organized into a northern and southern battalion. The *shotai* units, including the Kiheitai, were reorganized into standard units of 150 men. In addition, certain lower ranks of the samurai class were organized into rifle companies. These newly formed units were trained and drilled along the lines of Western military methods.[82]

A major problem in the military reorganization was the procurement of adequate arms and ammunition. There were foreign firms in Nagasaki eager to sell military equipment, but Nagasaki was under the control of the bakufu and the latter watched suspiciously every Chōshū move. Some efforts were made to manufacture ammunition in Chōshū and plants were built at Yamaguchi and Kinguchi, but this was no solution

81. Murata, *Ōmura Masujirō*, p. 63.
82. For a description of some of these changes, see *Ishinshi*, IV, 368–370.

to the immediate problem. Ōmura went to Shanghai aboard an American ship to purchase weapons,[83] and Chōshū agents were sent disguised to Nagasaki to negotiate with foreign agents[84] for modern weapons. In Nagasaki, Satsuma had agreed to operate as agents of Chōshū in return for a commission paid in rice. This cooperation established an important bond between the two han. By August 1865, Chōshū was able to purchase some 7,000 rifles of the Minie (Minieru)[85] type from the British firm of Glover at a cost of 150,000 ryō[86] (Ōmura had estimated that Chōshū required 10,000 rifles). In addition, ammunition as well as two foreign ships were purchased by Satsuma agents for Chōshū, the latter through the newly established Chōshū Naval Bureau. Protests by the bakufu to the foreign nations and direct efforts to halt the trade were to no avail. It is of crucial importance that amidst a rapidly deteriorating national political situation Chōshū was thus able to rebuild her military power. The unity and military modernization through the purchase of Western weapons were the secrets of this successful reorganization — indeed, they were perhaps the key to Chōshū's successful role in the national upheaval that lay ahead.

While Chōshū increased her strength and gained new confidence through military reforms, another more important gain in the preparations to meet the bakufu was the conclusion of an alliance with Satsuma. The urgency of such a move was made plain by the bakufu's mobilization of forces; elaborate preparations were underway for a campaign, and even foreigners in Yokohama observed that godowns and stores "were emptied of every gun, rifle, pistol, and keg of powder which was for sale. All the disposable canvas has been bought up for

83. Tōyama, *Meiji ishin,* p. 161.

84. British traders in Nagasaki reported that they met Chōshū agents who were anxious to make purchases and extend trade to their han ports but that the bakufu would not allow it. In the Nagasaki trade paper appeared the statement: "Chōshū is also greatly in favor of foreign trade extending to its ports, but he [the Chōshū daimyo] declares the Tycoon will not consent." This was quoted in a memorandum of a conference between the British chargé d'affaires and bakufu officials on May 2, 1865. *Accounts and Papers,* LXXVI (1866), 458–459.

85. Norman, *Peasant and Soldier in Japan,* p. 33, footnote 47.

86. *Yamagata den,* I, 575–576. An indication of another method used to acquire weapons, as well as a footnote on a foreign adventurer better known for his activities in the Taiping rebellion in China, was the report that "The 'Monitor' with General Burgevine on board, who had formerly been in the service of the Imperialists and gone over to the rebels, had left this port [Yokohama], and gone to Choshiu, and taken from there the 'Lancefield,' one of Choshiu's steamers, over to Shanghae, and sold her there under a power of attorney from Choshiu, and that now the 'Monitor' was loading arms from Japan, probably for Choshiu." *Accounts and Papers,* LXXVI (1866), 459.

tents." [87] As the shogun prepared for the assault on Chōshū, han representatives attempted to arrive at a secret understanding with Satsuma. Negotiations moved sluggishly because Satsuma's cooperation with bakufu forces in 1864 in expelling Chōshū warriors from Kyoto had caused deep wounds that healed slowly. However, as in the case of Chōshū, Satsuma extremists had dropped their violent antiforeign policy and had sought foreign trade and aid through British agents at Nagasaki to embark on their ambitious program of modernization.[88] These same extremists had influenced the han to withdraw support from the bakufu's efforts to cooperate with the court, and they opposed military measures against Chōshū. By virtue of the fact that the young leaders of both han now shared a common distrust of the bakufu and both were engaged in military reforms through foreign purchases, they drew closer. But it was finally through the intercession of Sakamoto Ryōma and Nakaoka Shintarō, two Tosa samurai, that Satsuma and Chōshū leaders were able to resolve their differences and conclude a secret alliance. The object of the alliance, signed on March 16, 1866, was to bring about the military cooperation needed to defeat the bakufu and restore the power and prestige of the emperor. To this end, Satsuma agreed to exert her influence toward the reinstatement of Chōshū in the good graces of the court. In case the bakufu opened hostilities against Chōshū, Satsuma pledged to restrain Tokugawa forces by assembling troops in Kyoto and Osaka.[89]

With a military alliance with Satsuma and her own military power vastly improved, Chōshū faced with greater confidence the crucial test of strength with the bakufu, which commanded less authority than ever before. In June 1866, in hostilities known as the "Four Borders War," Tokugawa forces, half-hearted and disunited, invaded Chōshū at several points. With only one of its units drilled in European tactics, the bakufu's forces were no match for the Chōshū rifle units. During this

87. Report from chargé d'affaires to foreign secretary, June 10, 1865, in *Accounts and Papers*, LXXVI (1866), 465–466.

88. See Thomas Smith, "The Introduction of Western Industry to Japan," pp. 130–152. One of the students Satsuma secretly sent to England suggested to the British foreign secretary that the han, directly under the court, rather than the bakufu should conduct foreign relations. Saigō repeated this idea to a British agent who visited Kagoshima. Satsuma also showed its independence by exhibiting separately at the Paris Exposition of 1867. Tōyama, *Meiji ishin*, pp. 161–162.

89. *Ishinshi*, IV, 470–471. In support of these pledges Satsuma asked the court to pardon Chōshū and carry out reforms. Again when the bakufu ordered Satsuma to send troops against Chōshū, Saigō, commander of Satsuma troops refused, reportedly claiming that it was a "private war." Tōyama, *Meiji ishin*, p. 182.

action Takasugi, who also commanded the Chōshū navy, was responsible for the force defending the southern approaches to Chōshū. Bakufu naval units took the island of Ōshima in the Inland Sea, but Takasugi, leading a *shotai,* successfully recaptured it within a week. Ōmura Masujirō commanded the forces on the northern coast along the Japan Sea who were protecting the northern approach to Hagi. He successfully drove back the invading forces in the north deep into the neighboring fief. In the central sectors the bakufu forces also suffered a series of severe setbacks.

Yamagata, who had participated in the military reorganization of the han, was in command of the Kiheitai which protected the Shimonoseki port. He expressed his eagerness to serve the interests of Chōshū in a poem written in the summer of 1866.

> Like dew on the road
> I would like to sacrifice myself
> for the han
> in order to get rid of
> the threat facing us.[90]

His opportunity arrived when Kiheitai forces boldly crossed the Shimonoseki straits to attack troops of several han gathered in the domain of the Kokura daimyo. In a series of engagements the Kiheitai routed the enemy; Kokura castle was burned; guerrilla warfare continued for some months until, at the end of 1866, the han surrendered.

By September Chōshū forces had decisively triumphed on all fronts. The weakness of the Tokugawa military units was clearly exposed and the sudden death of the shogun served as a welcome pretext for the withdrawal of bakufu forces. The power of Chōshū was now revealed, and, with the home front secure, the han schemed for the defeat of the power of the bakufu throughout Japan.

There were many plans set forth for the best way to accomplish this objective. Yamagata's own ideas on what action Chōshū should take are included in notes he set down during the fighting against Kokura. "Since the enemies have been overcome," he wrote, "the situation has changed so that each major han will assert its own influence. Tokugawa power is steadily declining while Chōshū's military strength resounds throughout the nation vindicating long years of loyalty to the Court. But still some changes desirable for the han have not been brought about." At this point in his notes Yamagata describes the punishment which he be-

90. *Yamagata den,* I, 635.

lieved should be meted out to Kokura han to prevent it from threatening Chōshū again. "Under the present circumstances," he continued, "we must mobilize our strength for all contingencies by strengthening our determination and securing adequate arms." He proposed an expansion of the han army and navy, and, "most important of all, we must select able people, send them abroad in order for them to become intimately acquainted with world conditions and to acquire practical knowledge about warships, artillery, military systems and administration." Surprisingly, he also calls for the training of businessmen who could develop Shimonoseki to replace Osaka as a commercial port. He concluded his plan by advocating the destruction of Osaka castle and the pro-bakufu forces. "Then afterwards with our emperor above us let us spread his true will, reform political conditions, and thereby bring about a stable order." [91]

In the development of Yamagata's thinking, these views are enormously significant. They indicate that by late 1866 he had moved decisively from his zealous antiforeign attitude to the advocacy of bold measures, even including the sending of members of the han abroad to gain practical knowledge, in order to fulfill the plans to strengthen Chōshū. They not only visualize building up Chōshū power to defeat the bakufu but call for innovative reforms under a new national order — a foreshadowing of early Meiji policy. The further strengthening of the han's military by Westernization, the defeat of the bakufu, and the creation of new order under the emperor — these objectives, outlined by Yamagata and made possible by the bakufu's military debacle, were hastened by fortuitous events.

Within six months of the death of the shogun, which had helped to end the bakufu-Chōshū war, the emperor died. Both events favored the political power of the court. In the first place, Emperor Kōmei, never a vigorous advocate of imperial power, was succeeded by his fifteen-year-old son who was to fall under the influence of nobles who favored bold action to raise the voice of the court. In the second place, Tokugawa Keiki, the new shogun, was an able, moderate man who favored a realignment of power. He proposed a council of twenty-four major daimyo which would act as an executive body whose decisions would be carried out by the Tokugawa administration. To lessen the criticism of that administrative structure, Keiki vigorously undertook a series of reforms. But against the background of military defeat, the shogun's new policy was treated as a sign of weakness, and most of the daimyo, assuming a

91. These notes, entitled "Eya no negoto," are reprinted in *ibid.*, I, 687–688.

cautious but freer stance, hesitated either to oppose or support the proposal. In the end few daimyo accepted the invitation and the plan was stillborn.

This failure stands in sharp contrast to the successful broadening of the Chōshū–Satsuma alliance and the advance of the loyalist movement. Satsuma and Chōshū had drawn closer as a result of the secret alliance, but the Satsuma daimyo still was participating in negotiations with the bakufu and Chōshū needed reassurance of what steps could next be taken to realize its program of winning influence in Kyoto. After word was received of the emperor's death, Yamagata was instructed to go to Kyoto, as he had been nine years before, "to investigate conditions in the Kyoto–Osaka area." [92] His departure for Kyoto was delayed for some days by his marriage to Yūko, daughter of Ishikawa Ryōhei of Hagi. But marriage was only a momentary intrusion.

From Shimonoseki, Yamagata traveled through the Inland Sea on a Satsuma steam vessel. In verse composed during this mission, he records how uncomfortable he was from the heat and the noise of the steam-driven propeller; he could not sleep nor could he feel wide awake. In Osaka, he indulged in the latest fad by having his photograph taken. This prompted the lines:

> After death,
> what will happen
> to this unworthy body
> being photographed? [93]

When Yamagata arrived in Kyoto he was using an alias, Akimoto Takanosuke, because, with their han still in disgrace at Kyoto, Chōshū samurai were required to move about secretly to avoid bakufu officials.[94] He went directly to the Satsuma residence which now served as headquarters for Chōshū loyalist activities. Here for the first time he met the Satsuma loyalist leaders, Saigō Takamori, Ōkubo Toshimichi, and Komatsu Tatewaki. With his Hagi companion, Shinagawa Yajirō, he had an important interview with Lord Shimazu Hisamitsu. It was just at the time that Satsuma had organized a coalition council of four leading daimyo but found the bakufu unwilling to accept its advice. Hisamitsu explained the current situation to the two young Chōshū samurai: "At

92. *Ibid.*, I, 756. The same orders told Yamagata "to get further instructions from Kido Junichirō [i.e., Takayoshi] regarding your specific duties."
93. *Ibid.*, I, 793.
94. *Gansetsu*, Part IV, p. 28. On this trip Yamagata recorded, often in verse, some of his experiences. This diary, known as *Hizakuri nikki*, was published as the last part of *Gansetsu*.

present I have come to Kyoto to consult with the daimyo of Tosa, Echizen, and Uwajima and to offer my services to the country, but our suggestions have gone unheeded and, since the bakufu is incapable of reconsidering its position, hereafter we must plan with your han anew for the benefit of the nation. Kindly convey these sentiments to your lords. I will give detailed instructions to Komatsu and Saigō and send them to your han. Please consult with them." [95]

To show his goodwill, Hisamitsu gave each of them a six-shooter.[96] In their subsequent talks with Saigō and Komatsu, the Chōshū men inquired what the daimyo had meant. Komatsu explained that they wished "to devote themselves to the protection of the Imperial Court and petition for an Imperial Decree to correct the long-standing crimes and offenses of the Bakufu in order to strengthen the Court's position in the future." [97]

The information that Yamagata garnered on his assignment pointed unmistakably to Satsuma's decision to overthrow the bakufu. After returning to Hagi, again incognito and on a Satsuma vessel, he reported the results of his mission to han authorities. What he had discovered in Kyoto was sufficient to convince Yamagata of the sincerity of Satsuma's intentions and that the critical period for military action to crush the bakufu was near at hand. Wanting Chōshū to be a part of that action, he put his mind to conceiving a suitable strategy and submitted a plan of action to the daimyo.

He prefaced his plan by brashly reminding the authorities that his suggestions for handling the crisis in 1864 had gone unheeded and the consequences were tragic. As in his plan of action for 1864, he again called for building up allies among the various han sympathetic to loyalist ends and added that "if our han wants to proceed to Kyoto we must cooperate with Satsuma." [98] He then outlined specific actions for overthrowing the bakufu. First he called for the capture of Osaka and

---

95. *Gansetsu*, Part V, p. 6.
96. Yamagata expressed his reaction to the gift in the lines:

mukai ada	I vow to use
araba ute yo to	this weapon given me
tamawari shi	to ward off those
tsutsu no hibiki mo	who threaten us.
yo ni ya narasan	

Yamagata den, I, 795.

97. This explanation appears in the report that Yamagata and Shinagawa submitted to han authorities upon their return to Hagi. Reprinted in *ibid.*, I, 783–785. A translation of the report appears in Mushakōji Saneatsu, *Great Saigo* (Tokyo, 1942), pp. 243–245.
98. The plan is reprinted in *Yamagata den*, I, 821–822.

the gun emplacements which controlled it, and then for the assassination of Tokugawa Keiki, which, he felt, would bring about the fall of the bakufu and lay the foundations for an imperial order. The key to his strategy lay in the early capture of Osaka, followed quickly by enlisting the aid of other western han in attacking Kyoto. He also advocated as permanent policies the return of Chōshū samurai to simple ways in order to regain the stern strength of the past. As he had suggested in his notes written during the fight against Kokura the previous year, he again wrote that "it is my hope that in order not to lag behind and in order to build a strong, stable han, talented men should be sent to various foreign countries."

This plan of action submitted to the han in August 1867 on the eve of the Restoration is of interest on several counts. It indicates Yamagata's propensity and ability to think through a military strategy. It is couched in cautious language, advocating careful planning before decisive action was taken. Furthermore, it clearly shows how completely committed he was to learning from the West and building on the knowledge which could be gained by travel abroad. Although some of his recommendations were later realized, his plan was rejected by the han authorities. The final resolution of the national conflict followed a somewhat different course.

The Meiji Restoration

In the autumn of 1867, political tension in Kyoto reached the breaking point. Two parallel movements developed for reducing the bakufu: one, led by Satsuma and backed by Chōshū, looked to the forceful overthrow of the bakufu with the aid of Iwakura Tomomi and other radical nobles; the other, a more moderate plan developed by Tosa samurai and widely supported by nobles and daimyo, was aimed at persuading the shogun to return the political authority of the bakufu to the emperor. It first appeared that the latter had succeeded when Tokugawa Keiki resigned as shogun on November 3 and asked that "administrative authority be restored to the Imperial Court." [99] By the terms of his agreement, the court's acceptance of his resignation still assured Keiki a leading voice in a proposed council of daimyo and, moreover, requested him to retain his authority as shogun temporarily. But the apparent success

99. Walter W. McLaren, ed., "Japanese Government Documents," in *Transactions of the Asiatic Society of Japan* 42.1:2 (May 1914). (Hereafter this will be cited as *Documents*.)

of this moderate scheme precipitated a more radical solution. Through the machinations of Iwakura Tomomi, secret edicts were issued to Satsuma and Chōshū calling for military action against the bakufu and to Chōshū pardoning her daimyo for traitorous acts in the Kyoto incident of 1864.[100] Satsuma troops had been increased in Kyoto and joint Satsuma–Chōshū plans were made to carry out the court order. Chōshū troops left their han, some by sea and some by land, and went into battle positions outside of Kyoto. Although startled by these developments, Tosa, realizing that temperate measures were no longer sufficient, reluctantly joined the plans of the Satsuma, Chōshū, and also the Aki loyalists.

On the morning of January 3, 1868, samurai of these han seized the gates of the imperial palace from loyal bakufu troops.[101] This assured the Iwakura court faction of military control of the capital and enabled them to have the emperor proclaim an end to the 265 years of unbroken rule of the Tokugawa house and the restoration of imperial rule through a new provisional government. In quick succession all nobles banished for their part in planning the Restoration were restored to their rank and office, the daimyo of Chōshū was officially pardoned, and the ban prohibiting Chōshū men from entering the capital was lifted. In still another decree, Keiki was ordered to surrender "his lands, his revenues and the private property of his house to his Sovereign." [102] Keiki found it impossible to comply with this order and left for Osaka.

A few days after Keiki retired to Osaka, which was now a bakufu stronghold, word was received that the Satsuma residence in Edo had been destroyed by loyal Tokugawa troops. This news inspired the bakufu troops in Osaka to attack Kyoto. In the crucial three-day battle at the village of Toba–Fushimi on the road to Kyoto, the combined troops of Satsuma and Chōshū decisively defeated the numerically superior enemy forces. Keiki, this time retreating to Edo, was persuaded that all was lost and decided to surrender his capital to the imperial forces. But in the north of Japan implacable allies of the Tokugawa, and the han of Aizu in particular, resisted to the bitter end.

Although Yamagata was not with the Chōshū unit that helped to de-

100. The edicts were secured by Iwakura through his influence over the emperor's grandfather, Nakayama Tadayasu, and were countersigned, as they should have been to make them legal, by the regent, Nijō Nariyuki. In the end, of course, the legality of the edicts was quite irrelevant. For these events I have followed the concise account given by Tōyama, *Meiji ishin*, pp. 199–209.
101. The best description of this episode occurs in Nobutaka Ike, *The Beginnings of Political Democracy in Japan* (Baltimore, 1950), pp. 3–6.
102. Murdoch, *History of Japan*, III, 771.

feat the Tokugawa forces near Kyoto, he participated in the arduous campaign to subjugate the northern han holding out against the Restoration. As chief of staff of the expedition, and as leader of the Kiheitai unit in the northern battles, he fought for long, arduous months before victory was won. Not until July 1868 did the castle stronghold of Nagaoka in the province of Echigo capitulate;[103] four more months were required to force the surrender of the Wakamatsu castle of the Aizu han. The surrender of this castle, accompanied by the beating of drums and the flying of imperial banners, marked the end of the resistance of all Tokugawa forces on the main island. A few bakufu followers refused to give up and withdrew to Hokkaido for a final but vain effort to keep the old regime alive.

Yamagata's gifts as a military leader had already been proven in the more limited struggle in Chōshū; the northern victories made those talents now more widely known and the recognition of this ability was to determine his role in the new government. As Yamagata was returning from these victories, he encountered quite by chance the emperor's procession making its way to the new imperial capital of Tokyo,[104] as Edo was now renamed. This was a fitting symbol of the dawn of a new era, and as he reverently watched the long procession he might well have viewed it as an appropriate ending to a chapter of his own life.

For ten full years Yamagata had devoted all his energy to the loyalist movement which had finally triumphed. As a Chōshū revolutionary loyalist of lesser rank, he had engaged in political schemes and military actions which culminated in the Restoration of 1868. Accepting the *sonnō jōi* doctrine, he had identified himself with a national program of action; and while he had never lost sight of his obligations to the Mōri daimyo, he had also developed a burning loyalty to the nation as personified in the emperor. He did not hold a position in the han bureaucracy or rise through its ranks. His advance came wholly through his association with the *shotai* which served as the instrument of the loyalists' success. Yamagata was carried to prominence with the upsurge of the Kiheitai, first in its ill-fated antiforeign action, then in its intra-

103. The long struggle to reduce Nagaoka castle resulted in one of Yamagata's best-known poems:

Ada mamoru	I feel the summer breeze
toride no kagari	of the Echigo pass
kage fukete	as the shadows of torches
natsu mo minishimu	fade into the night at
koshi no yama kaze	the fortress defended by the enemy.

Yamagata den, I, 757.
104. *Ibid.*, I, 758.

han struggles, and finally in the wars against the bakufu. He did have personal qualities which helped to launch him on an eminent career: education, devotion to samurai virtues, ability to lead men and win their confidence, talent for planning and organizing, and courage.

These and other traits, however, were to be found in many of the idealistic and adventurous extremist leaders of the day. In fact, Yamagata's emergence as a local military leader was similar to the experience of most of the men who later provided national leadership. They were restive, young, low-ranking samurai in whom the spirit of militant action, long tempered by the bureaucratization of the samurai under the Tokugawa order, was resuscitated first by the foreign crisis and then by teachers who inspired them to transform local loyalty into a national sacred cause. When traditional vendetta-like acts against the foreigners proved futile, their action was redirected to bringing about internal changes to strengthen han power and to reduce the national authority of the bakufu. In these changes Western technology was of prime importance. It might be said that the revival of the samurai spirit combined with the spirit of innovation to provide the foundations for national leadership.

Yamagata's progress was also imbedded in the larger triumph of Chōshū's successful conversion of economic strength and a tradition of pro-court and anti-Tokugawa sentiment into a military advantage. In the end it was vigorous leadership and han unity combined with bold military innovations — the use of Western arms and techniques and a willingness to use commoners — that achieved Chōshū's superior position. When this superiority was allied with Satsuma power, there was created the decisive element that enabled the rebellious han to take over the task of guarding and guiding the emperor. These were the steps that led to the inauguration of a new era — so well illustrated by the emperor's transfer to Tokyo. These were the lessons of Chōshū's leadership in the Restoration that Yamagata carried with him into the next chapter of his career.

2

Consolidating

the Imperial Rule

It would be inaccurate to claim for Yamagata a leading role in the Restoration; he was cast instead in a supporting role. He was rewarded by his han for his services in the Restoration, but he was given a stipend of 600 *koku* of rice while Ōmura Masujirō and Kido, leading Chōshū figures, received 1,500 and 1,800 *koku* respectively; Saigō and Ōkubo, the Satsuma leaders, received 200 and 1,800 *koku* respectively, and Gotō Shōjirō of Tosa was granted 1,000 *koku*. Yamagata was representative of a group that gave significant support to a movement planned by others, and the scale of his reward was a measure of his part.

In the first decade of the Meiji era, however, Yamagata achieved the stature of a leading actor and participated with ever increasing influence in the decisive measures adopted by the new government. The most pressing problem facing the government was to organize sufficient strength to buttress the new regime against internal opposition and external pressure. While the emperor was restored to nominal power in 1868, it took a full decade to liquidate the old political and social order. The growing opposition of the samurai or, as they were to be known, the *shizoku*, was evidence of resistance to the policies designed to abolish old privileges and institutions. At each stage, however, the government was successful in mustering sufficient strength to overcome the opposition and enforce its orders.

In the development of a modern-style army, Yamagata held to the conviction that the nation's security should be based on a system of universal obligatory military service, and he was the prime mover in the organization of Japan's Westernized conscript army. The first decade in Yamagata's career after the Restoration is marked by three major achievements which we must consider: the adoption of conscription, the defeat of internal opposition led by Saigō Takamori, and the subsequent re-

first meeting of Yamagata and the emperor with whom he was to become so closely associated in future years.

The Birth of the Modern Army and the "Second Restoration"

Within a month after his return, Yamagata was asked to become assistant vice minister of military affairs. His selection was based partly on the military ability he had shown during the Restoration fighting and partly on the strength of the knowledge he had gained of foreign military systems. But perhaps more important in his nomination was the fact that the assistant minister of military affairs was Ōmura Masujirō, the brilliant administrator who had carried out military reforms in Chōshū after the han civil war. Ōmura, who knew of Yamagata's military reputation, favored his Chōshū colleagues.

Yamagata was eager to apply his knowledge and experience in organizing the nation's military system, but he was chary of the complex problems of which military reform was merely a component. He was aware that the formation of a unified army would weaken han allegiances; at the same time he believed that the power of the han could not be reduced and political power centralized without the support of a loyal imperial army under the Meiji government. Through his own description of the situation, we can see how the complexity of the problem at first discouraged him from accepting office:

> The Imperial Restoration was an unprecedented undertaking. The Court regained both civil and military authority from the Tokugawa government and sought to unite the nation and strengthen the foundation of the central government. The first requirement of the new government was to establish its authority by assembling actual military power. However, in spite of the fact that in the beginning it was decided to have troops from Chōshū, Satsuma and Tosa form the military strength of the central government, Satsuma and Tosa, dissatisfied with their role under the Council of State, withdrew their troops to their han. Saigō Takamori returned to Kagoshima as if never to return. Yanagihara Sakimitsu and Ōkubo Toshimichi proceeded there to encourage him to return to the capital but failed. In the military department, the center of our military activities, Prince Arisugawa was fortunately serving as minister, but Vice Minister Maebara Issei had already resigned over certain matters and chief secretary Kuroda Kiyotaka had taken another post. Furthermore, the military system at the time of the Restoration was extremely varied: the Osaka Military Academy adopted the French

organization of the army along German lines. In his achievements we find illustrated the capacity of the Meiji leaders to comprehend the mainsprings of Western military superiority and to apply this learning in the construction of new institutions. Yamagata became an apt pupil of the West, and some of his lessons were learned firsthand.

First Travel Abroad

Yamagata and his companion, Saigō Tsugumichi, younger brother of Saigō Takamori, were the first prominent Japanese to go abroad after the Restoration. The West had approached Japan with its military face forward; it was the technological advancement of the West as proven by its superior arms which had made such a lasting impression on the minds of the audacious samurai of the western han. It was appropriate, then, that Yamagata of Chōshū and Saigō of Satsuma, who were to contribute to the Westernization of the army and navy respectively, should be among the first to seek "wisdom and knowledge" from the West.[1] The necessity for adopting Western knowledge was realized by the new leaders and a variety of means were used: wide use of Western writings, employment of foreign experts and advisers, and the sending of individuals and missions abroad to gain firsthand knowledge of the West. Within a few years almost all of the high government officials had traveled abroad, and Yamagata's trip was part of the process of learning from the advanced Western nations.

In May 1869, Yamagata submitted to Lord Mōri a request to travel abroad. It was motivated in part by a wish to realize the unfulfilled ambitions of his teacher Yoshida Shōin, who had failed in his attempt to stow away on one of Perry's ships, and of his comrade Takasugi Shinsaku, whose premature death cut short his hope to go to England. In part, also, it was an expression of his belief in the desirability of foreign travel which he had declared in 1867 to his han superiors. In a sense, he was seeking permission to satisfy his own recommendation that able men be sent abroad "in order for them to become intimately acquainted with world conditions and to acquire practical knowledge about warships, artillery, military systems and administration."[2] In June 1869, the Meiji government recognized Yamagata's desire and requested Lord

1. Article Five of the Charter Oath taken by the Meiji Emperor in the spring of 1868 said: "Wisdom and knowledge shall be sought all over the world in order to establish the foundations of the Empire." Yanaga Chitoshi, *Japan Since Perry* (New York, 1949), p. 48.
2. *Yamagata den*, I, 687

Mōri to send him abroad "to travel around Prussia and France in order to observe current conditions." [3]

Joined by Saigō Tsugumichi and an interpreter, Yamagata sailed from Nagasaki in August 1869, bound for Marseilles. After a brief period in Paris, where everything he observed from political institutions to the local zoo deeply impressed him, he crossed over to London to spend the remaining winter months. During the spring he traveled through France, Belgium, Holland, Prussia, and Russia, carefully observing the private customs and public institutions of Europe and studying, in particular, the military systems of each country. Wherever he went he recorded his inner thoughts in the poems he jotted down. For example, after visiting the battleground of Waterloo he wrote:

> Snow fell
> on the batlefield
> where they fought
> with such fury.[4]

On another day he honored the memory of Napoleon in these words:

> Defeating all
> who challenged him,
> was he not
> the rarest of humans? [5]

He also noted, how, through universal military service, all males were given military training, instilled with the habits of soldiers, and made active defenders of their countries. Since he traveled as a private citizen, he was in no position to meet any heads of state and was forced to rely on the introductions and guidance of the Japanese students then studying in Europe.

While Yamagata agreed with the generally accepted belief that Paris was the true fountainhead of European culture, it was the militaristic spirit he sensed in the German people to which he responded most naturally. Berlin aroused him to write:

> This is the capital
> of Germany,

---

3. *Ibid.*, II, 13.
4. *Ibid.*, II, 31.
5. *Ibid.*, II, 32.

> where the military bearing
> is not rare.[6]

This favorable response to the Berlin environment predisposed him to believe in the strength of Germany. A trivial incident on the train en route from New York to San Francisco illustrates the point.

Yamagata and his traveling companion Saigō had heard about the outbreak of the Franco-Prussian War and struck up a friendly argument over which nation would win. Saigō, who had spent most of his time in Paris, was impressed by France's power and confidently predicted her victory. Yamagata, on the other hand, remembering the martial spirit of the Germans, speculated that "stubborn France would probably fall." [7]

It is difficult to measure the impact of this foreign travel on the mind of Yamagata, but his experience must have provided a powerful new stimulus. Although it left no doubt in his mind of the necessity for adopting modern ways and, in particular, a modern military establishment, from the outset he recognized that "knowledge gained abroad must be digested well before it will help in nourishing our institutions." [8]

In one noteworthy respect doubts were raised in his mind by his experience in Europe. Everywhere he went he heard praise of the recent changes which had been brought about in Japan. Yet he himself was deeply alarmed by the development of political institutions in Europe which tended to undercut the absolute authority of monarchs. In a letter to Kido dated December 19, 1869, he observed that everywhere the representative form of government was extolled and taken for granted. "Even in England," he wrote, "the King has lost much of his former power." [9] Disturbed by this development, he added that it would be most undesirable if the emperor's unlimited authority should similarly be reduced.

In early September 1870, after a year abroad, Yamagata returned to Tokyo. The day after arriving in the capital, he and Saigō were privileged to pay a visit to the imperial palace and make a personal report of their experiences and observations. This was the first time persons without rank or title had appeared before the throne. It was also the

---

6. *Ibid.*, II, 33.
7. Watanabe Ikujirō, *Jimbutsu: Kindai Nihon gunji shi* (Tokyo, 1937), p. 104.
8. Interview with S. Sheba, in the *Japan Times and Mail* (weekly edition), Feb. 19, 1921, p. 70
9. Reprinted in *Yamagata den*, II, 29.

system used by the Bakufu, the Satsuma han used the English system, the Kii han the Prussian system and others used the Dutch system or the Naganuma system. Not only was there this variety and disunity but Yamada Akiyoshi, adopting the plan of Ōmura Masujirō, established Osaka as the heart of military power and centered all military administration there. In view of these conditions it was clear that I could do little by becoming Assistant Vice Minister in the military department. Therefore, I refused the appointment.[10]

Despite the fact that the daimyo had voluntarily turned over their land registers to the new government in 1869, the political power of the han was still little impaired. The ex-daimyo still ruled their realms as governors and retained their right to levy taxes and maintain armies. The leaders of the Meiji government realized that the major step required to centralize power and to unify the nation was the reduction of the autonomy of the han. But this important step required sufficient authority in the hands of the government to assure its success. "Upon my return to Japan," Yamagata recalled, "I felt that the han must be abolished, but at that time the new government lacked the power to enforce such a measure. Feeling that there was no choice but to await the proper time, I dedicated my efforts to the unification of military strength which I felt to be the most important task." [11]

Without a central army the supporters of the imperial Restoration realized that political unity and power would remain a myth. A sentence in the 1867 memorial of the Tosa han, which successfully pleaded with the shogun to abrogate his political power, mentioned that "military preparations being one of the primary requirements, we need surplus soldiers as guards for the Imperial court and a military headquarters established somewhere in the Kyoto–Osaka area." [12] Itō Hirobumi had suggested that the troops returning from the northern expedition at the close of the Restoration should form a regular national army.[13] Kido had foreseen the importance of a national army when he suggested that three-fifths of the national income should be spent to establish an army and navy.[14] Ōmura believed that fundamental military reforms required

10. Yamagata Aritomo, "Chōhei seido oyobi jichi seido kakuritsu no enkaku," in *Meiji kensei keizai shiron* (Tokyo, 1919), p. 377. (Hereafter this work will be cited as *Shiron*.)
11. Yamagata, *Shiron*, p. 384.
12. Quoted by Osatake Takeshi, *Meiji bunka sōsetsu* (Tokyo, 1934), p. 172.
13. See Itō's letter of Dec. 14, 1868, addressed to the Council of State, reprinted in *Ishinshi*, V, 511–512.
14. *Yamagata den*, II, 54.

the abolition of the han, the end of the samurai's privileges, and the introduction of universal military conscription.[15]

In March 1868, a preliminary move was made to form a central military organization. A guard unit composed of contingents from several han and totaling some 400 men was organized under a court bureau.[16] Two months later all the han were ordered to limit the size of their armies and contribute to the expenses of a national officers' training school in Kyoto.[17] These measures were the first cautious steps toward the creation of a central army, but suggestions for transforming this joint force into a national standing army met with little response. Progress awaited a fundamental reform of the political order.

Yamagata believed that the first step toward unification was to persuade Satsuma to place its troops under the direct authority of the Tokyo government. Satsuma troops, the strongest military contingent in the nation, had been led back to Kagoshima by Saigō Takamori after friction developed between himself and other leaders of the Restoration. This peevish action had rekindled doubts in the minds of some Chōshū men whose suspicions of Satsuma intentions ever since the Kyoto incident of 1864 had not been completely extinguished. Ōmura Masujirō, for example, favored stern measures to restrain the Satsuma forces, and it was in anticipation of trouble from Satsuma that the first military headquarters had been established at Osaka. Yamagata, on the other hand, favored broad compromise to secure the cooperation of Satsuma forces in building a national army. So when Iwakura, chief minister of state, pressed him to accept a position in the military department, Yamagata placed two conditions on his acceptance: first, that the various han military systems would be unified and, second, that Saigō Takamori would be invited to take charge of military affairs.[18] These appeared to him to be the minimum conditions for success and so he made them the price of his active participation in the government. He felt that the unification of military forces sufficient to enforce the reforms of the new government required the influence, prestige, and support of Saigō in order to forestall the potential opposition to the government that Saigō

15. *Ibid.*, II, 148–150.
16. Matsushita Yoshio, *Wadai no rikukaigunshi* (Tokyo, 1937), p. 31.
17. The government order limited each han to sixty soldiers for each 10,000 *koku*, eighteen of whom were to be sent to Kyoto for training and service in a regular standing army. Each han was to pay 300 *ryō* (one *ryō* was later made equivalent to one yen) per 10,000 *koku* to the government, payable in January, May, and September. *Ishinshi*, V, 612.
18. Yamagata, *Shiron*, p. 378.

represented at that time.[19] Iwakura agreed that the two conditions were necessary for effective military unification and succeeded in persuading Yamagata to work toward fulfilling those conditions.

Yamagata agreed to join a government delegation going to Kagoshima on a mission to regain Satsuma support for the Tokyo government. His specific task was to persuade Saigō Takamori to rejoin the government as supreme military commander. Years later Yamagata recorded the conversation in which he urged Saigō's cooperation. He remembered saying, "Since the palace was shifted to Musashino, the guards have included only two battalions from Chōshū. I am sure you recognize the danger of this situation. Therefore, I beg you to lead a Satsuma army to the capital at once to become guards of the Imperial court and strengthen the foundations of the new government." [20] When Saigō replied, "I will consult Kido, urge the Tosa han's cooperation and organize an Imperial Bodyguard (Goshimpei) with troops from Satsuma, Chōshū and Tosa," Yamagata pressed the point further, commenting, "When soldiers from the three han are organized in an Imperial Bodyguard they would naturally lose their status as han vassals. Satsuma men must be willing even to turn against the Satsuma lord if the occasion demands it. Similarly Tosa and Chōshū troops must be prepared to disobey their lords. In other words, we must organize an Imperial Bodyguard in reality as well as name." To this demand which, if accepted, would cut deep at the root of the major problem facing the unification of the nation's military strength, Saigō replied with a curt, "Of course." After Saigō was assured that adequate funds would be available for training the troops, he "nodded his head in approval and decided to return. Thus one of my conditions was fulfilled." [21]

Saigō's promise to return met the most important condition Yamagata placed on his acceptance of office and so on September 23, 1870, at the age of thirty-two, he agreed to join the Meiji government as assistant vice minister of military affairs (hyōbu shōyū).[22] At the same time he was given the Junior Fifth Rank by the court. "Immediately upon entering the military department," he recalled, "I undertook to reform the military system."

19. Watanabe Ikujirō, Jimbutsu, p. 108.
20. Yamagata's account of this dialogue appears in Shiron, p. 379.
21. Ibid., p. 380.
22. Reprinted in Matsushita Yoshio, Chōheirei seitei shi (Tokyo, 1943), p. 41. This is the fullest treatment of the subject by the leading Japanese military historian. (Hereafter cited as Chōhei.)

A month after Yamagata assumed office, major steps were taken toward a modern national army. Standardization of the varying military systems employed by the leading han was the first measure in the unification process and was the object of the October 26, 1870, order of the Council of State which stated that "since in the regular government forces the navy is to adopt the English system and the army the French system, each han army should first change its organization and adopt the French system." Before the order was issued, a problem arose within the government over which Western military system should be adopted. Yamagata advocated the Prussian model on the basis of his favorable impressions of that system. The majority preferred the French system not only because several of the fiefs and the Tokugawa government had already introduced the French system with the aid of a French military mission but also because few Japanese had learned German, making it difficult to translate German materials and interpret for German experts. Moreover, Ōmura Masujirō, who conceived the basic outlines of Japanese military reforms, had favored the French system and used it in his planning. Consequently the decision was made to adopt the French system for the army.

The second major step in the unification of military power was achieved on April 17, 1871, when an imperial bodyguard (*goshimpei*) was organized constituting the first important military unit under the direct command of the emperor. The three major han supporting the Restoration each contributed organized units: Chōshū, three infantry battalions; Satsuma, four infantry battalions and two artillery units; Tosa, two infantry battalions, two artillery units, and one cavalry group. While this bodyguard totaled no more than 10,000 men,[23] it did represent the cooperation of three of the most important han. Furthermore, with this nucleus of military power it was possible, for the first time, to undertake drastic political reforms with greater assurance. In fact, in the early years of the Meiji era the new army functioned primarily as a police force to protect the new government against opposition and provide an instrument for enforcing political changes.

The organization of the *goshimpei* provided the opportunity for abolishing the han, and Yamagata joined Kido and others in working for the approval of this major political reform. "In order to realize the aim of the restoration of the Emperor," Yamagata reasoned, "all orders must come from one source. If all orders are to emanate from one source we

23. Yamagata, *Shiron,* p. 385.

must first abolish the han . . . In abolishing the han and establishing the prefectures it will be difficult to prevent the opposition of certain ex-daimyo and vassals. In some cases it will probably require suppression by military force."

Kido receives credit for taking the leadership in this important change. He first influenced Lord Mōri to submit a memorial to the throne in May 1871, which asserted that the "Imperial will has not yet been realized and much of feudalism remains." [24] This initial step was followed by many meetings of the young leaders of the government to arrive at common ground for the all-important step. Although Iwakura and others considered such a radical departure from old political forms premature, Kido's resolution, strengthened by the work and support of Yamagata and others, won the day. Saigō's support was crucial and he expressed to Yamagata his willingness to follow Kido's initiative on this issue.

At a meeting held at Kido's residence in Tokyo on August 9, 1871, the young leaders of the government decided to have the emperor summon the ex-daimyo, order the han abolished, and rid the nation of "government proceeding from multi-form centers." [25] Three weeks later, on August 27, an imperial rescript was issued which abolished the han and converted them into 302 prefectures. This decisive measure ended the feudal political structure which had existed in Japan for many centuries. Feudal autonomy was superseded by centralized authority and fiscal control became the exclusive function of the imperial government. Yamagata appropriately labeled this event the "Second Restoration," [26] and he was to be convinced that "it made possible for the first time the actual realization of the Imperial Restoration." [27] On the same day that the "Second Restoration" was achieved, he was promoted to the post of vice minister of military affairs (*hyōbu taiyū*).

The Enactment of Military Conscription

Yamagata's role in the abolition of the han was minor, although his work in the organization of an imperial military force had helped to

---

24. *Ibid.*, p. 384.

25. This is the wording used in the rescript abolishing the han. McLaren, ed., *Documents*, p. 33.

26. From a letter to Yamada Akiyoshi, dated Jan. 15, 1889, in *Yamagata den*, II, 1060–1061.

27. Yamagata, *Shiron*, p. 386.

ensure its success, but he was to be a major contributor to an even more far-reaching reform — the construction of a Western-style army based on a system of nationwide conscription. The plans for introducing it did not originate with Yamagata; rather he adopted the ideas of others and gained acclaim by the vigor with which he pushed them to completion. It even won the encomium of Yoshino Sakuzō, a leading spokesman for the social democratic movement in the 1920's and a bitter critic of the army, who wrote, "If Yamagata were to receive the thanks of the Japanese people a hundred years from now it would be for this one thing alone." [28] The ultimate objective of establishing a conscription system was to provide the nation security in an unfriendly world, but the immediate aim was to devise the most satisfactory method of organizing a national military force loyal to the emperor, which would maintain internal order and solidify the control of the central government. And indeed it was, as Sir George Sansom concluded, "the most effective single measure that the government was able to take in its campaign to consolidate authority." [29]

The introduction of conscription proved vastly more difficult than the abolition of han. There was, in the first place, no complete agreement among those intimately concerned. Furthermore, the issuance of conscription orders was greeted at first with resentment, evasion, and opposition. Serious uprisings of farmers and die-hard *shizoku* threatened to ruin the system before it was firmly rooted. Fully five years were required before all opposition was overcome.

Ōmura Masujirō, who served as vice minister of military affairs until he was assassinated in October 1869, gains credit for having developed the original plan for national conscription. Soon after he became vice minister, he suggested that an army under imperial command should be organized by selecting healthy men between the ages of twenty-five and thirty-five from each han for five years' service. These troops would be supplied and clothed by the government and given one-third of their pay — the other two-thirds, to be given to them when they completed their service, would enable them to start some enterprise. He further proposed the revolutionary idea that troops should elect their own commanders and officers.[30] Most of these objectives were realized, but Ōmura's insistence that feudal bonds be ended immediately, his im-

28. Yoshino Sakuzō, "Rekishigan ni eizuru Yamagata kō," *Chūō kōron* 37.3:71 (March 1922).

29. Sir George Sansom, *The Western World and Japan* (New York, 1950), p. 326.

30. These suggestions were included in Ōmura's memorial of July 1869, reprinted in *Yamagata den*, II, 149–150.

patience with han military authorities, and his bitter anti-Satsuma feeling aroused personal opposition which led to his assassination.[31]

Success required that the nationalization of armed forces be gradual; radical changes could not run ahead of the government's power to enforce its viewpoint. Yamagata seemed temperamentally suited to the cautious but steady approach which seemed necessary. Some opposition had already been encountered in the government's first move — the standardization and reorganization of the han armies[32] — even though samurai privileges were protected by the phrase "only samurai and foot soldiers may be selected to become the new soldiers." [33] In 1870, when Yamagata went to Kagoshima to persuade Saigō to contribute Satsuma troops and his services to the government, preliminary plans for conscription had been drafted. Saigō's approval of a composite force of troops from three han was viewed by Yamagata only as a necessary preliminary step in carrying out those plans. For it was not until the goshimpei had been established and then the fiefs abolished that the first real opportunity for conscription arrived. Four months following the dissolution of the han, in a joint memorial with the two assistant vice ministers, Kawamura Sumiyoshi and Saigō Tsugumichi, Yamagata suggested specific measures which should be followed to strengthen the nation's military power. The memorial called for the construction of warships and an expanded coastal defense system, the development of a military academy, and the building of arsenals and storage depots for arms and ammunition.

The heart of the memorial, however, was the proposal to develop a system of universal military training and to organize regular and reserve forces for internal defense. Invoking the experience of European nations, the authors of the memorial argued that "although standing armies vary with each country, even such small countries as Belgium and Holland have at least 45,000 regulars and . . . all European countries have reserves." [34] The memorial suggested that:

> The establishment of a permanent force is the most urgent task and should not be delayed a single day. Courageous, healthy youth should be selected from each area in proportion to its size and

31. *Ibid.*, II, 150–151.

32. In December 1869, while Yamagata was overseas, Chōshū ordered the abolition of the *shotai* in order to establish four companies of a regular han army. Some of these units, including the famous Kiheitai, refused to obey. A clash, known as the *dattai sōdō* (secession disturbances), ensued in which the han regulars defeated the *shotai* and forced their submission. *Ibid.*, II, 95.

33. Order to the han is reprinted in Matsushita Yoshio, *Chōhei*, p. 40.

34. This memorial may be found in Watanabe Ikujirō, *Jimbutsu*, pp. 135–140.

trained and drilled in Western tactics and used in any emergency. The so-called reserve troops would return to their homes in time of peace and be called for duty when the occasion arose. If we adopt this national system now, all males who have reached twenty years of age, are healthy and without home problems would be called to service. They would be organized into units regardless of whether they be samurai or commoners. After their service they would return as soldiers so that in each settled district there would be those who could defend. By doing this we will develop a means of defense.[35]

But the authors of the memorial went beyond the immediate need for internal security and emphasized the importance of a trained military reserve for external defense.

The immediate concern of the military department is with domestic affairs while external matters are of future significance. Upon reflection, however, these are aspects of a single problem. That is to say, if adequate preparations are made against the outside world, there will be no cause for anxiety over internal matters. At present our military strength, aside from the Imperial Bodyguard established merely to protect the Palace and Emperor, includes only the troops of the four garrisons numbering twenty battalions. These are assigned to maintain internal security not external defense . . . but with the significant changes resulting from the dissolution of the han armies and the collection of weapons, circumstances are appropriate for determining a policy for external defense.[36]

Alternative plans were presented by those opposing the immediate inauguration of universal conscription. Yamada Akiyoshi, a Chōshū samurai and follower of Ōmura Masujirō, proposed that conscription be postponed for eight or ten years during which time a corps of noncommissioned officers would be trained. At the same time, he argued, the rudiments of military training should be introduced to the entire population through schools and villages.[37] The idea of military service

35. *Ibid.*, p. 137.
36. *Ibid.*, p. 136.
37. Yamada's opinion appears in *Yamagata den*, II, 200–205. He called for the training of 14,000 officers and noncommissioned officers in schools attached to each garrison. Training would be for one year and include regular educational courses as well as military training, "which will not only strengthen the army but will contribute to the education of all the people." Upon completing their work, they would take an examination and then join the reserves. Thereafter they would return to the garrisons once a year to train for forty to fifty days. He recommended that basic military training in school be given to boys between the ages of ten and sixteen for thirty minutes to one hour daily. This training plus the drilling in the villages every Sunday would be under the supervision of a professionally trained officer residing in that area.

regardless of class was objected to in a memorial submitted by Tani Kanjō of Tosa. He proposed that all the sons of the *shizoku* (ex-samurai) should serve as soldiers, with no exceptions and punishment for those who refused. According to his plan, the common people would be selected for service only after all the *shizoku* were trained.[38]

There was no disagreement in the government over the nation's need for a strong military organization; difference of opinion developed over the best means of achieving that end. The strongest opposition to the idea of universal conscription came from the group which doggedly held that a standing army should be made up exclusively of *shizoku*. This approach attracted considerable support among Satsuma and Chōshū men. Maebara Issei, a Chōshū clansman and the vice minister of military affairs following Ōmura's assassination and prior to Yamagata's promotion to that office, favored this conservative plan. Of the Satsuma group the ex-daimyo, Shimazu Hisamitsu, and two of Saigō's able subordinates, Kirino and Shinabara, opposed universal conscription. Kirino later bitterly cursed Yamagata saying, "He makes dolls of these damn peasants. What possible use are they?"[39] The main argument of these men was that peasants could not become the high-quality soldiers the nation required, and, as Torio Koyata, a Chōshū general who opposed Yamagata's plan, argued, the spirit of the samurai would be weakened. Underlying this point of view was the resentment of many ex-samurai who realized that their accomplishment in defeating the bakufu was now to be rudely rewarded by the loss of their ancient birthright.

Despite this disagreement over the best method of mobilizing the nation's military strength, Yamagata's basic plan prevailed. His position in the military bureaucracy and his unyielding determination had much to do with his success. A key factor, however, was the role played by Saigō Takamori. Saigō, the most powerful military figure in the nation, maintained a stern silence while the arguments for and against conscription were being exchanged, never openly expressing himself on this issue. Doubts had entered Saigo's mind about the efficiency of an all-*shizoku* modern army, and it is known that he privately encouraged the idea of conscription through his support of his younger brother, then the assistant vice minister to Yamagata, and worked to weaken the most violent opposition of his own clansmen. Although evidence on this point is not extensive, it is sufficient to have convinced the most eminent authority on the conscription system that "without Saigō's private support

38. Excerpts from Tani's memorial appear in Matsushita, *Chōhei*, p. 119.
39. *Ibid.*, p. 198.

Yamagata's plan would probably not have been adopted; with Saigō's opposition it certainly would have failed."[40]

Yamagata persisted in his proposal to introduce immediately a universal system of conscription. He was conscious that the privileges of the ex-samurai, his own class, would be reduced by universal conscription. What in his experience made him its determined spokesman? For Yamagata there were convincing reasons. He argued that controlling an army of ex-samurai would present insurmountable problems and that such an army would be far more expensive than a conscript army. Furthermore, he was unmoved by the argument that only the hereditary samurai could become efficient fighters, capable of enduring the rigors of combat. His experience as a leader in the Kiheitai and the rudimentary conscription system adopted in other fiefs prior to the Restoration[41] satisfied him that the non-samurai classes were just as adept at learning the methods of modern warfare.[42] Some writers have suggested that since Yamagata himself came from the very lowest level within the samurai class he did not have the traditional samurai disdain for the lower classes.[43] Lastly, his feeling that peasants and townspeople could be made into efficient soldiers must have been reinforced by his observations abroad. He had noted that most European nations built their armies on the foundation of a universal conscription system. Since the ultimate purpose of a modern army was to protect the nation from foreign threat, it was by its nature a comparative institution, and unless it compared favorably with foreign military forces it did not fulfill its purpose. Both European precedents and his own military experience convinced Yamagata that the burden of national defense should be shared by all classes.

The urgency for conscription in Yamagata's mind was owing primarily

40. *Ibid.,* pp. 189–190. General Torio Koyata claims that Saigō agreed with his advocacy of an all-*shizoku* army but that such an important change should await the return of the Iwakura mission. Watanabe Ikujirō, *Jimbutsu,* p. 147.

41. In 1868, the Wakayama fief inaugurated a form of conscription under which members of several classes were trained together in Western methods. The Tosa fief organized a small conscript army the following year.

42. *Yamagata den,* II, 205. Yamagata concurred wholeheartedly with the opinion Takasugi had expressed some years before: "Battles which depend on gunfire increase the importance of group training and the problems of the individual's combat strength. The hereditary samurai who boast of their hand-to-hand combat strength have grown accustomed to inaction during years of peace. It is from the ranks of the lower samurai and foot soldiers, the peasants and villagers where vigor and vitality appear. If we now select the most capable of these classes, give them light equipment and rifles and group training, they will be able to resist the foreign barbarians." Quoted by Matsushita Yoshio, *Chōhei,* pp. 92–93.

43. Yoshino, "Rekishigan ni eizuru Yamagata kō," p. 75.

to his concern for internal security,[44] and it led him to submit a second proposal, entitled "Opinion Favoring a Conscript Army," in which he outlined in greater detail a system of conscription. This "Opinion" in effect became the draft of the conscription law.[45] It called for the conscription of all twenty-year-old males and stipulated service for two years in the regular service and an additional four years in the reserves. Yamagata strengthened his argument by proposing that the conscription be viewed as an integral part of the national educational process. He maintained that "If boys enter grammar school at six, high school at thirteen and graduate at nineteen, after which, from their twentieth year, they spend a few years as soldiers, in the end all will become soldiers and no one will be without education. In due course, the nation will become a great civil and military university." [46]

Before the conscription law was enacted, it was preceded by both an imperial rescript and a special announcement from the Council of State. These pronouncements, published on December 28, 1872, paved the way for conscription and attempted to win support for the law by giving it clear imperial sanction. The rescript, citing the experience of the past and the lessons learned from the West, declared that in ancient times "there was no distinction between soldiers and farmers, and now, based on the system of our ancient past and taking into consideration foreign methods, it is desired to maintain the nation's security by establishing a system of universal military service." [47] The announcement of the Council of State bitterly denounced members of the samurai class "who wear two swords . . . are indolent and arrogant and in extreme cases irresponsibly murder innocent people with impunity," and declared that "the samurai is no longer the samurai of former times and commoners no

44. In his February 1872 proposal, Yamagata enumerated five branches of the army which should be established and then declared, "all personnel of each branch will be assigned some duty and constitute the regulars. They will be assembled from the district under the jurisdiction of each garrison and . . . will be called up to defend each locality." (At the time there were four garrisons, at Tokyo, Sendai, Osaka, and Kumamoto.) Matsushita, *Chōhei*, p. 122.

45. This "Opinion Favoring a Conscript Army," which included revisions of his ideas by two officials of the military department, appears in Matsushita, *Chōhei*, pp. 119–125. Yamagata explained, "The Conscription order as outlined by the Imperial Rescript of December 28, 1872, and the announcement of the Council of State of the same day were based upon our ancient system and the laws of various Western nations and established a new method of conscription. The scholars Miyamoto Shinjun and Nishi Amane were responsible for drafting it." Yamagata Aritomo, comp., *Rikugunshō enkaku shi*, new ed. (Tokyo, 1942), p. 97.

46. Matsushita Yoshio, *Chōhei*, p. 121.

47. Rescript appears in *Yamagata den*, II, 194.

longer the commoners of the past; all are now equal in the empire and without distinction in their duty to serve the nation." The peasant and soldier should be unified to "bring about equality and make the rights of the people uniform." [48] For all twenty-year-old men to enter the service of their nation was to be regarded as a duty and obligation, a "blood-tax" payment, as the Westerners referred to it, in support of the nation's defense.

The Conscription Act was promulgated on January 10, 1873. Taking much of its wording from Yamagata's proposals, the law provided for seven years of military service after the age of twenty, three years in the regular army and four years in the reserves. This added one year of regular duty to Yamagata's original plan. In addition to the regular and reserve service, all males between seventeen and forty were required to register as part of a national army which could be organized in case of a foreign attack or an extreme emergency.[49] Those who proved their superiority in military training would be transferred to the imperial guard.[50] At this same time six garrisons were established to serve as centers for training the troops and as military headquarters of the six military zones into which the nation was divided.

In the outline of the principles and organization of the conscription system and in the details included in the method of conscription there were very few major departures from Yamagata's plan. In the provision for liberal exemptions, however, there was a conspicuous difference. The final law provided for various types of exemption: the physically un-qualified; household heads and their heirs; students in military schools; hardship cases; criminals; those in certain stipulated professions; government officials and all teachers and students of prescribed schools; and, finally, all who could pay 270 yen.[51] These exemptions were included as a concession to those opposed to conscription. They favored the *shizoku*

---

48. The announcement of the Council of State is reprinted in *ibid.*, II, 195–196.

49. The full text of the Conscription Act is found in Matsushita Yoshio, *Chōhei*, pp. 137–166. In English, the law is analyzed and important provisions translated in Gotarō Ogawa, *The Conscription System in Japan* (New York, 1921), pp. 10–15.

50. On April 16, 1872, the name *goshimpei* (imperial bodyguard) was changed to *konoetai* (imperial guard) as a result of Yamagata's memorial disapproving the old name as unrefined. A separate *konoe* bureau was maintained at the palace to supervise the guard. *Yamagata den*, II, 168–169. Yamagata desired to reorganize the imperial guard because, organized as it was of *shizoku* units from three units from three han, it proved difficult to control. In the conscription law it stated that "outstanding men would be selected from each garrison to serve in the Imperial Guard for a period of five years after which they would be placed outside the reserves and exempt from further military service." This proposal, however, was successfully resisted by the officers of the unit and proved to be a minor cause of the Satsuma rebellion in 1877.

51. Matsushita Yoshio, *Chōhei*, pp. 169–170.

class and the well-to-do. The exemption for household heads and heirs, designed to give stability to families, did not in itself favor the *shizoku;* however, the fact that the *shizoku* class monopolized the professions and officialdom exempted a large group of the class, while the substitution of money clearly favored the wealthy. These exemptions infringed the equality of the national duty proclaimed of all citizens, but such compromises seemed necessary to assure enforcement of conscription. Furthermore, the government, in financial difficulties, welcomed additional sources of income at a time when it had only limited training facilities. Although Yamagata did not favor such broad exemptions, he did suggest that conscripts from the wealthier classes be selected first as they could more easily bear the burden of the soldier's low income.

The Opposition to Conscription and the Korean Crisis

The successful enactment of a conscription law, which in time became the basis of Japan's modern military power, was preceded by vigorous debate and considerable opposition within the government; it was followed by four years of serious resistance and open defiance. To make the exclusive duty of one class the right and obligation of all classes was bound to arouse deep resentment. At times it seemed that the system would fail, but those who had inaugurated it held staunchly to their conviction, advocating firm measures against all anticonscription demonstrations and disapproving any premature use of the new conscript army in overseas ventures that might weaken the whole system.

Opposition appeared in several forms. Among the peasants there was at first widespread evasion and opposition based on the sentiment that it was an oppressive law. Already heavily taxed to support the government, many peasants found the loss of a strong arm from the farm work intolerable. Service was often evaded by arranging for a favorite younger son to be adopted by a childless friend for a few years, thus making him an heir in another household.[52] Many eligible for service fled to the unsettled areas in the north to become pioneers in the development of Hokkaido. Antagonism among the peasantry was also caused by ignorance and misunderstanding of the aims of conscription. By late spring, 1873, the Council of State found it necessary to publish a special notice to dispel the fears of the peasants arising from a literal interpretation of the term "blood tax" which appeared in the conscription order. The term, adopted from Europe, where it served as a symbol of military

52. *Ibid.,* p. 174.

service to one's country, was often taken to mean the forced sale of one's blood. The blood was to be sold to the foreigners, so the rumors went, or to be used for dye for the army's red hat bands.[53]

The inclusion of the pariah or *eta* class in the conscript army proved another cause of trouble. Prior to conscription, the government had proclaimed social equality for the *eta* and renamed them the "new commoners." Yamagata had taken the precaution of assigning the new commoners to work in repairing shoes in the army, since *eta* traditionally worked with leather, but these measures were inadequate to offset the social attitudes of centuries, which erupted in violent demonstrations in Hiroshima, Himeji, and Kyoto, where peasants and townsmen reacted against the inclusion of *eta* in their army units.

It is difficult to distinguish anticonscription feelings from other motives in the many agrarian uprisings of the early Meiji period.[54] Often these were caused primarily by economic grievances, with conscription merely providing an additional motive. Nevertheless, it is estimated that opposition to conscription was the primary cause of at least fifteen major peasant unrisings.[55] Had these been coordinated, they might have proved disastrous to the conscription system, but government counteraction was successful in each instance. Relying upon ex-samurai stationed in garrisons or on those who had become policemen, the government easily quashed the disturbances.

While the resistance of the peasantry placed obstacles in the way of conscription, these were in time removed. The opposition of the *shizoku* class posed a far greater threat. Many of the ex-samurai who fought conscription from within the government organized opposition outside official circles after its enactment. In the case of the *shizoku* class as in the case of the peasantry, it is often difficult to point to anticonscription as the sole or primary cause for its increasing opposition to the policies of the central government. But whatever the forms the opposition took, it indicated a refusal on the part of a growing number of the *shizoku* class to make the shift into a new era. For four years the government faced a series of crises in which its policies were openly challenged by disgruntled and discontented ex-samurai, who through conscription and other measures were deprived of the feudal prerogatives.

The first of these, the Korean crisis in 1873, faced the government eight months after the enactment of conscription. When the Meiji Em-

---

53. *Ibid.*, p. 211.
54. Peasant uprisings numbered 277 by 1877. *Ibid.*, p. 219.
55. Each major revolt is described in *ibid.*, pp. 211–219.

peror ascended the throne, a mission was sent to Korea to announce the change and was discourteously refused recognition. Three separate missions were later sent to open friendly relations, but each time the Koreans refused to receive the emissaries. These repeated humiliations caused a growing resentment within Japan and provided a pretext which the disaffected elements in Japan could use to force through their demands for action and change in the government's policies.

The agitation for a punitive expedition against Korea came to a head during the absence abroad of Iwakura, chief of the Council of State, and an important party of government leaders who sought to combine a goodwill mission, a search for appropriate foreign models for the reconstruction of Japanese institutions, and preliminary action toward the revision of the unequal treaties.[56] To those dissatisfied with domestic developments, the subjugation of Korea seemed not only an appropriate way to divert the government from carrying out further legislation which struck at the heart of feudal practices but also a method of asserting Japanese power abroad.[57] Saigō Takamori, leading military figure in the nation and a councillor, served as the spokesman for the frustrated and disaffected *shizoku*. His strong position, supported by a majority in the Council of State, produced a decision in the summer of 1873 to take aggressive action against Korea. The decision could not be acted upon, however, because the council had been pledged to undertake no major changes in policy before the return of the Iwakura mission.[58]

During the early months of 1873, Yamagata, as head of the army, was preoccupied with plans for carrying into effect and for overcoming any resistance to the conscription law. He traveled about the country to check the operation of the new system, and when the Korean crisis came to its crest, he was on an inspection trip of the garrisons in western Japan. He had become the army minister when a government reorgan-

---

56. The mission of forty-nine officials included Kido, a member of the Council of State, finance minister Ōkubo and Itō, then vice minister of industry. The mission was as much, if not more, concerned with the aim of establishing goodwill and studying the West as with the revision of the treaties — the objective usually attributed to the mission. In fact, the intention was merely to explore in a preliminary fashion the question of treaty revision. Marlene Mayo, "The Iwakura Mission to the United States and Europe, 1871–1873" (unpublished Master's thesis, Columbia University, 1957).

57. Maruyama Masao has suggested that in addition to relieving the discontent of the ex-samurai class, demands for action in Korea were motivated by: the desire to assert national strength as a method of ridding Japan of the unequal treaties; the conviction that Asian alliances should be built up to check the European powers; and the wish to imitate on a small scale the imperialism of the Western powers. Maruyama Masao, "Meiji kokka no shisō," in *Nihon shakai no shiteki kyūmei* (Tokyo, 1949), pp. 189–191.

58. *Yamagata den*, II, 308.

ization in April 1872 established separate war and navy ministries, but he was not yet a councillor. Consequently, he had not participated in the discussion within the Council of State which led to the acceptance of Saigō's proposal for action against Korea.[59] Nevertheless, he had made his views known on the question. Although he shared Saigō's view of the desirability of a strong policy on the continent, he opposed any premature action which might cripple the growth of the new army. From this conviction he did not deviate, and before leaving on his tour of inspection he had written Saigō: "Our army is presently in the midst of reorganization. After one or two years when the foundation of the military system is established, there will probably be no obstacles to sending troops to the continent." [60] Little did Yamagata realize that this was the beginning of a split with Saigō.

Yamagata's argument received decisive support from the councillors returning with the Iwakura mission in September 1873. The opposition to Saigō, led by Ōkubo, based its objections on faulty timing, not on final objectives,[61] arguing that the heavy taxes and the foreign loans required to finance an expedition would jeopardize the nation's finances and risk foreign intervention.[62] All the members of the mission had received a sobering lesson on the distance Japan would have to travel to rival the strength of the major Western states. To dissipate the nation's energy so soon and to risk the ill will if not the opposition of foreign powers, they felt, would be foolhardy. In a crucial meeting of the council on October 14, the "war party" held a majority of one, but with the sudden illness of Sanjō, who had become chief of the council when Iwakura went abroad, and Iwakura's assumption of that post, the decision for war was reversed. Iwakura refused to approve the scheme and had the emperor revise his earlier sanction of belligerent action.

On October 25, 1873, the advocates of war within the Council of State all resigned, an act which marks an important juncture in the political history of the Meiji period.[63] The leadership of the nation was split; the coalition which had been formed to defeat the bakufu was shattered;

59. Text of the agreement and the names of those who signed it appear in *ibid.*, II, 308.

60. *Ibid.*, II, 308.

61. Ike, *Beginnings*, pp. 52–53. Ike includes an excerpt from an interesting letter from Kido to Ōmura, p. 51, footnote 16.

62. Kiyosawa Kiyoshi, *Nihon gaikō shi* (Tokyo, 1942), I, 199.

63. Chapter 5, "The Crisis of 1873," in Ike's *Beginnings*, as well as the same author's "The Triumph of the Peace Party in Japan in 1873," *Far Eastern Quarterly* 2.3:286–295 (May 1943), gives a good account of this crisis. A leading Japanese account is Tanaka Sōgorō, *Seikan ron: seinan sensō* (Tokyo, 1939), pp. 1–76.

the process of narrowing the ruling group had begun. From this event dates the development of two strong antigovernment forces. One force, represented by Saigō and composed of disgruntled *shizoku*, raised the threat of armed revolt. The other force, best represented by Itagaki, demanded a share in authority through elected representatives. Yamagata's efforts both as a political and military figure were directed, after the resolution of the Korean crisis, at containing the threat these two forces posed to the development of a militarily strong, politically stable government. The victory of the "peace party" saved the conscription system from a premature test, but the price of victory was, as we shall see, high.

The Aftermath of the Korean Crisis

One of the first problems facing the government in the wake of the Korean crisis was dissension in the ranks of the imperial guards. The sudden resignation of Saigō, at the time commander of the imperial guard, seriously affected the morale of its officers. Many of them were Satsuma men who immediately withdrew to follow Saigō. Among other things, these officers attacked Yamagata's integrity and the influence of Chōshū in the guards.[64]

The government was alarmed by the weakening of the guard. Kido feared that the unrest would spread to the garrisons, training camps,[65] and police,[66] within whose ranks there were a great number of Satsuma ex-samurai, and he therefore urged that the imperial guard be completely reorganized. Ōkubo and Iwakura succeeded in having the emperor address its officers to prevent them from leaving. With little regard for the truth, the officers were told that Saigō had resigned because of ill health, and that although he could not serve as a councillor or as a commander of the guard, he retained his rank of general and would be a pillar of the state. But this effort, and even a second plea by the emperor,

---

64. Yamagata had assumed command of the imperial guard in 1872 but he was forced to give up the post as a result of the "Yamashiroya Affair." Yamashiroya Wasuke had become a merchant in Chōshū many years after he had fought in the Kiheitai under his real name, Nomura Michizō. Relying on his friendship with Yamagata, he had received loans from the army to expand his business of producing military supplies. When it was discovered that Yamashiroya had embezzled these funds, Yamagata demanded that the loans be repaid. Unable to do this, Yamashiroya was driven to desperation. On the morning of Dec. 29, 1872, he entered the army department and in the waiting room committed suicide. Yamagata felt obliged to bear responsibility for this affair and returned the command of the guard to Saigō. Tanaka, *Seikan ron*, p. 37.

65. *Ibid.*, pp. 78–79.

66. See entries from Kido's diary reprinted in *Yamagata den*, II, 315.

failed to halt the withdrawal of over 100 officers, most of them from Satsuma.[67]

The Korean crisis marked an important step in Yamagata's rise to power within the military service. Saigō's departure left him indisputably the leading military figure in the government. He reassumed command of the imperial guard and, with a grant of 36,000 yen from the emperor's private funds, he set about its reorganization.[68] In doing this he placed many Chōshū men in important posts, a step which paved the way for the domination of the army by Chōshū men inasmuch as most of the important generals of the Japanese army were to come from the ranks of the guard officers. To assume command of the guard he resigned as army minister but became head of the Sixth Bureau, the operations section of the army department. In June 1874, he reassumed the army ministry post, but retained his field command; in August he was appointed a councillor of state.

The imperial guard was brought under control but other threats to the government developed. In February 1874, Etō Shimpei of the "war party" seceded from the Council of State and led 2,000 shizoku in an uprising in the han of Hizen. Calling themselves the Seikantō, or "Party to Chastise Korea," these ex-samurai assembled weapons and supplies and launched an attack which succeeded in capturing Saga castle, the capital of the han.[69] The insurgents hoped to spark a large uprising which would challenge the government's control. Fearing that they might be successful, the government moved quickly to defeat the insurrection. Ōkubo, head of the newly formed home ministry, was charged with its suppression, but Yamagata was directly responsible for the army's counteraction. Ordering the Kumamoto garrison to suppress the revolt and the Osaka and Tokyo garrisons to send reinforcements, he personally led a regiment of the guards and a company of the Tokyo garrison to Hizen. His force had reached the port of Kobe when word was received that the revolt had been suppressed.[70] Swift countermeasures, and later the summary execution of the leaders of the revolt, succeeded in preventing the spread of the antigovernment movement.

But there remained continuing danger of insurrections, complicated by the growing pressure from the second source of government opposi-

67. In January 1874, *The Far East,* a foreign newspaper published in Japan, reported that 500 Satsuma men on the Tokyo police force had demanded money to return to Kagoshima.
68. *Yamagata den,* II, 321.
69. Tanaka, *Seikan ron,* pp. 100–101.
70. *Yamagata den,* II, 328.

tion — that group of the *shizoku* who sought a share in authority through elected representatives. In January 1874, a Tosa group under the leadership of Itagaki, who had resigned from the Council of State over the Korean issue, submitted a memorial demanding the establishment of representative government.[71] This memorial and subsequent suggestions of the same character were parried by the government. But the political and military pressures continued to mount until Ōkubo, the most forceful member of the government after Saigō's withdrawal, felt sufficiently pressed to seize upon a new crisis in foreign relations as a way of diverting the growing threats to the government and its program.

The foreign crisis grew out of the slaying of sailors from the Ryūkyū Islands by Formosan aborigines late in 1871. Diplomatic efforts to seek a settlement with China foundered on the rival claims of China and Japan to sovereignty over the Ryūkyū Islands. Direct action in Formosa was advocated by a growing number of *shizoku* already irritated by the lack of an expedition to Korea and disgruntled at the loss of old privileges. On this occasion Ōkubo, who had been the key figure in the defeat of the Korean expedition, became the main advocate of a punitive expedition to Formosa to force China to pay an indemnity. The shift in Ōkubo's stand can be explained only by the need to divert the pressure exerted against the government's policies. But when these pressures threatened to get out of hand, it was decided to make concessions to the advocates of representative government as well as to send an expedition to Formosa. On April 14, 1874, an imperial decree called for an assembly of prefectural governors, and in May a contingent of over a thousand men, including a regular army unit from the Kumamoto garrison and voluntary *shizoku* from Satsuma, landed on Formosa.

The decision in favor of an expedition to Formosa was opposed by Yamagata and vigorously disapproved by Kido who finally resigned in protest. Following Kido's example, Yamagata submitted his resignation but it was not accepted. Yamagata opposed the action because, as he argued in the Korean crisis, such a move was premature and subjected the embryonic army to an unnecessary test. The clearest expression of Yamagata's reasoning is found in a memorandum dated July 8, 1874. The chief minister of state (*daijin*) had requested his views on the Formosan affair and so he wrote out his opinions in the form of a statement to his subordinate officers in the army ministry.

Since the Restoration we have certainly strived energetically to build

71. The memorial appears in McLaren, ed., *Documents*, pp. 426–432.

73

a national military system and since the day I assumed responsibility some progress has been made. Nevertheless, from the standpoint of my long-range plans, we still have not achieved our objective. Officers have not yet been well trained, soldiers are still trained inadequately, and equipment is still insufficient; furthermore, no plan for defense of the homeland has been developed. I believe that unless for the next several years we endeavour constantly to dedicate ourselves to the unfinished task we cannot build the foundations of our Imperial army and demonstrate to all our nations dignity. If we should commit more troops and from this situation a clash with China should result, the disadvantages would be beyond description. These are the grounds on which I have taken my position.[72]

In these words Yamagata argued that priority should be given to building internal strength and warned that adventurous acts might provoke a war with China for which Japan was not prepared.

Yamagata remained in office during the Formosan affair and resigned himself to the expedition. In the above memorandum he makes it clear that he had not been a party to the plans for the Formosan adventure but added that the decision for war was not within the power of the army minister. However, he was a dissatisfied public servant, as shown by his serious concern with the nation's future and by such social activities as his membership in an informal social club known as the *Yūhōsha* or "Like-Minded Group." [73] Opposed to the Formosan expedition, the club members, who never exceeded a dozen, met informally to exchange views on current questions, religion, art, and so forth. The last records of the group are dated September 1874; the club was significant only in that it was a reflection of a measure of discontent within the ranks of the bureaucracy.

Doubtful of the wisdom of the government's course of action, Yamagata turned his attention to formulating a broad plan to increase the nation's preparedness. In August he submitted to the emperor the first of many written judgments he was to offer on the state of the nation's defenses. These opinions usually included an appraisal of Japan's international strategic position. The stages in the growth of Japan's military strength may be traced through these documents. As we shall see, the constant theme running through these memorials was the continuing

72. The memorandum appears in Hirata Tomotarō, comp., *Ōkuma monjo* (Tokyo, 1958), I, 75–77.
73. The founders of the club included Yamagata, Itō, Yoshikawa Akimasa, Tanaka Kōken, and Mutsu Munemitsu. *Yamagata den*, II, 386–398.

need for strengthening the nation in order to face the international situation. A second constant theme was the identification of Russia as the power most threatening to the nation's security.

"We have achieved our independence," Yamagata wrote in his August 1874 memorial, "but still lack the power to oppose threats from abroad, particularly the Russian threat from the north." [74] He declared that the nation's strength depended as much upon economic development and a rising level in the people's welfare and intelligence as it did upon the military adventures. He pointed to four specific weaknesses in the nation's military power: brave officers were available but their training was inadequate; able troops were available but they required greater discipline; arms and ammunition were insufficient; and coastal defenses were still inadequate. Yamagata apologized for these unsamurai-like observations but justified his realism on the grounds of the overriding importance of the nation's security. Even if the Formosan expedition were successful, he added, it would contribute little to solving the nation's basic problems. In actual fact, it had committed untrained officers and green troops and increased the serious problem of enforcing discipline.[75]

Meanwhile military operations in Formosa continued; these consisted of patrol activity and minor skirmishes against unequipped natives by a motley force of Satsuma *shizoku* and a few regular army units. Most of the 1,300 troops suffered from malaria before the six-month operation was terminated.[76] As reinforcement for the diplomatic exchange proceeding in Peking, however, the landing was useful. Negotiations in Peking were tortuous, with the Chinese refusing to take responsibility for the acts of the natives yet claiming jurisdiction over Formosa. During these negotiations, Yamagata readied plans for possible eventualities, including direct action against China. In Japan, the nation became aroused; volunteer groups mushroomed and prepared for sacrifices to support the government. The negotiations, however, were successfully concluded; China agreed to pay an idemnity covering the cost of the expedition and the sums to be paid the families of the murdered Ryūkyū sailors, and also agreed that the expedition had been justified. By declaring the punitive action legitimate, the Chinese thereby unwittingly supported Japan's claims to suzerainty over the Ryūkyūs.

The Formosan affair had not received Yamagata's support and had

74. The memorial is reprinted in *ibid.*, II, 346–352.
75. Paraphrased from the memorial, *ibid.*, II, 350.
76. Edward H. House, *The Japanese Expedition to Formosa* (Tokyo, 1875), p. 160.

caused the resignation of Kido, the senior Chōshū statesman. Moreover, Ōkubo's success in negotiating with China had further strengthened his position and along with it the influence of Satsuma officials in the government. To consolidate unity at the highest level and restrain the Satsuma influence, Itō and Inoue of Chōshū initiated a meeting for the purpose of reorganizing the government.[77] Itagaki Taisuke was invited to this Osaka conference of January 1875, and Yamagata encouraged Kido to attend.[78] The conference resulted in the reorganization of the government, and Itagaki and Kido both returned to Tokyo.

Yamagata supported Itō and Inoue in their objectives, but his actions were of marginal significance. He was still preoccupied with the need to increase the nation's armed strength and he came to believe that the main obstacle to building up a modern conscript army was the recalcitrance of the *shizoku* class and its reluctance to support the domestic policies of the government. The Formosan expedition had indeed provided a means of deflating the growing pressure against the government. But deflecting the interest of the nation and particularly that of the disgruntled *shizoku* outside of the country had not, nevertheless, decreased the opposition to internal reforms.

The Last Challenge of Feudalism

Internal reforms which aimed at strengthening the nation required full-scale modernization and the consequent dissolution of feudal institutions which had outlived their usefulness. The enactment of conscription was only one among many measures which undercut the privileged position of the ex-samurai class. In August 1871, the government had suggested that the traditional samurai hairdress, clothes, and swords be given up voluntarily, but few relinquished their badges of social standing so readily. On December 7, 1875, Yamagata, in his capacity as army minister, proposed the abolition of the ancient sword-carrying privilege of the samurai class. In his view, the development of conscription and national garrisons for defense and a police force for the protection of citizens obviated the carrying of weapons by a single group. His charge was that many surly and reckless individuals, unaware of the changing times, flaunted their pride and committed reckless acts in the name of defending their nation. "In this way," he concluded, "they inevitably

77. Oka Yoshitake, *Kindai Nihon no keisei* (Tokyo, 1947), pp. 197–198.
78. *Yamagata den*, II, 408.

impede the political development of the nation";[79] and so he proposed that all weapons outside of the army should be placed under military control and the wearing of swords should be abolished at once.

Others had already given similar advice; among them was Mori Arinori, the Japanese minister to the United States. On March 28, 1876, the government responded to these recommendations and ordered an end to the practice of wearing swords. Opposition to this order was widespread and was increased a few months later by the compulsory commutation of the hereditary stipends received by the *shizoku* class from the government after the abolition of the han in 1871. These measures added fuel to the continuing opposition to universal conscription, and in 1877 thousands of *shizoku,* organized, led, and inspired by Saigō Takamori, rose in open rebellion in the southern island of Kyushu.

After the Korean crisis of 1873, Saigō had withdrawn to Satsuma, organized schools which trained military officers, and attracted many disaffected *shizoku* in the country who opposed the reforms of the government. As a symbol of the virtue of the feudal samurai and as a rallying point for the antigovernment sentiments, Saigō attracted followers from all over the country and organized them into a force of approximately 40,000 men.[80] He was skillfully aided by a group of able officers, many of whom had withdrawn from the imperial guards in 1873. "The situation in the southern corner is critical," wrote Yamagata in February 1877, shortly before the outbreak of the rebellion; "it is difficult to measure how serious the situation will be and what sort of cataclysm will follow when the crisis breaks." [81]

As army minister with the rank of lieutenant-general, Yamagata was called upon to serve as field commander of the government troops. When the cataclysm came, his first concern was that many southern areas would follow the lead of Saigō. He predicted that the rebels would pursue any one of three strategies: raid Tokyo and Osaka from the sea; attack Nagasaki and the Kumamoto garrison, establish control over the southern island, and then proceed north; or build up an impregnable defense in the Kagoshima area and await a favorable opportunity to move to the north. To counter these possibilities, Yamagata suggested that gov-

79. *Ibid.,* II, 435. The text of the whole petition is found on pp. 434–435.
80. Augustus H. Mounsey, *The Satsuma Rebellion: An Episode of Modern Japanese History* (London, 1879), p. 91.
81. The quotation and Yamagata's analysis of what might be expected are found in a memorandum he wrote on Feb. 12, 1877, reproduced in *Yamagata den,* II, 514–516.

ernment forces move into Kagoshima Bay, destroy the castle, which was the nerve center of the rebellion, and later reduce the other centers of resistance.

The government hope for the capture of Kagoshima was delayed for many months, but the rebels followed, in general, one of the approaches Yamagata anticipated. The immediate objective of the Satsuma forces was to capture the castle town of Kumamoto, important as one of the major military garrisons of the national army and a training center for conscripts. But the stout defense of the defenders of the castle caused a fifty-day siege to fail and forced the attackers to withdraw. For the government the success at Kumamoto was significant for several reasons: it blunted the powerful surge of the Satsuma army; it provided valuable time for mobilizing government forces; and it proved the fighting ability of the conscript soldiers, who numbered two-thirds of the 2,000 defenders.[82] Tani Kanjō, the general commanding the Kumamoto garrison, claimed that "The siege of the castle was withstood because of the peasant conscripts." [83] The conscripts proved disciplined and controllable under heavy strain; even Saigō admitted his surprise at their bravery.[84]

The Satsuma forces had been frustrated in their first objective but not defeated. The government's need for more troops raised a difficult problem. It was true that more conscript soldiers could be mobilized, and their efficiency in suppressing local uprisings had proved their worth. But the available number of conscript soldiers was inadequate, and it would take too long to train a sufficient number of new conscripts. For a few there were even lingering doubts about the effectiveness of the conscript soldiers against the Satsuma samurai army in the crucial battles that were ahead.

Yamagata, however, firmly opposed all plans to recruit *shizoku* forces. Convinced that such a move would undercut the conscription system, he suggested another solution. In a letter to Ōkubo and Itō, dated May 18, 1877, he declared there must be strict enforcement of the conscription law.[85] He contended that it was preferable to suffer a delay in the training of adequate numbers of troops than to weaken conscription by re-

---

82. Matsushita Yoshio, *Chōhei*, p. 427.
83. Quoted by Sakata Yoshio, "Meiji dōtoku shi," in *Meiji bunka shi* (Tokyo, 1956), III, 509.
84. See quote from *Yūbin Hōchi* (The Post-Dispatch newspaper) in Matsushita, *Chōhei*, p. 472. Saigō was reported as being pleased at the enemy's strength because it bade well for the nation's future if commoners could be trained to fight with such skill.
85. Reprinted in *ibid.*, pp. 434–439.

cruiting *shizoku* units outside of the system. He countered the doubts of the adequacy of conscripts by reasserting his faith in the ability of the ordinary citizen to become a good soldier and by asserting that *shizoku,* good as individual fighters, were not prepared for large-scale warfare without group training. The prospect of *shizoku* uprisings in sympathy with Saigō's revolt elsewhere in Japan could, he suggested, be reduced by taking more *shizoku* into the prefectural police forces. After that was done, and after other leaders of dissatisfied groups were given official positions in the government in order to win their loyalty, the *shizoku* in the police forces could be organized into military units for fighting against Satsuma. This would constitute enlisting *shizoku* for special military service but only after they had been made government employees as policemen under central authority. This plan was accepted and provided a scheme which supplied some of the manpower needed for the emergency and at the same time prevented the undermining of the conscription system by the mass direct recruitment of *shizoku* for military service.

The police brigade of over 3,600 men which resulted from this plan contributed significantly to the government's successful suppression of the Satsuma rebellion. Among the Satsuma soldiers there was a song which concluded: "Were it not for the Imperial Guard artillery and the Police Brigade we could advance to beautiful Edo." [86] The bitter fighting continued for seven and a half months; each side suffered serious losses, and more than once rebel forces surrounded by government armies escaped to fight another day. In the end, the government's superiority in arms and ammunition, its numerical and naval strength, and the strong showing of its green conscripts doomed the rebellion.

The victory of the government armies in the Satsuma rebellion marked the end of open hostilities to the Meiji government. Civil war had not spread to other areas and the strength of the Tokyo regime was demonstrated. It was the last episode in a decade of *shizoku* opposition to government policies and to the changing times. The inauguration of conscription, one of the measures which cut at the heart of the military and social prerogatives of the ex-samurai class, was resisted and openly opposed. But the government's victory justified Yamagata's unbending confidence in the conscription system as the best means of organizing the nation's military strength. Although augmented by other hastily organized special units which bear the major credit for suppressing the rebellion, the conscripts fought exceedingly well. Saigō acknowledged be-

86. *Ibid.,* p. 452.

fore his death during the final battle at Kagoshima in September 1877 that the ability of the conscripted farmers and merchants was in no way inferior to that of the traditional samurai class. Thus the Satsuma rebellion terminated the armed threat to the Meiji regime and dissolved all arguments against the conscription system.

For Yamagata the joy of victory was mixed with sorrow. The imperial forces had triumphed, and as field commander of those forces he received much of the credit for the final victory. Nevertheless, the fall of Saigō wrenched his heart. Throughout the war Yamagata steadfastly refused to believe Saigō was a traitor. He so prized his former friendship that he insisted on attributing the rebellion to those around the great warrior. Even after the rebellion had raged for several months, Yamagata continued to hope that a personal appeal to Saigō might terminate hostilities. In an eloquent plea addressed to Saigō in April 1877, Yamagata said: "Although I have not seen you personally since you returned to your native area several years ago, I have not passed a day without recalling our former friendship. Who would have dreamed that circumstances would lead us to meet on a battlefield? Since you returned home, those who have expressed views on the unusual behavior of the men of Kagoshima prefecture declare, 'Saigō is the chief plotter and schemer.' I alone have opposed these views . . . believing that the present incident is an unavoidable product of circumstance. I am well aware that it was not your intention." Later in the letter Yamagata made a plea for the ending of the war: "Several months of fighting have already passed; hundreds of casualties on both sides occur daily; friends kill one another, kinsmen are pitted against each other . . . yet the soldiers bear no hatred. The Imperial troops are fulfilling their military obligation while Satsuma men say they are fighting for Saigō . . . I entreat you to take measures to end the fighting both to prove that the present situation is not of your doing and to eliminate casualties on both sides as quickly as possible." [87]

The plea was in vain, lost in the heat of civil strife. But Yamagata's admiration and respect for Saigō and for his leadership in the Restoration never waned. He prohibited his own subordinates from speaking ill of Saigō and insisted that rebel prisoners should be treated respectfully as loyal vassals of his adversary. After the final battle in which Saigō, mortally wounded, requested an aide to behead him, Yamagata ordered that Saigō's head be found so that it could be buried ceremoniously with

87. Letter reprinted in *Yamagata den,* II, 741–742.

his body. When Saigō's head was brought to him, he had it washed and then holding it in his hands he is reported to have said, "Alas, your face looks serene. For your sake I have not been at ease for half a year. Now I am at peace; but you were one of the greatest heroes of our land . . . It is a pity that this should be your fate." [88] In these words Yamagata helped perpetuate the legendary life of the popular hero of the Restoration. On the evening of the last battle, he celebrated the fallen hero thus:

> With only the autumn moon
> where is any trace of the skies
> which saw the mountains burst
> and the oceans dry up? [89]

The Reorganization and Expansion of the Army

The suppression of the Satsuma rebellion marked the end of the early uncertain period of the Meiji government when the new regime was still insecure and vulnerable. As chief exponent of conscription, Yamagata had helped to develop the army into an instrument of central authority and had thereby contributed to the construction of the new order. But internal control was no longer the primary aim of the army following the Satsuma rebellion. In the years thereafter Yamagata's efforts were devoted to strengthening, expanding, and reorganizing the national army. By reorganizing its administration and by trying to isolate the army from political influences and control, Yamagata attempted to give the army greater unity and discipline. In the course of the reorganization, it should be noted, a number of prominent generals, such as Tani Kanjō of Tosa and Miura Gorō of Chōshū, left the army in opposition to the measures adopted. These ex-generals formed the nucleus of a conservative opposition to many of the government's policies.[90]

In this reorganization the most conspicuous reform was the separation of the command from the administrative function through the creation of the General Staff as an independent body within the army. In 1873, the Sixth Bureau had been established within the army department with the function of developing plans and operations. In the following year it was renamed the Staff Bureau. Prior to the Satsuma rebellion, the

88. *Ibid.*, II, 752–753.
89. *Ibid.*, II, 755.
90. The growth of this opposition has been studied by Barbara J. Teters in "The Conservative Opposition in Japanese Politics, 1877–1894" (unpublished Ph.D. dissertation, University of Washington, 1955).

bureau functioned as an integral part of the department under the jurisdiction of the army minister who, in turn, was subordinate to the Council of State. In combatting the Satsuma rebellion, Ōkubo, the home minister, was actually given total authority over all departments including the military administration. However, during the course of the operations the government established separate field headquarters under the Staff Bureau to carry out the command function. The organization of this independent staff section was the first step in the evolution of a more specialized military bureaucracy.

A more important step was the shift from the French to the German military system as a model for the development of the army. Yamagata, as we have seen, had originally favored the German military system and he continued to favor it even after the French had been adopted. The defeat of France in the Franco-Prussian War added strength to his arguments. In the end it was the assistance of Katsura Tarō, a brilliant young Chōshū officer, which enabled Yamagata to win his way. In 1870, Katsura had been sent by the government to study the French military system. When he arrived in London, he was informed that Paris had just fallen to the Germans so he was forced to alter his plans. He proceeded instead to Berlin where he spent six years, three as a student and three as a military attaché. He became deeply impressed by the efficient German military system and lost no opportunity to persuade his superiors in Japan that the Japanese army should be reorganized along German lines. In Yamagata he found a natural ally for this cause.

In the autumn of 1878, Katsura returned to Japan and immediately submitted a detailed blueprint for reorganizing the army. On October 8, Yamagata adopted this plan and submitted a proposal to the government calling for the establishment of an independent General Staff Headquarters. Two months later the Staff Bureau of the army department was replaced by the General Staff Headquarters. To indicate the importance of this post, Yamagata resigned as army minister to become the chief of the General Staff. At forty years of age, as state councillor and supreme military adviser to the emperor, Yamagata enjoyed the highest position of military authority in the nation.

The creation of the General Staff as a separate and independent body reflected a major shift away from the concept of military power resident within a single executive authority. The new organization did not merely expand the Staff Bureau but gave it independent status. Professor Nakano, an authority on the independent role of the military, wrote of this significant change:

By fundamentally changing the principles of administration, the Chief of the General Staff was made the Emperor's chief adviser on problems relating to military policy and strategy. Under this regulation the Chief of the General Staff not only became independent of the army minister but furthermore . . . was given a position superior to that of the army minister. Like the other ministers of departments at that time, the army minister had no privilege as direct adviser to the Emperor. Those appointed to assist the Emperor were the three leading ministers of the Council of State, in particular, the Prime Minister. Consequently, the Chief of Staff as the supreme military adviser directly under the Emperor not only was made independent of the army minister but independent of the *dajōkan*, and the duty of advising the Emperor on matters relating to the supreme command shifted from the Prime Minister to the Chief of Staff.[91]

Yamagata's desire was both to make the army independent of political influences and control and to discourage military interference in civil matters. The establishment of the General Staff accomplished this at the highest level of command by removing the command function from the office of the war minister where the Cabinet might be able to influence it. Independence from political affairs at the individual soldier's level was another problem and an aspect of the broader issue of morale and discipline. In the early years of the army, a new absolute loyalty to the nation had not yet fully developed. The method used to counter this was to develop rigid discipline among the troops by inducing the strictest obedience and loyalty to the emperor, symbol and center of the nation.

As early as 1872 the army had issued regulations defining the duties of each soldier. In the handbook of each man were entered the "Soldier's Rules," the first article of which read: "The army is established for the purpose of executing the will of the Emperor, to strengthen the foundations of the country and protect the people and the nation. Thus, those who become soldiers must make loyalty to the Emperor their guiding principle." [92] But success in developing military discipline came slowly. Even the great Saigō admitted that commanding the imperial guards was like "sleeping with a powder keg." [93] It was not until after all *shizoku* opposition to the government was overcome that the authorities were in a position to enforce strict discipline.

The lingering vestiges of such opposition, together with political agita-

91. Nakano Tomio, *Tōsui ken no dokuritsu* (Tokyo, 1934), pp. 362–363
92. Matsushita Yoshio, *Chōhei*, p. 377.
93. Matsushita Yoshio, *Meiji gunsei shi ronshū* (Tokyo, 1938), p. 240.

tion against the ruling oligarchy, played a part in a mutiny in August 1878 within the ranks of the imperial guard. Known as the Takebashi Mutiny and described as "the most conspicuous blemish in the history of the Imperial army, the most disgraceful event to scar the glorious Meiji era," [94] the uprising resulted in the punishment of 218 soldiers and the execution before a firing squad of fifty-three. The immediate pretext was a reduction in pay and a delay in the rewards received by the guards for their part in the Satsuma rebellion. But the underlying cause was two-fold. In the first place, the guard was composed mainly of ex-samurai, proud of their inheritance and not unaffected by the collapse of the prestige of the feudal warrior. Insofar as there was a lingering distrust of the conscripts with whom they were now joined as a unit, the mutiny represented the last gasp of discontent among the *shizoku*. In the second place, some of the officers involved gave their support to representative government, as part of a growing political agitation directed against the oligarchy. The only two officers sentenced by a court martial for their participation in the mutiny were found guilty because of their political influence among the mutineers.[95] The nature of the regulations promulgated following this mutiny makes it clear that the subversive influence of political agitation had been a contributing cause.

Yamagata was deeply shocked by the mutiny and moved quickly to improve and tighten discipline. Thirty-nine days after the mutiny he issued an order known as the *Admonition to Soldiers* (*Gunjin kunkai*). These instructions were drawn up by Nishi Amane, vice minister of the army, before the mutiny broke out, but the mutiny made apparent the urgency of measures to inculcate discipline in the army.[96] Congratulating the army on its meritorious service in battle but reminding it of its "spiritual weakness," the declaration set forth what Yamagata felt should be the three guiding ideals of all military personnel: loyalty, bravery, and obedience. Further, it defined the proper manners and deportment of the soldier and explained his general duties and obligations. Of particular interest in the "Admonition," and in the subsequent orders of both the army department and the Council of State, was the warning of all military personnel against political activities and influences.

94. Matsushita Yoshio, *Wadai*, p. 42. The essay on the Takebashi Mutiny in the volume is one of the most complete studies available.

95. *Ibid.*, pp. 54–55. See also Itō Jintarō, *Meiji rimenshi* (Tokyo, 1927), pp. 94–114.

96. On the career and influence of Nishi Amane, see Roger F. Hackett, "Nishi Amane: A Tokugawa–Meiji Bureaucrat," *Journal of Asian Studies*, 18.2:213–225 (February 1959).

Such behavior as questioning Imperial policies, or expressing private opinions on important laws, or criticizing the published regulations of the government, runs counter to the duty of a soldier. If there should be one such person, then the whole mass will imitate him and clearly it will sow the seed of contempt for superiors . . . But if one gives free rein to chatter and argumentation, then one is prone to deplore the times, to shout about people's rights, and so forth, and thus violate one's basic duty; for an officer to talk recklessly like some discharged government officials, to imitate the scandalous behavior of students, to give himself up to gross exaggeration, this is absolutely impermissible.[97]

But the warnings did not dispel the government's fear of political subversion within the army. As a consequence, instructions issued by the government reiterated the warning for military personnel not to participate in politics. The "Regulations for Public Meetings and Political Associations" issued by the Council of State on April 5, 1880, warned that: "No military and naval men now on active service or in the first or second reserves, police officers, teachers and students of government, public, or private schools, agricultural or technological apprentices, may attend any meeting where politics form the subject of address or deliberation. Neither may they become members of any political association." [98]

The army took steps to enforce these warnings. On January 4, 1881, the military police (*kempei*) were organized by order of the Council of State because "the movement for popular government is spreading throughout the country and clashes are occurring between the citizens and the authorities as well as between soldiers and police." [99] Soldiers from each garrison were selected to form the first military police unit and assigned the duty of administrative police overseeing the thought and activities of all military personnel.

In December 1881, following a governmental crisis which resulted in the promise of a constitution and the formation of new political parties, the army moved quickly to prohibit its personnel from political activity. Army Regulation No. 100 issued on December 29 read: "Regarding the participation of soldiers in political matters: all those who engage in debates or speeches or use the written word to spread political ideas will

97. Reprinted in *Yamagata den,* II, 774–779.
98. *Ibid.,* II, 775.
99. Quoted in Matsushita Yoshio, *Meiji gunsei shi ronshū,* p. 215.

be sentenced to not less than one month nor more than three years imprisonment." [100]

The disciplinary decrees and orders and the exhortations against political activity among the soldiers were an accurate reflection of Yamagata's own thinking. He was extremely anxious to develop habits of loyalty and service to the new regime. And the final step in achieving this end was to bring together the previous instructions in an imperial rescript. Anxious to give this rescript a special position, and motivated by the desire to distinguish clearly the independent political and military lines of authority, Yamagata submitted the following suggestion to the throne in December 1881: "In rescripts concerning the Emperor's position as commander of the military forces . . . there is no reason for them to be issued by the authority of the Prime Minister, as in the case of other rescripts. Therefore, I respectfully request that the Emperor personally hand down such rescripts directly to the military services outside the authority of the Prime Minister." [101] In response to this request, the Meiji Emperor in an unprecedented ceremony presented to the army and navy ministers on January 4, 1882, the "Rescript to Soldiers and Sailors."

This rescript reiterated the preceding pronouncements defining the duties and obligations of the military man, his moral and spiritual values. But the earlier three cardinal virtues were expanded to five: loyalty, propriety, valor, righteousness, and simplicity. Included in the elaboration of these ideals was the warning that political activities must be eschewed by all military personnel. The first article of the rescript proclaimed loyalty as the essential duty of the soldier and sailor and warned him "neither to be led astray by current opinions nor meddle in politics, but with single heart to fulfill your essential duty of loyalty." [102]

This rescript justly has been called one of the major documents of the Meiji period. The ideals it prescribed were instilled in the thousands of new recruits yearly to give cohesion to the army. At the same time, by advocating the virtues of the traditional warrior class—ideals which had permeated all Japanese society—the rescript helped to form the basis of the official popular ideology: duty and loyalty to the emperor, the spirit of courage and sacrifice. This compound of the traditional samurai

100. Matsushita Yoshio, *Wadai*, p. 134.
101. Quoted by Osatake, *Meiji Bunka sōsetsu*, p. 182.
102. The rescript appears, among other places, as an appendix in Hillis Lory, *Japan's Military Masters: The Army in Japanese Life* (New York, 1943), pp. 229–234.

ethic and imperial nationalism might well be identified as the "Meiji spirit."

External problems, as well as the problem of discipline within the army, concerned Yamagata after the government's victory in the Satsuma rebellion insured domestic order. To meet these problems he took steps which finally brought to completion the military reforms begun in 1878 and established the army as more than an instrument of domestic harmony. Soon after he became chief of staff, the problem of Japan's relation to the continent of Asia occupied his attention. In particular, he was concerned with the rapidly changing military and political situation in China. To gain more information, he sent Lieutenant-Colonel Katsura on a secret mission to North China and Korea to study and report on conditions, attached an officer to the Japanese legation in Peking, and, in the following year, sent ten officer-students to survey the situation in various areas in China. After their return the officers submitted, on the basis of their observations, analyses and reports bearing titles such as "The Military Preparedness of Neighboring Countries" and "The Geography of China." Using the information in these reports, Yamagata formulated a plan regarding the need for greater military preparedness. First in 1880, and then again in 1882, he expressed his opinions in personal audiences with the emperor, and then through formal statements he submitted his views on the need for greater national security and the means to achieve it. As in similar memorials he had submitted in the past, he preceded his recommendations with a broad survey of Japan's strategic position. In his proposal of July 15, 1882, he warned of potential continental enemies and urged greater military preparation. He argued, in part:

> The nation with which our country must be concerned and must compete in terms of strength is not a remote country but one situated closeby. In the present situation there is imminent danger. Naturally I dislike war but I desire not to forget the possibility of war. When I say I do not forget the possibility of war I only mean that I do not for a moment forget that we might be attacked by a foreign enemy. If we fail now to recover our martial spirit, expand the army and navy to make a veritable floating fortress of our Imperial nation, extend our strength to all corners of the state in the spirit of steadfast valor, our nation, which in the past has experienced trouble with nations in the immediate vicinity, will unquestionably suffer again from weakness. If we remain inactive in this situation how are we going to maintain our independence and talk

of our strength and prosperity? Thus, the expansion of the army and navy is the most urgent task at hand and the government must devote itself to this aim.[103]

Proposals for greater preparedness were acted upon on December 12, 1882, when an imperial edict was issued calling for military expansion. The edict was read to the prefectural governors who were meeting in Tokyo at that time; it was not printed for distribution to newspaper editors nor made public. A new reorganization and expansion program was immediately put into effect. Garrisons were reorganized into field divisions and expanded; in 1883 the conscription law was rewritten limiting exemptions and expanding the period of service. The original conscription law had been revised in 1879 to lengthen active and reserve service from seven to ten years; now it was extended to twelve years. Yamagata's aim was, his biographer notes, "to complete the changes in the organization of the national army, which hitherto had been established with the maintenance of internal order as the prime objective but was now aimed at continental strategy." [104]

In the twelve years since Yamagata had become a member of the Meiji government, dramatic changes had been brought about. A national army had been created to preserve, protect, and promote the national interest. It had helped to achieve the first and vital need — unity. Yamagata and his colleagues in the government recognized that national security required revolutionary reforms; they also understood that the process of unifying the nation politically was intimately linked with the centralizing of military power. And the measure of their success was the ability of the new army to defeat all armed opposition to the regime and to secure internal order without which a unified, stable state would have been impossible.

At the root of this success was the system of universal military service. It was perhaps the most important reform undertaken to fulfill the motto of the guiding architects of the new order—*fukoku, kyōhei* (rich country, strong army). Equal but required military service provided training and indoctrination to a major segment of the population. It helped to reduce class lines and local loyalties. More important, it developed a sense of involvement in national affairs and a heightened feeling of identification with the state. In the future the conscript army would provide the basis for the ascendency of Japan in the world.

103. *Yamagata den,* II, 816.
104. *Ibid.,* II, 821.

Of the many activities with which Yamagata was to be associated in the construction of the new nation, all are eclipsed by this military reform. Many contributed to its realization; it was nevertheless his decisive energy and persistent labors that assured its success. So successful was this reform that Yamagata, and many others, tended always to view the problems of internal government and foreign policy from the standpoint of the efficiency of the military establishment. His whole attitude toward the life of his nation was fashioned by this early experience. The effectiveness of the military reform also elevated him to unquestioned leadership of the army and beyond that to a prominent position in government councils. He could not have built a more secure foundation for his future. Through his commanding position he built up a coterie of loyal army followers: Katsura Tarō, Kodama Gentarō, Terauchi Masatake, Tanaka Giichi — all fellow clansmen from Chōshū who were to rise to prominence, like himself, first in the military and then in the civil bureaucracy. Yamagata's control of the army was always the heart of his political strength.

3

Entering the

Political World

The dissidence and unrest which led to Yamagata's organization of the military police in 1881 and called forth the imperial rescript of 1882 also had important political consequences. The first of these, the imperial decree of 1881 promising a constitution, may fairly be called a major landmark in Meiji history. The unexpected rise of popular demands for representative government, reinforced by Ōkuma's disclosure of scandal in high places and his subsequent proposal for the immediate election of a national assembly, constituted a crisis the government could not ignore. To meet it the government made its first positive move toward the adoption of a constitution — a problem to which it had given only desultory consideration since 1873, when Kido had returned with the Iwakura mission emphasizing the need for constitutional changes. The decree of 1881 promised a constitution in nine years, the length of time deemed necessary to work out an appropriate system. In so promising, it marked the end of that hurried and self-preservative adoption of Western military and economic techniques that characterized the the first phase of Meiji history, and inaugurated a second phase characterized by the adoption of political forms that gave a more ordered direction to the forces released by the Restoration, an age of less hurried reforms.

In the early phase of the Meiji period, while the life of the nation was being slowly molded into new forms, no clear lines separated the military, political, and economic aspects. Personalities dominated the stage, moving like Ōkubo, Ōkuma, Itō, or Inoue from one critical problem to another regardless of its particular place in the task of reconstruction, or concentrating like Yamagata on a single major problem — the development of modern military power. With the ensuing change to overall political planning, such leaders as retained their ascendency were obliged to assume new roles in the evolving machinery of constitutional government. This was what Yamagata did when, in 1882, at the age of forty-five, he assumed the presidency of the Legislative Board during Itō's absence. As head of the board, a body which had been created to study and advise the government on measures deemed necessary in preparing for the constitution, he moved to the center of the political stage where he was to remain until his death forty years later.

It can be fairly said that the key to Yamagata's political growth rested on the fact that his shift into politics was not accompanied by any loss of influence among the military. Although Yamagata's ascendency in the political world during the second phase of Meiji history depended to some degree on his assumption of new civil positions, his influence in this realm was firmly based upon his military achievements before 1881. His part in building a modern conscript army and the withdrawal and final demise of Saigō had elevated him to an uncontested position of military leadership. He had enjoyed the independent authority of the position of chief of staff of General Headquarters ever since that office had been created in 1878. Furthermore, as the nation's ranking active general, retaining the loyalty of his appointees and followers in the army, he continued to maintain his authority in all matters relating to the military growth of Japan.

Nevertheless, the next chapter of Yamagata's career is primarily the story of his part in the development of a new political synthesis, first as head for sixteen months of the Legislative Board and then, more significantly, as minister of home affairs. In seven and a half years as home minister, he reorganized that ministry to make it the heart of the internal administration both through police reforms and changes in the system of local government. In so doing, he firmly implanted the roots of his authority in the civil bureaucracy. It was a period when he developed a loyal following of civil bureaucrats who formed the nucleus of a trusted personal clique, an attainment which furthered his political influence in subsequent years.

With his military background, it is not strange that Yamagata approached his new task with the thought that the political activities and authority of the people as expressed in the popular party movement should be restricted by law. He tended to conceive of protection of the government from political attack as a continuation of his efforts to guard the government from internal military threats. He frankly distrusted the popular party activities and strove to increase the centralized power of the state. Both the Imperial Constitution of 1889 and the local government system established through legislation in 1888 and 1890 were to become the main pillars of the new political structure. Yamagata's major work in erecting the new political framework was the development of a local government system. Yet his cautious, conservative attitude and his uneasiness over the growing strength of the popular party movement are to be seen first in the earliest consideration of the question of introducing into Japan a Western-type constitutional system.

The Question of a Constitution

In June 1879, Prince Arisugawa, the ranking imperial prince, asked all state councillors to submit their views regarding a constitution. This was not the first time that the government had shown an interest in the eventual adoption of a constitution. Kido's proposal of 1873 calling for the progressive development of a constitutional system was followed, in 1875, by an imperial message announcing that in due course a constitution would be granted to the people. Then in 1876 Prince Arisugawa was instructed to draft plans for a constitution, but the domestic crises of the following year demanded the total energy of the government and postponed concrete action.

Yamagata was the first to respond to Arisugawa's request and in December 1879 presented his views on the state of the nation as well as his suggestions for the gradual evolution of a system of representative government.[1] His analysis of general conditions, as well as his specific proposals, was an indication of his attitude toward the progress of events under the government.

After reviewing the far-reaching changes of the twelve years since the beginning of the Meiji period, changes such as the postal system, land tax, conscription, and the school system, Yamagata observed in his memorial that the people had little respect for and often disobeyed the government. He was satisfied with the material advances of the nation but disturbed and perplexed by the restless discontent of popular sentiment. Why, he queried, do the people distrust a government striving for their welfare? To his own question he suggested four answers: first, the Restoration occurred so swiftly that the people were not yet accustomed to the change; second, old abuses were discarded but the new ways were still superficial, the results of reforms still not discernible;

1. The complete text from which I have quoted and paraphrased appears in *Yamagata den*, II, 841–848. George M. Beckmann has included a translation of Yamagata's opinion as an appendix to his *The Making of the Meiji Constitution* (Lawrence, Kansas, 1957). I have used my own translation which agrees with Beckmann's.

third, while many gained from the changes, others — members of the old samurai class and merchants and landlords with reduced wealth — had suffered and become discontented; and fourth, "since the Restoration, we have adopted foreign laws, and the whole nation knows that we must have laws to preserve society, but it has been completely forgotten that society must also be maintained by good morals and manners." [2] The moral fiber of society had weakened; this could be observed in loss of respect of children for their parents, pupils for their elders. In the place of proper respect he saw contempt, crude competition for wealth and position, arrogant acts justified by the principle of freedom. His diagnosis of the nation's ills was phrased in strong terms: "Insincerity is everywhere apparent with the driving motive now to make money. Those without self-discipline are impudently boastful and conceited, readily resisting officials. Furthermore, the foreign word 'freedom' is mouthed without any understanding of the principle of freedom. Respect and love for superiors and kindness toward others have disappeared; infatuation with fashions and thoughtlessness are now common." [3]

It was his contention that moral deterioration was attributable to an overdependence on laws. Not that the orders of the government had been wrong, but that the tendency to rely solely on laws had caused the moral cement, the beliefs and practices holding society together, to crumble. The most alarming manifestation of this he saw in the withdrawal of the people's support for the government's efforts.

The major external problems he identified were the revision of the treaties and relations with neighboring countries. In meeting these problems he advocated no drastic shift in policy. Yet, with the question of treaty revision in mind, he admitted the need for an organized body of law which would gain the acceptance of the foreign powers. He recognized the inevitability of a national constitution but insisted that it must evolve gradually. Rather than formulate precise laws, he felt it was first necessary to determine the main principles and spirit of the policy to be pursued. "Although today we have a semblance of a structure with three separate powers, the executive, legislative and judiciary, we must avoid contradictions in the constitution, making it more rigorous by defining the boundaries so that executive power is not allowed to restrain the other two powers." [4]

2. *Yamagata den,* II, 842–843
3. *Ibid.,* II, 843.
4. *Ibid.,* II, 844–845.

Speaking to the specific problem of a national assembly, he advocated extension to the national level of prefectural assemblies which already existed as advisory bodies to the governors. This he would accomplish by establishing a special assembly (*tokusen kaigi*) composed of members of the local assemblies. Members would be either elected by their bodies or selected by the government "to make this assembly the foundation on which to erect a popular assembly in the future." [5] As he phrased it:

> It would not be difficult to select the leading men from among the members of the prefectural assemblies, which, fortunately, already exist. These distinguished men could first discuss the provisions of a constitution and then proceed to a consideration of national legislation. If, after some years of experience, it is felt that legislative power should be granted to this body, it would then be transformed into a popular assembly. Or perhaps we should not adopt a specially selected assembly and have a single assembly composed of two or three members elected from each prefectural assembly. Again, after some experience had been gained and time had elapsed, direct and indirect elections could be combined to convert this body into a popular assembly. Of course, initially such an assembly should not be called a popular assembly and the power of convening and dissolving it should be held by the government. Furthermore, it should be determined that its decisions may not necessarily be carried out.[6]

Yamagata's opinion as expressed in this document is revealing on several counts. His concern over the decay of older values pointed to his conservative outlook. While on the one hand he favored borrowing Western methods, as he did in the adoption of the conscription system and the German-style military command system, on the other hand he desired traditional values to constitute the substance of political and military forms, as evidenced by his encouragement of military discipline and morale through the revival of the vigor of traditional values. As a realist, he was aware of the need to adopt Western-type laws but he was equally alive to the dangers they presented to age-old values.

Above all he wanted an orderly, controlled evolution. He thought of broadening the authority of the government by gaining popular support without relinquishing power to an assembly which would represent the popular will. Despite his assertion that the executive should not be "allowed to restrain the other two powers," it was his greatest fear that

5. *Ibid.*, II, 848.
6. *Ibid.*, II, 846–847.

imperial authority would be weakened by a popular assembly. The popular assembly would represent the meeting place of imperial powers and the powers of the people and hence should be constructed with care, so that the latter would in no way infringe upon the former.

We glimpse here the central tenets of Yamagata's political philosophy: the differentiation of the rights of the people and imperial rights and the need to safeguard the power of the government as executor of the imperial prerogative. He conceived of the government as master, not as servant, of the people; of bureaucracy as a servant of the state, not as representative of the people. So his proposal for an elite assembly is in accord with the desire, shared at this time by most of the oligarchs, for strong executive control of political developments. The assembly he proposed would be an advisory group to assist in administration without power to limit the authority of the government. He did recognize, however, that after a gradual evolution a representative assembly under a constitution would be desirable. In fact, on March 17, 1880, he wrote his friend Suematsu Kenchō, "If we wish to be sure of the future it will be necessary to enact a constitution, open a national assembly and establish foundations for a nation based upon laws." [7]

The majority of the councillors responding to Prince Arisugawa's request advocated a gradual, cautious advance toward the establishment of a national assembly. Only Kuroda, a senior Satsuma statesman, considered talk of an assembly entirely premature. At the other extreme, Ōkuma Shigenobu, the finance minister, not only called for a nationally elected assembly to be opened by 1883 but thought that the majority party should be responsible for conducting the nation's business.[8] In addition to his drastic proposals, Ōkuma disclosed to the public in an open meeting in Tokyo the scandalous squandering of government funds by certain prominent officials who were seeking to purchase land formerly controlled by the government's Hokkaido Colonization Commission.[9] To counter the pressures for constitutional government, a commitment had been made, but the cost was a further narrowing of the ruling group. The Korean crisis of 1873 had been the first stage in that process; the crisis of 1881 leading to Ōkuma's resignation was the second. At each stage Yamagata moved closer to the center of the policy-forming group.

7. *Ibid.*, II, 838.
8. Smimasa Idditti, *The Life of Marquis Shigenobu Ōkuma* (Tokyo, 1940), pp. 210–211.
9. Yamagata was among those in the government who encouraged Kuroda to give up his project of purchasing land in Hokkaido. *Yamagata den*, II, 858.

Yamagata and the Popular Party Movement

The years between 1881 and the proclamation[10] of the constitution in 1889 were the busiest years in the period of constitutional development. Yet even before 1881 the fight for and against the idea of a constitutional assembly formed a main thread in the political history of the early Meiji era. The movement toward a constitution had been sluggish and the obstacles many, but after internal security had been achieved, each crucial political issue reflected in some degree a basic struggle between those who held state power and those who had been excluded from sharing that power. The agitation for popular rights and representative government was an aspect of this struggle. It was a movement inspired largely by certain elements among the former samurai who had aided and participated in the formation of the new nation but who had lost their position of real authority as a result of the factional contest for power within the new government. In that contest the Satsuma and Chōshū factions had triumphed, so it was not strange that the leadership of the popular movement came from the Tosa and Hizen groups. It began as demands by the "outs" in opposition to the "ins" for representation within the government, and from there it was not a long step to an appeal for representative government regulated by a constitution. The rank and file of the movement included a variety of middle- and lower-class elements who joined a growing body of dissatisfied citizens prepared to turn any issue into a contest for greater privileges and a larger voice in government.

To some extent foreign pressures stimulated the development of a constitutional system. However, although government leaders recognized that ending the compromise of sovereignty through revision of the treaties with foreign nations awaited legislative reforms, the main pressures spurring this development were largely internal. As antigovernment agitation became organized and more effective, the government took steps to adjust itself to the hostile political pressures being built up. Ever since the split in the government occasioned by the Korean crisis in 1873, one group had opposed the government through the formation of political societies advocating liberal democratic principles. Led mainly by *shizoku* of Tosa, such societies had proliferated and considerably strengthened the movement for popular rights. We have already seen how Yamagata's fears of the effect of this development led him to adopt

10. McLaren, ed., *Documents*, pp. 86–87.

stringent regulations warning all military personnel against participating in the movement.

To counter the growing popular pressure, the government established local representative assemblies, relieving the stress without actually granting powers which would reduce its authority. In 1875, for example, an assembly of governors (*chihōkan kaigi*) was convened and three years later local assemblies (*fuken kai*) were organized. While these bodies diverted some of the pressure for a national representative assembly, they were given only advisory privileges.[11]

The creation of local representative institutions appeased popular opinion while the actions of the people were rigidly restricted. The government hoped to contain the political movement within narrow limits through laws restraining the press and by limiting the people in all political activities. For example, the newspaper regulations of 1873 prohibited any attack on the government and warned citizens not even "to discuss the laws, or to cause obstacles in the way of the working of national institutions by the persistent advocacy of foreign ideas."[12] The press law of 1875 further restricted the expression of opinion.[13] These laws were followed, in 1880, by the regulations concerning public meetings (*shūkai jōrei*).[14] We have already seen how these regulations proscribed all political activity for military personnel, teachers, students, and police officers. So many restrictions were placed on the holding of political meetings, and the latitude given the police authorities in controlling them was so great, that the continued growth of the popular movement was indeed remarkable.

The growth of the popular movement was considered a real and present danger by the oligarchs. When Itō had succeeded to the position of home minister after Ōkubo's assassination, Yamagata expressed to him such fears and encouraged him to take determined steps to control political activity. "Itagaki's scheme," he wrote, "is to call for the people's rights, slander the government, abuse officials with reckless and groundless attacks and thereby arouse disgruntled *shizoku* and spread unrest throughout the land. By prolonging this situation he hopes to unite the

11. A good account of the government's policy is available in Chapter 6 of Walter W. McLaren, *A Political History of Japan During the Meiji Era, 1867–1912* (New York, 1919).
12. McLaren, ed., *Documents*, p. 534. The text of the newspaper regulations is given on pp. 534–535.
13. *Ibid.*, pp. 539–543.
14. *Ibid.*, pp. 495–499.

people and overthrow the government at an opportune moment. Therefore, every day we delay the evil poison will spread farther and penetrate
the minds of the young and produce, inevitably, incalculable harm." [15]

This opinion was indicative of the attitude shared by the government
leaders and led logically to the enactment of harsh laws. Despite these
laws the imperial announcement promising a constitution injected new
life into the popular movement and with the formation of the Rikken
jiyūtō (Constitutional Liberal party) in October 1881 and the Rikken
Kaishintō (Constitutional Progressive party) in March of the next year,
the movement reached a new height. To counter the influence of these
parties the government inspired the formation of the Rikken Teiseitō
(Constitutional Imperial party) on March 18, 1882.

The Teiseitō was organized at the suggestion and encouragement of
leading Chōshū statesmen. Itō, Inoue, and Yamada Akiyoshi were all
secretly involved in its formation, although they had no intention of
joining the party. The plan was to organize nonofficial support for the
government and thwart the development of the other parties. Fukuchi
Gen'ichirō, one-time secretary to Kido, editor of the pro-government
newspaper *Tokyo Nichi Nichi,* and one of the drafters of the "Rescript to
Soldiers and Sailors," was the active organizer of the party. Editors and
publishers of three prominent metropolitan newspapers helped to draft
a party platform. A strongly nationalistic group formed about Sasa Tomofusa also supported the party.[16]

Yamagata was not directly involved in the development of the Teiseitō,
but along with Itō and Inoue he read and approved its platform before
it was adopted. He encouraged Itō and Inoue in their more active efforts
and shared their belief, as expressed in the platform, that gradual progress
and order should be carefully balanced, that the nation needed a strong
central government supported by a vigorous nationalism.[17] Furthermore,
the organization of a third party responsive to the oligarchs was seen
by Yamagata as sound political strategy. The organization of two basically
antigovernment parties was cause for alarm and required countermeasures.
Although Yamagata articulated his belief in a three-party system many
years later, his encouragement of the Teiseitō was his first effort in that

15. From a letter dated July 4, 1879, quoted in Osatake Takeshi, *Nihon kensei shi
taikō* (Tokyo, 1938–1939), II, 527–528. (Hereafter this work will be cited as *Kensei shi.*)
16. For the formation of these parties, see Ōtsu Jun'ichirō, *Dai Nihon kensei shi*
(Tokyo, 1927–1928), II, 249–259. (Hereafter cited as *DNKS.*)
17. *Yamagata den,* II, 882. The eighth plan of the platform must have been particularly satisfying to Yamagata. It read: "Army and Navy personnel must not get
involved in politics." Ōtsu, *DNKS,* II, 551.

direction. He wished to keep the strength of the two major parties divided so that they could not combine to thwart the policy of the government. "I believe in a plan," he confided, "to establish a three-party system in the Diet which would eliminate excesses and bring about moderation." [18] He advocated organizing pro-government groups, men he considered "impartial and moderate, with intelligence and sincere concern for the welfare of the country," who would be loyal allies of the oligarchs moved by patriotic devotion rather than narrow party and personal ambitions. The party need not be large; all that was necessary was "a sufficient number capable of standing between the two large parties and of checking their excesses." These were thoughts expressed in 1917, but in 1882 Yamagata was thinking and advocating actions along the same lines.

On February 27, 1882, Yamagata resigned his position as chief of the General Staff to assume the duties of the president of the Board of Legislation during Itō's absence in Europe.[19] The board had been established to study and advise the government on various measures deemed necessary in preparation for the constitution. The sixteen months Yamagata spent in this new position marked his first full-time experience in political affairs.

Our knowledge of Yamagata's activities and views during his time in office is derived largely from his correspondence with Itō who was then in Europe. He kept Itō informed about latest developments and sought his approval for the various measures the board had drawn up. The main subject of his letters, however, was the growing strength of the popular party movement and the need for more drastic laws to control it. On June 3, 1882, for instance, Yamagata reported on the political turmoil in Japan and a revised law which had been decreed to limit political activities.

> As you may be aware, general interest in political matters has risen sharply. Political talks, speeches, gatherings and associations increase daily throughout the nation, and recently there has been a marked increase of undesirable results. Although the Regulations for Public Gatherings were formulated to control just such activity in 1880 and sufficed to maintain control during that time, since then, as a result of rapid shifts in the social current, developments have occurred outside the jurisdiction of the present law which cannot go unnoticed. If we do not make revisions now, conditions will result

18. Takahashi, *San kō iretsu*, pp. 136–141. These remarks, made in February 1917, are the clearest statement of Yamagata's consistent belief in a three-party system.
19. *Yamagata den*, II, 910.

prohibiting the enforcement of the spirit of the present law. Since spring there have been requests from the Home Minister for revisions. Recently at an advisory meeting at the Home Ministry, to which the Police Chiefs of the various *fu* and *ken* were invited, in reply to the Home Minister's inquiries about gatherings and political speeches in various areas, it was declared that the present law was inadequate to maintain control. Therefore, because of this inadequacy, the subject of revising the law arose and it was discussed in the Board of Legislation and the *genrōin* [Council of Elder Statesmen]. Under separate cover I am sending you the revised law today and desire your approval of our action.[20]

On June 15, 1882, Yamagata again wrote to Itō on the activities of the two main parties. "The Gifu incident[21] has attracted wide sympathy for the Jiyūtō and resulted in increasing their strength, but the violent and lawless acts of the party members will lose them the confidence of the people. Therefore, the middle and upper class people of intelligence and wealth will not participate in this party."[22] Yamagata also reported a serious lack of harmony within the Jiyūtō. "Most of the Jiyūtō members," he observed, "dislike Itagaki's propensity to be excessively theoretical. Thus, while Itagaki advocates a unicameral system the Jiyūtō has decided upon a bicameral legislature."[23]

In the same letter he included an analysis of the rival Kaishintō, which he said was "first, attempting to organize upper-class elements and establish a source of revenue; second, training a group of speakers at Waseda University; and third, organizing the wealthy merchants and farmers throughout the nation." And he added, "behind the scenes the Mitsubishi interests are giving monthly financial support to Ōkuma." The Kaishintō, he concluded, was no great threat at the moment but would, in the future, constitute an important faction in the political world.

If the popular parties constituted less of a threat than might have been expected, it was partly because the government showed great cunning in dealing with them. We have already seen how concessions in the form of local assemblies were in a sense offset by a combination of repressive laws and the organization of a pro-government party. Another tactic employed by the government leaders was to deflate the political

20. Reprinted in *ibid.*, II, 919–920.
21. At Gifu a young fanatic failed in an attempt to assassinate Itagaki, leader of the Jiyūtō. The incident allegedly prompted Itagaki to declare, "Itagaki may die, but liberty will never die." Ike, *Beginnings*, p. 151.
22. The letter appears in *Yamagata den*, II, 883–885.
23. *Ibid.*, II, 884–885.

pressure simply by bringing the leadership of the opposition into the ranks of the government with bribes of office or other advantages. Itō was the master behind a spectacularly successful plot to send abroad Itagaki and Gotō Shōjirō, the real leaders of the Jiyūtō. Gotō, in collusion with the government, received funds for the journey overseas. Itagaki never knew that it was the government that paid him to leave with the object of weakening his party.[24] During Itagaki's absence of seven months, his party declined and its quarrels with the Kaishintō wrecked all hope of a united popular movement. In a letter to Itō on June 16, 1882, Yamagata announced triumphantly, "Your plan has been realized, and Itagaki has decided to go." [25]

The threat of the party movement was a continuous theme in Yamagata's correspondence with Itō. In his report of January 22, 1883, one of his last addressed overseas to Itō, he again disclosed his concern over the radical, subversive activities of the popular movement. "Although we are taking steps daily," he wrote, "the laws are too theoretical and inadequate and, tossed about by the changing currents, are extremely difficult to apply precisely. With this condition prevailing at present I am apprehensive that unless we take drastic measures to deal with the political parties it will prove hopeless to attempt to achieve the goal of preserving the independence of our imperial nation." [26]

Financial problems and factional disputes within the leading party, the Jiyūtō, combined with the devious means adopted by the government to force its dissolution in October 1882. It was later to reappear and again challenge the concept of government held by the oligarchs, but momentarily the government gained a reprieve and, as if to signify victory in the first round, the government caused the Teiseitō to be dissolved in September 1883.[27]

Yamagata as Home Minister: Police Reform and Peace Preservation

On December 12, 1883, Yamagata became minister of home affairs; it marked a firm step up in his climb to the political summit. The home

24. Osatake Takeshi, "Itagaki Taisuke yōkō mondai," *Meiji seiji shi tembyō* (Tokyo, 1938), pp. 152–179. It is interesting that the government tried and failed to induce Ōkuma to go abroad and offered one of his important lieutenants a diplomatic post. The government also helped to establish a transport company to compete with the Mitsubishi Company with the object of weakening a major source of Ōkuma's financial support. See Oka, *Kindai Nihon*, pp. 248–250.

25. *Yamagata den*, II, 928.

26. *Ibid.*, II, 928.

27. Oka, *Kindai Nihon*, p. 256.

ministry was one of the original administrative organs established after the Restoration, but it was the Korean crisis of 1873 which caused the government to increase its authority as the central agency of the civil bureaucracy. Seventeen days after the split in the government over Korea, a new home ministry was created with vast powers over the internal administration of the country and given rank next to the department of foreign affairs.[28] Ōkubo, the most powerful oligarch until his assassination in 1878, shaped the ministry's policy of repressing all antigovernment activities. In succession, Itō and then Yamada, who had served as home ministers before Yamagata, followed the policy laid down by Ōkubo before his death. In preparation for the establishment of a parliamentary system, the central government was reorganized in 1885 and all executive authority was shifted from the Council of State to a Cabinet in which each minister was made responsible for his own department and accountable to the premier. This reorganization of the central organs of the state provided Yamagata with an opportunity to reform the home ministry.

Yamagata was by all accounts an industrious and able administrator. He was impatient with inefficiencies and demanded of himself and his subordinates thorough study and knowledge of actual conditions, and he sought expert assistance whenever he felt it was needed. Each of his major undertakings during his more than six years as home minister was calculated to build a more efficient agency of control. In view of his anxiety over the political currents of the day — so frequently expressed to Itō — it is not surprising that through the reorganization of the home ministry, and in particular the police system, and through the introduction of a new system of local government, the heavy hand of central government control was extended down to the local village.

Compared to his modernization of the Japanese army, Yamagata's part in the formation of a new system of local government and in the reorganization of the police system is relatively uncelebrated. Yet there is a striking parallel between the two. In both developments he was impelled by a desire to erect a strong, unified imperial order and driven by the conviction that the free play of political forces was detrimental to this end. The army and the police force represented the instruments of centralized authority. A further parallel also suggests itself: in his tenure as home minister he attracted a group of followers who thereafter formed the hard core of his political clique, just as Katsura, Kodama, Terauchi, and Tanaka, his military protégés, formed the heart of his military fol-

28. McLaren, ed., *Documents*, pp. 36–41.

lowing. But the analysis of his following among the bureaucrats is best seen in connection with his later assumption of the prime ministership.

After a complete reorganization of the home ministry, a procedure which enabled him to select men of his own choosing as bureau heads, Yamagata addressed himself to the problem of reorganizing the police system. The Police Bureau had been established first in 1872 under the department of justice.[29] Originally it was made up of some 6,000 recruits, mostly *shizoku* of Satsuma and Chōshū. Two years later the police of Tokyo were organized under a separate Metropolitan Police Board. Garrison troops were relied upon for maintaining order in the countryside during the early Meiji years, but by 1885 this work had become the responsibility of the national police, which by that time had been nominally placed under the home ministry. Actually, local police were still largely under the control of prefectural authorities, while the Metropolitan Police Board remained a semi-independent and semi-autonomous section of the home ministry.

Yamagata's aim was not only to modernize and standardize the nation's police force but to bring it under the firm authority of the home minister. The first step was to establish a training school for police officers. To introduce modern methods Yamagata relied on the German model. Two German police officials were invited to instruct at the school and assist in reorganizing the system.[30] Through their efforts the discipline and standard of police officers were raised. "In order to bring about the realization of the constitution and the revision of the treaties . . . we must constantly encourage the education, discipline, and training of policemen," [31] declared Yamagata.

As director of the Police Bureau, Yamagata selected Kiyoura Keigo who, in time, was to become his political heir. An imperial ordinance in 1886 defined the organization of the Metropolitan Police Board, making its head "subject to the direction and supervision of the Home Minister." [32]

Centralization of the ministry's administrative structure was accompanied by a spread of the influence of the police in local areas. Prior to this reorganization police had been organized into units of eighty to a hundred men and stationed in strategic localities throughout the land, from where they were sent out on call, much like a small-scale military

29. See Ōura Kanetake, "The Police of Japan," in Ōkuma Shigenobu, ed., *Fifty Years of New Japan* (London, 1910), Chapter 11.
30. *Yamagata den*, II, 996.
31. Quoted in *ibid.*, II, 995.
32. McLaren, ed., *Documents*, p. 312.

garrison system. This meant that the areas between these localities were not under continual surveillance. Under the new system, police were placed at more frequent intervals in branch stations and local village police boxes,[33] making it possible for the central government rapidly to reach into the smallest village to enforce its laws. As the efficiency of this system increased, it became a powerful instrument in the hands of a government deeply suspicious of any activity which might be interpreted as injurious to the state.

It was not long before the efficiency of the police system was put to a test. Economic grievances and political opposition led to serious public demonstrations against the government during Yamagata's tenure as home minister. Guarantees of free speech and assembly and revision of the treaties were demanded by one section of the politically conscious public. At one point, nationalistic groups protesting the official policy favoring Europeanization of the social as well as political life of the nation strangely joined proponents of civil rights in denouncing the government. Stringent laws led to the arrest and detention of many but failed to halt the flow of petitions, memorials, and demands. Leaders of the opposition, such as Itagaki and Gotō Shōjirō, insisted on submitting memorials of protest to the premier. Eventually the situation led to a series of local revolts.[34] Thus, just as the government was working on the draft of the promised constitution and completing work on a local government system, it felt seriously threatened by a wave of opposition.

To Yamagata those protests and outbreaks posed as serious a threat to the state as the imperial guard mutiny had posed to the army. He instinctively thought in terms of harsher controls and greater restrictions on the life of the people. "It was at this time," wrote one of Yamagata's biographers, "that he demonstrated a policy of blood and iron." [35]

In September 1886, regulations were issued prohibiting the free petitioning of government officials.[36] One month later Yamagata further restricted political gatherings by issuing an order which declared: "Those who participate in public meetings and demonstrations, no matter what the reason, must submit three days in advance to the local police the names of the leaders and officers, place of meeting, route of the parade and date . . . If this is not fulfilled, the leader and officers of the meeting

---

33. Kiyoura's account of this is in *Yamagata den,* II, 997–999. See also Osatake Takeshi, "Keishichō monogatari," *Meiji Bunka sōsetsu,* pp. 330–349.
34. The major revolts are described in Ike, *Beginnings,* Chapter 13.
35. *Yamagata den,* II, 960.
36. The home ministry order is reprinted in *ibid.,* II, 961.

will be held by the police for not more than ten days and not less than three and be forced to pay a fine of not more than 195 or less than 50 yen." [37]

Yamagata planned with military precision to meet the threat. In the spring of 1887 he had instructed Kiyoura Keigo to draft an even more drastic law which would effectively deal with the political agitation, which was then concentrated in Tokyo. In a letter dated August 1, 1887, he wrote to Kiyoura indicating that he favored action more uncompromising than that advocated by the head of the Police Bureau: "Regarding the matter about which I spoke to you the other day, how do you propose to put into effect my stubbornly held old-fashioned idea of expelling people from the capital? Please make a decision on this today or tomorrow and forward your complete plan as soon as possible. Because you are opposed to the idea it is, I realize, difficult for you, but we are in a hurry so I ask you to act upon it with dispatch." [38]

By the end of December 1887, the Peace Preservation Ordinance had been drafted. It is interesting to note that Itō Miyoji, who at this time was one of the small group engaged in drafting the constitution, was one of the authors of this ordinance.[39] Aimed at permanently crippling the liberal movement with one blow, the ordinance (1) forbade all secret societies and assemblies, (2) conferred on the police authority to halt any meeting or assembly, and (3) gave the home minister authority to expel, within a fixed number of days or hours, any person residing or sojourning within a seven and one-half mile radius of the Imperial Palace who was judged to be inciting disturbances or disrupting public tranquility.[40]

With the law drafted, preparations were completed for putting it into action. First, Yamagata was forced to bring his own forces into line. The severity of the law disturbed even the hardened chief of the metropolitan police, Mishima Michitsune. When Mishima, who had already gained an unsavory reputation for his ruthless acts in suppressing anti-government demonstrations in one of the prefectures and who was popularly known as "Chief of the Devils," hesitated in carrying out the ordinance, Yamagata threatened to lead the police and soldiers himself. At that, Mishima changed his attitude.[41]

Reports and rumors which came to the government toward the end

37. This was Police Order No. 20; it is reprinted in *ibid.*, II, 961–962.
38. Letter in *ibid.*, II, 966.
39. Suzuki Yasuzō, *Jiyū minken: kempō happu* (Tokyo, 1939), p. 296.
40. McLaren, ed., *Documents*, p. 503. Text of the ordinance is on pp. 502–504.
41. Tokutomi Iichirō, *Sohō kanmeiroku* (Tokyo, 1944), p. 147.

of December prompted the decision to issue the order on December 26, through a special edition of the *Kampō* (Official gazette).[42] The day before the ordinance went into effect, Kiyoura invited the governors of prefectures surrounding Tokyo to a meeting at which he instructed them to prepare lists of political extremists in their areas. That night Yamagata took charge of what he seems to have considered a military operation. Imperial guard troops were stationed around the Akasaka Palace. Military police were mobilized to reinforce the metropolitan police. Extra guards protected official residences, arsenals, and military depots. Special communication lines were laid and doctors were assembled at army hospitals to await developments.[43]

Yamagata's private secretary leaves us an account of how the general conducted a personal front-line inspection of his preparations. For over six hours he walked around the city to assure himself that all sensitive points were adequately protected. He ended his inspection at two in the morning by reporting to Itō at the premier's official residence that all preparations had been completed.

Yamagata's view of the strength of the antigovernment movement was grossly exaggerated, and such elaborate and extravagant measures were unnecessary, but the ordinance was so unexpected and so sweeping that the momentum of the popular movement was decisively broken. In all, over 570 people who were classified as dangerous were ordered to leave the capital. Ozaki Yukio, one of those expelled, recounts his surprise when he read of the ordinance on the morning of December 26. Returning to his home that evening, he discovered it surrounded by policemen and he was ordered to the police station. When he asked what the problem was, he was handed instructions which read, "Under article four of the Peace Preservation Ordinance you are ordered to withdraw three *ri* (seven and one-half miles) from the palace by 3 p.m. December 31, for a period of three years." [44] "Instead of being placed in prison," Ozaki adds wryly, "I was ordered out into the wide world." [45] This harsh measure, graphically described in the American press as a "flash of light-

42. Ozaki Yukio recalls that at a meeting at the house of Gotō Shōjirō on Dec. 24, he had jokingly suggested that they form units to put the capital to flame and rob the finance ministry. Ozaki Yukio, *Nihon kensei shi o kataru* (Tokyo, 1938), I, 173. This incident was undoubtedly reported to the police through their highly organized informer system and perhaps accounts for Osatake's statement that "the outrageous Peace Preservation Ordinance was brought on by the incorrect reports of a spy." Osatake, *Meiji Bunka sōsetsu,* p. 342.

43. Oka, *Kindai Nihon,* p. 276, note 2.

44. Ozaki, *Nihon kensei shi o kataru,* p. 179.

45. *Ibid.,* p. 179.

ning followed by a roar of thunder out of a blue sky," [46] was an indication that Yamagata and other ministers were prepared to take drastic action to preserve order and suppress what they considered to be dangerous developments. And reforming the police system improved the main instrument of suppression.

The Development of Local Government

Internal unity was also served by the reorganization of the local government system. Following the Restoration, the system of local administration of the Tokugawa period had been radically altered. At the very outset of the Meiji period, areas which were controlled directly by the Tokugawa family had been converted into administrative districts under the direct jurisdiction of the Tokyo government. Then when all han were abolished in 1871, they became prefectures under the nominal authority of Tokyo, but actually a large degree of autonomy remained. Thereafter, each successive step in reorganizing local government was aimed at creating local bodies more susceptible to centralized control. In 1872 the number of prefectures was reduced from 302 to 72, and each prefecture was subdivided into urban areas (*fu*), towns (*chō*), and villages (*son*). The supervision and control of the local government system were placed under the home ministry when it was created in 1874.[47]

Changes in the hierarchy of local government were prompted partly by a desire to satisfy the growing demands for greater participation and self-government at the local level. Elective assemblies were formed at the prefectural level in 1878 and later at the city and town levels. In each case, however, the assemblies were limited to advisory powers and placed under the final authority of the central government. A locally elected mayor could be rejected by the prefectural governor who in turn was appointed by and reflected the policy of the home minister. Although the word "autonomy" was often used in speaking of local government units, the word had little meaning since all local units were subject, within the area of authority delegated to them, to centralized supervision.

Although advances had been made in developing a local government system, by 1880 there was little local self-government, no standardization, and no legal framework specifying the rights and obligations of local units. The standardization and codification of local government laws

46. *Nation*, Feb. 16, 1888.
47. Fujita Takeo, "Meiji shi ni okeru chihō jichi seido no igi," *Meiji Bunka shi ronshū* (Tokyo, 1952), pp. 711–760.

along with the adoption of a constitution were considered necessary steps in constructing a new political framework. Itō had listed local government as one of the problems he should investigate during his European travels.[48] Yamagata wrote Itō during his absence in Europe that "The development of a local government system is something which cannot be entered into lightly, and present economic conditions prevent immediate action. But I thought I would mention it to you because it is something I have always advocated." [49] It is not certain how much attention Itō was able to devote to the problem, but he did listen to lectures on the subject from the German jurist Albert Mosse, a leading pupil of Rudolf von Gneist, and from the Austrian scholar, Lorenz von Stein.

Yamada Akiyoshi, who had preceded Yamagata as the home minister, had requested that a law be drafted covering the administration of towns and villages. This was presented to Yamagata when he assumed office but he rejected it as inadequate. He immediately organized a committee to investigate foreign laws concerning towns and villages and suggest a plan. At this point another problem arose. Among those engaged in the task of constructing the new political framework, there were some, including Itō, who held that the constitution should be written before a local government system was worked out. Yamagata, on the other hand, maintained that the reorganization of the local government system first would be the "best preparation for a future constitutional system . . . Thus," he recalled, "I vigorously advocated the adoption of a local government system prior to the promulgation of the constitution, and I was finally able to achieve that purpose." [50] Indeed, one of the characteristics of the Meiji constitution was that it included no provisions relating to local government.

Although the committee appointed to draft local government laws submitted its plans in June 1885, it was not until the arrival of Albert Mosse from Germany that the final law took shape. Itō brought back from Europe the conviction that the Prussian political forms were best suited to the type of government favored by the ruling oligarchs. Hirata Tōsuke, a close friend and political adviser to Yamagata who had studied in Germany under Gneist, encouraged the invitation of Gneist's leading pupil, Mosse, to act as adviser to the Japanese government on the development of local government laws. Through his friend Aoki Shūzō, the Japanese

48. *Ibid.,* p. 741.
49. Letter dated June 16, 1882, appears in *Yamagata den,* II, 892.
50. Yamagata, *Shiron,* pp. 398–399.

minister in Berlin, Yamagata was successful in obtaining the services of Mosse as an official adviser to the Japanese government.

Albert Mosse arrived in Japan in May 1886 and remained until March 1890.[51] During those years he was intimately connected with the drafting of the constitution and acquired the title of "father of the local government system." [52] Two months after his arrival Mosse submitted a memorandum containing his views on local government. Pointing out that town and village administrations were inseparable from the development of higher organs, he suggested that a special committee should be formed to determine the basic principles to be followed in reconstructing local administration. In his statement, Mosse supported Yamagata's contention that local government must be built up first as a foundation for the nation's administration:

> Since there is a close relationship between regional organizations and the articles of a constitution, in order to institute a constitutional system it is necessary, first, to build a system of local self-government and thereby construct a firm foundation for the nation.

> Thus the local system must precede the realization of the constitution. Care must be taken not to allow too great a separation between the town and village system and the next level of self-governing organs. There is a marked interconnection between the regional branches of national organs and the local self-governing bodies. Consequently, to make a complete study of local self-government we must set up a special committee which will outline a plan for a draft. Once the general principles are formulated the detailed articles should not be difficult.[53]

Accordingly, a committee for drafting a local government system was established on January 27, 1887, with Yamagata serving as its chairman. The committee requested Mosse to suggest rules to guide the committee in its work. By February 1887, these guiding rules were completed, accepted by the committee, and then approved by the Cabinet. Mosse then proceeded to draft a local government law on the basis of these principles, using as a model the Prussian laws for village self-government. One of the three secretaries attached to the committee translated Mosse's draft, and it was ready to be considered by the full committee on July 13, 1887. The only major revision made on Mosse's proposal was to

51. *Yamagata den,* II, 1013.
52. Osatake, *Kensei shi,* II, 681.
53. Quoted in Yamagata, *Shiron,* p. 400.

separate the city system from the town and village government system, which were not differentiated in Mosse's draft.[54] "If you ask why I had a European, Mr. Mosse, draft the law," wrote Yamagata, "even though there was to be found the spirit of self-government in the *goningumi* [neighborhood association], *shōya* [village headman], *nanushi* [village chief], and *toshiyori* [village elders], it was in order to be in step with the institutions extant among the great powers of Europe and America . . . and the German system was adopted as the model because it was the most suitable." [55]

Yamagata's decision to adopt the German model is an instructive instance of the Meiji government's policy of following Western experience, for the main principles for local government reform were adopted from continental Europe. In the person of Mosse, firsthand guidance and assistance were readily available. A secondhand source of acknowledged value was a biography of Heinrich Friedrich Stein, the great Prussian statesman, by J. R. Seeley, Regius Professor of Modern History at Cambridge. Completed in 1878, his three-volume study came into Itō's possession in the 1880's. Immediately seeing its application, he sent the work to Yamagata who had it translated. The latter waited impatiently to read installments as it was translated. Through it he gained greater knowledge and insight for his own task; so much so, that he wrote a laudatory preface to the completed translation and ordered that it be circulated to officials concerned with the administration of local government.[56]

In spirit and substance the reforms of Stein were close to those advised by Mosse, himself a direct descendant of Stein's school of thought. A close examination of Stein's problems and their solutions afforded specific suggestions in the writing of the new laws. Seeley outlined in great detail the origin and aims of Stein's municipal reform, reproducing many of the 208 sections of the law.[57] One reference in particular must have found a sympathetic response. Seeley wrote: "There is, indeed, something in the law which reminds us of the great principle of the military reorganization of which Scharnhorst was meditating at the very same time. As the military reform ended in the state taking possession of three whole years in the life of every citizen, and partial possession of four more, so does this law enact that a citizen may be called upon to serve

54. *Ibid.*, p. 401.
55. *Ibid.*, p. 401.
56. *Yamagata den*, II, 1024–1027.
57. J. R. Seeley, *Life and Times of Stein* (Boston, 1879), II, 223–247.

his town gratuitously for three years, and, as a general rule, that he may be expected to serve for six." [58] In Yamagata's mind too, conscription and local self-government were clearly related: both represented service to the state; both bound the people to the central government, strengthening unity and contributing to stability. In Japan, Yamagata played the part of both Stein and Gerhard von Scharnhorst.

Stein's broader purposes likewise suited Yamagata's beliefs. Before the adoption of his municipal law, Stein argued that participation in local affairs "is a most beneficial manifestation of patriotic national feeling; if all cooperation is refused the result is discontent and opposition, which will break out in manifold forms or must be suppressed by violent measures which are destructive of the spirit." [59] Yamagata, guilty himself of suppression, echoed these words: "To my mind the influence of local autonomy contributes to the workings of constitutional government because it tends to develop public spirit and political knowledge and experience." [60] Moreover, to the extent it contributed to a civic spirit, it naturally lessened dissatisfaction with the government and its leaders. Albert Mosse had stressed this very point in a series of lectures he delivered to officials interested in local government. Outlining the advantages of local self-government, he pointed out that it was vital for the government "to attract men of ability into local government work, because, if left out, they often became the instigators of anti-government activities." [61]

It was one of Yamagata's aims to lure men of ability from the popular party movement into the administrative organization of the nation. Once brought in, he sternly warned them, as he had previously admonished military personnel, to remain aloof from political activities. This article of his political philosophy is perhaps most explicitly stated in instructions to local government officials after the enactment of the new laws and his appointment as prime minister. In January 1890, local officials were called to Tokyo for instruction. On this occasion they were lined up before Yamagata according to their civil service rank,[62] and he may easily have thought of himself as the supreme military figure of the nation addressing the garrison and local military commanders, as he had done

58. *Ibid.*, II, 244–245.
59. Quoted by Guy S. Ford, *Stein and the Era of Reform in Prussia* (Princeton, 1922), p. 226.
60. Yamagata, *Shiron*, p. 406.
61. Tokyo Shisei Chōsakai, *Jichi gojū nen shi* (Tokyo, 1929), p. 115.
62. Miyake Setsurei, "Yamagata Kō Ichidai no seijiteki kōka," *Chūō kōron* 37.3:65–69 (March 1922).

so frequently in the past. Indeed, his phraseology was almost the same: "Upon you, each in his own sphere, have devolved the arduous functions of local government, and your task is to determine the best way of performing them. Before everything, what you have to consider is that the people may be directed into the route most conducive to their interest, and that you yourselves may follow the path of duty without error, favour, or affection. The executive power is of the Imperial prerogative, and those delegated to wield it should stand aloof from political parties and be guided solely by considerations of the general good in the discharge of their duties." [63]

Thus many factors encouraged the adoption of a modern system of local government. There was the desire to give knowledge and experience to the local levels of administration in preparation for a constitutional system; there was also the wish to stabilize the administration of local areas and thus protect them from the adverse effect of the constant changes in the national political situation; and there was the hope that people could be drawn into local affairs, become preoccupied with local administration and less interested in the liberal party movement. As in the case of most Meiji reforms, the drive to become a modern, "civilized" nation was also present — the determination to meet a standard of political administration which would earn the respect of foreign powers and equality with them. For Yamagata, local self-government was desirable also for the salutary effect it might have on local morale; he hoped it would foster a heightened civic sense and stronger national feeling.

In September 1887, the two plans were submitted to the Cabinet. They were approved after minor revisions and passed on to the *genrōin* on November 16. At this juncture obstacles arose. Several of the members of the *genrōin* favored delaying the adoption of a local system until the constitution was completed; one member explained that since things were always done from the top down in Japan it was unwise not to wait for the organization of the national organs first.[64] In reply to these objections Yamagata declared, "Local self-government has always been the foundation of the nation. No time must be lost in securing it for the future. If we commit ourselves to it now, great opportunities lie ahead." [65] Yamagata won his point and patiently argued against other objections. Whether local officials should be elected or selected was another controversial issue. Yamagata advocated the election of the lower-echelon

63. McLaren, ed., *Documents*, p. 420.
64. Yamagata, *Shiron*, pp. 402–403.
65. Quoted in *Yamagata den*, II, 1012.

officials, arguing that the spirit of local self-government required it. The issue was settled in his favor so that village and town heads were to be elected by a selected electorate, but city mayors, district heads, and governors were to be appointed directly or indirectly by the government.

By January 1888, the law had been completed, and on April 14 it was issued as Law No. 1 of the nation, entitled "Organization of the Government of Towns and Villages." [66] The law governing the prefectures and that governing the districts were completed in 1890. These elaborate laws established the form of local government which remained essentially unchanged for half a century. The latter law brought into being the districts (*gun*) as an administrative area between the prefectures and the towns and villages. They were never to become a vital link in the local government system, although district heads, appointed by the government, formed another layer of the bureaucracy,[67] centrally appointed and controlled, strengthening the local power of the national government.

While the laws of 1888 and 1890 increased the areas of jurisdiction of local officials to a degree and allowed the local citizenry to select some of their representatives, in no real sense did they represent an important extension of local political responsibility. The democratic features of both of Yamagata's major reforms—universal conscription and election of village and town heads—has sometimes been stressed.[68] Both were measures which involved a broader segment of the population in the affairs of the state and, as a consequence, undoubtedly increased the citizen's identification with the state. And this concern to give the masses a greater sense of responsibility is an important characteristic of the Meiji leadership.

Yet it is difficult to escape the conclusion that Yamagata's interest in organizing the countryside was mainly inspired by the expectation that orderly government would be served by granting a modicum of local

66. Full text of the law is in McLaren, ed., *Documents*, pp. 367–404.

67. At intervals attempts were made to abolish the districts. When Hara Takashi was home minister (1906–1908), he was opposed by Yamagata in his efforts to eliminate the districts. Yamagata's supporters in the House of Peers defeated the proposals. See *Hara Kei nikki* (Tokyo, 1950–1951), IIA, 391. (This diary will hereafter be cited as *Hara nikki*.) In 1912 pressure again developed to abolish the districts, but again Yamagata thwarted the attempt. The districts were finally abolished in 1933.

68. Maeda Tamon has written that Yamagata's "two great accomplishments were the creation of conscription and local self-government systems. In the former there is a type of democracy associated with military duty; in the latter, the foundations of constitutionalism. It is interesting that he insisted on the election of town and village heads." Maeda Tamon, *Chihō jichi no hanashi* (Tokyo, 1930), p. 45. For the favorable impression of a foreign observer in Japan, see John H. Wigmore's reports in *Nation*, July 3, 1890, pp. 8–10, and July 10, 1890, pp. 25–27.

responsibility. And a second reason was his desire to erect a protective dike against the spreading strength of the political parties organized in opposition to the government. If centralized authority could control local areas through the lower echelons of administration before the constitution was granted, the strength of the liberal movement could be limited before the establishment of a national representative assembly.

In general, an authoritarian political system was made more rigid and efficient. The subjection of each administrative level to the supervision and control of the next gave the central government a higher degree of control than before. The broad powers reserved for the home minister at the apex of the pyramid left little room for real decisions or initiative at the local level. Decentralization was carried out in a very limited sense: towns and villages were given the responsibility for their local budgets and land assessments for local taxes, thus unburdening the national government of these less significant decisions. But as the laws were conceived and carried out, they were means by which duties were delegated and policies were executed from above rather than measures to register and carry out the will of the people from below. Local policy was shaped far above. A governor could block all local initiative: he could suspend the prefectural assembly, he could order taxes collected even if not approved by the assembly, and he could recommend that the home minister veto any measure passed. Since the participation of the people in local administration was very limited, the local government system in its modern garb became a main pillar of the political power of the central government.[69]

What is striking is that the reorganization of local government presaged the form of the national assembly. In a sense, the latter became an extension of the local assemblies with similar limitations in its power. It can be said that the local government laws and the constitution became the twin pillars of the new political synthesis.[70] Both aimed to foster unity and stability by securing power in the central government; both aimed to regenerate the state as a better instrument of national authority under imperial rule.

Yamagata had enlisted the aid of many others in the cause of local gov-

69. Fujita Takeo, *Meiji Bunka shi ronshū*, pp. 759–760. See also Nagahama Masahisa, *Chihō jichi* (Tokyo, 1952), p. 21.

70. Mizuno Rentarō, home minister in several Cabinets between 1915 and 1928, wrote in praise of Yamagata's work, "I hereby pay my tribute to these people, headed by Prince Yamagata . . . who established local government. The adoption of local government system was, along with the promulgation of the Constitution, the greatest Civil enterprise of the Meiji Restoration." Mizuno Rentarō, "Chihō seido no kako narabi ni genzai ni okeru sho mondai ni tsuite," *Kokka gakkai zasshi* 51.10:7 (October 1938).

ernment reform but, as was the case with military reforms, its actual completion was in large measure the result of his persistence. And the thought and work he put into this reform led him to convictions which, as we shall see, fashioned his attitude toward the national assembly. He was to advocate the same relationship between the prime minister and the national assembly as the governors had to a prefectural assembly. But he was not to face the national assembly before he had renewed his firsthand experience with the West. Significantly, unlike the chronology of events in most other modern nation-states, the modern army of Japan was organized and the local government system firmly fixed (as, indeed, were other essential organs of the central administration) before the constitution, under which the legislature was elected, was written. In both developments Yamagata had been the key figure.

Second Trip Abroad

On December 2, 1888, eight months after the enactment of the first local government laws, Yamagata went abroad on his second trip to Europe. The main purpose of his journey was to observe in action the various local government systems in the countries of Europe. This would explain the presence of three officials of the home ministry in his suite. But it would hardly explain the presence of three or four army officers. It has been noted that regardless of the position Yamagata held in the political administration of his government, he always retained his active interest as well as his authority in the military camp. His second tour of Europe illustrates this point. His secondary objective was to observe again the military developments in Europe.

The substitution in Japan of German military instructors for French proved a real embarrassment when Yamagata requested permission to observe the French army. In a letter dated January 16, 1889, addressed to Matsukata, he recounted: "When I had an interview with the [French] Foreign Minister it was evident that he was considerably influenced by the return of the instructors, and when I spoke of inspecting a unit of the army, the suggestion was received coldly." [71] Resentful of the growing German influence in Japan, the French showed the visiting party little enthusiasm and treated perfunctorily their request to observe the local government system in France.

There were marked differences between this trip and Yamagata's first trip almost twenty years before. Now a leading minister of state, he en-

71. Reprinted in *Yamagata den*, II, 1032.

joyed a status which permitted him to move among the higher circles of European governments.[72] From France his party proceeded to Berlin where Yamagata, through an interpreter, listened to a series of lectures by Rudolf von Gneist on the principles of local government. After Germany the group visited Austria, Russia, Italy, Holland, and then England. In London, Yamagata was cordially entertained by the Lord Mayor, Count Roseberry.[73]

In letters to his associates in Japan he reported the remarkable changes which Europe had undergone since his last visit almost two decades earlier. The conviction that Japan had some distance to travel to catch up with European nations was recorded in a Chinese-style verse he wrote during his tour:

> When I reflect on the brilliant and enduring
> culture of Europe
> to which I now return
> I realize, though I am already turning grey,
> that half my life's work is still undone.[74]

As a result of his months of investigation, he returned home with a clearer idea of the functioning of local governments in foreign countries. At the same time he had been able to observe military advances from which Japan could benefit.

During Yamagata's sojourn in Europe important events took place in Japan. On February 11, 1889, the Imperial Constitution was promulgated, and, at the Kaiserhof Hotel in Berlin, Yamagata gathered his party together and in celebration drank a toast to the emperor. He recognized that the enactment of the constitution marked a decisive stage in the nation's development. "The first decisive step after the Restoration," he wrote Yamada Akiyoshi, "was the abolition of the han and the establishment of the prefectures, an event which could be called the second restoration. In that sense, the promulgation of the constitution could be regarded as the third restoration. In slightly over twenty years our political and cultural life has made great progress . . . an advance unparalleled in the world." [75]

The completion and promulgation of the constitution prompted Yamagata to reflect on the practice of constitutional government. As he trav-

---

72. Hara Takashi was in charge of the Japanese embassy in Paris and assisted Yamagata in meeting government leaders. *Hara nikki*, II.
73. *Yamagata den*, II, 1040.
74. *Ibid.*, II, 1040.
75. Letter, dated June 15, 1889, in *ibid.*, II, 1060–1061.

eled about Europe he had concerned himself with such practice, and he related his observations to his closest friends at home. His letters of the spring of 1889 reveal his attitude toward the policy he felt the government should favor under the new constitution. Retaining the skepticism toward popular government which we noted in his first trip to Europe, he encouraged the government leaders to set a clear policy and hold to it with a firm hand.

In a letter written from Berlin on April 5 and addressed to two of his close friends, Yoshikawa Kensei, vice minister of home affairs, and Tanaka Kōken, then the vice minister of the Imperial Household, he summarized his doubts about parliamentary government and suggested the proper course for Japan.

> In observing the various assemblies and election methods during my travels in Europe, I find that calm, mature discussion generally arouses little response while the reputation and influence of those advocating the empty theories of extremism gradually increase, the phenomenon varying in proportion to the development of the culture. Although the historical growth of each nation produces varying traditions prohibiting generalizations, it seems odd that in European society of today, liberal politicians cultivate the spirit of absolute monarchism, while monarchists, on the other hand, advocate liberalism. Both groups are extreme. Administrative power is centralized, but in practice executive authority shifts to the legislature, with both groups advancing selfish policies doing untold damage to the state.
>
> Although parliaments could be called the flower of civilization and the spirit of politics, most unfortunately this abuse makes a plaything of a nation's welfare. Considering our present state and the immediate future, many unanticipated problems will surely arise. For these we must be fully prepared. I hope that in the various preparations to which you are devoting yourselves you will give careful attention to this problem.[76]

Three weeks later Yamagata wrote Matsukata his views on the policies which the government should pursue, stating his advocacy of a strong government: "As we have already become a constitutional state, unless we first of all define our goals and principles and fix a steady course we will be faced with many unexpected problems. Unless the government's foundations are first firmly established, no matter how good the laws, unsatisfactory results will not be prevented. Furthermore, politics will be-

76. *Ibid.*, II, 1051–1052.

come chaotic, giving rise to a hopeless situation, and in the end even the question of where sovereignty resides may be introduced." [77]

These ideas were further developed in a letter to Yamada Akiyoshi, the minister of justice, on June 15, 1889: "If the administration fails now to formulate quickly a fundamental policy which will not bend to every wind, and [does not] prepare to work towards its realization, it is doubtful that tranquility can be preserved in the nation. Unless there is unity in the cabinet and the foundations of the government are solid, one could predict that regardless of how good the policy, it would certainly fail." [78]

In these reflections on constitutional government we gain further insight into his attitude just prior to the time he was to assume the office of the prime minister. It was his constant conviction that unless a united and determined government grasped unquestioned authority, hopeless conditions would ensue. The duty of leadership, he believed, was to provide the force which might enable the country to advance, strong and united.

The Problem of Revising the Treaties

During Yamagata's absence the recurrent problem of revising Japan's unequal treaties reached a critical stage. The readjustment of the treaty system with the Western powers was the central question demanding the attention of every foreign minister after the Restoration. The Iwakura mission in 1872 had made a tentative start on the problem. In 1874 a special bureau was organized to study possible approaches to freeing Japan from extraterritoriality and unfavorable tariffs. After Inoue Karoru became foreign minister in 1885, he made some progress in negotiating with the powers. Feverish efforts were made to convince the Western countries that Japan had advanced to a stage in her modernization which would enable her to carry out the obligations and responsibilities of a sovereign nation under the accepted legal arrangements between nations. During the year from May 1886 to April 1887, twenty-eight conference sessions were held with the American and European treaty powers. Inoue was satisfied to advance slowly toward the objective of equality, but his efforts were opposed by those who demanded a complete rewriting of the treaties. Thus when it became known that Inoue's plan would con-

77. *Ibid.*, II, 1054.
78. *Ibid.*, II, 1060.

tinue the practice of appointing foreign judges to adjudicate cases involving foreign residents, a tide of opposition rose which crippled negotiations for six months and forced Inoue's resignation in 1887.

Ōkuma, who succeeded to the ministry of foreign affairs in January 1888, renewed efforts to negotiate a satisfactory settlement with even greater vigor.[79] He shifted from a conference method to secret bilateral negotiations with each nation. Initially his methods met with spectacular success. In succession Mexico, the United States, Germany, and Russia signed revised treaties of amity and commerce. But negotiations with Great Britain ran into difficulties which finally wrecked all of Ōkuma's efforts.

On April 19, 1889, the London *Times* published Japan's terms, and a month later the terms appeared in a Japanese newspaper. The leak in the secret negotiations revealed several features which immediately aroused a violent reaction among those opposing the general policies of the government. The stipulations that foreign judges would sit on the Supreme Court and that foreign residents would be permitted to own land outside of the settlement areas touched off demonstrations and demands for the withdrawal of the proposals. Opposition within the government developed on legal grounds. Inoue Kowashi, head of the Board of Legislation, objected to the terms on the grounds that they violated several articles of the constitution. Opposition both outside and within the government led to a serious split within the Cabinet when Ōkuma's proposal was brought up for Cabinet discussion in July 1889.

Yamagata was aware of Ōkuma's proposed plan before he went abroad because of his participation in a Cabinet meeting when the plan[80] was originally presented.[81] During his absence Yamagata assumed that the treaty negotiations were progressing satisfactorily. He wrote Yoshikawa from Berlin in April that he was pleased that a plan for treaty revision had been formulated.[82] And while traveling in the United States several months later, he sent instructions to all governors that treaty revisions were about to be effected.[83] He was not aware of the serious split within the Cabinet until his return; and he could not have known that by his very absence he had become the key to the solution of the crisis.

79. For the account of Ōkuma's negotiations, see Idditti, *The Life of Ōkuma*, pp. 256–267.

80. Watanabe Ikujirō, *Monjo yori mitaru Ōkuma Shigenobu kō* (Tokyo, 1932), p. 176.

81. Watanabe Ikujirō, *Meiji shi kenkyū* (Tokyo, 1934), p. 233.

82. Letter dated April 5, 1889, in *Yamagata den,* II, 1053.

83. Watanabe Ikujirō, *Meiji shi kenkyū*, p. 232.

The government leaders were divided into two factions: one favored carrying out the negotiations (popularly identified as the *danko ha,* or "faction for decisive action"), and the other demanded that the negotiations be halted (known as the *chūshi ha,* or "faction to halt action"). Ōkuma stubbornly refused to halt his progress and received the full support of Kuroda, the premier, of Yamada, minister of justice, and of Enomoto, the minister of education. Saigō, the minister of navy, Ōyama, the minister of war, and Matsukata, the minister of finance, gave their nominal support but were in fact opposed. The problem was that they were all Satsuma men, and inasmuch as Kuroda was a senior Satsuma statesman as well as premier, they found it difficult to exert their opposition openly. Gotō Shōjirō, the minister of communications and ex-leader of a popular political party, the Jiyūtō, was the chief opponent in the Cabinet, and he had the support of Inoue within the Cabinet and of Itō, who was then serving as president of the Privy Council.

An intense contest was waged by both factions to gain Yamagata's support.[84] Opinion in court circles and within the Privy Council favored the *chūshi ha.* Sugiura Jūgō and Sasa Tomofusa, prominent among Yamagata's followers within the civil bureaucracy and members of the *chūshi ha,* prevailed upon Shinagawa Yajirō,[85] privy councillor and close clan associate of Yamagata, to write a letter which would be delivered to the home minister before he disembarked at Yokohama on October 2. In this letter, the basis for the opposition to Ōkuma was to be explained. On September 26, Shinagawa wrote the requested letter, indicated the impasse which had been reached over the question of revising the treaties, and explained that Itō and Inoue were helpless in the existing situation. He appealed for Yamagata's aid, stating that "a single word from you will determine the issue," and added the interesting observation that "both government and opposition groups were unanimous in feeling that Yamagata was the only logical successor to Kuroda."[86]

Four days after Shinagawa wrote his letter, Yamada, the justice minister and the only Chōshū man to support Ōkuma, followed the same course and presented the other side of the argument in order to solicit Yamagata's support. Playing upon Yamagata's known distaste for the

84. I have followed Watanabe's account, *ibid.,* pp. 235–236.

85. According to one author, "Shinagawa was the originator of the movement opposing Ōkuma's treaty revision plan." This may well be the case with regard to opposition within the government, but diverse groups joined in the general opposition, from the Jiyūtō to the ultra-nationalist organization Genyōsha, represented in this agitation by Toyama Mitsuru. Okutani Matsuji, *Shinagawa Yajirō den* (Tokyo, 1940), p. 249.

86. Letter is reprinted in *Yamagata den,* II, 1064.

parties, he pointed out that the parties opposing the treaty revision were considering only their selfish ends and not the people's welfare.[87]

Rarely had the return of a minister been awaited with such anxious expectation. The treaty question was posing a real threat to the unity of the central administration, and Yamagata was looked upon as the only person who could save the situation. The press accurately reflected the situation. The newspaper *Chōya's* headline read, "Whole Nation Anxiously Awaits Return of Count Yamagata." [88] He is, said the *Jiji Shimpō,* "the cynosure of such high hopes and expectations." [89] *Kokumin no Tomo* stated, "We believe that Count Yamagata is one of the most important elements of power in the government, and consequently his return will be equivalent to the addition of so much personal weight to the cabinet." [90] On October 6, the *Tokyo Nichi Nichi* asked in its headline, "Will Situation Change Completely with Yamagata's Return?" [91] On October 4, the *Tokyo Nichi Nichi* had written, "On the basis of the Count's previous behavior, no matter what the problem he does not act simply after hearing one side's explanation." [92] This was quite evidently a general feeling, and an interesting race developed between Cabinet ministers to reach Yamagata first and express their views in private. Matsukata and others proceeded to Yokohama on a small boat the night before the ship was due to arrive. He hoped to express in private his real views on the issue, which he had not felt in a position to do in the Cabinet meeting. On the morning of October 2, war minister Ōyama was surprised when he met both Ōkuma and Kuroda at the Shimbashi station. They were all traveling to Yokohama for the same purpose. Realizing that Matsukata would have little opportunity to talk with Yamagata if Kuroda and Ōkuma arrived on the scene, Ōyama quickly fabricated a story. He claimed that the arrival time of the ship on which Yamagata was crossing the Pacific was still not known but it appeared that it would be late. He encouraged the premier to await reply to an inquiry he had just sent requesting the exact time of the ship's arrival. As a result of this stratagem, Kuroda and Ōkuma left Tokyo on a later train and were able to do no more than briefly welcome Yamagata home at Yokohama.

87. *Ibid.*, II, 1064.
88. Nakayama Yasumasa, comp., *Shimbun shūsei Meiji hennen shi* (Tokyo, 1935), VII, 315. (Cited hereafter as *Meiji hennen shi*.)
89. As quoted in the *Japan Weekly Mail*, Oct. 5, 1889, p. 304.
90. *Ibid.*, Oct. 5, 1889, p. 302.
91. *Meiji hennen shi*, VII, 317.
92. *Ibid.*, VII, 316.

While it is not known whether Matsukata was able to have a satisfactory talk with Yamagata, it seems certain that the *chūshi ha* reached him first. Shinagawa's letter followed by his long visit with Yamagata on the night of October 2 were the first detailed accounts Yamagata received and were the basis of his first impressions. Kuroda was aware of the influences being brought to bear on Yamagata and suggested that Ōkuma call on Yamagata and present the arguments in favor of treaty revision.[93]

Itō Hirobumi wrote to Yamagata on October 4, two days after his return, explaining his position and his inability to settle the dispute. "I have been waiting expectantly for your return," he wrote, "and fondly hope that after acquainting yourself with the situation you will arrive at a policy best suited to the nation's welfare and the cooperation of the other ministers." [94]

A week after his return the press was unanimous that "the final decision as to the fate of the Treaty Revision still rests with Count Yamagata" and spoke of "the impatience with which the public awaits Count Yamagata's decision." The *Jiji Shimpō* drew a parallel between the prevailing situation and the split which occurred over the Korean problem in 1873 and reminded Yamagata that he could repeat Kido's service by working vigorously for harmony within the ruling circle.[95]

Characteristically, Yamagata approached his delicate position with caution and care. He refused to commit himself immediately, and after a few days in the capital he retired to Ōiso, a fashionable seaside resort south of Tokyo where he had built a small house, and invited Inoue Kowashi to brief him thoroughly on the problem. Inoue, who had shifted to the opposition on the grounds that the Ōkuma treaty plan conflicted with the constitution, provided himself with supporting documents and proceeded to Ōiso to acquaint the home minister with the background of the problem.

On October 10, Itō resigned as president of the Privy Council, a move which not only caught Kuroda and Ōkuma off guard but precipitated a settlement of the crisis. Ōkuma attempted to dissuade Itō from resigning, but the latter refused to withdraw his resignation. When Itō explained that it appeared Yamagata would oppose the treaty revision, Ōkuma disagreed and suggested that the three hold a conference at Yamagata's residence the next day.

93. For this see letter from Kuroda to Ōkuma quoted by Watanabe Ikujirō, *Meiji shi kenkyū*, p. 236.

94. Quoted in *Yamagata den*, II, 1070.

95. *Japan Weekly Mail*, Oct. 12, 1889, p. 322.

At the resulting conference on October 12, Ōkuma discussed both the treaty plan and Itō's resignation. Apparently Yamagata joined in encouraging Itō to remain in office, but he did not give any clear indication of his stand on the treaty question. Although friends of Yamagata were aware of his views, Ōkuma and Kuroda were not informed because he had submitted no official view. Even when the question was brought to an imperial conference before the emperor on October 15, with Ōkuma defending and Gotō attacking the treaty plan, Yamagata did not make known his views. He pleaded insufficient acquaintance with all the issues involved and requested further time for consultation and study.

Finally, at the second imperial conference called to settle the deadlock on October 18, Yamagata submitted his opinion in writing to the emperor. He openly disclosed his opposition to the Ōkuma treaty plan, but he did not do so on the grounds that it violated the constitution. He argued that until the nation's legal code had been formulated and enacted, the real heart of the treaty problem, extraterritoriality, could not be dealt with. Therefore, he concluded, revision of the treaties, as proposed by Ōkuma, would not be helpful because in actuality it would have to be postponed until the legal code had been completed.

In addition to the political rivalries it aroused, this dispute represented the dilemma of treaty revision. All wanted to gain total independence and end the humiliation of the treaties by freeing Japan of foreign customs control and extraterritoriality. Yet it was generally acknowledged that final revisions must await legal reforms. On the other hand, the lack of reforms in the laws was often used to counter foreign demands for concessions of more travel and residence privileges in the interior. Furthermore, Japan's moral justification for equality was claimed on the basis of Western international law; yet she was forced to admit that her lack of Western-type laws inevitably weakened that claim.

Yamagata's hesitation in committing himself reflected his dilemma, his normal caution, and, added to this, his sensitivity to the fact that his position would be decisive and, if adverse, would cause Kuroda to resign. In the end, however, he took a firm stand conscious of the consequences. On October 15 in a letter to Matsukata he said, "Even if it leads to the downfall of the cabinet, I cannot approve of Ōkuma's plan, so please convey my feelings to Saigō and Ōyama." [96] The meeting of October 18 broke up with Ōkuma's plans effectively defeated and no new plan adopted. At this point another event intervened to end all of Ōkuma's efforts.

96. Reprinted in *Yamagata den,* II, 1080.

As Ōkuma was returning to the Foreign Office from the meeting at the palace, an extremist of a newly formed patriotic society threw a bomb at his carriage. The bomb shattered Ōkuma's right leg, necessitating amputation, but he survived the attempt on his life. Yamagata's stand and the attack on Ōkuma forced Kuroda to admit his failure. The premier proceeded to the palace and submitted his resignation, recommending Yamagata as his successor.

This episode in the story of treaty revision is recounted not because it was of such great consequence in the effort to rewrite the treaties. It is told because Yamagata's role in it placed him in a position to be the logical person to form a new government. His absence in Europe had removed him from the emotional entanglements and animosities arising out of the treaty problem. Yet his opinion on this key question had determined its outcome at the moment. In addition to this, however, Yamagata stood as Kuroda's logical successor as a result of his enhanced position within the civil government. Ever since his formal entry into the political world in 1882, he had moved closer to the center of the narrow policy-forming group within the government. His noted record and accomplishments as home minister, added to his achievements in organizing the army, had won for him wide respect. "The Count," it was, therefore, not surprising to read in a newspaper of the time, "is a statesman of prudence and moderation. It would be impossible to find anyone better qualified to assume leadership of the Government at this juncture." [97]

97. *Japan Weekly Mail*, Dec. 28, 1889, p. 594.

4

Leading the Nation

In December 1889, Yamagata reached a new point in the steady rise of his career. In that month, he agreed to serve as the emperor's prime minister. With this act he opened a new chapter in his eventful life during which he not only increased his power in the domestic field but, as a result of Japan's startling victory over China, became the symbol of strength of a nation which suddenly joined the first-rank powers of the world. With his authority now deeply rooted in both the civil and military bureaucracies, he helped to lead the country through the early uncertainties of constitutional government. It was a period which brought together the authority which he had acquired in successive steps in the civil and military camps.

Yamagata's First Cabinet

Two months passed between the demise of the Kuroda government and the inauguration of Yamagata's administration. There was no opposition within the government to his selection; on the contrary, he was the unanimous choice of the leading statesmen.[1] The delay was caused, rather, by his own refusal to accept the invitation. Yamagata was fond of saying "I am merely a soldier" (*yo wa ikkai no buben*) in response to requests to serve in high political positions. Many have taken this to represent deception, a façade behind which he schemed and plotted for greater power. But it is just as reasonable to conclude that it reflected a genuine lack of confidence in dealing with the political problems of the nation and in particular in handling the delicate question of foreign

1. See letter of privy councillor Motoda Eifu to Itō Hirobumi (dated Oct. 28, 1889) and from Itō Miyoji, chief secretary of the Privy Council, to Itō Hirobumi, in Fukaya Hiroji, *Shoki gikai: jōyaku kaisei* (Tokyo, 1940), pp. 154–156.

relations, for which he felt himself inadequately prepared. His natural cautiousness made him reluctant to step into the top political position, and he did not relish exposing himself to the sharp political winds.

To counter his colleagues' entreaties he pleaded political inexperience, unfamiliarity with diplomacy, and his heavy responsibilities as home minister in preparing the government for the opening of the Diet in 1890.[2] In this instance, however, his refusal was overcome by persistent pleas. Sanjō Sanetomi, who had formed an interim Cabinet following the collapse of the Kuroda Cabinet, eagerly sought the aid of Chōshū bureaucrats in pressing Yamagata's acceptance. Yamagata's wish to avoid the problem of facing the first Diet and his conviction that Itō, more familiar than he with the workings of parliamentary government, was the logical person to face the Diet were overcome by pledges of support and assistance from the other oligarchs. He had a general's fear of defeat, and when he finally assumed the premiership he carefully planned his tactics as though he were engaged in a military campaign. The phrase "I am merely a soldier" did point to one truth: that when he accepted office his conceptions of political maneuverings were placed in a military framework.

The first Yamagata Cabinet was the third in a long line of Cabinets monopolized and alternately led by men from Satsuma and Chōshū. A conspicuous feature of his Cabinet was the retention of all the members of Kuroda's Cabinet with the exception of Kuroda, Ōkuma, and Inoue. He himself retained the home ministry post while serving as premier, and nominated the vice ministers of agriculture and commerce and of foreign affairs in the previous Cabinet to ministerial rank in the same departments.[3]

Yamagata's Cabinet represented a continuity with previous Cabinets in philosophy as well as personnel. He fully subscribed to the concept of *chōzen shugi* (the principle of aloofness), which meant in practice that the government should remain above and aloof from political parties. This policy, favored initially by all the major leaders of the Meiji government, had first been enunciated by Kuroda in instructions given the governors in 1889 on the day following the promulgation of the constitution. The followers of *chōzen shugi* did not oppose the formation of

2. *Tokyo Nichi Nichi*, Oct. 26, 1889, in *Meiji hennen shi*, VII, 330.
3. Yamagata's Cabinet included three from Chōshū: Yamagata (premier and home minister), Aoki Shūzō (foreign minister), Yamada Akiyoshi (justice); three from Satsuma: Saigō Tsugumichi (navy), Ōyama Iwao (army), Matsukata Masayoshi (finance); two from Tosa: Iwamura Michitoshi (agriculture and commerce), Gotō Shōjirō (communications); and one ex-Tokugawa bureaucrat, Enomoto Takeaki (education).

political parties; they accepted the inevitability of associations of the like-minded in political organization. However, as Kuroda said, "the government must always, with a single policy, pursue a fair and correct course and stand above and outside the parties." [4] Three days later, Itō, in a speech to the heads of the prefectural assemblies, repeated the same point: "It would be dangerous for political parties to organize a cabinet, it would jar the nation's foundations." [5] Yamagata reiterated this principle in his instructions to the governors one day after taking office. "The executive power is of the Imperial prerogative," he declared, "and those delegated to wield it should stand aloof from political parties." [6] *Chōzen shugi* was in keeping with the tradition in Japan of a hereditary class holding ultimate political authority, by legal right. But by their social reforms, the Meiji leaders had made it difficult to re-create the sinking autocracy of the past. The new political elite that emerged came from a slightly wider segment of society than the old, but in espousing *chōzen shugi* they were perpetuating the political philosophy that had guided former rulers. That is, they were claiming that those now chosen to rule, as opposed to those born to rule, should govern by standing above the self-serving factions of the populace and exercise authority, on behalf of the emperor, in the interests of the whole nation.

The government, according to Yamagata, should not only stay clear of political rivalries but also maintain unity in the face of party pressures. The deep split within the Kuroda Cabinet had distressed him; it represented to him a weakening of the government's strength. Disharmony, he feared, would disable the Cabinet at the very time when its effectiveness should be improved in order to face the Diet.[7] This concern for unity prompted him, even before he assumed office as the first minister, to formulate rules to govern the conduct of the Cabinet. He recommended four principles: first, the Cabinet should be a balanced and stable organization; second, it should present a single, unified policy; third, strict secrecy should be maintained by the cabinet regarding its discussions; fourth, each Cabinet minister should be accountable directly to the emperor.[8]

The last of these recommendations reflects Yamagata's concern with the excessive power held by the prime minister. "According to the principles laid down in the constitution," his memorandum read, "the au-

4. Quoted by Oka, *Kindai Nihon*, p. 293.
5. Quoted by Watanabe Ikujirō, *Meiji shi kenyū*, p. 103.
6. McLaren, ed., *Documents*, p. 420.
7. Rōyama Masamichi, *Seiji shi* (Tokyo, 1942), p. 265.
8. *Yamagata den*, II, 1094.

thority to manage all the affairs of state is an Imperial prerogative and all of the ministers should be held responsible for the acts of their respective offices. At present, the prime minister supervises each minister and, with the minister concerned, countersigns all Imperial laws, placing excessive power in his hands. The cabinet procedures should be changed so that each minister will be entirely responsible for the acts of his office. This would be a more complete realization of the principles of the constitution." [9] On the question of the secrecy of Cabinet deliberations, he felt they should be kept confidential even after a minister left office. "In spite of the fact that constitutional government is aimed at open councils and the Diet designed to be public, Cabinet deliberations must be completely secret so that the opinions of no minister will leak out to become the seed of popular debate." [10]

These recommendations reveal some of Yamagata's notions of how a constitutional cabinet should function. The changes relating to ministerial responsibility which he recommended were incorporated in an imperial rescript on December 24, 1889, the day Yamagata assumed office. The area of authority of each minister was defined in greater detail.[11] The right of the chief of staff to report directly to the throne on important military matters, it should be noted, was explicitly preserved. Armed with these rules for the guidance of the Cabinet and his own understanding of the constitutional system, Yamagata prepared to put his policies into effect.

The Imperial Rescript on Education

Before considering the policies of the Yamagata Cabinet and its relations with the legislature, however, we must note Yamagata's part in an event of far-reaching importance — the enactment of the "Imperial Rescript on Education." The imperial rescript has been called "the most influential document produced in modern Japanese history." [12] Such a judgment is based on the fact that the rescript went far beyond a statement of principles for an educational policy. It was in fact a declaration of ethical principles which were meant to govern every aspect of the relationship between the people and the state; it stressed the Confucian doctrines of filial piety, loyalty to superiors, and duty to the state. The

9. *Ibid.*, II, 1095.
10. *Ibid.*, II, 1095.
11. The rescript appears in McLaren, ed., *Documents*, pp. 232–233.
12. Daniel C. Holtom, *Modern Japan and Shinto Nationalism* (Chicago, 1947), p. 77.

purpose of the rescript was to reassert, with imperial sanction, values which would buttress the allegiance of the people to the emperor and to precepts which would encourage traditional morality.

Yamagata did not originate the idea of such a rescript but at every stage in its evolution he gave encouragement and the support of his growing authority. In February of 1890 he had told the nation's governors that "the emperor has granted to his subjects a constitutional system in order to improve their morals and increase their happiness." [13] It was his hope to strengthen this purpose of the constitution by an official pronouncement on morals. The *Tokyo Nichi Nichi*, early in January, had predicted that one of Yamagata's policies would be to strengthen social morality.[14] This is not surprising since as early as 1879, as we have seen, Yamagata had already been disturbed by the effect of the adoption of a Western system of laws. He had observed then that "an overdependence on laws has weakened the social fabric with the result . . . that loyalty for those above and sympathetic regard for those below have vanished." [15] Similar concern for the moral foundations of the nation had been entertained in high government circles for some time. In particular, those about the throne were anxious to make the teaching of a national ethic part of the educational process. Yamagata and other conservatives realized that the indoctrination of youth with traditional values would tend to produce the sentiment of respect upon which the system of an absolute emperor ultimately rested.

Western influences had been strong in the sweeping educational reforms after the Restoration. The theories and practice of education had been freely adopted from both European and American models. By 1872 an educational bill had been enacted which laid the foundation of state-controlled compulsory education. The shift from the narrow class-based educational system of Tokugawa days to a system based on universal education was, along with the adoption of a universal conscription system, a measure which exerted the greatest influence on the lives of the people. The rapid change in education brought into conflict traditional ideas and the requirements of modern Western education.

The origin of the educational rescript is to be found in the minds of conservatives troubled by the conflict. The same officials who were skeptical about the liberal and egalitarian ideas which stirred the political

13. In a speech delivered to governors meeting in Tokyo on Feb. 13, 1890; *Yamagata den*, II, 1101. Text of speech is printed in *Yamagata den*, II 1097–1103.
14. *Tokyo Nichi Nichi*, Jan. 5, 1890; see *Meiji hennen shi*, VII, 358.
15. *Yamagata den*, II, 843.

world feared the influence of foreign ideas on the traditional ideals of Japan. Yamagata was prominent among those who had for some time favored the formulation of an ethical code to guide the people. His early Confucian training had set in his mind a moral code which had not been affected by his advocacy of certain Western ways. It was Motoda Eifu, however, a leading Confucian scholar and, more important, one of the emperor's tutors, who doggedly advocated that an imperially sanctioned national ethical code should be part of the education of all Japanese. More than any other single person, he was responsible for formulating and writing the "Imperial Rescript on Education." [16]

As early as 1879, Motoda, allegedly at the request of the emperor, had drafted a document designed to establish a moral framework for the education of the nation. He stoutly maintained that the erosion of public morals could be reversed only if education were "founded upon the Imperial ancestral precepts, benevolence, duty, loyalty, and filial piety, and Confucius were made the cornerstone of our teaching of ethics." [17] This document, entitled "Kyōgaku taishi" (the aims of education), was submitted to Itō for his comment. Itō agreed with the aims of the document but replied that the aims of virtue and morality could be accomplished only by example and great teaching, not by legislation.[18] Four years later Motoda wrote a "Yōgaku kōyō" (Primary school outline) which was heavily influenced by Confucian doctrine. The emperor, who had requested this outline, distributed the document to the governors and ministers of state, declaring that it should be regarded as containing the essentials of moral teaching. This caused Motoda to claim with satisfaction: "Since the compilation of 'Yōgaku kōyō' by Imperial order, the evils produced by American education have steadily been corrected, and the nation has again turned to the principles of loyalty to the sovereign and love of the country." [19]

In 1884, Motoda again attempted to press his views for a definition of a national moral code. He submitted an opinion to Itō who was then serving as Imperial Household minister, suggesting that a policy statement be made to clarify the purpose and philosophy of education. He emphasized that the lessons bequeathed by imperial tradition must form

16. For Motoda's career and influence, see Donald H. Shively, "Motoda Eifu: Confucian Lecturer to the Meiji Emperor," in David S. Nivisen and Arthur F. Wright, eds., *Confucianism in Action* (Stanford, 1959), pp. 302–333.
17. As quoted in *ibid.*, p. 327.
18. Quoted in *ibid.*, p. 328.
19. *Yamagata den,* II, 1120.

the ideals of the nation. Itō again was interested but not prepared to act.[20]

Motoda's desires had to await a shift in the climate of the times. In the early 1880's the country was making desperate efforts to become Westernized, feverishly adopting foreign customs and pushing Europeanization "into finical details." [21] The clamor for popular rights and the activities of the political parties reached their height about the time Motoda again submitted his views. The government was preoccupied with attempts to control political activity, while preparing for the constitution and negotiating for treaty revisions. Until the swing to extreme Westernism had generated its own reaction, the time was not yet ripe for a sacred text on virtue. Dissatisfaction over the treaty revision plans generated a patriotic upsurge which perhaps marked the turning point in another of Japan's classical swings from a period of importations from abroad to a period during which it assimilated these importations. In the present alternate swing, traditionalism, which had been alive but submerged by the wave of Westernization, reasserted itself. Nationalism gained strength and ancient symbols were given renewed significance. The problem gradually shifted from an exclusively educational matter to a political concern of major proportions. It fell upon the Yamagata ministry to find a satisfactory solution.

Events took place within court circles as well as in the government to hasten matters. At the end of 1889, Nishimura Shigeki, a conservative, nationalistic court adviser, addressed a letter to Hijikata Hisamoto, the Imperial Household minister, in which he urged an imperial pronouncement on morals. He argued that the emperor must be the source of all moral standards and consequently the court should be responsible for drawing up a suitable document. This view coincided with those held by Motoda and other court advisers. As a consequence, a group of scholars began to study the questions involved.[22]

In February 1890, Yamagata, in his capacity as home minister, invited the prefectural governors to a conference in Tokyo. During the course of the conference, the local leaders raised the problem of the nation's moral standards and the ideological confusion into which it had fallen. Yamagata answered these queries by saying that the minister of education would take the problem under consideration. After discussing this ques-

20. Watanabe Ikujirō, *Meiji Tennō no seitoku: kyōiku* (Tokyo, 1941), p. 263. This is a good brief source for the story of the writing of the rescript; see Chapters 9 and 10.
21. Basil H. Chamberlain, *Things Japanese*, 6th ed. (London, 1939), p. 259.
22. Matsushita Takeo, *Kindai Nihon kyōiku shi* (Tokyo, 1949), p. 143.

131

tion with the Cabinet, Yamagata discussed it with the emperor. As a result, the education minister, Enomoto, was summoned to the palace and instructed to draw up a set of principles to serve as the basis of the nation's moral education. Enomoto left the education ministry before his assignment had produced any tangible results, and Yamagata nominated his own vice minister of home affairs, Yoshikawa Kensei, to succeed him. The emperor, who took particular interest in this appointment, at first hesitated to approve it but agreed when Yamagata assured him of Yoshikawa's competence. On a visit to the palace after his appointment, Yoshikawa received his instructions "to establish a basis for national enlightenment in consultation with Premier Yamagata." [23]

The writing of the rescript went through a number of stages. First, several drafts and many revisions were written under the responsibility of the education department. Inoue Kowashi, head of the Legislative Board of the government, when then asked to comment on a draft, rejected it as unsatisfactory and wrote a new draft which he submitted to Yamagata. The latter placed this in the hands of the emperor who, in turn, asked Motoda to rewrite whatever parts of the draft the Confucian scholar found unsatisfactory. It has long been supposed that Motoda did little more than alter the style of Inoue's draft without changing its substance. It is now known, however, that Motoda, who had secretly written a draft of his own, virtually substituted his for that of Inoue.[24] How much of a change this actually involved is not known. At any rate, it is clear that while several people had a part in this work, Motoda was the chief author of the final rescript. The official translation of the text is as follows:

> Know ye, Our Subjects:
> Our Imperial Ancestors have founded Our Empire on a basis broad and everlasting and have deeply and firmly implanted virtue; Our subjects ever united in loyalty and filial piety have from generation to generation illustrated the beauty thereof. This is the glory of the fundamental character of Our Empire, and herein also lies the source of Our education. Ye, Our subjects, be filial to your parents, affectionate to your brothers and sisters; as husbands and wives be harmonious, as friends true; bear yourselves in modesty and moderation; extend your benevolence to all; pursue learning and cultivate arts, and thereby develop intellectual faculties and perfect moral powers; furthermore, advance public good and promote common

23. Quoted in Ōtsu, DNKS, III, 482.
24. Watanabe Ikujirō, Meiji Tennō no seitoku: kyōiku, p. 279.

interests; always respect the Constitution and observe the laws; should emergency arise, offer yourselves courageously to the State; and thus guard and maintain the prosperity of Our Imperial Throne coeval with heaven and earth. So shall ye not only be Our good and faithful subjects, but render illustrious the best traditions of your forefathers.

The Way here set forth is indeed the teaching bequeathed by Our Imperial Ancestors, to be observed alike by Their Descendants and the subjects, infallible for all ages and true in all places. It is Our wish to lay it to heart in all reverence, in common with you, Our subjects, that We may all thus attain to the same virtue.

> The 30th day of the 10th month
> of the 23rd year of Meiji
> (October 30, 1890).[25]

An interesting sidelight on Yamagata's part in the writing appears in a letter he wrote Inoue Kowashi on September 30, 1890. In this letter he asked Inoue to include in the rescript the thought that "the maintenance of the nation's independence is dependent upon military preparedness, and the peace which happily prevails in the Far East at present is based upon friendly relations with neighbouring countries." [26] The closest thing to this thought in the rescript is the phrase, "should emergency arise, offer yourselves courageously to the State."

A problem arose over the phrase, "always respect the Constitution and observe the laws." Motoda considered this sentence unnecessary, but Yoshikawa disagreed. Finally the decision was left to the emperor who ruled in favor of its inclusion. Another problem related to the manner in which the pronouncement should be issued. Inoue suggested that it should be kept free from any political flavor and should not include the signature of the minister concerned. This view prevailed.

Special efforts were made to have the rescript promulgated before the opening of the first Diet. This was accomplished. The emperor, on October 30, 1890, called Yamagata and Yoshikawa to the palace and handed down to them the "Imperial Rescript on Education." [27] It was printed and distributed to all schools throughout Japan, where it became required reading. Its profound importance rested not only in the principles it laid down for the education of all Japanese but in the fact that it became a leading text of Japan's state religion.

25. Robert K. Hall, *Kokutai no Hongi* (Cambridge, Mass., 1949), p. 192.
26. Reprinted in *Yamagata den*, II, 1128.
27. Watanabe Ikujurō, *Meiji Tennō no seitoku: kyōiku*, p. 288.

Yamagata presided at the birth of this important document. The educational rescript was designed to inspire an attitude of loyalty to the state among the entire population similar to that promoted in the armed services by the "Rescript to Soldiers and Sailors." It expressed his own profound reverence for the imperial institution and his desire to revive traditional values. His part was to encourage the undertaking and guide it through to its final fruition. Motoda, the real "author" of the rescript, in a letter written two days after its promulgation, acknowledged the role played by Yamagata in the following words: "I am aware that your achievements are many in both the civil and military fields. Nevertheless, with admiration and respect I express the thought that the support given this Imperial Rescript by the Premier is the greatest achievement of your life." [28]

Prime Minister of the First Diet

The year 1890 was also a crucial year from the point of view of another major development of Meiji political history: the establishment and growth of constitutional government. The first general election was held in July, and in November the Diet was scheduled to open its first session. These were the events for which Yamagata prepared himself after taking office. His genuine doubts about his own ability to cope with the anticipated problems plunged him into the study of the workings of constitutional government. In facing any major task, he always prepared himself carefully, using the knowledge and seeking the guidance of those with greater experience. In the military field, for example, he kept up with the latest developments abroad by reading reports and by inviting recently returned officers to his residence in order to interrogate them on their experiences and observations. As a statesman he followed the same plan.

Kaneko Kentarō, one of those who worked on the drafting of the constitution, has left an interesting story which illustrates the way in which Yamagata attempted to educate himself to face the problems ahead. He recalled:

> In the spring of 1890 I was observing the parliaments of various European countries and planned to cross to the United States and observe that nation. While in London I received an urgent telegram requesting my return home by June so I cancelled the rest of my

28. Reprinted in *Yamagata den*, II, 1134.

plans in order to carry out this request. Upon returning, I called on Yamagata at his official residence and he said to me, "In your absence I have unavoidably become premier. From the beginning I have been a soldier without the competence of a premier who is to face the important first Diet. Moreover, I have no confidence in myself whatever. Therefore at present, I am concentrating all my attention on a study of the constitution." (Glancing at the shelf I noticed [Itō's] *Commentaries on the Japanese Constitution* and various documents regarding the Diet piled high.) "Since you fortunately have been investigating the parliaments of each country, I should like you to talk to me in detail about them." [29]

Yamagata invited Kaneko to spend evenings with him to instruct him on "how a premier should handle a parliament . . . and act towards the parties and the members of the assembly." [30] Patiently, Kaneko discussed the problems of constitutional government and submitted in writing a detailed account of his observations overseas. In this way Yamagata was able gradually to build up his own confidence.

Personal study of the problems of constitutional government was only one step he took to prepare for the opening of the Diet. In May 1890, he made some minor but very significant changes in his Cabinet. He dropped the home ministry portfolio he had held concurrently with his premiership and moved Saigō Tsugumichi to that post. As vice minister of home affairs he appointed Shirane Sen'ichi, an important member of his own fast-growing political clique. The most interesting changes, however, were the promotions of Yoshikawa Kensei to education minister and Mutsu Munemitsu to agriculture and commerce minister. These were significant appointments because through them, for the first time since the beginning of Meiji, men from outside the four western han and the old Tokugawa government were included in the highest political councils of the nation. For that very reason and the additional reason that in the case of Mutsu a person without rank was being brought in, Yamagata's nominations were not fully approved of by court circles.[31] These objections were overcome, however, by Yamagata's personal endorsement and the weight of his prestige. As a result, these two new ministers became personally indebted to the premier.

Yoshikawa's promotion can be explained by the fact that he had been

29. Irie Kan'ichi, *Yamagata kō no omokage* (Tokyo, 1930), p. 207.
30. Quoted by Osatake, *Kensei shi*, II, 823.
31. See Fukaya, *Shoki gikai*, pp. 174–177. Actually only Katsu Awa and Enomoto Takeaki were from families who served the Tokugawa administration. Mutsu was from the former Wakayama han and Yoshikawa from Awa. See Ōtsu, *DNKS*, III, 321.

associated with Yamagata in the home ministry. But the selection of Mutsu can be explained only on other grounds. Mutsu was a friend of Inoue Kaoru and under the latter's sponsorship had been sent to Washington, D.C., as the Japanese minister. Mutsu had cordial relations with many party members, a fact which Yamagata hoped might prove to be useful to the Cabinet in negotiating with the parties in the Diet.[32] At the same time, these two appointments strengthened Yamagata's hand against the parties. The parties had centered their attack against the government on the grounds that it represented a han oligarchy (hambatsu), a monopoly of power held by a small group of Restoration leaders from the four western han. By introducing men from other areas, Yamagata hoped to nullify one of the slogans used by the opposition. His willingness to depart from the established pattern also indicated a flexibility, a realistic calculation of the advantages to be gained in facing the Diet.

On the morning of July 1, 1890, male Japanese of over twenty-five years of age paying a direct national tax of at least fifteen yen a year cast their votes in the first general election in Japan's history. Over 95 percent of the more than 450,000 eligible voters, or approximately 1 percent of the 40,000,000 population, went to the polls to elect 300 representatives to the House of Representatives.[33] More than a third of the successful candidates could be classified as pro-government, but over half who were elected were members of political parties opposed to the government. These included many representatives of the revived Jiyūtō and Kaishintō which had struggled for power in the 1880's but which had been suppressed by governmental pressure and cunning and weakened by internal strife.

In view of the election results, Yamagata moved quickly to strengthen his hand and to block the consolidation of antigovernment delegates into a united party. There was some evidence that the two major antigovernment parties were secretly planning to form a working relationship in the Diet. The government moved to halt such cooperation on July 25, 1890. It issued a revision of the harsh "Regulations for Public

32. In the first election Mutsu was elected to the House of Representatives from the first district of Wakayama prefecture. On Sept. 20, 1891, he resigned from the Lower House explaining, "On the one hand I am a member of the cabinet, on the other, with the representative system of our country still inadequate, grave problems are present. Thus, I fear I invite the suspicion of both the government and the people." Shinobu Seizaburō, *Mutsu Munemitsu* (Tokyo, 1935), p. 193.

33. Oka, *Kindai Nihon*, p. 301. It is noteworthy that in a report to the home ministry it was pointed out that 191 of those elected were commoners, and 109 were *shizoku*; thus the *shizoku* electorate supported candidates from their social group, and commoners (*heimin*) supported commoners.

Meetings and Political Associations," specifically forbidding any party from combining or even communicating with another party.[34] To further buttress his position against the Diet, Yamagata secured the services of Itō as president of the House of Peers. Itō pledged his active support in return for a promise that he could resign his position at the end of the first session and be allowed to take a pleasure trip to China. With Itō's appointment, the way was cleared for the opening of the first Diet. Months of preparation during which laws and regulations governing the election system were enacted had now been completed.[35] Yamagata had studied his strategy, had revised the rules governing the conduct of policy, had assembled his forces, and now stood ready to enter combat.

In a stately ceremony on November 29, 1890, the emperor opened the first session of the Imperial Diet by reading a message to a joint assembly of the House of Peers and the House of Representatives. One week later Yamagata, who a short time before had been promoted to the rank of a full general on active duty, delivered the opening address to the Lower House in which he laid down the broad outlines of the government's policy.

Several weeks before the Diet opened, Yamagata had been uncertain when he should deliver the speech and to which house if not both. After considerable correspondence between Yamagata, Itō Hirobumi, and Itō Miyoji, secretary of the Privy Council and drafter of Yamagata's speech, it had been decided that it should be delivered to the Lower House just before the budget address by the finance minister.[36]

Yamagata detested public speaking. It was not to his liking to have to rely on persuasive speeches to arouse the support of men; he was never an effective public speaker, relying on other means to assert his influence. His thin voice was ill-suited to oratory and the rich classical flavor of his writing made listening difficult. The novelty of addressing a large audience disturbed his composure, and he must have experienced considerable anguish anticipating his maiden speech. It is said that he methodically memorized his speech and rehearsed it several times before a mirror.[37] His speeches were criticized because he could not be heard throughout the house, and his listeners would, therefore, interrupt him to beg him to speak louder and crowd forward to catch his words. When

34. Ōtsu, *DNKS*, III, 322–327.

35. See Ōtsu, *DNKS*, III, 333–335, for a listing of nineteen major regulations issued between June and October 1890.

36. Oka Yoshitake, "Dai ichi gikai ni kansuru jakkan no kōsatsu," *Kokka gakkai zasshi* 60.2:63–65 (February 1946).

37. Tokutomi, *Sohō kanmeiroku*, p. 169.

he relied on a manuscript it could be seen that his hands shook with nervousness, a fact which occasioned comments of how he trembled "as he would not have done in the face of bullets and bayonets." [38]

In his first speech as prime minister on December 6, 1890, Yamagata outlined the broad objectives the nation should pursue. He declared that the Restoration had marked an important shift in the nation's course. Ever since then, he asserted, the continual goal of all endeavors was to redeem what had been lost by nearly 300 years of Tokugawa isolation and to come abreast of the progress of the world. "Thus, while domestic affairs cannot be neglected for a single day, at the same time we must preserve our independence and enhance our national position." [39] In order to accomplish this he called for a large allotment to the armed forces in the national budget.

Premier Yamagata was clearly thinking in the mental framework of the military man when he defined the nation's security in the following terms: "The independence and security of the nation depend first upon the protection of the line of soverignty (*shukensen*) and then the line of advantage (*riekisen*) . . . If we wish to maintain the nation's independence among the powers of the world at the present time, it is not enough to guard only the line of sovereignty; we must also defend the line of advantage . . . and within the limits of the nation's resources gradually strive for that position. For this reason, it is necessary to make comparatively large appropriations for our army and navy." [40]

In the remainder of the speech he advocated the repayment of foreign debts, reorganization of the administration, and greater production, but the significant point was the concept of security he laid before the house. It was the first time that terms such as "line of sovereignty" and "line of advantage" had been used in speaking of the nation's security. The "line of sovereignty" referred to the territorial limits of the nation, but the precise extent of the "line of advantage" was not made clear in the speech. It could be inferred to refer to an area beyond the territorial boundary of the nation in which Japan should seek dominant influence. It perhaps indicated a buffer zone of protection, a strategic area, which, if in unfriendly hands, would threaten the nation's security. This was indeed the case. In March 1890, Yamagata defined his concept in a written opinion. Korea was the area he had in mind. And it was an area

38. *Japan Weekly Mail*, Feb. 21, 1891, p. 218.
39. *Yamagata den*, III, 4.
40. *Ibid.*, III, 5.

which he predicted would become the center of conflict when the Russian trans-Siberian railway was completed. Because Korea's independence would then be threatened, and because the loss of that independence would push back the "line of advantage" to the Tsushima Island, he argued for an agreement between China, England, Germany, and Japan to guarantee Korea's independence. For Yamagata, the essential pre-requisites for a policy aimed at securing the "line of advantage" were military expansion and stronger patriotism among the people through education. He was convinced that to secure the "line of sovereignty" and "the line of advantage" and insure the nation's independence would require twenty years of arduous effort.[41] At any rate, the "line of advantage" became a concept which future militarists could define to suit the convenience of an expansionist policy.

With the government demanding large appropriations and the opposition pledged to reduce the cost of government and lighten the tax burden, the battle over the budget became a major test of strength. The problem of the budget, which was to arise in succeeding Diets, became the focus of the long struggle between the centrifugal force of the popular movement working to reduce power at the center and the centripetal force of the government and its supporters working for greater consolidation. In this instance the budget committee of the house reduced the budget by over 10 percent, but the government refused to recognize this cut.

In disagreeing with the budget committee, the government based its position on an interpretation of Article 67 of the constitution. The article declared, "Those already fixed expenditures based by the Constitution upon the powers appertaining to the Emperor," which included expenditures arising from legal obligations or such "as may have arisen by the effect of law," could not be reduced by the Diet "without the concurrence of the Government." [42] In anticipation of problems which would arise from this vague phraseology, Yamagata had, in February 1890, issued a circular giving an official interpretation to the article. He was careful to include, under the fixed expenditures, appropriations for the army and the navy.[43] Under the guarantee of this interpretation, the figure for the military budget was set at a level sufficiently high so that

41. See Yamagata's opinion in *Nihon gaikō shi kenkyū: Meiji jidai* (Tokyo, 1957), pp. 183–203; especially pp. 192–195.
42. McLaren, ed., *Documents*, p. 142. Constitution appears on pp. 134–144.
43. *Ibid.*, pp. 234–236.

when it was renewed it would underwrite a seven-year plan of expansion.[44]

The opposition parties refused to accept the government's interpretation and maintained that they were free to make basic revisions in the budget. Yamagata conceded them the right to suggest changes but argued that the acceptance of the basic revisions of the committee in effect transferred the prerogative of initiating action from the government to the Diet. In this sense, the conflict over the budget was one to determine the area of authority of the executive and legislative branches of the government.

Yamagata was not skilled in the intricate problems involved in working out questions with the Diet. He relied heavily on both Itō Miyoji and Itō Hirobumi to guide his acts, although he reserved for himself final judgment. The necessity of bargaining with the House of Representatives was irritating and irksome to one who felt that the prime minister's relationship with the Diet should be similar to that between governors and prefectural assemblies: he believed he should be amenable to suggestions but unimpeded in final decisions. In responding to queries from Diet members, Yamagata made clear the Cabinet's condescending attitude, and he encouraged Cabinet ministers to refuse to give more than vague and indefinite answers when questioned. This approach to the Diet was natural when the ministers felt in no way responsible to the legislature. "If the cabinet is responsible to the Diet," Yamagata once remarked, "it is impossible for the government to have a fixed policy." [45]

This attitude on the part of officials, of course, spurred on those dedicated to weakening the oligarchy. The *mintō,* or popular parties, which held a majority over the *ritō,* the pro-government faction in the Diet, concentrated their attack in the budget committee of the house. Despite the fact that Yamagata had a tacit agreement of support from the seventy-five or so members of the pro-government Taiseikai,[46] this group was ineffective in opposing the *mintō.* The budget committee cut out over nine million yen from the over eighty-three million yen budget.[47]

Defiance on the part of the Diet stiffened the attitude of the government. On February 16, both Yamagata and Matsukata addressed the Diet strongly opposing their action on the budget question. Matsukata warned

44. Shinobu Seizaburō, *Meiji seiji shi* (Tokyo, 1950), p. 18.
45. *Jiji shimbun,* as quoted in *Japan Weekly Mail,* Nov. 29, 1890, p. 528.
46. *Yamagata den,* III, 7.
47. Oka Yoshitake, "Teikoku gikai no kaisetsu," *Kokka gakkai zasshi* 58.1:48 (January 1944).

that the government would be forced to take decisive steps, the inference being that dissolution of the Diet would be inevitable.[48] "The representatives have been extremely obstreperous," declared Itō, "and taking measures which disregard the constitution and the Law of the Houses is unavoidable." [49] Yamagata sought advice and received divided counsel. Responding to those who urged an uncompromising stand, he received imperial permission to dissolve the Diet at his discretion.[50] At the encouragement of those who advised patience, on the other hand, he decided against such a drastic step. In the end compromise seemed to be the most sensible solution.

Neither the government nor the opposition wished to see the nation's first attempt at parliamentary government end in failure. The parties feared that such failure would destroy the people's confidence in representative government. In the government there was concern over the effect that failure would have on the Western powers which were carefully observing Japan's experiment. Within the Cabinet, both Gotō and Mutsu encouraged a harmonious settlement. When a move for a compromise was made by a group within the Jiyūtō,[51] Mutsu and Gotō were the government officials used to exploit this soft spot in the hitherto solid opposition, and the two entered into secret conferences with Itagaki, leader of the Jiyūtō. The government's aim in these negotiations was to separate enough votes from the Jiyūtō to bring a majority when they were added to the pro-government vote. Success was achieved, and, as a result of these meetings, a group of liberals pledged their support to a compromise bill. In the compromise bill two and a half million yen were restored to the budget, which meant that the government was still forced to sacrifice about seven millions from their budget. In the final vote in the Lower House, twenty-nine liberals defected and the budget was passed 157 to 125.

In March 1891, Yamagata became ill and was placed under the care of Doctor Erwin Baelz, the famous German physician and professor of medicine at Tokyo Imperial University, who attended the most prominent leaders of the day.[52] It was this illness that prevented him from attending the closing ceremonies of the first Diet on March 7, 1891. Two months later he asked to be relieved of his position for reasons of health. Actually there were other grounds for desiring to end his tenure as premier. The

48. See *Yamagata den*, III, 12.
49. Quoted by Shinobu, *Meiji seijishi*, p. 20.
50 *Yamagata den*, III, 13.
51. Oka, *Kindai Nihon*, p. 65, note 1.
52. Toku Baelz, ed., *Awakening Japan: The Diary of a German Doctor, Erwin Baelz* (New York, 1932), p. 94.

Cabinet had not always acted in complete harmony, a fact which distressed Yamagata. Furthermore, the long duel with the opposition parties in the Diet was a distasteful and enervating episode. There is also evidence that Itō, dissatisfied and impatient with Yamagata's conduct of office, had used his wide influence to interfere with the activities of the Cabinet. Whatever the relative importance of the factors, these combined to convince Yamagata that he should resign.[53]

Yamagata's first Cabinet had lasted less than a year and a half. But during this period he had given evidence of some skill and flexibility in meeting political problems. From the start he had shown himself to be a man of strong unchanging convictions, but he had always favored a wide variety of tactical measures to protect those ideas. As an administrator he had already shown his competence. "Especially noteworthy is your vigorous assiduity which knows no relaxation," wrote one friendly newspaper editor in analyzing his qualities; ". . . when all the other ministers of state are light-hearted and fickle like butterflies, you alone preserve a soldierlike gravity and regularity in your every step." [54] This partisan appraisal of his leadership need not obscure the fact that he had successfully led the nation in its first step into an era of parliamentary government. On the first Diet he had imposed the view that adequate military strength was the prime requisite in order to "preserve our independence and enhance our national position" — an aim with which few disagreed.

His first experience in directing national policy and securing its acceptance by the Diet indicated several significant things. Most important it reflected his methodical way of preparing carefully before entering combat. He first strengthened the hand of government through new definitions of the executive authority, a favorable interpretation of a financial clause in the constitution, and the sponsorship he gave to the educational rescript. These measures increased the power of the bureaucracy. At the same time, he attempted to weaken the parties both by including in his Cabinet people not exclusively associated with the government and by forbidding the union of the opposition parties.

Upon entering into political combat, within the arena of the constitution he showed an ability to maneuver. He established the precedent of

53. Rōyama Masamichi lists four causes for Yamagata's resignation: difficulties in carrying out the administrative reorganization promised the liberals as a condition of the compromise; disagreement with the parties on the expenditure of money saved by the reorganization; Cabinet disunity caused by Yamagata's dissatisfaction with the delay in the enactment of a commerical law; and, fourth, the restraining hand of Itō and Itō's anger at the unskillful maneuvering of the ministers toward the Diet. Rōyama, *Seiji shi,* p. 275.

54. *Kokumin no Tomo,* as quoted in *Japan Weekly Mail,* July 21, 1889, p. 29.

a compromise solution despite advice not to give an inch. Nevertheless, the pattern established by the first Diet was not a healthy beginning for the parliamentary system. For one thing, it was widely believed that bribery had been used to buy votes and that the so-called compromise was in fact a sell-out by one section of the leading party.[55] Also, in receiving imperial permission to dissolve the Diet, Yamagata indicated the high-handed method to which the oligarchs were to have recourse in the future.[56] That he did not use the weapon and cause the first experiment in parliamentary government to fail, and thereby suffer foreign charges of being incapable of operating a constitution system, was perhaps owing to his desire to subordinate lesser objectives to major ones. The initial success of parliamentary government, he felt or was persuaded to feel, was more important than complete victory in the budget battle. But this consideration was no longer present when the second Diet convened. The dispute over the budget as a test of strength set a pattern, as Yamagata correctly predicted it would. On December 14, 1890, he wrote the finance minister about the problem saying, "No matter what is decided as a result of the debate, I am apprehensive that this will be a source of grave difficulty in the future." [57] With the government's insistence that larger fixed expenditures, including military appropriations, were beyond the control of the Diet, it was hardly surprising that the demand for the right of major revisions in the budget continued throughout Meiji history to be the central dispute in the Diet.

Yamagata's belief that friction would continue between the Diet and the Cabinet suggests another result of the first experience with constitutional politics. This was the lesson that even with all the advantages favoring the executive branch of the government under the new constitution, the Meiji leaders could no longer contain the pressure of the opposition which had received a legal channel of expression in that same constitution. High-handed decrees and oppressive laws to control party activities were no longer sufficient to reduce antigovernment actions. With a legitimate role in the political process constitutionally sanctioned, the opposition parties

55. Tanaka Sōgorō, *Kindai Nihon kanryō shi* (Tokyo, 1941), p. 231. Mutsu, Gōtō, and the vice minister of war, Katsura Tarō, were reportedly active in the bribery.

56. Ōtsu's conclusion on the first Diet session are worth quoting: "From the point of view of constitutional government several bad precedents were established. First, bribes were used to corrupt Diet members. Second, compromise politics were abused for political advantages. Third, for these reasons the evils of the oligarchs were not corrected, the notion that the popular parties could be easily used by the oligarchy gained strength. These three bad precedents were set. In truth, the blame for this must rest with those who betrayed their party." Ōtsu, *DNKS,* III, 597.

57. Reprinted in *Yamagata den,* III, 8.

to some degree were able to force the government to adjust its policies to party demands. Although the parties were required to make the greater concessions in their program, compromise was accepted and practised as a method of resolving differences and as a way of making the newly adopted constitutional system work.

Finally, during the first Diet there were differences of view among the Meiji leaders on how the government should operate within a constitutional regime. Yamagata's hard-line approach contrasted with Itō's more moderate approach to the parties. Although they were not as serious as the factional strife that weakened the Diet parties, cracks were observable at the highest level of the ruling group and presaged more serious divisions within the leadership.

Yamagata's Clique

Free from the battles of the government and removed from the necessity of balancing forces and conceding to others small advantages in order to make major gains, Yamagata tended to become less flexible and more dogmatic in his attitude. As if to celebrate his withdrawal from the toils of political office, Yamagata purchased a house in Kyoto. He called this home Murinan (lit., "hermitage without a neighborhood,"), a name reflecting his desire to remove himself from the turbulence of political life. In actuality, however, he borrowed the name from a small home he had built in Hagi when he was a leader in the Kiheitai. In Kyoto, he busied himself with the landscaping of his new villa; for many hours with loving dedication and considerable talent he planned his garden. An added diversion was his interest in a geisha by the name of Yoshida Sadako, who was to join his household after the death of his wife in 1893.

His detachment from governmental affairs in May 1891 was never complete, however, for he worked through loyal members of his following to encourage his point of view in government councils. Each of the oligarchs had developed a following of loyal supporters. It particularly suited Yamagata's temperament and his political strategy to utilize increasingly the services of faithful adherents of his views. Indeed, a key to his lasting impact on national policy is the remarkable number of prominent bureaucrats who counted themselves among his followers and through whom he was able to exert his ideas when he was not in office. Accounts of Meiji politics are peppered with references to the "Chōshū clique," usually meaning Yamagata's faction.

It is true that factionalism was a feature of Meiji politics. However, analysis of these factions should never be allowed to obscure the truth that the nation's leadership as a whole was remarkably cohesive, sharing the same overriding objectives for the nation. Nevertheless, it was in the nature of Japanese political life for every prominent figure to gather around him a group of followers whose activities were governed more by personal loyalty than the merits of any given issue. Yet to speak of a "Chōshū clique" which would include Itō, Yamagata, and Inoue is to disguise the real differences in the approaches that these three statesmen followed. To talk of a "Satsuma clique" and to pretend, for example, that Matsukata and General Ōyama operated effectively together in furthering a particular policy is to bind their very casual relationship. It is more exact and meaningful to speak of personal cliques, and no leader in modern Japan succeeded in attracting so large, so loyal, so effective a clique as Yamagata.

Yamagata's following developed in several ways. During his work in establishing the modern army he favored certain subordinates who showed, like himself, administrative capacity as well as military competence. His four leading protégés, Generals Katsura Tarō, Kodama Gentarō, Terauchi Masatake, and Tanaka Giichi, were all, furthermore, from Chōshū. All were to serve as war minister, all were to occupy other ministerial posts, and, with the exception of Kodama who died in 1906 at the relatively early age of fifty-four, all became prime minister. They carried on the soldier-statesman tradition established by Yamagata. It was General Tanaka who once remarked, "Yamagata achieved most of his success through the willing toils of his loyal followers who would stick with him through thick and thin." [58]

Yamagata's satellites in the civil bureaucracy were Chōshū clansmen, relatives, or men who had been selected to work under him during his long tenure as home minister. Of five prominent Chōshū men who were his dependable allies, two were related. One was Shinagawa Yajirō, a comrade from Hagi and Yoshida Shōin's school and the Restoration movement, who married his sister's daughter. He had held many minor government posts before becoming home minister, through Yamagata's recommendation as we shall see, in 1891. The other was Yamagata Isaburō, his own nephew and adopted son, who became a member of the home ministry and served as governor of several prefectures, vice resident general of Korea, and eventually governor-general of Kwantung. Shirane Sen'ichi, Aoki Shūzō, and Nomura Yasushi were Chōshū men, civil bu-

58. Saito Man, "Yamagata: Life and Death," in *Japan Times and Mail*, Feb. 11, 1922, p. 134.

reaucrats of prominence, and members of Yamagata's clique. Shirane and Nomura became respectively, but at different times, vice minister and minister of home affairs. Aoki, son of the physician to the Chōshū daimyo, served as Yamagata's foreign minister in 1889 and again in 1900. Two non-Chōshū followers were perhaps Yamagata's most important political associates. Hirata Tōsuke, from Yonezawa han and often called Yamagata's political chief of staff, was a high-ranking bureaucrat, privy councillor, and member of the House of Peers. He was the son-in-law of Viscountess Shinagawa, Yamagata's niece. Kiyoura Keigo, from Kumamoto, drew close to Yamagata during the latter's home ministry days. In 1922, Kiyoura became prime minister after serving for many years in other ministerial posts. Ōura Kanetake of Satsuma, Hijikata Motohisa of Tosa, Yoshikawa Kensei of Tokushima, and Komatsubara Eitarō of Toyama were other non-Chōshū followers of Yamagata. Each rose to positions at the top of the civil bureaucracy; all had begun their careers in the home ministry during Yamagata's incumbency.

These civil and military bureaucrats, and many others, rose under Yamagata's patronage and support, believed in their leader's political philosophy, and through their own activities enhanced the position of Yamagata and the influence of their clique. At first it may appear strange that the frugal, stern, taciturn soldier succeeded in holding such a large following of loyal supporters. Itō, who had great talent and a natural flare for political life, never had so impressive a following. The answer to why this was so must be sought in Yamagata's character.

Yamagata's unwavering adherence to certain fixed principles was a rallying strongpoint for conservative bureaucrats. More than Itō he relied upon the assistance and collaboration of others; he sought others' opinions and made them feel that they shared in his own decisive acts. To his many followers he must have represented the finest traits of a samurai hero: humble, strict in conduct, bold in action, repaying loyalty with loyalty. As a rule, he yielded his trust slowly and cautiously but once given he gave it generously. Takahashi Yoshio, for many years a close acquaintance, recalls that when in 1890 Inoue Kaoru first introduced him to Yamagata, he was warned that Yamagata's tactic in approaching a person was to become friendly in gradual stages, opening only one area of his interests at a time. Takahashi relates his initial meeting in these words:

> In this first interview he listened with only an occasional interruption to observations on my tour of Europe. In three hours he

said little more than humbly claim, "I am a mere soldier and although I should know something of civil affairs I am completely ignorant." So my first impression was that Yamagata was not only taciturn but most incompetent to speak on any nonmilitary subject. Later however, when I became well acquainted with him I discovered he could speak with brilliance not only on military and political affairs but on such topics as education, religion, Nō songs, poetry writing, landscape gardening and architecture.[59]

Irie Kan'ichi, Yamagata's private secretary, has also disclosed how he was first able to perform only the most elementary tasks for him, but that when they became close he was entrusted with all manner of secret information and Yamagata's complete confidence.[60] As we shall see, Yamagata was always able to count on a devoted band of followers anxious to please him. This was to become obvious after the formation of his successor's Cabinet.

Relations with the Matsukata and Itō Cabinets

The Matsukata Cabinet's inclusion of figures best known for the fact that they represented the point of view of a senior governmental figure marked the beginning of a development which was to increase in importance, and one which complicates greatly the analysis of the sources of political moves. As the oligarchs grew older and as they developed a larger following sharing their essential outlook, they relied more and more upon their faithful supporters to spread their opinions and implement their policies. The precise degree to which any given policy was the product of the thinking of some oligarch on the one hand, or the result of the initiative of a subordinate on the other, is extremely difficult to determine.

When Yamagata decided to resign after the first Diet session was completed, he nominated Itō as his successor. This was the first performance of a scene that was to be reenacted many times. The reigning oligarch nominated a colleague to the court after exchanges of views with the other leaders whose support he solicited. The nominee usually rejected the offer, suggesting one or more other oligarchs as possible successors to the resigning premier. Meanwhile court officials entered the act to attempt to expedite the procedure, sounding out and encouraging one oligarch after another to accept the post. It was only a question of enough of the small

59. Takahashi, *San kō iretsu,* pp. 5–6.
60. Irie, *Yamagata kō no omokage,* pp. 30–31.

circle of oligarchs agreeing on a single person who would be willing to shoulder the burden of the premiership. The pattern of alternation between Satsuma and Chōshū members was not rigidly set, but it was commonly adhered to, one suspects, because in addition to providing a balance wheel, it was also a useful rule in the game of selecting a successor.

In this particular case, Itō was urged to accept the nomination by Inoue and others but refused in a forthright statement to the emperor in which he said, "Since I believe that it would not be in the best interest of the nation, I could not accept even if you were to order me to do so a hundred times." [61] So saying, Itō nominated both Saigō and Matsukata, and the latter finally accepted. Itō agreed to serve again as head of the Privy Council.

Yamagata's influence was felt in the new Cabinet through the home minister. In organizing his Cabinet, Matsukata had sought the advice of the outgoing premier in his selection of men for some of the portfolios. Yamagata's important part in building up the home ministry made it natural for Matsukata to request his opinion on a suitable home minister. Working through his political aid Hirata Tōsuke, Yamagata endeavored to satisfy Matsukata's request by persuading one of his followers, Shinagawa Yajirō, to accept the post. At first, Shinagawa demurred, but after a personal visit from Yamagata he changed his mind. In this interview, Yamagata outlined the political situation and tried to indicate the need for Shinagawa's services. At one point Yamagata is alleged to have said, "You may consider this an order from your senior." [62] Shinagawa entered the Cabinet and rapidly became the central figure in the Cabinet's clash with the political parties. In addition to Shinagawa, the vice minister of home affairs, Shirane Sen'ichi, who was a holdover from the last Cabinet, was also one of Yamagata's political disciples.[63]

After the close of the first Diet, government strategists, alarmed at the strength and recalcitrance of the parties, drew up plans for strengthening the Cabinet's effectiveness by closer coordination between the activities of the ministries.[64] When the second Diet opened in November

61. Quoted by Shinobu, *Meiji seiji shi*, p. 21.
62. Quoted by Okutani, *Shinagawa den*, p. 257.
63. Home minister Shinagawa, giving the annual instructions to the governors, carried on Yamagata's concept of local government when he said, "The extension of the Home Ministry into the local areas is like the link of a body. Unless there is a spirit common to both [a logical connection between both] the administration cannot hope to succeed." Quoted in Ōtsu, *DNKS*, III, 64.
64. Mutsu led these efforts and succeeded in having a separate office established to

1891, the Matsukata Cabinet, determined to give no quarter, prepared to take aggressive action. The opposition parties had also decided to take a firm stand against the entrenched leadership of the government and demand a reduction in administrative expenditures and an alleviation of the tax burden. When the government submitted a budget which included increased expenditures for steel works and national defense, the battle was again joined over the annual budget. Thirty-five days after its opening, the second Diet was dissolved by the government in retaliation for the intransigence of the parties in refusing to approve the budget.

Yamagata gave active encouragement to this drastic step. In a letter addressed to Matsukata on December 26, the day after the dissolution, he wrote: "Since the scheming of the political parties has caused this critical situation, the parties must bear the blame. As I mentioned to you last spring, unless the government is prepared to use even two dissolutions in succession, it is very doubtful that this aim [i.e., forcing the parties to retreat] can be achieved." [65]

In theory, Yamagata's concept of constitutional government was very similar to the concept Itō expressed in drafting the constitution. This "Japanese constitutionalism" retained the concept of the primacy of the official governing group; within the new framework of Western political forms, the traditional power of officialdom was to continue to operate. The Diet's powers were narrowly restricted so as not to undermine this predominance. As representatives of the people, the Diet members were to be consulted and allowed to advise and give support to measures proposed by the government. That they should question the essential rights of the executive and deny officials the ultimate power of decision was not part of this scheme. To insure this unequal relationship the first principle was for all Cabinets to remain outside of the parties. To Yamagata, a conflict of loyalties was involved in the notion that parties should lead the government. The party member, he felt, was pledged to support a program, his first loyalty was to his party, whereas an official or Cabinet minister was pledged to support an official policy as a servant, not of the people, but of the emperor. In this scheme those who served

---

plan and coordinate Cabinet activities. Shinagawa disapproved the idea, and his home ministry work conflicted with the work of this office. This, as well as other reasons, led Mutsu to object to Shinagawa's election interference plans and resulted in his resignation in September 1891. See Shinobu, *Mutsu Munemitsu*, pp. 199–201.

65. Reprinted in *Yamagata den*, III, 53–54.

in the name of the emperor must be masters of the people and not their representatives. And the master-servant relationship could hardly countenance equality of rights or responsibility, let alone the radical notion that the servant could question, disobey, and attempt to undermine the position of his master. In sum, Yamagata refused to trust the parties with political responsibility.

Itō's thoughts, we have already seen, were originally stated in these terms. After two Diet sessions, however, it was plain to him that the application of these theories was unsatisfactory. Basically a progressive conservative, he gradually drew away from the rigid stand of his colleagues. Disappointed by the first two Diets, he gave considerable thought to the problems of the practice of constitutional government. One piece of evidence of his changing attitude is a report he submitted to the emperor upon returning to the capital after spending some of the winter of 1891 in Hagi. "Unless we rely on political parties we cannot put constitutional government into practice. I am thinking of resigning my position as president of the Privy Council to organize a united party as a commoner . . . and lead it to assist the government. Please allow me to do this." [66] He was not permitted to resign, and ten years were to elapse before he would carry out his plan of forming a party.

For the moment, Itō encouraged the use of the pro-government party, the Taiseikai, as a basis for the organization of a large government party. This, he thought, would be the most effective way of reducing the strength of the opposition parties. When he told the other oligarchs of his plans, they were all opposed to the idea and dissuaded him from taking such rash steps. For some years he made no attempt to carry out these plans, but his changed ideas were important for they marked the time at which he began to draw away from the concept of constitutional government leadership held by the other oligarchs.

Prior to the Sino-Japanese War, the oligarchs ruled through a Cabinet and bureaucracy relatively free from the influences of the liberal parties. They prepared to meet the opposition of the Diet by proroguing and dissolving that body and, in addition, by interfering in the elections. We have already seen the dissolution of the Diet used as a weapon to intimidate the opposition. Interference in elections was to follow quickly.

In the latter part of the letter in which he congratulated Matsukata for his stalwart stand against the Diet, Yamagata included a remark which anticipated what was to be attempted within exactly two months.

66. Quoted in Watanabe Ikujirō, *Meiji shi kenkyū*, p. 104.

"If in the next election," he suggested, "a majority is returned which is loyal and sympathetic to the government, holds practical views, and plans for ordered progress, it would be a great fortune for the country and the government." [67] It would be unsound to exaggerate the relation of this remark to what was to follow, but the central role of his political protégés in the election interference of February 1892 makes his statement of December 1891 most significant.

Over the objections of some members of the Cabinet, the home minister set a policy for the election which did more than give encouragement to pro-government candidates. As one historian of this episode has concluded, "for the maintenance of the nation's tranquility, Shinagawa planned various measures which were to be used to prevent the election of 'advocates of destructive policies' — as the various antigovernment parties were referred to — and determined to interfere in the election to have 'loyal men' elected." [68] Orders were sent down to prefectural police officials to impede the election of "disloyal" candidates. Money was distributed by the government to assist "loyal" candidates. Even the old han daimyo families were asked to help in the selection and support of friendly candidates.[69] There is no doubt who was directly responsible for this flagrant election interference. Shinagawa's biographer was forced to the conclusion that "the election interference was instigated primarily by Home Minister Shinagawa and Vice Minister Shirane . . . and the cause of the ruthless interference was, of course, the Shinagawa–Shirane policy." [70] From the fact, however, that they consistently reflected Yamagata's political attitude and often acted on his behalf, and in view of Yamagata's known attitude toward the parties and his past record in attempting to control them, we may deduce that the ex-premier gave wholehearted encouragement to crippling the strength of the antigovernment parties.

Interference in the election indicated the lengths to which the government would go to halt the popular parties. It is significant that the parties had shown sufficient vigor to force the oligarchs to such steps, when the latter thought that they had written a "fool-proof" constitution. Even more significant, however, was the failure of the harsh policy. For the most naked use of the government's coercive powers, which resulted

67. *Yamagata den,* III, 54.
68. Hayashi Shigeru, "Rikkensei no bōei," *Kokka gakkai zasshi* 55.4:486–487 (April 1941).
69. *Ibid.,* p. 487.
70. Okutani, *Shinagawa den,* p. 277.

in twenty-five deaths and nearly 400 injuries, was inadequate to gain its ends.

The popular parties (*mintō*) succeeded in returning a majority.[71] This fact split the Cabinet and released a flood of criticism from within the government as well as from without. As the parties attacked the government with renewed vigor, Itō sharply criticized the interference and demanded the punishment of the responsible officials. He emphasized his stand by resigning from the Privy Council in protest, and two members of the Cabinet, Mutsu and Gotō, threatened to resign.

As criticism mounted, Shinagawa submitted his resignation. This he did despite Yamagata's active effort to dissuade him. The latter felt that the home minister did not deserve the censure he was receiving, and he objected to creating the impression that the election returns had forced the government's hand, indeed, had caused its disruption. Writing to Matsukata on March 4, 1891, he described his efforts to prevent Shinagawa's resignation on the grounds that "it would adversely effect the confidence of public sentiment, and as a result both parties [i.e., Jiyūtō and the Kaishintō] would gain advantages, causing untold damage to the government." [72] Yamagata's insistence that Shinagawa remain in the Cabinet indicates that he approved the latter's policy. However, Shinagawa finally stepped out of the Cabinet and instead was appointed to the Privy Council.[73]

Yamagata's attitude, that the government should not retreat in the face of party pressure, prompted his stand when Matsukata subsequently threatened to resign. When the third Diet met, it was concerned primarily with the government's interference in the elections earlier that year. Protests over the elections became a new weapon for the parties to use against the government. Vituperative speeches were made against the Cabinet, and petitions were submitted to the emperor denouncing the government. To this attack Matsukata responded by proroguing the Diet for one week in May and then threatening to resign. Both Itō and Yamagata worked vigorously to prevent such a move, arguing that if the Cabinet resigned because of a decision in the House of Representatives,

71. Pro-government forces numbered 137 against an opposition of 163. See Hayashi, "Rikkensei no bōei," p. 497.

72. Reprinted in *Yamagata den*, III, 58.

73. Shinagawa never disavowed his methods. Touring the prefectures after his resignation, he explained, "If the obstructionists were re-elected it would endanger the nation's safety; therefore, various means were used to influence the election so that they would be defeated and loyal representatives would be elected. If similar conditions should prevail in the future, I would do the same again and exterminate the obstructionists." Okutani, *Shinagawa den*, pp. 286–287

it would weaken the executive power and the position of supremacy held by it under the Meiji Constitution.[74]

Matsukata agreed to remain in office, but when the Diet met again a new deadlock immediately developed. Conflict arose over the budget submitted to the Lower House. The budget was sharply cut by the House of Representatives, but when it was sent to the House of Peers the items cut from the budget were promptly restored. A dispute arose over the powers of the House of Peers to restore money cut by the Lower House. To break the stalemate, the dispute was referred to the Privy Council for a decision. The Privy Council thus suddenly became a court to which constitutional questions could be referred, and since it was filled by members or close associates of the oligarchy it naturally ruled in favor of the House of Peers. Despite this aid to the government in meeting the challenge of the parties in the Diet, the continued attacks on the Cabinet plus the irreparable harm that resulted from interference in elections proved insurmountable. When the new home minister attempted to ease the antigovernment pressure by punishing guilty local officials involved in the election interference, several Cabinet ministers resigned and the Matsukata government collapsed.

The Matsukata Cabinet had been dubbed the "behind-the-scenes cabinet" (*kuromaku naikaku*) because of the influence exerted in the background by Itō, Yamagata, Inoue, and others.[75] There was serious concern among the oligarchs with the unsatisfactory way in which constitutional government, as they conceived of it, was functioning. Itō, realizing that greater support was needed in the Diet, had proposed forming a party to surmount the problem, but his plan had been blocked by the other oligarchs because it violated the principle of Cabinets remaining aloof from the parties and, more than that, it would undermine their whole position in the long run. The attempt to gain public support by obstructing the election of unfriendly candidates had failed and had caused a split in the Cabinet. After Matsukata resigned, there was a period of frequent meetings and frantic exchanges of letters between the leading statesmen. Various plans were suggested for meeting the problem of the Cabinet's relations with the Diet, but no Cabinet member was willing to undertake them personally from the exposed position of the premier. Finally, Itō agreed to take the responsibility of forming a new Cabinet; his condition was the active cooperation of the other oligarchs

74. Hayashi Shigeru, "Dai san gikai to dai ichiji Matsukata naikaku no gakai," *Kokka gakkai zasshi* 62.4:17 (April 1948).
75. *Ibid.*, p. 15.

in the Cabinet. Yamagata, extremely reluctant to join the Cabinet, held out the longest but finally agreed to join Itō's second Cabinet as minister of justice. This Cabinet was popularly known as the "veteran statesmen's cabinet" (*genkun naikaku*); this was not an inaccurate label, for the senior statesmen, who had remained behind the scenes during the previous Cabinet, now stepped through the curtains as a group to form the new Cabinet.[76]

Yamagata's period of service as minister of justice was short — eight months — and relatively uneventful. As his vice minister he appointed Kiyoura Keigo, a member of his clique. He had not been eager for office and served more for the stabilizing effect it would have than for any other reason. He did undertake, however, one major act during his incumbency — prison reforms. The prison system was antiquated and badly in need of improvement. To complete this reform would give Japan one more modernized institution, providing further proof to foreign nations that treaty revision could not long be deferred on the grounds of Japan's backwardness. Adhering to the procedure he had used in the other reforms with which his name was associated — conscription, the police system, and the local government system — he ordered a careful study of the prison systems of European nations, including the construction of prisons and their management. He also invited a leading German authority to assist in the task of prison reform and to help establish a school for training prison wardens.[77]

In meeting the problem of the Diet, the new Cabinet was no more successful than its predecessor. As might be expected, Yamagata encouraged Itō to take a strong stand and not to hesitate to dissolve the Diet at any time. He even went so far as to suggest that if Itō did not dissolve the Diet the Cabinet might proceed to use the appropriations requested for naval construction without Diet authorization and have the money, already put to use, approved in the next Diet. But Itō found his own solution. Reaching an impasse with the hostile Diet, he took the unprecedented step of gaining approval for the budget by means of an imperial rescript. Thus the opposition was brought in line by a word of warning from the throne.

Upon the completion of the fourth Diet in March 1893, Yamagata submitted his resignation. Yamagata stood firm against all of Itō's efforts

76. The veteran statesmen included: Itō (prime minister), Yamagata (justice). Kuroda (communications), Inoue (home), Ōyama (army), Gotō (agriculture and commerce), Mutsu (foreign).
77. *Yamagata den*, III, 83–84.

to dissuade him, and Itō finally was forced to be satisfied with Yamagata's agreement to become president of the Privy Council when he left the Cabinet. When he resigned as minister, he was successful in having one of his political protégés, Yoshikawa Kensei, appointed to succeed him. Under Yoshikawa, and later when Kiyoura was head of the justice ministry, Yamagata's influence spread into still another area of the bureaucracy.

The autumn of 1893 was filled with personal tragedy for Yamagata. In September his wife Yūko, whom he had married in 1867 when she was only sixteen, died after a protracted illness. In twenty-six years of marriage she had given birth to three boys and four girls, but only two daughters lived beyond three months; one of these daughters died at seven leaving the other the only surviving child. She was married and became the mother of Isaburō who was adopted as Yamagata's legal heir. By all accounts Yamagata was devoted to his wife and grief-stricken by the succession of family deaths. His fortune in his family life stood in stark contrast to his good fortune in all other spheres.

5

The War with China and

Yamagata's Second Government

By the summer of 1893, at the age of fifty-five, Yamagata stood at the midpoint of his career as a major figure in post-Restoration Japan. In the quarter century since the Restoration the nation had undergone far-reaching changes; a radical rearrangement of her institutions had been adopted to enable Japan to catch up with the strength of the Western powers. In the 1870's, waves of outside influences had produced startling changes in almost all areas of society. By the 1880's, the reawakening of cultural traditions had reduced what one observer called the "foreign fever," [1] and the 1890's were characterized by a stable new synthesis of old and new elements. The foundations of the modern military system, the educational system, the political structure, and many other institutions had been firmly fixed. By the mid-1890's, the leaders of the nation, vigorous and full of confidence, turned their attention more to the fixing of Japan's place in the international order. This effort to assure Japan's international position led the nation to its first large-scale military encounter abroad. In keeping with this development, we observe how Yamagata's career after 1893 was more influenced by the problems of Japan's foreign relations.

Foreign Affairs and the Sino-Japanese War

When Yamagata left the justice ministry to take up his task as president of the Privy Council, he received a message from the emperor saying, "As you are a General on active duty . . . on all important military matters I will seek your advice, so please reply candidly." [2] With more leisure on

1. Chamberlain, *Things Japanese*, 259.
2. Quoted in Watanabe Ikujirō, *Meiji Tennō to hohitsu no hitobito* (Tokyo, 1938), p. 275.

his hands than when he was serving in the Cabinet, he was able to devote time and thought to the question of the nation's position in the Far East. The product of this study was a recommendation he submitted to the government in October 1893. His proposals were preceded by a detailed analysis which indicated which of the problems faced by the country in the developing Far Eastern situation he considered of greatest significance. Because of this it is worth analyzing in some detail.

Viewing with alarm the activities of the European powers in the Far East, Yamagata predicted that within ten years there would be a war. He was concerned over the aggressive imperialism of France and England, who were profiting, he claimed, from the decay of China. But his main fear was the specter of Russia extending its influence across the Asian continent into the Far East. In 1891 Russia had started the construction of the Trans-Siberian Railway aimed at linking the maritime areas in the Far East with European Russia. Yamagata's fear of Russia hinged on the development of this railway. "The progress in its construction," he concluded, "poses an immediate threat to the Far East." [3] In due course, he predicted, Russia would be able to wrest Manchuria from China and move in on Peking. "At any rate ten years from now when the Trans-Siberian has been completed, Russia will undoubtedly seize Mongolia and extend its hand into China." [4] It was on the basis of this forecast that he made his recommendations. "As any one can plainly realize with a little common sense," he summarized, "the completion of the Trans-Siberian will sharply alter the situation in the Orient and exert a strong influence on our nation. It is not only for this reason that we must prepare adequate military power within the next eight or nine years; we must also be prepared to grasp any opportunity which may present advantages. This is a truly critical juncture in the fortunes of our nation." [5]

How must Japan prepare itself for this eventuality? The army and the navy, he answered, must be expanded. He argued that, "in order to defend oneself by remaining stationary, one must have enough strength to launch an attack. The advocates of a stationary force without the power to attack and defend do not know the real meaning of a defense. This has been my constant thought, and history is replete with supporting examples. At present our country's military strength is, of course, inade-

---

3. *Yamagata den*, III, 100. The text of the memorandum appears in *ibid.*, III, 98–108. Much of his information regarding Russia came from a report submitted to the army by a Major Fukushima after a fact-gathering mission to Manchuria and Siberia.

4. *Ibid.*, III, 101.

5. *Ibid.*, III, 104.

quate for any offensive action. Moreover, it is even inadequate for what is commonly known as a stationary defense. Consequently, we must take measures gradually to increase the army and the navy." [6] As it had been in his memorial to the throne in 1882 and again in his message to the Diet in 1890, military expansion was the unchanging conviction on which Yamagata based his hopes for the nation's development as a major power.

What were the obstacles to achieving this expansion? The popular political parties, he answered, which recklessly impede the passage of budgets and disrupt the domestic scene. He disagreed with those who used the argument that Japan's military expenditures should be cut because proportionately they exceeded those of Britain and France, who allotted a third and a fourth of their respective budgets for military use. This was fallacious, he argued, because the European countries had generations of development. He was obviously thinking not merely of defense but of the desire to place Japan among the first rank of world powers. He disagreed with the contention of the liberal parties that any surplus in the budget should be used to reduce the tax burden. He agreed that it was a laudable goal but should not receive serious thought until external problems were solved and prosperity was enjoyed at home. Therefore, he contended, whatever was saved from the annual budget should be used for immediate military preparations, particularly for naval expansion.

He ended his recommendations with a statement of what he considered to be the aim of the government. "At the time of the Restoration when the nation was opened up, the aim of the Meiji government was to establish the independence of our country and increase the nation's strength in facing the Western powers. Thus, the Meiji government cannot shirk its responsibility for completing the revision of the treaties and the preparedness of the army and navy. No matter what difficulties may be encountered there must be no swerving from the resolution to advance." [7]

It is interesting that Yamagata did not include China as the immediate threat nor foresee, at this time, the war which was to break out only nine months later. His attention was fixed on the encroachment of the Western powers in the Far East. His memorandum is of significance, however, in revealing the framework within which Yamagata viewed Japan's situation. Developing the nation's military strength to defend more than what he had called the "line of sovereignty" was necessary; it must include the

6. *Ibid.,* III, 104.
7. *Ibid.,* III, 108.

power to advance and protect the "line of advantage," the undefined line of security.

With these overriding considerations in his mind, it is not surprising that he objected to the conduct of the Diet. It represented a concrete obstacle to the strengthening of the nation. He constantly thought and wrote in that vein. In the spring of 1894, when Itō was attempting to overcome the obstacles placed in the way of his policies by the popular parties in the Diet, Yamagata wrote to him saying, "As anticipated, the Diet is boisterous with intemperate and violent language. Under such circumstances it is pointless to confer with a Diet of this nature on the affairs of state." [8]

In January 1894, Itō had already dissolved the fifth Diet. When the sixth Diet opened in May, as Yamagata indicated in his letter, nothing had been changed. Attacks on the government were persistent and unrestrained, more often than not unrelated to the pressing problems at hand. Itō's efforts to deal with the Diet had followed the general pattern of his predecessors. Although he disagreed with the election interference scheme, which had proved so ineffective, he had introduced the method of imperial intervention to gain his objectives and freely dissolved the Diet. Frustrated by the sixth Diet, Itō sought Yamagata's advice on the question of handling the parties. Yamagata replied on June 1, 1894: "Since the opening of the sixth Special Diet there have been persistent efforts to oppose the national policy, attack the cabinet and interfere with the positive measure of the government. It is useless for the government to consult this kind of assembly. No matter how conciliatory the approach may be, the Diet has no desire to listen. If this Diet continues, the dignity of the government will suffer and the confidence of the people will be shaken. Under these circumstances, I believe there is no other course than to settle unhesitatingly on a policy of dissolution." [9] The Diet was dissolved the next day.

Although Yamagata had written in his memorandum of October 1893 that "our nation's adversary is not China nor Korea but England, France and Russia," [10] less than a year later Japan was at war with China. Early in 1894, when problems over the balance of power between China and Japan in Korea were aggravated by internal strife in the Korean government, Yamagata became convinced that war plans should be drawn up

8. Letter dated May 17, 1894, is printed in *ibid.*, III, 113.
9. Reprinted in *ibid.*, III, 114–115.
10. *Ibid.*, III, 106.

which could be acted upon in an emergency. He stood as a leader of those forces advocating war with China and spent his time formulating broad strategic plans of action.[11] "He was," Tokutomi contends, "the first to advocate sending troops to Korea."[12]

Korea had been a constant problem in Japan's foreign relations since the Restoration. As Japan's strength grew, she was able to exert greater influence on the peninsula and challenge China's age-old claims of suzerainty. In the Treaty of Tientsin in 1885, an attempt was made to balance Sino-Japanese power in Korea; both recognized Korea's nominal independence and agreed to increase their military strength there only after notifying the other. But internal strife in Korea continued through a tug of war between rival factions supported by the two neighboring states and became the focus of the Sino-Japanese struggle for influence. In Japan, ultra-nationalist organizations were active in building up friendly action groups among the Koreans as well as in influencing highly placed officers in the Japanese command.[13] An increasing body of opinion, disgruntled by the sorry display of constitutional government during the early Diet sessions, was attracted to the panacea of heroic action abroad.

It was during the Cabinet meeting of June 2, at which the decision was made to dissolve the sixth Diet, that Mutsu, the foreign minister, produced an urgent dispatch from the Japanese minister in Korea stating that the Korean government had requested the reinforcement of Chinese troops. At this meeting of the Cabinet, at which both Yamagata and the chief of staff were present,[14] it was agreed that when China sent troops to Korea, Japan should do likewise in order to maintain a balance of power.[15]

In the face of anti-Japanese outbreaks in Seoul and the increase in the number of Chinese troops in Korea, steps were undertaken by the army to mobilize forces to be sent to Korea. At the same time, efforts were made by the militarists to prevent Itō from getting reports on the favorable turn in negotiations at Seoul for fear that he would deprive them of an opportunity for action. General Kawakami, the army assistant chief of staff, realizing that the army's actions might be halted, kept information

11. *Ibid.*, III, 118.
12. *Ibid.*, III, 120.
13. See Shinobu's reference to conversations between General Kawakami, assistant chief of staff, and Hiraoka, a leader of the super-patriotic Genyōsha, in *Meiji seiji shi*, pp. 42–43.
14. Sterling Tatsuji Takeuchi, *War and Diplomacy in the Japanese Empire* (New York, 1935), p. 111.
15. Shinobu, *Meiji seiji shi*, p. 47.

from Itō. When Itō discovered this, he threatened to resign. Kawakami apologized with a false statement that it had been an oversight. This, it has been stated, was the first example of the army's attempt to circumvent political authority to conduct its overseas plan.[16] While negotiations to avert a war deteriorated, Yamagata submitted, on June 24, a plan of action because, as he wrote, "It appears the negotiations with China will fail." [17] In these plans, Yamagata suggested that supreme headquarters be shifted to the palace, that Pusan be established as an army base, and that the fifth division, the third brigade, and the imperial division be used in that order.[18]

Yamagata's plan reflected his willingness to wage war. The practical ground upon which he had argued against military ventures in 1873 and 1874 no longer existed. The organization of the modern army was well advanced and the foundations of the new government were firmly established. Furthermore, the Diet's opposition to the oligarchs was limited to domestic issues; there was no genuine opposition to an aggressive foreign policy. There was a desire on all sides to join the European powers in acquiring territories and economic privileges on the mainland. The unstable conditions in Seoul, where Japan and China stood face to face, coupled with conditions in Japanese politics encouraged Yamagata and other military leaders to seize the initiative and test the new army of Japan in a major engagement.

At a meeting attended by the emperor, Cabinet members, army and navy representatives, and leading councillors three days after Yamagata submitted his plan for mobilization, the decision was made to go to war. On August 1, 1894, war was declared.

Like most military men, Yamagata most enjoyed duty as a commander in the field. Recalling in later years his appointment to command on August 30, 1894, he said, "The happiest moment of my life was when I became commander of the First Army at the outset of the Sino-Japanese War, with the duty of leading three divisions against the Chinese." [19] His part in the Satsuma rebellion had earned him great prestige, but it was his participation in this war that gave him the satisfaction of operating the military machine he had done so much to create. When he received his order to lead the First Army, he also received a sword from the emperor. He was moved to write:

16. *Ibid.*, pp. 49–50.
17. Reprinted in *Yamagata den,* III, 131.
18. *Ibid.*, III, 131–132.
19. Quoted in *ibid.*, III, 238–239.

I know that pine trees
live for a thousand years.
So if I should return
I will see them again.[20]

Yamagata's glory as a field commander was cut short by a serious illness. He arrived in Korea in mid-September, entered P'youngyang after its capture, and actually was in direct command during only one short engagement at the Yalu River. After crossing into southern Manchuria, he fell seriously ill with dyspepsia. He had never been physically robust and often suffered from digestive troubles, but this attack was most serious and he was forced to remain on a cot in his field tent. For days he refused to consider the advice of his associates that he should return to Japan for treatment. Finally, Hirata Tōsuke was sent over as the emperor's messenger to order his return.[21] Now he had no choice, and he was carried off the field on a stretcher. His sadness at having to leave the war was expressed in a Chinese-style poem he addressed to his division commanders.

To die in battle is the attitude with which I came,
One shouldn't return in the midst of war.
But since the Emperor orders me to hurry home,
            it can't be helped,
Yet weeping tears on one's uniform can't be helped
            when parting from comrades.[22]

Yamagata never gained the reputation of a brilliant military commander. It was not Yamagata's but Yamada Akiyoshi's able stroke which saved the besieged Kumamoto castle during the Satsuma rebellion and turned the tide of battle. And it was Kawakami Soroku who was generally regarded as the military mastermind of the Sino-Japanese War. Under him there was an able group of divisional commanders, Generals Nozu, Koroki, and Katsura. Yamagata's military reputation rested on his ability as a strategic planner and organizer. Nevertheless, inasmuch as he was the senior military figure, the army's success brought added prestige to his name.

Upon Yamagata's return to Japan, he was highly honored by a special imperial rescript lauding his service to the nation. The rescript also called him to serve as senior adviser to the emperor, upon his recovery at the

20. *Ibid.,* III, 137.
21. The emperor's message is reprinted in Alfred Stead, ed., *Japan by the Japanese* (London, 1904), p. 13.
22. *Yamagata den,* III, 188.

imperial headquarters which had been established in Hiroshima during the war. After recuperating, Yamagata used his time to formulate broad strategic plans for the army in the field. Away from the heavy pressure of combat, at his leisure he drew up plans designed to bring an end to the war. One of his plans called for a daring assault on Peking to force China's surrender. The plan anticipated the landing of army divisions at Shanhaikwan north of the Chinese capital and on the Shantung peninsula to the south. From north and south the divisions were to converge on Peking. The emperor in person, according to this plan, was to lead the army into enemy territory.[23] This broad strategy did not proceed beyond the planning stage.

Diplomacy intervened to bring the Sino-Japanese conflict to an end. Japan's startling victory over China had bared the weakness of China; it was also disquieting to the leading European powers who now had to contend with another competitive power to the possible detriment of their own interests. Since November 1894, Japanese peace negotiations with China had been carried on intermittently but only half-heartedly. After Japan's successive victories on land and sea, however, foreign powers pressed the two nations to end hostilities. Continually distrustful of each other's designs in the Far East, the great powers urged an end to a war which accentuated the struggle for power, and which now introduced another participant in the struggle.

Despite Yamagata's grandiose schemes for victory, he believed that it would be reckless not to heed the foreign pressure and respond to overtures for peace. In this he shared the view of both the prime minister, Itō, and the foreign minister, Mutsu. Unlike many of the other military leaders, Yamagata rarely allowed his patriotic enthusiasm to blur a careful appraisal of the existing military situation. He did not succumb to the traditional fault of generals — that they fight wars with the sole objective of destroying an enemy without thought of winning an advantageous peace. He tended to hold a clear and steady view of the immediate military situation in the light of the nation's long-range needs. He based his approval of peace negotiations on the conviction that Japan's strength must be conserved for more difficult crises ahead. "It is certain that the situation in Asia will grow steadily worse in the future," he wrote his friend Shinagawa on April 12, 1895, after negotiations got under way, "and we must make preparations for another war within the next ten years. Considering the recent past and the future, now is the opportune time to end the war. By ending hostilities in our present condition, be-

23. The plan, dated December 1894, is printed in *ibid.*, III, 193–194.

fore exhausting our resources, we have promises of great progress for the future of our nation — of that I am very pleased." [24] In the back of Yamagata's mind was also the fear of joint foreign intervention. Believing that Japan was not yet prepared to meet the foreign powers on equal terms, he cautioned against arousing their suspicion by pushing ahead recklessly.

Negotiations for peace began in earnest in March 1894, at Shimonoseki, after the arrival of Li Hung-chang, the Chinese plenipotentiary. Just prior to this Yamagata again had been appointed army minister. His illness had forced him to reduce his responsibilities — he had resigned as president of the Privy Council and commander of the First Army — but upon recovering his health he took on the Cabinet post and also served as inspector general of the army. During the negotiations he was consulted by both Itō and Mutsu, Japan's representatives. He fully endorsed the terms of surrender which they submitted to the Chinese on April 1, in which the Japanese government demanded territorial concessions, including Formosa, the Pescadores Islands, and the whole of the Liaotung Peninsula; wide commercial advantages at seven new ports to be opened up in China; a large indemnity to cover the cost of the war; and China's recognition of the complete independence of Korea.

During the negotiations over these terms, Yamagata was particularly irritated by the reckless statements and unrealistic demands of members of the main popular political parties. Their call for a continuation of the war enraged him. In his view the parties had done little to bring victory and, indeed, had hindered the development of Japan's military strength, which alone had produced the favorable outcome which the parties were now irresponsibly misusing. The extremes to which the parties pressed stood in contrast to Yamagata's own moderation and must have added to his low opinion of the popular parties. In the letter to Shinagawa, quoted above, he reported a favorable turn in the negotiations and his disapproval of party statements. "For the last five or six days it seemed as though the negotiations at Shimonoseki were on the verge of collapsing, but yesterday, in a five hour session, the main provisions were agreed to, and today it will probably be ready for signing. This is a fine thing for the nation. Naturally I disapprove of the immature proposal of the members of the Kaishintō, calling for the total destruction of China and feel that this [the treaty] will bring us most satisfactory results." [25]

During the negotiations Yamagata also showed himself to be sensitive to the reaction of foreign powers to Japan's action. He predicted that the

24. Reprinted in *ibid.*, III, 220.
25. *Ibid.*, III, 220.

Western powers would disapprove of some of Japan's demands. In anticipation of such developments, he advocated diplomatic measures which, if they had been accepted, might have prevented the eventual foreign intervention. Both his analysis of developments and his suggested measures were contained in a revealing and lengthy letter to the foreign minister on April 5, 1895.

Now that negotiations have been resumed I am keenly interested in what the reactions of the various European powers will be. In agreeing to a truce we have been widely praised for our generous gesture, and the news indicates that popular sentiment in both Europe and America has been favorable. This is gratifying. However, when we disclosed our peace conditions to the Western powers, the reaction of the Russian government was not favorable, a factor which will surely prove a hindrance to our demands. Although there is no word from England yet, she will certainly consider the proposal unjust and, as is her habit, maneuver to extract some advantage for herself. If this be the case, these two great powers will clearly join hands in opposing our demands. If so, this will be a tremendous disadvantage for us. Therefore there appears to be no other course than to take advantage of the present situation, resolutely join hands with Russia and discuss her future policy in Siberia . . . and negotiate for our mutual advantage. If we do not pursue this course, even if we gain control of Korea in the future, ominous problems are liable to arise. Even with the present war ended, a look at the future indicates that it would be impossible to maintain our strength in the Far East independently. Therefore, this decision is the most important condition for the future of our nation. We must not lose the present opportunity, and shifting our foreign policy should be the responsibility of the Meiji government and must be undertaken with determination. The Russian Crown Prince's tour of our country before was certainly not undertaken with any view that in the future our nations would be enemies. I believe it represented a genuine desire for friendly relations. Why? Because her relations with China have been unfavorable for many years; moreover, Sino-British relations have long been friendly. Thus it is plain to see that Russia can gain no particular advantage from the point of view of its interest in seeking friendly relations with China. So it seems that she has set her policy to cultivate our nation and remain on lukewarm terms with China. Unfortunately the Ōtsu incident [the attempted assassination of the Russian crown prince] occurred, but happily the sincerity shown by the Emperor and the deep feeling shown by our people prevented it from becoming a disastrous affair. Since then our relations have been amicable and friendly. With this friendship I believe our best course is to change our foreign policy now. In the present situation, clearly we must by all means win one of these nations as a supporter and prevent their joining forces. At the present time we should unite not with England but with Russia. There would be no future advantage in casting our lot with England under the present circumstances.[26]

Mutsu's reply two days later indicated that he was thinking along similar lines, but he felt it difficult to make a fundamental shift in the nation's policy before the government had agreed to such a change. It is interesting to speculate on what the result might have been had Yamagata's bold idea been accepted. Yet it is difficult to believe that Russia would have favored an entente with Japan at the moment Japan was demanding the Liaotung Peninsula, an area Russia coveted.

Although the Treaty of Shimonoseki, signed on April 17, 1895, gave Japan all her demands, the European powers were dissatisfied with the settlement. Specifically, the annexation of the Liaotung Peninsula by Japan was viewed with alarm, and Russia in particular regarded such a move as directed against her interest. While Britain stood aloof, Russia, France, and Germany joined forces in "advising" Japan to retrocede the peninsula because it "would be a constant menace to the capital of China, would at the same time render illusory the independence of Korea, and would henceforth be a perpetual obstacle to the peace of the Far East." [27]

Yamagata and other military leaders in Japan were forced to admit that resistance to the three powers was beyond possibility. The government, therefore, was forced to give up one of the greatest war prizes. It was an onerous assignment for Yamagata to have to proceed secretly to Port Arthur to deliver news of the retrocession to the field commanders. Several of the field commanders had demanded that hostilities be reopened rather than accept such a humiliation. So Yamagata was called upon to use the great weight of his influence among the military leaders to force down the bitter pill.

Aftermath of the Sino-Japanese War

The victory of Japan had profound consequences both for the international relations of the Far East and for Japan's internal affairs. Internationally, the world's powers were forced to recognize a new situation.

26. The letter appears in *ibid.*, III, 230–232.
27. Quoted in W. L. Langer, *The Diplomacy of Imperialism* (New York, 1935), I, 186.

Military victory accomplished for Japan what years of negotiation had failed to achieve — equality in her foreign relations. Negotiations for the revision of the unequal treaties received a decisive impetus. Domestically, the war stilled internal battles; it was a useful diversion in the deadlock between the government and the Diet. A Diet which twice had been dissolved met after the outbreak of war at a special session in a temporary building in Hiroshima and proved docile, even eager to approve government measures. The magic charm which a state of national emergency had over the Diet was not forgotten by the authorities.

Underlying this cooperation was the surge of nationalism. The rise of national consciousness which was accentuated by the treaty revision issue united the nation in a single effort. The party members, in a way, adopted the attitude of the leaders of the nation who strove to achieve "national prosperity and a strong army." The urge for expansion had been kept alive by the ultra-nationalist groups ever since the days of Saigō Takamori. Now the whole nation was sharing some of these sentiments, sentiments which dissolved disunity and produced a strong united effort. "The Sino-Japanese War," wrote Yamagata, "was not only the first foreign war but was also the final resolution of the crisis over Korea in 1873. My elders who passed on would have been pleased. At that time our military preparations were incomplete, and even during the Sino-French War of 1885 there was a proposal that we ally ourselves with France to subjugate China, but I turned this down because it was premature." [28]

Thus, success in the war with China was both the resolution of a domestic problem of long standing and the expression of growing nationalism. Victory gained for the army the praise and confidence of the people who were shown that large investments in constructing naval and military forces were sound and profitable. And the prestige accorded to the military of Japan gave them the role of the instrument of the nation's destiny. Victory also gave the leaders of the government a new confidence and assurance. Among the leaders none gained greater prestige than Yamagata. He had become a world figure. The foreign correspondents covering the fighting mentioned his name whenever they mentioned the First Army. This was so despite the fact that his actual participation in the battles of the war was extremely limited. It was well known, however, that he was the supreme military personality of Japan, and his career was a symbol of the sudden rise of Japan as a military power in the Far East. This prestige, as we shall see, preceded him on his travels abroad the following year

28. Quoted in *Yamagata den,* III, 239.

It was under the impetus of an aroused nationalism, glorying in victory and embittered by the humiliation of the retrocession of Liaotung, that the army planned its next steps. Yamagata put forth the views which formed the basis of a demand for increasing the number of the army divisions from seven to thirteen. The aim of this expansion was not only to implant Japan's influence in Korea but to prepare to participate in the maintenance of peace in the Far East.[29] Underlying these aims, however, was the conviction that Japan's power must be built up to the point where it could act as a counterbalance to Russia's rapidly increasing strength in the Far East, as evidenced in the progress of the Trans-Siberian Railway.

On April 15, two days before the signing of the Treaty of Shimonoseki and ten days after Yamagata had proposed, in the letter to Mutsu quoted above, a shift in foreign policy, he submitted a petition outlining the reasons for the contemplated expansion of the army and the navy.

> Although the war with China has not been concluded, it has already been about a year since hostilities began . . . During this period we have been consistently victorious against the Chinese . . . Of course this was made possible by the benevolent virtue of the Emperor, but it must also be attributed to our superior military organization and discipline.

> Nevertheless, if we are to maintain peace the present military organization is inadequate. As a result of the present war we have gained new overseas territories which require expanded military forces for their defense. Beyond that, it is necessary, if we are to ride the wave of victory, to become a leader in the Far East. It is, furthermore, natural to plan adjustments in our military preparations to be alert for the revenge China will seek. Of course, Russia, England, France, and other powers with a stake in the Far East will surely alter their policies and strengthen their military forces in the Far East. At present, the construction of the Trans-Siberian Railway is progressing and will be completed in a few years. We must be alert to this prospect.

At this point in his petition, Yamagata utilized the concept of national security which he had introduced in his first speech to the Diet in 1890. At that time he had laid down the concept of a "line of advantage," a strategic line or zone, the defense of which should govern the military expenditures of the nation. The war, he now maintained, had radically

29. *Ibid.*, III, 240.

altered the strategic line which should be defended. In his proposal he argued:

> If we expand our military forces, national expenditures are increased, but if we do not do so at once, our superior position with respect to our neighbors will be reversed . . . It would be a greater loss to be invaded by an enemy than to train a million men . . . Our military preparedness up to this time has been used chiefly to maintain the line of sovereignty. However, if we are to make the result of the recent war something more than a hollow victory and move on to become the leader of the Far East, it will be absolutely necessary to extend the line of advantage. Our present military strength is inadequate for maintaining our new line of sovereignty. It follows that it is inadequate for extending the line of advantage and being dominant in the Far East.[30]

Yamagata's views represented the high-level thinking which resulted in the request for a drastic expansion of the military establishment. In November 1895, Itō agreed to the request and, as prime minister, submitted to the Diet a budget providing for an increase of six divisions and four brigades in the army and a comparable expansion of the navy.[31] The expenditures were approved and the army's budget jumped from ten million to over fifty-two million yen, increasing the percentage of the army's share of the national budget from 10.5 percent to over 30 percent.[32]

The working agreement Itō had concluded with the Jiyūtō during the war made it possible for the government to carry out its plans. But in the Diet there were some objections to such a sizable increase in the army and the navy. The Kaishintō proposed an increase by three divisions while the Jiyūtō suggested limiting the increase to four. Some opposition was expressed even in the House of Peers. By scheduling the increase in divisions over a period of years, the government won approval from the Diet for an increase of six divisions. This accomplished the army's objectives, the details of which had been drawn up by Kawakami, the

30. The petition is reprinted in *ibid.*, III, 241–242.
31. Matsushita Yoshio, *Kindai Nihon gunji shi* (Tokyo, 1941), p. 159.
32. For a tabulation of the yearly rise in army and navy expenditures, see Matsushita Yoshio and Izu Kunio, *Nihon gunji hattatsu shi* (Tokyo, 1938), pp. 365–379. To justify the expansion of the army, Yamagata once claimed, "During the feudal period there were about 400,000 samurai with the task of defending the nation. Now with the loss of the professional samurai, if we are to call up soldiers we must train 400,000." *Yamagata den*, III, 244. The statement was made years before the Sino-Japanese War; the army was to achieve that size after the war.

chief of staff, but for which the overall policy had been formulated by Yamagata.[33]

Soon after Yamagata returned from his mission to Port Arthur, undertaken to explain to the field commanders the decision to retrocede the Liaotung Peninsula, he resigned his position as army minister. By imperial order he was to be accorded treatment as a minister and senior statesman. On August 5, his great services to the nation were recognized in the honors he was given. He received the Order of the Paulownia, the Order of the Rising Sun, and the Order of the Golden Kite, Second Class, with an annual stipend of 1,000 yen. On the same day he was raised to the rank of marquis and received a personal gift from the emperor of 50,000 yen for his service to the nation.

During the months following the final settlement of the Sino-Japanese War, Yamagata had no administrative responsibilities. Always deeply concerned with the military preparedness of the nation's defenses, his thoughts now turned more frequently to the nation's foreign policy. At the same time, however, Yamagata's influence in domestic affairs was exerted to achieve what he considered to be desirable ends. An example of this occurred in February of 1896.

In Korea, Japan attempted to assert her influence by pushing reforms. Opposition of the Korean court led, first, to the murder of the queen by a pro-Japanese faction under Japanese direction and, second, to the king fleeing to the Russians for protection. These events increased anti-Japanese feeling, and consequently Russia's influence in Korea, and unleashed a storm of protest in Tokyo. The usually pro-government but intensely nationalistic faction in the Diet, the Kokumin Kyōkai (National Unionists), submitted a petition to the Diet to impeach Itō's Cabinet. Itō immediately prorogued the Diet and turned to Yamagata for aid.

The Kokumin Kyōkai was formed in 1892 by Shinagawa Yajirō and Saigō Tsugumichi, soon after Shinagawa's forced resignation from the Cabinet over the election interference incident. These highly placed bureaucrats organized their political group (they refused to admit it formed a party) to support a nationalistic policy and the principle of nonparty Cabinets. The group "was established on the basis of a tacit understanding between Yamagata and Shinagawa,"[34] and many of Yamagata's followers had joined the group.

33. Shinobu, *Meiji seiji shi*, p. 97.
34. Okutani, *Shinagawa den*, p. 293.

It was natural, therefore, that Itō should appeal to Yamagata to have the petition of the Kokumin Kyōkai withdrawn. Yamagata himself was not satisfied with the government's policy in Korea, but he was convinced of the greater importance of the military expansion program, which the Diet was delaying. Yamagata invited Shinagawa to his residence and impressed upon him the undesirability of the Kokumin Kyōkai's position in the Diet. In obedience to Yamagata's wish, the group was assembled and was advised by its leader that "although the Korean problem is urgent, not a single day can be lost in working for the postwar plans. Therefore, after these projects have received our approval there will still be time to discuss the Korean problem." [35] In this way the crisis was averted and the Itō government continued.

Mission to Moscow

On February 21, 1896, Yamagata was appointed minister plenipotentiary and instructed to attend the coronation of Tsar Nicholas II in Moscow, in company with Prince Fushimi who had been selected as Japan's formal representative. The real purpose of Yamagata's attendance, however, was to negotiate an agreement with Russia regarding the Korean problem on which the two nation's interests were in open clash. This was made clear to Nishi Tokujirō, the Japanese minister to Russia, by foreign minister Saionji in a dispatch of February 24: "In view of the special circumstances in which Japan finds herself in regard to Russia, the Japanese government must first consider profiting from the exceptional occasion of the Coronation." [36] Nishi was instructed to keep this information from the Russians until a later time.

Itō was first chosen to carry out this task, but, when opposition developed to his appointment, he agreed to withdraw and nominated Yamagata himself.[37] Mutsu, who had served Itō as foreign minister, was instrumental in getting Yamagata to accept the appointment. In a letter to Yamagata he wrote that he was better qualified than Itō for the mission. Mutsu had been impressed by the reasoned suggestions he had received from the general, encouraging an understanding with Russia.

35. Quoted in *Yamagata den,* III, 253.
36. Gaimushō, *Dai Nihon gaikō bunsho* (Tokyo, 1936–), XXIX (1896), 808. Nishi reported to Saionji that the Russians expressed a preference for Itō, but the public announcement had already been made designating Yamagata minister plenipotentiary to attend the coronation of the tsar.
37. See letter in *Yamagata den,* III, 263.

Knowing that Yamagata had previously recommended a Russo-Japanese coalition, Mutsu pushed his nomination. Yamagata pledged his service, writing:

> Though I may exhaust
> my aging body
> I will not falter
> until my mission is achieved.[38]

Accompanied by representatives from the Foreign Office and the Imperial Household ministry, army officers, including a Lieutenant-Colonel Tōjō Hidemori, father of General Tōjō Hideki of later fame, and a personal physician, the party left Japan for San Francisco on March 15, 1896. Yamagata, the hero of the Sino-Japanese War, as the foreign press called him, was now on an international stage. And his thoughts were naturally turned to solving the problems of international relations in the Far East. "Since sailing," he wrote Tanaka Kōken, vice minister of the Imperial Household, "I have been wondering how the Korean situation is developing. I am constantly concerned with the policies of the various European nations. On the other hand, I haven't given a single thought to the situation at home both in the Diet and in the cabinet." [39]

Yamagata's "trip overland from San Francisco has been a sort of triumphal march, and everywhere he has been received and entertained lavishly," reported the *New York Daily Tribune*.[40] He was acknowledged to be the real hero of the Sino-Japanese War and, "next to the Mikado, the most influential statesman and soldier in the Empire." [41] From Chicago the train took him to Niagara and from there to Buffalo, from where a special train and a reception party, including Governor Morton of the state of New York, escorted him to Albany. In Albany, where he was officially entertained, a local problem was overcome when "an enterprising citizen, after much research, managed to find a Japanese flag and this was hung in honor of the visitor." [42] When he was told about the American Indians, en route to New York City from Albany, "he surprised the other members of the party by declaring through the interpreter that the Japanese Empire contained within its borders Indians

---

38. *Ibid.*, III, 266.
39. The letter, dated March 29, 1896, was sent from San Francisco. Reprinted in *ibid.*, III, 267.
40. *New York Daily Tribune*, April 13, 1896.
41. *Ibid.*, April 13, 1896.
42. *Ibid.*, April 14, 1896. The same article explained that "the flag of Japan has a large red ball in the middle of a white field. If such a flag was floated on top of the Fifth Avenue stage it would mean there was skating in Central Park."

like those which once roamed over the hills and prairies of America," [43] and that they presently occupied the extreme northern end of Japan.

Despite Yamagata's plea for no display in his honor, he was entertained at a dinner and reception every night during his six days in New York City. He impressed his hosts with his simplicity, and, surprisingly, his speeches were reportedly filled with wit and hospitality. The local press was pleased to quote his remark: "It was you Americans who introduced Western civilization. You were the harbingers of civilization to my country." [44]

From New York the delegation proceeded to France. In Paris, Yamagata was entertained by the president of France and had several interviews with the foreign minister and other important French officials. The cordiality of the French, in striking contrast to the behavior of the French on Yamagata's last visit to Paris in 1889, was duplicated by the Germans during a brief stopover in Berlin. The party arrived in Moscow on the 17th of May and entered into the gay festivities provided for the galaxy of foreign representatives gathered for the coronation ceremonies.

After the formal functions surrounding the coronation had been concluded, Yamagata made the initial overtures for negotiating a settlement. Fortunately, a few days prior to the party's arrival in Moscow the Russian and Japanese ministers in Korea had negotiated a local settlement of disputes.[45] This smoothed the way for Yamagata, whose aim was now to confirm the agreement made in Korea and extend its scope by establishing two spheres of influence on the peninsula. Colonel Vogak, the Russian military attaché in Tokyo and a friend of Yamagata's, had encouraged a plan to partition Korea into Russian and Japanese zones of influence.[46] Vogak had been an observer during the Sino-Japanese War and was impressed by Japan's strength. He was convinced that Japan posed a formidable threat to Russia's interests in the Far East and would fight for her position in Korea. Fearing a clash, Vogak encouraged a scheme for partition,[47] a scheme which had Yamagata's support because it would, he felt, provide the stability and time required for Japan to bring her military forces into equilibrium with Russian forces in the Far East.

Yamagata's general instructions were to conclude an agreement which would stabilize the situation in Korea and promote law and order. Be-

43. *Ibid.*, April 14, 1896
44. Quoted in *ibid.*, April 11, 1896.
45. Kiyosawa Kiyoshi, *Nihon gaikō shi* (Tokyo, 1942), I, 280.
46. Takekoshi Yosaburō, *Prince Saionji* (Kyoto, 1933), p. 142.
47. Langer, *Diplomacy of Imperialism*, I, 405.

fore leaving Japan, Yamagata also received specific instructions which said, "In order to avoid a clash between the armed forces of Russia and Japan, the area into which each shall be permitted to send its troops should be delineated and, moreover, a protective neutral zone between the two armies should be established." [48] With this objective in mind, Yamagata entered the negotiations. On the specific question of where the north-south boundary should be drawn, some sources have claimed that Yamagata proposed the thirty-eighth parallel. In reality, neither Yamagata nor Ambassador Nishi had any specific plan. It is reported that during the first interview Yamagata only laughed in response to the question of where the boundary line was to be drawn.[49] At later meetings the Japanese mentioned the Taedong River as a possible dividing line, but evidently this was suggested more to sound out the Russians than to fix a firm line. For their part the Russians suggested that the expression "north-south partition" be eliminated and the Japanese agreed.[50]

The final agreement, known as the Yamagata–Lobanov Agreement, said both powers would recognize Korea's independence, guarantee foreign loans for internal reforms, and support the king of Korea in maintaining order and in carrying out reforms. More specific and important matters were covered in two secret clauses. The first said that until Korea developed adequate military forces of her own the provisional arrangement for equal numbers of troops worked out by Russian and Japanese representatives in Seoul would be in effect. According to the second, both parties could dispatch troops to maintain their lines of communications and order. In such cases, it was stated that "in order to avoid clashes between the armed forces of both Imperial Governments there will be an unoccupied area between the armies of both states and spheres defined for their respective armies." [51] Aside from a natural north-south division of areas of greater interest to the two powers, the designation of a sphere of action remained vague.

Both nations profited from this agreement, which established, in effect, "something in the nature of a condominium, a joint protectorate." [52] Russia gained solid footing in the peninsula and at the same time con-

---

48. Nagaoka Shinjirō, "Yamagata Aritomo no rokoku haken to Nichi-Ro kyōtei," *Nihon rekishi* 59.4:17 (April 1953). See dispatch of foreign minister Saionji to Yamagata, dated March 13, 1896, in *Dai Nihon gaikō bunsho*, XXIX (1896), 810–811.

49. A full report on the conversations was submitted on August 15, after Yamagata returned. *Ibid.*, XXIX (1896), 832–845.

50. *Ibid.*, XXIX (1896), 836.

51. The French and Japanese texts of the agreement are included in *ibid.*, XXIX (1896), 815–818.

52. Langer, *Diplomacy of Imperialism*, I, 407.

cluded agreements with Japan. On the other hand, the agreement gave Japan assurance that she would be allowed time to complete her military expansion program. The agreement, however, did nothing to correct the friction and rivalry which were eventually to lead to a major clash.

On July 28, 1896, Yamagata and his party returned from abroad. This was to be Yamagata's last trip overseas. In less than twenty years he had been around the world three times, in 1869–1870, 1889, and 1896, spending over two and a half years abroad. The increased prestige with which he traveled on each successive trip was an interesting reflection of his growing stature in Japan: he had gone abroad as a young, wide-eyed samurai in 1869, then as a confident minister of state in 1889, and finally as a suave world figure in 1896. Each of these trips marked a period in his career, though after his return from the last there was to be a pause of several years before he took his next decisive step. In the interim, the completion of a new home in Kyoto absorbed his attention. As before, the landscaping of the new, slightly larger residence was the product of his planning and careful supervision. The name Murinan, which he had used for his previous house in Kyoto, was transferred to the new.

Postwar Political Developments

As we have seen, the Sino-Japanese War had produced a period of striking internal unity. Itō had given continuity to the government's leadership by serving as premier for the unprecedented term of four years. Yet the humiliating aftermath of the military victory caused a serious break in domestic harmony, and many party members attacked the government with charges of "diplomatic defeat." Ignoring these denunciations, the government maneuvered to avoid in the postwar period the clashes between the Diet and the government that had marked the prewar period.

Itō took the leadership in inaugurating a new phase in Meiji political history: a period of alliances between the Cabinets and one or the other of the leading two parties. Cabinets had succeeded in the past by gaining the aid of a block of party votes on crucial issues. The new tactic extended that expedient practice to a broader compromise between the aims of the premier and the demands of the party with which an alliance was formed. Itō, aware of the government's failure to avoid serious clashes with the Diet over key issues and more inclined to operate through a government party, decided a new policy was necessary. Thus in November 1895, Itagaki, leader of the Jiyūtō, which had supported the government during the 1895 Diet session, was made a member of the Cabinet as home minister. On the one hand, government hoped to achieve its plans by this new policy of compromise and cooperation. On the other hand, the Jiyūtō agreed to cooperate because it appeared to be in keeping with its aim of forcing the government to share its administrative power.[53]

Yamagata was abroad when Itō formed his alliance with Itagaki, but his followers kept him closely informed, and what he heard troubled him. On April 30, 1896, Kiyoura Keigo reported: "Since your departure the most radical change has been Itagaki's entry into the cabinet . . . as a natural consequence of the alliance with the Jiyūtō." [54] He added that Itagaki had made it clear that he would not secede from his party in order to assume the Cabinet post. He further reported that members of the home ministry were displeased to work under a party politician and that several governors had threatened to resign because of Itagaki's appointment. Kiyoura expressed the displeasure, even alarm, of the Yamagata clique with what appeared to be a drift toward party government.

Itō's new policy had not adopted without opposition. Some factions in the government opposed Itagaki's entry into the Cabinet because they feared that it would create a bridgehead for the eventual formation of a party Cabinet. Yamagata shared his sentiment, but he had still other reasons for being alarmed. Ever since the reorganization of the home ministry in 1885, it had been directly or indirectly subject to his influence. In the Itō Cabinet, Nomura Yasushi, a Chōshū bureaucrat in Yamagata's faction, had served as home minister, and in February 1896 he was succeeded by Yoshikawa Kensei, another member of Yamagata's clique. Now a party man had assumed this sensitive Cabinet post, troubling the mind of Yamagata and his conservative followers.

Little could be done from abroad to press his views. Displeased but resigned to Itō's party alliance, Yamagata was able to see the immediate advantages of such an arrangement. He had himself made a less formal arrangement with politicians in the Diet to gain his ends. Smooth passage of the budget was the valuable reward of Itō's alliance, an accomplishment Yamagata was glad to see, for it assured the postwar military expansion program which he anxiously desired. In the end, Yamagata minimized the threat of the alliance to his view of the proper conduct of government and gave his support to the Cabinet. Nevertheless, it is from this time that we must date the rift between the two giants of the Meiji

53. Shinobu, *Meiji seiji shi*, pp. 93–97.
54. Reprinted in *Yamagata den*, III, 283.

government. They were never to lose respect for each other, but what had previously been an insignificant crack in their attitude toward constitutional government widened to a gap; this was shortly to force a major contest for authority.

The countercurrents within the political party movement, rather than conservative resistance, ended Itō's new approach. The advantage gained by the Jiyūtō from its entente with the government spurred its rival, the Kaishintō, to new activity. In March 1896, Ōkuma organized the Shimpotō (Progressive party) by bringing together the Kaishintō and several smaller factions. Supported by business firms which had profited from the sudden economic expansion generated by the Sino-Japanese War, the Shimpotō pressed for representation in the Cabinet. Ōkuma, noting Itō's new strategy, succeeded in establishing a working agreement with Matsukata, the oligarch who had gained a reputation as an able administrator of the nation's finances and a man in whom the business community had considerable confidence. Business circles insisted that Matsukata be made finance minister, and, in turn, Matsukata declared that his acceptance of office must be accompanied by Ōkuma's simultaneous entry into the Cabinet. However, Itagaki refused to approve the seating of his rival party leader, and this created a crisis which was finally resolved only by the resignation of the Cabinet.

Yamagata had been home only a week from his excursion into foreign affairs when the Cabinet crisis came to a head. A quiet rest in the peaceful setting of his Kyoto home was interrupted by an urgent message from Inoue, which explained the events leading to the resignation of the Cabinet and informed him that the emperor desired the advice of the elder statesmen in selecting a new premier. Itō had already recommended that either Matsukata or Yamagata should succeed him. The latter hastened to the capital to engineer Matsukata's appointment and escape the responsibility. In his maneuvers he was counseled by his friends at court.

A year earlier, Itō had already expressed his desire to resign to Hijikata Hisamoto, Imperial Household minister. Tanaka Kōken, the vice minister of the Imperial Household and Yamagata's ally at the court, was able to discover and report this, although Itō had warned Hijikata against disclosing it. This whole incident illustrates the way in which Itō and Yamagata worked closely with their own allies in court circles; each had an intelligence agent at court. Tanaka, in a letter to Yamagata dated November 14, 1895, warned Yamagata against assuming office at this time. Itō's long and triumphant tenure as premier, he claimed, would make any succeeding Cabinet suffer by comparison. "In my opinion," cautioned Tanaka, "since at present the questions of the Liaotung Retrocession and Formosa are settled and things in Korea are calm, there would be little to gain in becoming Itō's successor. By all means persuade Matsukata to take office and postpone assuming office until a time when the nation is confronted by perilous problems." [55]

Yamagata, joined by the other elder statesmen, persuaded Matsukata to accept the premiership. As in earlier Cabinets, Yamagata was able to exert his influence through those he nominated for Cabinet posts. When the Cabinet was being formed, Yamagata recommended Nomura Yasushi, Kiyoura Keigo, and General Katsura Tarō for Cabinet posts. Katsura, at the time serving as the governor-general of Formosa, was acceptable to Matsukata, and Yamagata was entrusted with the task of encouraging him to accept the position of army minister. For his part, Yamagata was anxious to have Katsura included in the Cabinet to make sure a non-party person would guard the authority of the army in carrying out the government's policy. Nevertheless, he had reservations about the Cabinet, because Matsukata had allied himself with Ōkuma and the Shimpotō in forming the new Cabinet.

Kiyoura and Nomura joined the Cabinet, as justice and communications ministers respectively, and Katsura was finally persuaded to head the army ministry. Yamagata reported his success in a letter to Matsukata. He revealed that he had instructed Katsura that the army's basic plan should, in time, be realized, but in view of the difficult financial situation following the war boom modifications would be necessary. "Regarding the objective of expanding the army," he wrote, "the economic situation requires some reduction in expenditures, necessitating a difficult job of readjusting the nation's plan." [56] Yamagata felt Katsura was well qualified to handle the difficult work.

After Katsura's acceptance, however, a situation arose which forced Matsukata to reverse himself. General Takashima, the last colonial minister and a senior Satsuma general often at odds with Yamagata, demanded representation in the Cabinet. For over a month a tug of war was waged. Finally Matsukata felt obliged to appoint Takashima as war minister. Angered by this turn of affairs, Yamagata's support of the Matsukata–Ōkuma Cabinet became half-hearted.

The Matsukata Cabinet alliance with Ōkuma's party did not last long. Its failure was caused by the increasing demands of the Shimpotō. The

55. Reprinted in *ibid.*, III, 287.
56. Letter, dated Sept. 14, 1896, printed in *ibid.*, III, 290.

Shimpotō, as the Jiyūtō before it, had entered into an alliance with the oligarchs partially to form a wedge in the solid front of the bureaucracy, but the latter had refused to relinquish any significant amount of authority. After the fall of the Matsukata Cabinet, Itō, who again assumed the premiership, endeavored to ally himself first with the Shimpotō and then with the Jiyūtō. The parties' price for cooperation was control over the home ministry. Itō refused.

In May 1898, Itō faced the twelfth Diet with a plan for an increase in the land tax. Meeting solid and united resistance, he dissolved the Diet twenty-two days after it opened. This action afforded the antigovernment parties a common issue which led to a union of the Shimpotō and Jiyūtō on June 22. The new enlarged party was named the Kenseitō (Constitutional party), and its announced objectives were the protection of the constitution and the establishment of party government.[57]

The Challenge of a United Opposition

The formation of a single, large, opposition party presented the government with a serious challenge. For Yamagata it was a two-fold challenge: first, there was the new strength of the parties' opposition to the government resulting from their unification; and, second, there was a challenge from another direction—Itō's proposal that he form a government party. "Although there are several courses which can be followed in our present difficulty," Itō maintained, "it is certain that some policy must be decided upon before the opportunity passes. Thus the immediate task is to organize a new party in order to meet and solve our most pressing problems."[58] Inoue favored Itō's plan and, establishing an organizational headquarters at his residence, proceeded to build up financial support. Prominent industrialists freely contributed money to this enterprise.[59]

Yamagata first heard of these plans on June 12 and discussed the matter with Inoue and Yoshikawa the next day. On June 18, he wrote Matsukata about it:

> With the Shimpotō and Jiyūtō uniting to attack the government, unless we form an opposing party we will, in the end, be unable to continue the aims of the Restoration and preserve our national policy. So we have arrived at a point where the most urgent task

57. Shinobu, *Meiji seiji shi*, pp. 101–102.
58. Quoted in *Yamagata den*, III, 307.
59. Shinobu, *Meiji seiji shi*, p. 103.

of the cabinet is the need to form a Loyalist Party (*kinnōtō*) . . .
However, in forming such a Loyalist Party the following problems
must be solved.

(1) How would the Loyalist Party vary in principle from the
People's Parties (*mintō*)?

(2) Would cabinets be formed outside of the party or be organized
by it?

Unless we define our attitude toward such a party, it will lack principle and a solid membership. The only difference between the
kinnōtō and the *mintō* would be in the rejection of party cabinets;
aside from that there would be no distinction. If one views the future in the light of the present situation, the formation of a party
cabinet may some day be unavoidable, but, of course, this cannot be
approved in the light of the history of the Meiji government and
the spirit of the constitution. If a party cabinet is organized, unquestionably our nation would suffer the same fate as Spain and Greece.
If the *kinnōtō* is formed it must be led by someone outside of the
government. If someone within the government becomes its leader,
he should resign and accomplish the work in a non-official capacity
in cooperation with the government.[60]

This is a clear exposition of Yamagata's attitude on the problem of
forming a party. He staunchly held to the belief that a party should
support a government Cabinet, not replace it. For this reason he had
always rejected the principles advocated by the opposition parties which,
he felt, were aimed at defeating, not supporting, the government which
ruled at the pleasure of the emperor. For the same reason he had given
encouragement to the Taiseikai, the first pro-government political faction, and the Kokumin Kyōkai which he guided both openly and privately.[61] He was not opposed to the formation of popular parties, but
he disapproved of the British system — two opposing parties, one of
which would bear the responsibility of running the government. He advocated instead a triangle of three parties (*sambun teiritsu*) supporting
the bureaucratic government, with each party given certain rights and
privileges to suggest, criticize, and advise. He was strongly opposed to
opportunistic groups forming parties, without any clearly defined principles, in order to gain advantages through the temporary use of political
power. The crux of the problem, however, was that there should be a
clear distinction between the government ruling on behalf of the em-

60. Excerpts from the letter are printed in *Yamagata den*, III, 309–310. A copy of
the whole letter is in my possession.
61. *Ibid.*, III, 320.

peror and the parties owing loyalty to their own objectives. A Cabinet member should be responsible solely to the emperor whom he served as an adviser. It would be a violation of the constitution, he argued, if ministers were to be responsible to the Diet or to a party.

Itō's proposal sharply divided the government leaders. Kaneko Kentarō, agricultural minister, and even Kuroda, president of the Privy Council, joined Inoue in supporting the idea. On the other side, Shinagawa whose Kokumin Kyōkai hinged its activities on a nonparty Cabinet platform, opposed the project. Katsura, Saigō, and Yoshikawa, all members of Itō's Cabinet, disagreed with the prime minister. Aoki Shūzō, supporting Yamagata's stand, wrote to him, "Of course I believe this matter will soon pass over; it is no more than a childish rash action. I earnestly hope that for the sake of the nation you will take precautions to see that the Emperor's prerogatives are preserved and basic principles are maintained." [62]

On June 24, two days after the popular parties had joined to form the Kenseitō, the elder statesmen solemnly met to consider the government's policy. Itō had already received informal imperial consent for his project of forming a party, but early efforts to organize support had met with indifferent success. Furthermore, when he had announced his plans to the Cabinet on June 19, he had met resistance. With the formation of the Kenseitō, Itō was determined to carry out his plan and sought the counsel of the other oligarchs. Attending this meeting were Inoue, Kuroda, Ōyama, Saigō, Itō, and Yamagata. Itō opened the discussion on the question of a Cabinet member forming a party. In this discussion, as reconstructed by one historian, Yamagata was the first to reply and challenged Itō in the following exchange.

> Yamagata: No one opposes parties in a parliamentary system, but it is improper for a prime minister in office to organize his friends into a party. Beyond that, it is a poor policy because it accentuates the struggle between officials and the people. As a principle, the government must be impartial toward all parties. If the followers of the prime minister are to constitute a government party, a fair and just attitude cannot be maintained. Therefore, from the standpoint of reason or political policy, it is inadvisable for the prime minister himself to organize a political party.
>
> Itō: If it is improper to organize a party while in office, I resign the premiership without hesitation.
>
> Yamagata: Even if you left your post to form a party, I could not

62. Reprinted in *ibid.*, III, 314.

remain silent. You are a *genrō* (elder statesman). *Genrō* always bear the responsibility of passing judgment on the gravest issues confronting the nation. If a *genrō* becomes the leader of a party he loses his independent position.

Itō: If you absolutely oppose my forming a party either while I am prime minister or after resigning, then I have no alternative to withdrawing from my position as a state official and giving up my rank and organizing a party as merely citizen Itō Hirobumi. And as a member of the opposition it will not be necessary to reckon with the meeting of the *genrō*.

Yamagata: If you organize a political party, it will probably mark the beginning of party cabinets. Isn't the system of party cabinets opposed to our national policy, the spirit of the Imperially bestowed constitution and a descent to democratic politics? Why do you associate yourself with such people and plan such eccentric projects?

Itō: This discussion of the pros and cons of party cabinets is really an inconsequential issue. We must concern ourselves with the progress of the nation. You and I differ basically on our views toward constitutional government. There is nothing more to be said. I am only attempting to follow the course which, on the basis of my convictions, will best serve the country.[63]

After this sharp exchange, Itō declared he had already decided to resign his position and suggested that one of the other elder statesmen organize a new Cabinet. "Why don't you bear the responsibility?"[64] he asked Yamagata, but the latter replied that he was not prepared. Similarly, the others present refused to accept the task of forming a new government. Itō then declared that he was nominating the leaders of the Kenseitō, Ōkuma and Itagaki, to form the next Cabinet. The meeting abruptly ended; Itō returned to his official residence, wrote out his resignation, and asked to be stripped of his rank. In an accompanying note he submitted the names of Ōkuma and Itagaki as his successors.

Called before the emperor the next day, none of the *genrō* voiced any objection to Itō's nominations. They were unable to block Itō's maneuver for the simple reason that they were not prepared to shoulder the burden of leading the government against the united forces of the opposition. Yamagata was bitterly aware of his predicament. It was now unavoidable that the parties should form a Cabinet, but he was in no way surrendering his stand. In a letter to a friend two days after this *genrō* meeting, he

63. This is Shinobu's reconstruction of the conversation, *Meiji seiji shi*, pp. 109–110.
64. *Ibid.*, p. 110. For this meeting also see Komatsu Midori, *Itō Hirobumi den* (Tokyo, 1940), III, 377–380.

revealed his feelings. "Our political life has undergone a radical change. It is pointless to trouble you with the details of the nature of this change which has caused the downfall of the Meiji government. It is useless for a general of a defeated army to talk about his troops. I believe retirement is the only course open to me." [65] These words, however, were prompted more by momentary despair than by any firm resolution to surrender in the struggle to contain the influence of the political parties.

Yamagata's attitude was reflected in the increasing anti-Itō sentiment within the bureaucracy. In the view of most of the bureaucrats, Yamagata's position promised to keep their forces solidified, while Itō's moves threatened to destroy the unity of the civil and military bureaucracy in the face of party pressure. Indeed, this incident marked more than an important point in the divergence of Itō and Yamagata. For, although Itō's efforts to form a party were not realized for another two years, his resignation and the offer to forfeit his rank gave the party movement an impetus which tended more and more to divide the military bureaucrats from the civil bureaucrats. The old government-party rivalry gradually changed its form. A section of the bureaucracy, followers of Itō, now stood side by side with the parties. However, the section of the civil bureaucracy remaining loyal to Yamagata's leadership, the military bureaucracy, and his personal supporters in both houses were angered by Itō's plan and its divisive effect.

Outmaneuvered on the question of forming a party Cabinet, Yamagata took steps to retain what influence he could and, in particular, to preserve the independent position of the military ministers. On June 27, he wrote a note to Tanaka Kōken, who in February 1898 had been promoted to minister of the Imperial Household: "When the Emperor orders Itagaki and Ōkuma to form the next cabinet, the order must ask them to select cabinet ministers with the exception of the army and navy ministers." [66] Yamagata insisted that the army and navy ministers, to preserve their authority, should be completely disassociated from the party.

On June 30, Ōkuma and Itagaki formed their Cabinet, but the army and navy ministers of the outgoing Itō Cabinet were given special imperial orders to continue to serve. When Katsura received his separate or-

65. Reprinted in *Yamagata den*, III, 319. Hattori Shisō has suggested that the date of the letter, July 26, given in *Yamagata den*, is an error. Logic would seem to be on his side; it probably should be June 26, and Yamagata probably spoke to Tanaka Kōken because the letter addressed to Tanaka on June 27 refers to "yesterday's conversation" (see next footnote). See Hattori Shisō, *Meiji no seijikatachi* (Tokyo, 1950, 1954), II, 28–29.
66. Reprinted in *Yamagata den*, III, 328.

ders, he sought an interview with Ōkuma and Itagaki with the object of determining beforehand their attitude toward the projected military plans. Speaking for Saigō, the navy minister, and himself, Katsura said at this interview, "If we disagree with the policy of the new cabinet we would be unable to discharge our responsibility to the Emperor. The principle followed by Count Ōkuma is to reduce armaments. What policy does the Count intend to follow as prime minister of the new cabinet? As we enter the cabinet under special considerations, it is necessary to make some decision on this matter beforehand." [67] Following this statement, Ōkuma and Katsura had a significant exchange.

> Ōkuma: In regard to the defense establishment, the necessary projects must of course be continued.
> Katsura: In that case the new cabinet will not follow a policy of reducing military preparedness? You have resolved to provide the essential things?
> Ōkuma: Yes.
> Katsura: The post-war plans have not yet been completed as, for example, the Hokkaido coastal defense. Again, will you agree to supplement the shortage of funds for the post-war projects?
> Ōkuma: Yes.
> Katsura: In that case we will be able to remain in our present posts.

This important condition which the military was able to place on its participation tied the hands of the Kenseitō. Yamagata's request to have separate orders issued had been fulfilled, and the military was assured of support for its expansion program. The practice of the service ministers entering the Cabinets under special privileges developed from this time. In due course, as we shall see, Yamagata was to issue orders which made sure that even if it was not possible to prevent the formation of party Cabinets the independent authority of the military forces would still be preserved.

During the Ōkuma–Itagaki administration, Yamagata remained at his Kyoto villa to watch the political scene. But his quiet observation was short-lived. Internal dissension within the new party Cabinet was present from the outset as the two factions of the new single party competed for advantages. The unauthorized return of Hoshi Toru from his ambassadorial post in Washington for fear of being excluded from the political spoils added a major problem. Moreover, the already unsettled situation

67. This conversation is quoted in *ibid.*, III, 324–325.

was stirred into a turmoil by the innocent use of the word "republic" in a speech by the education minister Ozaki Yukio. These events combined to split the government and cause the Cabinet to collapse.

Such inept direction of the nation's affairs, along with the serious disunity of the government, only confirmed Yamagata in his expectations. But Katsura, Yamagata's voice in the Cabinet and increasingly the strong personality giving shape as well as force to the clique's position, did much to foster the conditions which resulted in the party failure. In reality, the Cabinet represented three distinct forces: one, the old Jiyūtō members; another, the old Shimpotō members (both now formally joined together in the Kenseitō but actually preserving their former identities); and the third, the service ministers, who were, in effect, the voice of the old line bureaucracy. Ozaki's speech opened a breach into which the bureaucratic conservatives rushed their forces. Katsura, from within the Cabinet, fostered an atmosphere which was calculated to cut short the party Cabinet's tenure. The effort of the parties to assume high administrative positions alarmed the bureaucrats and came under severe attack, especially among prominent members of the House of Peers who at one point planned for the impeachment of the Cabinet. Outside of the government the newspapers and publications favorably disposed to the oligarchs launched violent attacks on the party Cabinet.[68] Although the Kenseitō party collapsed primarily because of party factionalism, the pressure of the service ministers and, behind them, that of the bureaucracy contributed to the dissension and aggravated the disunity. A prominent party member singled out Katsura's intrigues as a major cause of the early collapse of the Cabinet:

> As a member of the *hambatsu* (oligarchy) he lost no opportunity to work behind the scenes to bring about the fall of the Ōkuma–Itagaki cabinet after it was established . . . I long ago perceived that he was not merely a soldier . . . He was without doubt scheming for the *hambatsu* . . . When the balance of power argument occurred within the Kenseitō and the struggle between the two factions became intense, he would adopt a fair, impartial attitude in public but in private he would act in concert with the *genrō* outside of the cabinet and continually attempt behind-the-scenes maneuvers. His plan was to organize the next cabinet during the disturbance over the split in the Kenseitō, and in this he was conspicuously successful.

68. One Tokyo newspaper, the *Keika Nippō,* was reportedly subsidized by Yamagata. *Japan Weekly Mail,* Nov. 12, 1898, p. 404.

As they were able to snatch political power out of the hands of the detested Kenseitō, you can imagine their elation.[69]

Katsura's scheming took into account the fact that Itō was absent in China. With the exception of Itō, the oligarchs all seemed involved in applying pressure to cause the downfall of the Cabinet. Katsura kept Yamagata informed of the situation in Tokyo, arrogating to himself the role of political strategist. In a reply to one of Katsura's letters, Yamagata wrote that the Ozaki Yukio affair would lead to a very grave situation.[70] On October 23, Katsura wrote Yamagata that he had been told confidentially that the emperor had ordered the prime minister to drop the education minister for his indiscretion. "It is difficult to say," he observed, "whether this affair will stop Ozaki or whether it will act like a fuse which will in the end destroy the whole cabinet. There will probably be arguments between both factions over his successor, but it is difficult to calculate whether it will end in an orderly adjustment." [71] He went on to report that he was keeping Ōyama and Matsukata informed of all developments, intimating that he thought the Cabinet might fall momentarily. His message ended with a sweeping attack on the Cabinet. "While we face today serious internal and external problems, this government spends its time in keeping the party power balanced and hunting for official positions . . . There is no hope that it will have a good policy for our internal and external problems. Indeed, the sooner it is ended the happier it will be for the empire." [72]

Outside of the Cabinet the pressures exerted by Yamagata's allies in the House of Peers also helped to shorten the life of the first party Cabinet. Through the vigorous activity of two of his closest followers, Yamagata's influence was solidly implanted in the major factions of the Upper House. Kiyoura Keigo, appointed to the House of Peers in 1891, was the leader of the largest faction, the Kenkyūkai (Study Group). Hirata Tōsuke, who became a peer in 1890, formed the Chawakai (Tea Conversation Group) in 1892. The latter, in turn, was affiliated with a group of independent members in a social club, the Saiwai Kurabu (Happiness Club). The members of these groups tended to reflect the attitude of

69. These were the words of Kōnō Hironaka, a Kenseitō stalwart. Quoted in Ōtsu, *DNKS*, V, 2.

70. Letter from Yamagata to Katsura dated Oct. 19, 1898; the original is in the Katsura Tarō monjo (Papers of Katsura Tarō), in the National Diet Library. A postscript to this letter reveals that Hayashi Yūzo, communications minister of the Kenseitō Cabinet, traveled to Kyoto to discuss with Yamagata the issues before the Cabinet.

71. Reprinted in *Yamagata den*, III, 331–332.

72. *Ibid.*, III, 332.

the most conservative bureaucrats and acknowledge the leadership of Yamagata.[73] These conservatives were shocked by the indiscretion of the education minister, alarmed at the infiltration of party men into high official posts, and opposed to the idea of a party Cabinet. Publicly and privately they made representations against the party Cabinet.

In the face of these multiple pressures and as a result of the inability of the major groups within the Kenseitō to resolve their differences, the Cabinet was unable to function effectively. On October 29, Itagaki submitted his resignation, and two days later the Cabinet fell. In the wake of the failure of the first tentative experiment in party government, the two factions of the Kenseitō gave up all pretense of unity and reverted to their separate organizations. The old Shimpotō took the name Kenseihontō (Real Constitutional party), while the old Jiyūtō retained the name Kenseitō.

At eleven o'clock on the night of November 1, 1898, Yamagata arrived at the Shimbashi station in Tokyo in response to an urgent message from the court. From there he proceeded directly to the official residence of the army minister. During a conversation which lasted several hours, Katsura informed him in detail of the events leading to the resignation of the party Cabinet. He also learned that Katsura, anxious to avoid another party Cabinet and fearful that Itō upon his return from China would encourage the continuance of Ōkuma in office, had taken actions to have Yamagata assume office. The *genrō* then in Tokyo, Ōyama, Kurada, and Matsukata, with whom Katsura had been in close touch during the four months of the party Cabinet, had unanimously agreed that Yamagata should be the next prime minister. Inoue, who was then in the Kansai area, also gave his support. Only Itō, then in Shanghai, was not consulted, and Katsura urged that the Cabinet should be formed as quickly as possible for the nation's welfare and that a possible split among the *genrō* should be avoided.[74]

Katsura has left an account of the opinions he expressed to Yamagata on this occasion. The ideas he outlined were important because they became something of a blueprint for Yamagata's future actions. In extolling the idea of a Cabinet placed beyond the reach of the parties, he showed how he thought that end was attainable through an expedient alliance with one of the parties. He believed that Itagaki and the Kenseitō could be enticed into an agreement and be used as an instrument of

73. The factions in the House of Peers are discussed by Shinobu Seisaburō in *Taishō seiji shi* (Tokyo, 1951–1954), IV, 1028–1031. (Hereafter cited as *Taishō shi*.)
74. Ōtsu, *DNKS*, V. 7–8.

government policy. It is difficult to determine whether Katsura was solely responsible for formulating this plan. In some measure it reflected the growing opinion among the bureaucratic leaders, both civil and military, and among the oligarchs, with the conspicuous exception of Itō, that granting responsibility to the parties was mere folly. In a real sense, however, he was the new strategist suggesting a plan of action which the weight and influence of an older statesman could carry through. In the political war, Katsura was becoming General Yamagata's chief of staff. He had already shown talent, free of scruples and restraint, in out-maneuvering the parties. In this conversation he allegedly expressed his views as follows:

> The next cabinet must adopt a firm policy toward the leading political party. If the party persists in its opposition, forcing the dissolution of the Diet several times in succession and even the suspension of the constitution, it would be a serious disservice to the nation to allow reckless and irresponsible conduct to continue. This must be the firm resolution of future cabinets. In the past, cabinets have vacillated because of the Diet and in the end a large united party has formed to organize a cabinet based on the popular parties. With the fall of the cabinet the most urgent need is for someone outside of the parties to form a cabinet. Thus the best plan for the government is to move ahead forthrightly while there is a definite split between the Kenseitō and the Kenseihontō, which were united but now stare at each other jealously.[75]

Katsura advocated what he called a "policy of assaulting the center" (*chūō tokkan no saku*), driving a wedge between the parties and keeping them apart; then one group, he argued, would go along with the government. In principle, Katsura favored the policy of aloofness (*chōzen shugi*) toward the parties, but he suggested it would be foolish to lose an opportunity to gain the support of a party or a large group in the Diet where the majority vote was crucial.[76]

Katsura discussed the need for an increase in taxes to enable the nation to complete its defense program. It should be an increase in the land tax, and not, as Ōkuma had proposed, an increase in the tariff. He predicted that this would present real difficulties, particularly with those Diet members representing agricultural interests. For this reason, he proposed joining hands with the Kenseitō, which represented largely

75. Reprinted in Tokutomi Iichirō, *Kōshaku Katsura Tarō den* (Tokyo, 1917), I, 838–839. This source gives a detailed account of Katsura's activities on this occasion. (Hereafter cited as *Katsura den.*)

76. Shinobu, *Meiji seiji shi*, p. 118.

agricultural interests. In addition, this group, he pointed out, was the same group with which Yamagata had successfully made an agreement during the first Diet in 1890. A secret agreement which promised some concessions could, he was inclined to believe, be worked out with Itagaki.[77]

Although there is no record of Yamagata's words during this meeting, Katsura has made it clear that Yamagata was prepared to assume the responsibility of forming a government. After four hours of conversation, Yamagata finally left Katsura's residence at three o'clock in the morning and proceeded to his own Tokyo home.

The *genrō* who were present in Tokyo met and formally recommended Yamagata as the next premier and on November 5, 1898, Yamagata was asked to form his second Cabinet. For the first time in Meiji history, Itō was not consulted on the appointment of a prime minister. When his Cabinet resigned, Ōkuma had cabled Itō to return immediately. Responding to this urgent request, Itō hurriedly left China but he was too late, for his ship arrived in Nagasaki on November 7, two days after Yamagata had received imperial orders to form a new Cabinet. Indignant that the selection of the new Cabinet was made before his arrival, he changed his plans and delayed his return to the capital.[78]

Yamagata's Second Government

Yamagata was always inclined to conceive of political life in the framework of military operations. One can imagine how he might have viewed the problems of political leadership: the "line of sovereignty" to be protected at all costs was the imperial institution, and the oligarchs were members of a supreme headquarters responsible for the strategy for defending the inner citadel. The civil and military bureaucracies, with top military personnel and the highest-ranking civil servants comprising an elite corps, constituted the major defensive forces to be maneuvered. The Privy Council, the House of Peers, certain groups within the House of Representatives, and other units might represent the "line of advantage," with permanent alliances formed with factions within each of these bodies sympathetic to his concept of government to bolster this protective zone. In this scheme, of course, the enemy was represented by the popular political parties and groups within the civil population questioning the legitimacy of the existing order and demanding greater political freedoms. Compromises with the opposition forces concentrated in the House of

77. Tokutomi, *Katsura den*, I, 841–842.
78. Idditti, *The Life of Ōkuma*, p. 322.

Representatives were an acceptable and sometimes necessary tactical move to gain limited objectives.

Within this framework, Itō's suggestion that he form a party which could assume the responsibility for government policy and the tenure of the Ōkuma–Itagaki Cabinet represented a penetration of the defensive system. The military, however, had remained unaffected by the party incursion and indeed became the lever for asserting the bureaucracy's power in the party Cabinet. Yamagata now felt responsible for reorganizing the breached defenses of the bureaucracy. As the elder statesman richest in the number of supporters of high standing, Yamagata embarked on a concerted effort to reassert the bureaucracy's full authority.

In January 1898, the Board of Marshals and Admirals had been established as part of the military expansion and reorganization program following the Sino-Japanese War. Generals Yamagata and Ōyama and Prince Komatsu Akihito were promoted to the rank of field marshal and Admiral Saigō was given the equivalent naval rank. Under the leadership of Yamagata, this group served as the highest military advisory body of the nation. So it was as field marshal and marquis that Yamagata undertook to form his second Cabinet.

One of the most significant facts in Yamagata's return to office was the increasing importance of General Katsura. Long an associate and trusted follower, Katsura, as we have seen, represented the military wedge in the party Cabinet. The line of action he outlined on the night of November 1 became the basis for action. Yamagata always preferred to work through others; unlike Itō and Ōkuma he never sought public favor personally. With the emergence of his military assistant as an astute political assistant, he increasingly relied upon his suggestions and entrusted him with important assignments. It was undoubtedly Katsura's arguments that persuaded Yamagata that an alliance with a party was necessary in order to weather the voyage through the Diet session. When Itō had followed such a course, Yamagata's followers were alarmed, but now a change had taken place. Persuaded that significantly larger expenditures were required to expand military forces and offset the Russian build-up in East Asia, convinced that larger taxes were the only source available to pay for expansion, and aware that the previous two Cabinets had failed to pass such a measure, Yamagata was persuaded that a departure from his previous practice was justified.

In an interview with the press, Yamagata explained that he felt it his duty to respond to the emperor's request to form a Cabinet after the resignation of the party ministry which, he added, "resulted in many abuses and the obstruction of State business." [79] In this same interview he made clear his unchanging attitude toward party Cabinets and the conditions for cooperating with the Kenseitō: "I do not consider the Cabinets organized on a party basis as consistent with the spirit of a Constitution enacted by the Emperor. Therefore, I did not think of forming a party Cabinet . . . People talk of a union with the Liberals (Kenseitō). If their policy and ours agree we may march in step. But there is no union." [80]

In forming his Cabinet, Yamagata for the most part relied on members of his following and a few senior Satsuma men. This was strikingly different from his first Cabinet which had continued in office many of the previous ministers and made an effort to balance representation between several former han. Now, while Satsuma support was solicited by the inclusion of four from that han in the Cabinet, the majority and more vigorous members were identified less with their area of origin than with Yamagata's own political faction.

All efforts to broaden the membership of the Cabinet did not meet with success. Katsura had suggested that Hoshi Tōru, a prominent member of the Kenseitō, might be persuaded to serve in the Cabinet as a preliminary move toward cooperation with that party, and that Itō Miyoji, a notable bureaucrat primarily associated with Itō Hirobumi's clique, might be brought in. Yamagata entrusted Katsura with the necessary negotiations. Both men, however, refused. The Kenseitō placed conditions on Hoshi's service unacceptable to Yamagata, and Itō Miyoji declined because he could not get Itō's permission while the latter was away. Yamagata's own efforts to persuade Prince Konoe to become minister of education also failed. In the end, the Cabinet was made up entirely of conservative bureaucrats sympathetic to Yamagata's aims. It included three admirals and two generals, and seven of the ten were titled; the Cabinet was thus tagged by the press as the "military bureaucracy cabinet" (*gunjiteki kanryō naikaku*).[81] As he had done when he organized his first Cabinet, Yamagata issued instructions that all discussions were to be kept confidential and the Cabinet was to act in unison.

79. Yamagata's interview with the *Jiji shimpō* translated in *Japan Weekly Mail*, Nov. 19, 1898, p. 500.
80. *Japan Weekly Mail*, Nov. 19, 1898, p. 500.
81. It included: Count Matsukata (finance), Admiral Marquis Saigō (home), Admiral Count Kabayama (education), Viscount Aoki (foreign), Viscount Yoshikawa (communications), Admiral Yamamoto Gombei (navy), General Viscount Katsura (army), Kiyoura (justice), and Sone Arasuke (commerce). In addition to Kiyoura, Katsura, Aoki, and Sone, two other reliable satellites of Yamagata were given important positions: Hirata Tōsuke became director of legislation and Ōura Kanetake, metropolitan police chief.

The most important problem facing Yamagata concerned his relations with the Diet. Unless he could devise some scheme for insuring a majority in the Diet, all urgent business of the nation, dependent upon increased expenditure, would be hampered. He could be reasonably sure of the support of the House of Peers, because of his many followers there. In the House of Representatives, however, aside from the support he could count on because of his influence in the Kokumin Kyōkai, he would have to be prepared for strong opposition.

During the middle of November 1898, special combined army-navy maneuvers were scheduled to be held near Osaka. Yamagata never missed important maneuvers and always accompanied the emperor if the latter were attending. The 1898 maneuvers attracted most of the other Cabinet members. On this occasion, Katsura received imperial permission to invite the leaders of the Diet to witness the event and was able to have Itagaki accorded the privileges of a minister and join the official party. Pleased by this honor, many of the party leaders journeyed to the Kansai for the event, and Itagaki received Katsura's special attention during the actual maneuvers.[82]

There was a purpose in these plans. They led to a significant meeting between Itagaki and Yamagata at which issues facing the Cabinet were discussed. On November 16, following the completion of the maneuvers, Yamagata, Saigō, and Katsura met with Itagaki, Hoshi Tōru, and Kataoka Ken'ichi of the Kenseitō. The meeting took place at the residence of Yamagata's friend, Fujita Densaburō, a wealthy industrialist, with whom he often stayed while in Osaka. What transpired at the meeting was recorded in Katsura's notes.

Yamagata's main intention was to convince the party men of the need for a fiscal policy which would enable the government to complete the armament program originally undertaken after the Sino-Japanese War. His suggested solution was a more equitable land evaluation followed by an increase in land taxes as well as other miscellaneous taxes. There was surprising agreement on these points and, indeed, on most of the others. In fact, on only one question was agreement absent. Yamagata rejected any suggestion that party members be included in administrative offices, including Cabinet posts. "In general," concluded Katsura, "although this evening's meeting adjourned without reaching any specific conclusions, it greatly increased the friendly feeling of the Kenseitō." [83] The meeting represented one more step in the courtship leading to a formal marriage.

82. Tokutomi, *Katsura den*, I, 854.
83. Reprinted in *ibid.*, I, 855.

Upon returning to Tokyo, Itagaki visited Katsura and expressed the desire of the Kenseitō to help the government and repeated the hope that an agreement would provide Cabinet positions for some party members. After being told that it would not be possible to reorganize a Cabinet which had so recently been formed, he reiterated that the times required completion of the government's plans and the party was anxious to co-operate. Nevertheless, in a meeting of all the party's Diet members on November 24, a decision was made to take a stand against the Cabinet because of its policy of exclusion. That evening a delegation called on Yamagata to disclose the decision and once again requested the entry of party men into the Cabinet. Yamagata refused to give any ground and turned the conversation to the subject of the problems facing the nation. After persuading them of the seriousness of the situation, he expressed his hope that an agreement could be worked out. The party delegation left the prime minister's residence but hurriedly returned later that night. This time they brought a proposal that the Cabinet ministers, with the exception of those who were prohibited by law from doing so, become members of the Kenseitō party. Yamagata firmly rejected this suggestion.

While adamant on the question of party members in the Cabinet, Yamagata realized that the cooperation of the Kenseitō had a price. He agreed to declare that his aim was not to pursue a policy totally unaffected by the party. The rather surprising extent of his ultimate concessions was made public on November 29, when the government announced its alliance with the Kenseitō and the three conditions it agreed to meet. First, the Cabinet would publicly announce that it would work in coalition with the Kenseitō in the Diet. Second, in fulfillment of the alliance, the government agreed to follow the basic platform of the Kenseitō, including nationalization of the railways and extension of the franchise. Third, the alliance was accepted as a permanent arrangement in which both sought the same ends and the Kenseitō would be accorded every advantage.[84]

In announcing its alliance with the Yamagata government, the Kenseitō declared, "As the present cabinet has declared its willingness to adopt our policy and support our party we will unite with it to seek passage of important bills and endeavor to fulfill constitutional practices."[85] This, translated into political facts, meant support for Yamagata's plan to increase the taxes to meet the enlarged budget. In order to be assured of this, Yamagata was prepared to make concessions which would not en-

84. Ōtsu, *DNKS*, V, 14–15.
85. *Ibid.*, V, 15.

danger his concept of government. Yet despite the declaration that the government would not be an independent Cabinet, there was a clear division between the government and the party. It was strictly a marriage of convenience, not a love match. Both parties to the agreement were determined to gain maximum advantages. Yamagata was fully aware of the dangers of party infiltration through his defensive system. While he was prepared to counter these dangers, he was at first determined to keep the alliance intact to support his legislation.

To strengthen the new-born alliance Yamagata departed radically from his usual practice and invited members of the Kenseitō for tea at his residence. He explained to the gathering that he was merely a soldier who, having been entrusted with the grave responsibility of leading the government, could not shirk his duty. He pleaded for cooperation in carrying out the government's policy in order that the nation might be able to "preserve its rights and advantages among the powers and not lag behind in general progress." [86] At the same time he assured his conservative allies both in the Diet and in public life that he had not, like Itō, changed his political position.

A few days later, members of the Kokumin Kyōkai and a group of industrialists were also invited to his official residence. In his talk to these conservatives he sought their confidence in and understanding of his alliance with the party. He is reported to have congratulated them for their "strict regard for the national duties, their principle object being to strengthen the Imperial prerogatives. They early advocated the urgency of the preparations to complete the national defense, and have taken the lead in supporting every important national work." [87] He expressed his full agreement with their aims and solicited their continued support.

Yamagata was uneasy on these social occasions. It was not the way in which he preferred to operate, although he entertained several more groups during the same week. But he seemed prepared to accept these inconveniences in order to move ahead. Previous Cabinets had failed in large measure because of their failure to meet the financial problems of the nation; so Cabinet tenure called for a political alliance which would assure passage of a tax increase. Yamagata appeared ready to secure such an alliance by any means, however personally repugnant.

Unlike his maneuvers during the first Diet, Yamagata was now seeking the active cooperation of a party rather than attempting to separate a faction of a party and gain its support. Both approaches, however, were

86. Quoted from a speech reprinted in *Yamagata den*, III, 356.
87. *The Kobe Chronicle*, Dec. 3, 1898, p. 475.

undertaken in large measure because of the pressure of external affairs. In the first instance, fear of failure in the eyes of the outside world had forced a compromise solution. Now, in 1898, it was being forced by external pressure of a slightly different sort — the demand that a military and economic level be achieved which would enable Japan to fill its newly acquired position in the world. It will be recalled that at the outset of the first Diet Yamagata had formulated his concept of the "line of advantage" beyond the "line of sovereignty." After the Sino-Japanese War he had advocated rapid expansion of the military power of the nation to defend the "line of advantage" which, as a result of victory, cut across the middle of Korea. In his speech at the reception for the party members, he again referred to Japan's rights and advantages which she must be prepared to defend. There is a clear continuity in his thought and his approach. Certain political concepts he held sacrosanct; nevertheless he was prepared to compromise to achieve the unity of action without which the "line of advantage" would lose its advantage. What he held to was the belief in the superior position of officialdom. But it was a conviction which had been modified to the point where he urged joint action with one of the enemy forces (Kenseitō) rather than splintering off one of its components. From this point of view the "policy of assaulting the center" was carried out by "capturing" one of the opposition forces, thereby weakening the total strength of the enemy by preventing its consolidation.

On December 8, 1898, Yamagata faced the Diet for his opening policy address, as he had done nine years before. Profound changes had occurred during those intervening years, but the main point of his speech in 1898 and that of this speech were strikingly similar. Both addresses were directed at justifying the need for increased expenditures for the nation's defense. "I have inherited the policy of the preceding cabinets," he now declared, "which was the program, inaugurated by the ninth Diet [1895], aimed at accomplishing the national defenses necessary for our security and the accompanying enterprises required for the progress of our country." [88] In order not to halt midway in carrying out this project of military expansion, he warned, we must strengthen the nation's finances. Later in his speech he observed that Japan's foreign relations had improved but that, "if in these days of rapid progress we do not wish to fall behind, we cannot relax for even a day from encouraging education, greater production, communications and trade." [89]

88. The speech is reprinted in *Yamagata den,* III, 358, and translated in full in *Japan Weekly Mail,* Dec. 10, 1898, p. 585.
89. *Yamagata den,* III, 359.

Again, as in 1889, Matsukata, the finance minister, followed him with the budget speech giving a detailed outline of the financial measures proposed by the government. The budget submitted by the government, which totaled 226,340,000 yen, would leave a deficit of 36,600,000 yen over the total income.[90] The large appropriations included the special expenses for organizing an army division in Hokkaido, developing Formosa, and expanding the railroads. One-third of the ordinary and over half of the special expenditures were earmarked for military purposes. In order to meet this deficit, the government submitted proposals for an increase in land taxes and taxes on specific products such as sake.

Yamagata followed the developments in the Diet's budget committee with eagerness. Itō Miyoji, after Itō Hirobumi had assured Yamagata of his support, worked as a liaison man between the government and the Diet. One of his reports to Yamagata, dated December 11, 1898, is of interest not only because it is phrased in military terminology but because it discloses the careful and devious methods being employed by the government to get the budget passed. Even with the Kenseitō alliance and the support of the Kokumin Kyōkai, the government could count on only 116 votes of a total of 300. It was necessary to win the support of the independents who held the balance.

> Matters are proceeding satisfactorily regarding the Diet with those agreeing with us working strenuously; victory is in sight. Until the battle is joined there will be small disturbances. But when our strategy is determined, the plan of the combined army completed, the fifth column (fukuhei) alerted and all preparations well in hand, we will have overpowering strength and await your order to advance. As I mentioned to you the other day, since until then we must have various emergency plans, we must be careful that all orders emanate from one headquarters, lest mistakes result from working at cross purposes along the front line . . . According to one of our spies (teishi shitaru hito), in a secret talk among the leaders of the enemy it was felt that the government will have a slight majority of some seven or eight votes, so they are increasing their efforts. Of course, unless we are assured of victory we will not join battle.[91]

The battle over appropriations was joined and, after a short fight, won; but the plan to increase the government's income met with

90. Ōtsu, DNKS, V, 32.
91. Reprinted in Yamagata den, III, 367.

greater difficulties. The original proposal of the government was to increase the rate of land taxation from 2.5 percent to 4 percent of the evaluation of the land. This proposal caused a wave of opposition. The opposition party in the Diet, the Kenseihontō, mobilized its forces, and all opposition groups joined forces in an Anti-Land Tax Increase League. Led by Ōkuma and a few prominent members of the House of Peers, the league held public meetings and sponsored speeches throughout the country in order to mobilize public opinion against the proposed law. In attempting to counter this effort, the government prohibited public speeches on the subject, ordered the league to disband, and prevented its supporters outside Tokyo from coming to the capital.

To build up parliamentary support, on the other hand, the government resorted to severe methods. First, Hoshi Tōru was treated with special consideration. In meetings with Yamagata another attempt was made to have him enter the Cabinet. While unsuccessful, the effort was not wasted because Hoshi became sympathetic to Yamagata's aims and promised the fullest cooperation in the name of patriotism. Special gatherings were held at hotels in Tokyo for members of the Kenseitō as another means of building up strength for the government. On one such occasion, Yamagata himself gave an emotional talk appealing to the national loyalty of his listeners as a basis for supporting the Cabinet's policy. A third method was less scrupulous. With the collusion of Hoshi Tōru, large funds were liberally distributed to buy supporting votes.[92] It seems probable that Yamagata was able to use funds appropriated for the Imperial Household ministry for this purpose.[93]

The opposition proposed that any tax increase should be limited to commodity taxes, but Yamagata refused. Finally, however, the government compromised and proposed that the tax rate for rural areas be raised only to 3.3 percent, and that the higher rates be limited to a period of five years. In this form the bill was passed with a majority of thirty-seven votes. Added to the tax increases on sake, soya sauce, and other consumer goods, the land tax increase provided sufficient revenue to meet the budgetary deficit.

Passage of these measures was a triumph for Yamagata's government. One writer has concluded that it "was the most successful administra-

92. For a description of Hoshi's activities, see Nomura Hideo, "Gumbatsu Yamagata Aritomo no zaiaku," *Bungei shunjū* 34.2:54–59 (February 1956). See also Miyake Setsurei, *Dōjidai shi* (Tokyo, 1950), III, 169.
93. For this important information, see *Hara nikki*, II, 456. Saionji informed Hara that that was the source of finances.

tion during the troubled domestic situation following the Sino-Japanese War." [94] Success reflected, in part, Yamagata's political leadership and his realistic handling of a difficult situation. But success had required a generous use of bribery and other means to muster a majority vote, detracting from the administration's accomplishments. Success had its price. "The assistance the government received from the Kenseitō," observed Katsura, "was of considerable advantage in the Diet, but, on the other hand, the inconvenience to the government was considerable. For example, in local areas the government could not avoid approving those connections which occurred in two or three cases out of ten between local officials and parties. Nevertheless, to accomplish the nation's plan it was an unavoidable situation and even the stern prime minister Yamagata grimaced and suffered through the ordeal." [95]

Yamagata suffered the ordeal no longer than was necessary. The alliance had justified itself in the passage of important measures in the Diet, but it had not been conceived as more than an expedient union. With budget in hand, Yamagata prepared to launch an offensive calculated to curb the advantages the party had gained through its alliance with the government. During the uneasy alliance with the Kenseitō, Yamagata had been concerned by the continual pressure exerted by the party for official jobs — "job hunting" (ryō kan), as it was popularly called. He had viewed with alarm the tendency to relax the restrictions placed upon qualifications for civil service appointments. During the tenure of the Ōkuma–Itagaki Cabinet even the highest appointments of civil officials had been placed outside the operation of various restrictive civil service regulations. This made him fear the demands which would be made by the Kenseitō after the Diet closed. They were bound to request rewards in the form of offices for their cooperation.

In addition to this fear, Yamagata was disturbed by the renewal of Itō's efforts to organize a political party. In anticipation of increasing pressure by party members to be given high positions in the bureaucracy, Yamagata devised a plan to close the ranks of the civil service to all party members. He formulated regulations which would make it extremely difficult for party politicians to meet the requirements necessary to qualify for the rigid civil service examination. Furthermore, he extended the prerequisite of an examination to include the highest civil service ranks, excluding only the Cabinet ministers. Before issuing these regulations, however, Yamagata maneuvered to have his views sanctioned by the emperor. In

94. Rōyama, Seiji shi, p. 343.
95. Quoted in Tokutomi, Katsura den, I, 865.

a secret message to the emperor on March 25 1899, he argued: "The affairs of state would be handled competently by a politician like Itō, but without Itō's ability I rely on your aid in the conduct of political affairs . . . My interpretation of the constitution differs from that of Itō and Ōkuma. I am absolutely opposed to a party cabinet. My only hope is that Imperial authority will be extended and Imperial prestige will not decline. I hope you approve of these things." [96]

Through the grand chamberlain, Yamagata learned that the emperor had reacted favorably to his message. On March 28, 1899, less than three weeks after the close of the Diet, he had three imperial ordinances issued.[97] These were: the Civil Service Appointment Ordinance (Bunkan ninyō rei), the Civil Service Limitation Ordinance (Bunkan bungen rei), and the Civil Service Discipline Ordinance (Bunkan chōkai rei). The Appointment Ordinance was a revision of an 1893 ordinance and abolished the free appointment of the highest rank of the civil servants by extending the same examination requirements for that rank that already applied to lower ranks. It was so worded that those who had been appointed to this rank during the previous administration could not remain in office because their term had been too short. The Civil Service Limitation Ordinance governed the qualifications for each rank and guaranteed status and security. The third ordinance outlined the regulations governing the discipline and conduct of civil servants and punishment for misconduct.

By requiring difficult examinations for all ranks of the civil service, Yamagata in effect closed the bureaucracy to political party members. Politicians could no longer be appointed to posts in the bureaucracy, with the exception of ministerial posts. They would have to take examinations for which, as a rule, they were not trained. Thus the bureaucracy would be limited to career bureaucrats. In the explanation accompanying the issuance of the ordinances, Yamagata said: "Our country has just entered the period of a constitutional system. Although the people's ideals have not yet developed, the laws are extremely detailed, reducing the arbitrariness of officials. Indeed, administration will gradually become a special skill. Administrative officials can no longer qualify for their duties on the basis of natural talent alone. Since administration requires specialized learning, the appointment of officials must be determined by special

96. Watanabe Ikujirō, *Meiji Tennō to hohitsu no hitobito*, pp. 278–279.
97. The ordinances are summarized in Tanake, *Kindai Nihon kanryō shi*, pp. 276–280, and are discussed by Sterling Tatsuji Takeuchi in "The Japanese Civil Service," in Leonard D. White, ed., *The Civil Service in the Modern State* (Chicago, 1930), pp. 515–555.

training as well as qualifications of loyalty. In the past, progress in administrative work depended upon the individual, now it depends mainly upon learning." [98]

This argument, justifying the ordinances because of the modern development of the administration, did not convince the hopeful members of the Kenseitō. They regarded it as a declaration of war and, indeed, it was an attack which came as a complete surprise. While bureaucrats, including those in Itō's faction, applauded the ordinances as "great measures enriching the nation," [99] there were strong sentiments within the Kenseitō for terminating the alliance with the government. First, however, an effort was made to have the ordinances withdrawn. Party leaders called on Yamagata in an attempt to influence such action. Although he was irritated by the demands of the party leaders, Yamagata nevertheless desired, if possible, to continue the alliance. In a move to appease the party, several officials involved in drafting the ordinances left office, but Yamagata doggedly refused to set aside the ordinances.

That the refusal of the government to compromise did not lead to a termination of the alliance seems strange. Preoccupation with intra-party disturbances is one explanation, but there is another probable reason. The alliance between the Kenseitō and the government had benefited the party in local areas. Elections for local assemblies returned more party members blessed temporarily by the sanction of officialdom. In Tokyo, party people had penetrated deeply into the municipal government, which in time was to be a strong base of party strength. The desire not to deprive itself of these admitted advantages was persuasive in holding the tenuous alliance together.

Broadening the government's support to include the Kenseitō had cut into the pro-government Kokumin Kyōkai, which before this time had enjoyed the advantage exclusively. With the Kokumin Kyōkai reduced in strength and the alliance with Kenseitō showing signs of weakness, Yamagata became interested in reorganizing the group with which he had so long been associated. As an organization it never had the recognized characteristics of a party and was in fact a coterie of conservatives prepared to support Yamagata's views of constitutional government. On July 5, 1899, the Kokumin Kyōkai dissolved itself and was reformed as the Teikokutō (Imperial party). Its platform stated that "the present

---

98. Reprinted in *Yamagata den*, III, 370.
99. In a letter from Kaneko Kentarō to Yamagata dated March 30, 1899, reprinted in *ibid.*, III, 374–375.

cabinet recognizes the same principles as our party" and advocated "alliances with political factions holding to the same political views and actions of our party." [100] While this party never became a powerful force among the parties, it continued to hold a bloc of votes in the House of Representatives for the conservative wing of the government.

Although politically successful, the government was by no means unchallenged or uncriticized. Bribery, misuse of political power, interference in elections, corruption of officials — these were the charges thrown at the government by antigovernment groups, and there seems to have been considerable evidence in support of these accusations.[101] On December 26, the opposition Kenseihontō submitted to the Lower House a bill impeaching the Cabinet.[102] The government's coalition proved capable of turning back this measure, but there was growing dissatisfaction with dishonesty shown in high office and the unashamed corruption of party politicians.

Before the fourteenth Diet ended, Yamagata had fulfilled his pledge to the Kenseitō that the franchise would be extended. A bill was enacted which enlarged the House of Representatives, abolished tax qualification for candidates, reduced the national tax qualification for voting from fifteen to ten yen, reorganized electoral areas, and guaranteed a secret ballot.[103] By means of a larger electorate and larger representation in the Lower House, Yamagata hoped to be able to garner greater popular support for pro-government candidates, thereby increasing the strength of a third party, responsive to the government, which might hold the casting vote on issues before the House of Representatives. These were notable achievements in the political development of Meiji Japan, and for Yamagata these concessions were the price for the alliance he had formed. Yet while these liberal measures were being achieved, he did not neglect to strengthen the foundations of both the civil and military bureaucracy.

As during the previous year, Yamagata waited until the Diet session was completed before adopting measures to offset the Diet's legislation and maintain the balance of power in the hands of the bureaucracy. The

100. Ōtsu, DNKS, V, 63.

101. Ibid., V, 63. Viscount Shinagawa, leader of the Kokumin Kyōkai, told his followers that they had formed out of "the necessity of weaning party politicians from the destructive habits into which they had fallen in the days when personal ambitions, not national interests, were their governing impulses." Japan Weekly Mail, July 5, 1899, p. 32.

102. McLaren, Political History, p. 262.

103. Ibid., p. 261.

most important laws in Meiji Japan were effected not by legislation but by ordinances prepared by the government and promulgated by the emperor. In this way laws were still written, as in traditional Japan, through the edict of the ruler. In the previous spring the civil service ordinances had effectively closed off the bureaucracy to popular party members. In April 1900, Yamagata advanced on another front. He submitted a secret request to the throne asking that the authority of the Privy Council be increased. His request was granted, and the Privy Council was authorized to extend its reviewing power to a wide variety of legislation. For example, all imperial ordinances relating to civil service status and regulations as well as changes in the educational system were to be reviewed by the Privy Council.[104] In this way Yamagata raised the Privy Council from an advisory to a supervisory body. An organ of government established originally to protect and interpret the constitution was, by this measure, made largely independent of any government in office. Furthermore, the conservative character of its membership, reinforced it as a bureaucratic stronghold protecting the government from the parties.

Yamagata was behind still another measure to strengthen the bureaucracy. As a result of his handiwork, Imperial Ordinances No. 193 and No. 194 were issued on May 15, 1900, attracting at that time surprisingly little attention. By these ordinances the regulations of both the army and the navy were revised so that only generals and lieutenant-generals, admirals and vice-admirals on active duty could serve as ministers. The first note to the table of organization attached to this revision read, "Those serving as Army (Navy) Minister and Head of the General Affairs Bureau will be general officers on active duty." [105]

The enactment of these ordinances has been called "a turning point in the development of Japan as a modern state and crucial in her international relations." [106] The significance of this revision was in the introduction of the words "active duty." Early in Meiji history the principle of limiting the service ministers to military men was established. The prac-

---

104. Suzuki Yasuzō, *Nihon seiji no kijun* (Tokyo, 1941), p. 284.

105. *Nihon genkō kitei hyō*, published by Naikaku shōkikanshi kiroku ka (Tokyo, 1906), pp. 134–135. Unaccountably confusion has surrounded the date of this ordinance: E. E. N. Causton, *Militarism and Foreign Policy in Japan* (London, 1936), p. 77, gives the date 1894; Norman in *Japan's Emergence as a Modern State*, p. 193, uses the date 1895, and Sir George Sansom repeats this date in *Japan in World History* (New York, 1951). The date 1898 is used by Kenneth Colegrove in *Militarism in Japan* (Boston, 1936), p. 22.

106. Sansom, *Japan in World History*, p. 86.

tice was written into the regulations in 1873 and again in 1888 when the posts of minister and vice minister of the army were limited to general officers. In the army regulation revisions of 1891 and 1896, however, military qualifications for the position of minister were not mentioned, although the rank qualifications for other posts such as head surgeon were listed. Actually no civilian was ever appointed to serve either as minister or vice minister of the army. Perhaps it was because the likelihood of such an appointment was so remote that no legal prohibitions were placed on a civilian becoming the army minister between 1891 and 1900.[107]

It was Yamagata's fear of the intrusion of the parties into the military bureaucracy which prompted him to place legal restrictions against any possible civilian control of the army and navy. But the qualification of "active duty" now prevented retired generals or those of the first or second reserves, generals such as Soga Yūjun and Tani Kanjō who, as members of the House of Peers, had opposed some of Yamagata's measures, from assuming a ministerial post as a friend or even a member of a party.

Although the importance of this ordinance has been greatly stressed by Western writers, Japanese authors, while not underestimating its influence during later Cabinets, nevertheless treat it as one among a long list of measures which secured for the army a position of independence and power. It is true that it was a measure which strengthened the army's authority, but the army had already achieved a position of unique authority by the establishment in 1878 of a General Staff Headquarters free from political control — a position confirmed by the constitution. Also, the right of direct access to the throne gave the military command immense power if it cared to use it. The army was now further protected from political control and the independence of the supreme command was made complete. These ordinances were to become more significant in the future, but it would be an exaggeration to claim that they mark a major departure or turning point in the relationship of military authority to the government. They could be regarded as such a major step only had they not been added to a series of measures dating back to the early days of Meiji which already assured the military a position of independent power. They were, however, significant in reinforcing that independence and, in a broader sense, in strengthening the bureaucracy against the slow but relentless growth in the power of the popular parties.

107. Matsushita Yoshio and Izu Kunio, *Nihon gunji hattatsu shi*, pp. 144–146, 164–165.

Much of the skill claimed for Yamagata as a political tactician rested upon the instinct he showed for the correct moment to pull one step backward before taking two steps forward. He was careful not to move ahead recklessly when the prospects for advancing were slim. He always prepared his withdrawal even as he calculated his maneuvers. Toyabe Shuntei, the able editor of the magazine *Taiyō*, observed in 1897, "The ups and downs of Inoue, Ōkuma, and Itō are very clear, but that is not the case with Yamagata. As a politician, he was neither a success nor a failure; he had the faculty for appearing and disappearing most skillfully, never being caught holding the bag." [108]

Withdrawal from Office

As early as March 1899, Yamagata had revealed to the emperor his intentions of remaining in office for no more than another year. After the completion of the Diet, he privately expressed his desire to withdraw from office. The Kenseitō was again seeking rewards for its cooperation; new requests were made in the spring for fuller payment for services rendered. Yamagata was still immovable. To the demand that Cabinet ministers be required to join the party, he replied that that was an individual and private matter for each minister to consider but that each was already pledged to serve under the emperor's prerogative.[109] These annoying demands added to his conviction that he should retire from office.

Through Tanaka Kōken, minister of the Imperial Household, Yamagata was informed that this resignation would not be popular with the emperor. Nevertheless, his attitude was firm and on May 25, 1900, less than a week after issuing the ordinances relating to the service ministers, he submitted his resignation. In succession, Yamagata recommended Matsukata, Saigō, and Itō. Each, in turn, declined to serve. On June 1, Tanaka wrote Yamagata that the emperor was still seeking his successor, adding that it would be desirable if he could remain in office until the situation in China (the Boxer Rebellion) was clarified.[110]

At this point, Yamagata made the suggestion that the time had arrived to allow the junior statesmen to shoulder the responsibilities of organizing a government. Invited to Yamagata's residence, Katsura was surprised to be told he was going to be nominated for the highest office.

108. Toyabe Shuntei, "Yamagata Aritomo," in *Shuntei zenshū* (Tokyo, 1909), p. 151.
109. *Yamagata den*, III, 397–398.
110. Letter reprinted in *ibid.*, III, 481.

Katsura hesitated, insisting that frequent changes in Cabinet were not good for the nation — an argument Yamagata had used on previous occasions — and pleaded with Yamagata to continue in office. With the insistent court requests for him to remain in office until the China situation was cleared up and the refusal of his nominees to assume office, Yamagata finally agreed to postpone his resignation.

During most of Yamagata's second ministry, the nation's foreign relations were steady and untroubled. The development and exploitation of Korea continued, and in this work Yamagata, over the objections of Itō and Inoue who feared that it might stimulate Russian acts, vigorously pushed for the construction of the Seoul–Pusan railway.[111] But late in 1899 the alarming growth of the Boxer movement in North China created a major diplomatic problem. Scores of foreign missionaries and hundreds of Chinese converts had been killed by the xenophobic Boxers. The movement posed a threat to the interests of foreigners in China and alarmed the capitals of Europe. The murder of a secretary of the Japanese legation in Peking suddenly placed Japan among the powers eagerly watching the Boxer movement. In Tokyo voices were raised demanding that troops be sent at once to avenge the death of the secretary and protect other Japanese.

Yamagata was cautious in his approach to the emergency. Above all he wished to avoid any complications which might result from precipitate action in a problem which was international in scope. In a letter to Matsukata on June 8, he expressed his position: "The outbreak in North China is far more complicated than it appears; it is complicated by the competitive race among the powers whose policies, geared to their future, aim to realize immediately their own advantages . . . This is not an incident which can be controlled easily by a few troops . . . In this instance our best foreign policy is to adopt a cautious attitude and refrain from sending [troops] ourselves unless the Powers request our assistance." [112]

Three days later Yamagata decided to take some preliminary steps. He summoned Katsura and his foreign minister, Aoki Shūzō, and the three drafted messages to be sent to the major European powers. The purpose

111. Yamagata persistently encouraged that the Seoul-Pusan railway be completed. In November 1899, he wrote Matsukata, his finance minister: "Although I am aware of the present economic and social conditions which render the plan to construct the Seoul-Pusan railway difficult, the future of our national strength is related to this project so I am deeply concerned. Please continue to work towards its realization." *Yamagata den,* III, 391. Financial problems slowed the work and at one point Katsura arranged a special private grant of 50,000 yen for the survey work. *Ibid.,* III, 392.

112. Reprinted in *ibid.,* III, 407–408.

of the messages was to inquire if Japanese troops were needed and to indicate Japan's readiness to cooperate. Yamagata wrote Matsukata on June 12 reiterating that "we have decided absolutely not to dispatch troops on our own";[113] but a few days later the powers agreed, albeit somewhat reluctantly, to call on Japan for military aid, and their call was answered.

Rapidly and efficiently Japanese forces were mobilized. General Terauchi, designated as commander of the Japanese force, proceeded to Tientsin in order to consult with the local military commanders of the foreign powers organizing a joint task force. To the international relief force, finally organized in August 1900 to lift the siege of Peking, the Japanese contributed the largest contingent. During and after the brief but sharp encounter with the Chinese forces before the lifting of the siege in mid-August, the discipline and conduct of the Japanese troops gained the respect of the other foreign troops.

Negotiations for settlement of the controversy arising out of the Boxer Rebellion began in July 1900 at Tientsin, before Peking had been invaded. Some of the foreign powers were inclined toward harsh terms. Japan took a moderate position. Japan acted in concert with the United States and France, fearing that the partition of China would allow Russia great advantages in future relations in the Far East.

Although the Boxer Protocol was not signed until September 7, 1901, by the end of the summer of 1900 the emergency in China had passed and Yamagata again turned to thoughts of resignation. Nothing in internal affairs had occurred to weaken his earlier intention and now the crisis which alone had forced him to defer action was over. On the other hand, developments had taken place which strengthened his resolution to withdraw. For one thing, an abortive action against Amoy in South China by Japanese adventurers aided and abetted by General Kodama, the governor-general of Formosa, was an annoying embarrassment.[114] There is little evidence that Yamagata himself was engaged in this scheme, but his army minister, Katsura, was involved.

But in addition to this event, there was another and more decisive factor hastening his resignation. On September 15, 1900, Itō Hirobumi organized the Rikken Seiyūkai (Constitutional Political Fraternal Asso-

113. Letter appears in *ibid.*, III, 415–416.
114. See Marius B. Jansen, "Opportunists in South China during the Boxer Rebellion," *Pacific Historical Review* 20.3:241–250 (August 1951), and the article by Ian H. Nish. "Japan's Indecision during the Boxer Rebellion," *Journal of Asian Studies* 20.4:449–461 (August 1961).

ciation) with the members of old Kenseitō constituting the majority of the new party. For many months Itō had been planning and talking about the necessity for a new political alignment, and in this activity he had steadily grown apart from the other oligarchs on the question of responsible government. Unquestionably, Yamagata's growing strength as the spokesman and leader of not only the military camp but also the conservative bureaucrats spurred Itō's actions. For their part, party members were quick to see the advantages of submitting to the leadership of one placed by his rank and accomplishments at the heart of the bureaucratic government.

Itō's activities were well known to Yamagata. In a letter of July 1, 1900, Itō wrote, "I am enclosing a draft of the party's policy about which I spoke when you visited yesterday. Please examine it." [115] Although Yamagata did not oppose outright the political policy Itō advocated, nor the organization of a party, he had serious doubts that any large party, such as Itō was organizing, could avoid abusing and misusing its power when it held a majority in the government. Furthermore, he maneuvered to embarrass Itō and his new party by his own resignation.

Itō sensed that Yamagata was going to resign. "I wonder if the prime minister isn't planning to withdraw suddenly," he said to Katsura one day. "If he does it will place me in a difficult position." To this Katsura replied, "Of course, I don't know for certain whether he is going to retire, but he most probably will. If you are concerned about the prime minister's withdrawal, why don't you have a meeting with him and discuss the situation?" [116] Itō was too busy with the final work of organizing the Seiyūkai to have a meeting, but he made it clear that he was going to be in trouble if forced to organize a Cabinet immediately. On June 9, Itō wrote Yamagata, imploring him not to withdraw, warning that he could not accept responsibility for forming a new Cabinet, and pointing out that it would disrupt the newly organized party.[117]

The actual formation of the Seiyūkai created a new political situation. Consequently, upon resigning, Yamagata shifted from Katsura to Itō as his recommended successor. On September 20, he visited Katsura to explain his resignation and his nomination of Itō:

> Since Itō has organized the Seiyūkai and leads this large party, it is only natural that in the future Itō himself should organize the cabi-

115. Reprinted in *Yamagata den*, III, 436.
116. Quoted in *ibid.*, III, 428.
117. See letter in *ibid.*, III, 430.

net and bear responsibility for domestic and foreign affairs. Besides, my ill health, as you know, prompted me to resign prior to the China incident. I remained as a loyal servant only because I felt I could not shun my responsibility during the crisis. But now Peking has been rescued and the mission has been completed. Now is the proper time for me to withdraw. Fortunately, as a successor, Itō, leader of a large party, is ready at hand. This will relieve the nation. What do you think? [118]

To this Katsura could only reply, "This would appear to be instructions rather than a question." [119] With the backing of the other elder statesmen, Yamagata was able to make it difficult for Itō to refuse. For many years after, Itō was deeply resentful of Yamagata's attitude and actions on this occasion. Itō attempted to persuade Prince Saionji Kimmochi, a prominent member of the Seiyūkai to accept the premiership, but the latter insisted that there should be a Seiyūkai Cabinet with its leader as the prime minister. Itō had no alternative, and Yamagata's action thrust political responsibility on the new party before it had an opportunity to muster its full strength.

Thus on October 19, 1900, for the second time, Yamagata officially ended his tenure as prime minister. His ministry had lived for close to two years, seven months longer than his first Cabinet. Weary of governing, tired of the constant discontent expressed by the parties, and irked by the necessity of placating the opposition to get measures passed in the Diet, he withdrew for the last time from service in the Cabinet. He stepped back with relief from the front line of fire and retired to his quiet villa in Kyoto. But as before, retirement to Kyoto did not mean that he was cut off from the political nerve centers of the nation. His followers served as tentacles sensitive to policies of which they believed he would disapprove; they were alerted to warn him and on guard to protect the interests of their faction.

Relations with the Itō Cabinet

Yamagata's life of leisure was interrupted by the financial problems plaguing Itō's administration. Increasing expenditures forced Itō to seek tax increases from the fifteenth Diet. A bill accomplishing this passed the House of Representatives without trouble but ran into serious ob-

---

118. Tokutomi, *Katsura den,* I, 932–933.
119. *Ibid.,* I, 933.

stacles in the House of Peers. Itō, who had served as the first president of the House of Peers, shared a position of influence and power among the peers with Yamagata until he undertook to organize a political party. His party activities, however, alienated many of his aristocratic friends, who joined the staunch antiparty peers to block the tax increase. Frustrated in his plans, Itō suspended the Diet and solicited aid in arriving at a compromise with the stubborn peers.

In a telegram to Yamagata in Kyoto, Itō sought his influence in overcoming the opposition to the government's policy. Clearly Itō suspected Yamagata's hand behind this act. "It is most regrettable," he wrote, "that members of the House of Peers who are your followers are to be counted among those who oppose." [120] It was after three o'clock in the morning on February 26, 1901, when Yamagata received the telegram. Before returning to bed, he wrote a reply assuring Itō of his support. He revealed that he was aware of the problem and added, "although I do not know who the leaders of the opposition are, I am sending a message to Yoshikawa, Kiyoura, and Sone, advising them to work on your behalf." [121]

In the letter of instruction addressed to the above-mentioned three peers, who were his close supporters, Yamagata acknowledged receiving word from the prime minister about the difficult situation that had been created. His message then continued: "Because at the present time we cannot foresee what changes will occur in the Far Eastern situation in the near future, it is, of course, improper to oppose the tax increase in the House of Peers . . . Of course, I don't believe you are opposing this measure, but as it is such an important matter, I cannot sit quietly at the side, so I am sending you my opinion. However, it is your responsibility to take a firm stand in the enforcement of official discipline when the administration and the foundation of the nation are being corrupted." [122]

While admonishing his followers to pass the tax increase, he left them valid grounds for opposing Itō. It was precisely the issue of corruption in government which was the peers' point of attack. In particular, the practices of Hoshi Tōru during the time he served as head of the Tokyo municipal government had been revealed to the public and provided grounds for the accusation of corruption among the politicians. As a prominent Seiyūkai member, Hoshi had been included in Itō's Cabinet as minister of communications. Outraged at Itō for having included

---

120. Reprinted in *Yamagata den,* III, 442.
121. Letter printed in *ibid.,* III, 443.
122. Reprinted in *ibid.,* III, 444.

Hoshi in the Cabinet, the peers heavily attacked Hoshi's dishonesty and were determined to oppose Itō's policy.

Yamagata and other elder statesmen were called to Tokyo from their country estates to help break the impasse. The different factions within the House of Peers often took varying positions, but now they were united in the anti-Hoshi drive, and they were also united in opposing the proposed tax increase. They solidly withstood the arbitration efforts of the elder statesmen, whose efforts in any case seemed to have been only half-hearted. Yamagata favored passage of the tax bill, reiterating his position in a letter to Matsukata on March 1: "As we cannot predict what shifts will occur in the Far East in the near future, the opposition, from that point of view, must be judged irresponsible." [123] Nevertheless, he felt Itō was mishandling the situation and aggravating the opposition. Itō, on the other hand, was apparently convinced that Yamagata's influence with the peers was primarily responsible for his trouble. Undeniably, to the extent that the opposition was based on resentment against the formation of a party Cabinet under a renegade bureaucratic leader, Yamagata's antiparty philosophy played a large part.

In the end, Itō resorted to the intervention of the emperor. As no one dared oppose an imperial decree, the peers were pleased to pass the tax increase. The immediate problem was solved, but disagreement within the Cabinet over other financial problems split the administration and caused Itō to resign early in May 1901.

Following Itō's resignation, the problem of selecting a successor to Itō occupied the minds of the elder statesmen for over a month. In the usual manner, Yamagata first recommended two of the oligarchs, Inoue and Matsukata, but neither was able to form a government. Yamagata wrote Itō that, "If this does not work out [i.e., Matsukata's nomination], I see no other choice than Katsura." [124] To this Itō replied, "Since I have no particular plan, you decide." [125] Katsura was agreed upon and, after he had received Yamagata's pledge of support, he undertook to organize a new Cabinet on June 2, 1901.

Yamagata assisted his protégé in the selection of ministers and was the Cabinet's main support among the elder statesmen. The Cabinet excluded Itō's followers and included the core of Yamagata's clique. Hirata Tōsuke, Yamagata's political chief of staff, became agriculture and commerce minister. There was evidence that the Cabinet was built on that

123. Reprinted in *ibid.*, III, 447.
124. Letter in *ibid.*, III, 465.
125. Itō's letter reprinted in *ibid.*, III, 466.

faction in the House of Peers which had opposed Itō's Seiyūkai. Three prominent members, Yoshikawa, Kiyoura, and Sone, the same three whom Yamagata had jointly addressed in his plea on behalf of Itō, took seats in the Cabinet. It was a thoroughly bureaucratic Cabinet, made up of the inner circle of Yamagata's faction. The Katsura Cabinet had still another special characteristic which was of greater significance.

6

The Elder Statesman

The inauguration of Katsura's Cabinet in June 1901 marked a new stage in Meiji politics. For the first time since the Restoration the government was not under the direction of one of the original Meiji leaders. Since the introduction of the Cabinet system in 1885, only five elder political leaders had served as prime minister, with only one, Ōkuma, not a Satsuma or Chōshū man. After Itō's resignation, no senior Satsuma or Chōshū statesman was to serve again. Instead, they stepped back from the front lines, spoke through the voices of their subordinates, and acted through their lieutenants.

However close the original Meiji leaders were to developments after 1901, however much one can claim their direction of policy, one must concede that the scene was now occupied by new actors. Yet the power now given leading junior statesmen did not mean that the dominant power of the elder statesmen was ended. Katsura, then Saionji, and the prime ministers who followed him showed deep deference to their opinions at each turn in the political road. Nevertheless, even if preponderant political power continued to reside, as in the past, in the hands of the oligarchs, before long it became clear that the new Cabinets represented a shift in the political balance of power within the framework of an all-powerful bureaucracy.

Although Yamagata, at the age of sixty-three, stepped aside from the main current of political affairs, his life beyond this point was not of steps going down. He retired from active political life only in the sense that he relied more than ever before upon his loyal followers to voice his opinions on the passing events. In the complicated politics of the elder statesmen, Itō and Yamagata were rivals in their attempts to influence policy. General Ōyama and Admiral Saigō were the least involved politically of the six *genrō*. Matsukata and Inoue were influential in the business and financial world, but in the political world they did not have the power of either Itō or Yamagata. In their personal contest for power, Yamagata's advantages remained impressive.

Yamagata continued to lead a fixed but informal bloc of men. This bloc had its defectors and it had its large circle of supporters both among the military and the civil bureaucrats, but in general it was made up of a limited number of close associates who adhered to the principles he advocated. The private nature of his inner circle of friends makes it difficult to analyze his following. He was, as one scholar has written, "surrounded by many large and small satellites — his own clique at Court, in the Privy Council, in the House of Peers and in the army — which he arranged in such a way so that by controlling them he continued to attempt to impose his will on the political scene." [1] Itō, on the other hand, with a small but loyal following at the court and in the bureaucracy, was disposed to base his main strength on a political party. His leadership of the Seiyūkai, as we have seen, alienated many bureaucrats and thus weakened the growth of a clique within the key areas of the bureaucracy. Itō, justifiably proud of his own talents, relied more on his own broad experience and less on the judgment and assistance of others. In competition with Yamagata this proved to be a weakness.

Although it was clear that Yamagata stood in a position of far-reaching authority, it is a difficult task to assay the precise application of his power in the political events that were to follow. His work could be judged less easily now that he had withdrawn from the active work of a government bureaucrat. This problem of evaluating Yamagata's activities is difficult today and it disturbed the political analysts of his day. An able contemporary observer, Toyabe Shuntei, editor of the magazine *Taiyō*, was frank to admit his predicament:

> Probably the most perplexing figure in modern Japan is Prince Yamagata. Unlike Itō and Ōkuma, his character, ability and policy are not clearly known. The public knows he has power in the political world without any knowledge of his true worth. For example, it is known that he represents the most obstinate conservatism but no one understands the exact nature of his conservatism. Again it is known that he is a statesman opposing a party cabinet system yet who has ever heard him speak publicly as an advocate of non-party cabinets? Again, he is called crafty and an oppressor yet what is that

1. Oka Yoshitake, "Gaikanteki rikkensei ni okeru seitō," *Shisō* 333.3:37 (March 1952).

actually based upon—the real facts? It is extremely doubtful. Nevertheless, his chief value lies in the fact that his real worth is not known.[2]

Toyabe attempted to solve this problem by suggesting that there were two types of politicians in Japan. First, he argued, there is the open and frank type, willing and eager to disclose his inner thoughts. Ōkuma was this type and, to a lesser extent, Itō. "The other type is quite the reverse —closed to the public, guarded, even secretive with accomplishments considered more important than honor, and more important than any criticism. Yamagata is the perfect example of this type, disclosing his thoughts to a select few . . . thinking of himself and his function as the central focus." [3]

Nevertheless, although the precise extent of Yamagata's influence in any single event during the last fifteen years of his life is difficult to determine, the direction of his influence on politics was what it had always been: to fortify the bureaucracy in order to prevent the popular parties from encroaching upon the government's responsibility to rule at the pleasure of the emperor. To this end he used his influence behind the scenes and through his followers to accomplish the policies he favored and to block those he disapproved. There were few Cabinets in the succeeding years which, even aside from the service ministers, did not have as one of their members a disciple of Yamagata. Katsura's ministry of 1901 was popularly referred to as the "curtain cabinet" (donchō naikaku), implying that those who sat behind the curtain or front line of political life manipulated executive power. It was also labeled the "apprentice cabinet" (kozō naikaku)[4] because of the inexperience of the new ministers and their dependence upon the genrō.

Yamagata's activities from this time on are best seen through the major political and diplomatic issues confronting the nation. Of the two, the problems relating to Japan's foreign relations became the over-riding questions in the first decade of the twentieth century. Not long after it was formally installed, the Katsura government was faced with a major foreign policy decision, a decision in which Itō and Yamagata from behind the "curtain" were deeply involved.

2. Toyabe Shuntei, *Shuntei zenshū*, pp. 230–231, written in January 1908.
3. *Ibid.*, p. 232.
4. Sugiyama Shigemaru, *Yamagata Gensui* (Tokyo, 1925), p. 195.

The Alliance with England

The continuing focus of Yamagata's concern in Japan's foreign relations was Russia's Far Eastern policy. His prediction that the advance of the Siberian Railway signaled an increasing intervention by Russia in the Far East proved to be accurate. The policy he had favored up to the turn of the century was one of negotiating an agreement with Russia. The major problem requiring settlement was the conflict in interests in Korea. During the Sino-Japanese War Yamagata had favored unilateral development of Korea. The intervention of the powers, however, had changed the picture radically. Bending to reality, he realized Japan could not exploit Korea by itself, and consequently he favored a new approach — an understanding with Russia. This line of approach was embodied in the Yamagata–Lobanov Agreement and later extended in the Nishi–Rosen Convention.[5]

When Russia occupied large areas of Manchuria in 1900, nominally to protect the Chinese Eastern Railway during the Boxer Rebellion, Yamagata felt that the nation could no longer rely wholly upon its agreements with Russia. The menace of Russia's increasing power in the Far East convinced him that new measures were necessary to counterbalance it. While he favored continuing the agreements with Russia, even extending them, he now advocated full support for the Open Door policy and a new alignment with Germany and England. On April 24, 1901, in a letter addressed to Itō, who was then prime minister, Yamagata enclosed an interesting document. Entitled "Argument for a Far Eastern Alliance" ("Tōyō dōmei ron"),[6] this document presented his case for an alliance with Britain as a means of counteracting Russia's power in the Far East. The argument is worth quoting at some length:

> Although the uprising in North China has ended, a peace treaty between China and the powers has not been concluded and the union of the powers will not necessarily be preserved . . . Russia has for many years harbored ambitions in Manchuria. The construction of the Chinese Eastern Railway and the development of Port Arthur and Dairen anticipate a permanent occupation. Henceforth, she will undoubtedly expand her sphere of influence whenever the opportunity arises until, in the end, she has occupied the three Eastern Provinces. Moreover, China's political order is decreasing, and the nation is already decaying with only its last breath

5. Yanaga, *Japan Since Perry*, p. 278.
6. The "argument" from which I quote appears in full in *Yamagata den*, III, 494–496.

remaining. Even though the powers manage to preserve her for a time in order to maintain the balance of power, the pressure of Russia and incessant internal uprisings will prevent the country from remaining united for long . . . If the fate of China is to be as expected, to handle this eventuality we must have a plan which, in the positive sense, will maintain peace in the Far East and, in the negative sense, will guarantee our borders . . . Although our relations with Russia are not yet seriously strained, sooner or later there will undoubtedly be a collision of major proportions. If Russia, overconfident of her strength, should penetrate our line of sovereignty (*kenrisen*) we must be resolute and prepared for such an eventuality. The only policy for avoiding this collision and preventing a war beforehand is to contain her southern advance by gaining support from among the powers . . . It would be advisable immediately to sound out the British and discuss with the Germans a plan to establish an alliance. The treaty should give us free action in Korea, and, although its precise extent is difficult to formulate, it should not conflict with our agreement with Russia. It would be most desirable if the treaty could avoid mentioning Korea, so no matter what agreement we later have with Russia, it would guarantee our free action . . . If this alliance is concluded, it will preserve peace in the Far East, enable us to expand our trade, develop our industry and plan for economic revival. Thus later, when an opportunity arises, it would not be difficult to establish spheres of influence in Fukien and Chekiang. What must be done now is to form an alliance immediately. If we lose this opportunity it will not return.

It was the privilege of the *genrō* to have access to diplomatic correspondence and Yamagata had been reading the reports of Ambassador Hayashi in London, where the latter was exploring the possibility of an alliance with the British and sounding out the German ambassador in London on his government's attitude. The sentiment for such an alliance was not new. It had grown stronger following the forced retrocession of the Liaotung Peninsula in which the British did not participate. In mid-April 1901, Katō Kōmei, the foreign minister, authorized Hayashi to explore the project of an alliance with the British foreign minister, Lord Lansdowne. Lansdowne was sympathetic and pointed out that Germany might be included. Yamagata was giving his powerful support to the sentiment favoring an alliance, and at the same time giving his analysis for the strategic reasons favoring its conclusion. The imminent collapse of China and the growing menace of Russia were the main factors. He argued, in effect, that new forces should be brought into play by Japan to contain Russian advances in order to allow Japan to continue her industrial and military development, gain a free hand in Korea, and participate in the exploitation of China.

Discussions exploring the possibility of an alliance with Britain were continued after Katsura succeeded Itō as prime minister, with Ambassador Hayashi in London conducting the negotiations. Germany had already indicated she would not participate. By the middle of the summer of 1901, British opinion favoring an agreement with Japan was increasing. When Japan was asked to submit its terms, hurried conferences were held among the elder statesmen to determine a course.[7] On August 5, the *genrō* met at Katsura's residence to discuss the question of an alliance. Only Itō was not present. At this meeting no objections to an alliance were raised, but it was Yamagata in particular who pressed for an alliance. Advocating it as the only basis for a solution to Far Eastern problems, he urged the government to move ahead with concrete proposals.

Itō, with some support from Inoue, felt this action was premature. Although he had not disapproved of the exploratory talks progressing in London, in general, he favored a further understanding with Russia as the cornerstone of Japan's foreign policy. He favored an agreement in which Japan would acknowledge Russia's prominent position in Manchuria in exchange for Russia's recognition of Japan's predominant position in Korea. Yamagata, on the other hand, regarded such an agreement most difficult to achieve and, in any case, undesirable. With Itō leading the move for a rapprochement with Russia, and with Yamagata favoring the alliance with Britain, the antagonism of the two most powerful *genrō* was highlighted. It is difficult to know to what extent their varying approaches to this problem issued from the growing political antagonism. Although Itō and Yamagata remained on reasonable personal terms, each was keenly aware of the political power and prestige of the other. With Yamagata's political ascendency, it is reasonable to deduce that Itō engaged in efforts to retrieve his losses and regain political control. Itō's formation of the Seiyūkai as an organized base for his power and his advocacy of an agreement with Russia in order to maintain his influence in the shaping of foreign affairs may be seen in this light.

Itō was scheduled to go abroad in the autumn of 1901, and he requested to be allowed to use the opportunity to approach the Russian government. On September 13, at Katsura's private Tokyo residence at

7. See Ian H. Nish, *The Anglo-Japanese Alliance* (London, 1966), Chapter 9.

Mita, Itō, Inoue, Katsura, and Yamagata held a meeting. During this conversation Itō first broached the question of an agreement with Russia. To this Yamagata replied: "The Anglo-Japanese alliance, within the framework of all the problems of the Far East, is aimed only at the maintenance of the territorial integrity of both Korea and China. I am not necessarily opposed to a Russo-Japanese agreement relating to part of our Korean problem and satisfying our demands there, but there are complicating factors in international problems which cannot be decided arbitrarily. Even if we try for a Russo-Japanese agreement, the attitude of Russia should be reported so the government can first decide whether or not it is acceptable." [8]

Itō grew indignant at this remark and is purported to have replied, "I am not going abroad for my own pleasure. If you make such fatuous requests I will call off my trip." [9] Itō did proceed to Europe and from Paris he moved on to Moscow, where he attempted to negotiate an agreement with Russia. Meanwhile, negotiations in London moved ahead rapidly. On December 7, Katsura invited the elder statesmen, Matsukata, Ōyama, Saigō, Inoue, and Yamagata, to meet at his summer villa at Hayama, a seaside resort settlement of Tokyo, to give final consideration to the revised proposal for an alliance. Only Inoue raised any objections, desiring to have Itō's opinion considered, but when he received no support he joined in the approval. Yamagata encouraged the immediate conclusion of the alliance without waiting for the outcome of Itō's efforts in Moscow. A telegram from Itō discouraging immediate action arrived too late for the *genrō* meeting.

On the basis of the unanimous approval of the *genrō* in Japan, negotiations proceeded rapidly to the conclusion of the Anglo-Japanese Alliance (announced on February 20, 1902). The choice of an alliance with Britain rather than an entente with Russia marked the hardening of Japanese foreign policy toward the tsar, for it was plain that the new alignment was meant to curb Russia's eastward expansion. This important decision was the accomplishment of many individuals. Katsura, his foreign minister Komura Jutarō, Ambassador Hayashi, and others were to receive credit for the achievement. At every turn in the negotiations, from the earliest conception to the determination to carry out the alliance, the figure of Yamagata loomed large in the background. His part in securing unity among the *genrō,* with the conspicuous exception of Itō, received Katsura's appreciation. "I certainly wish to congratulate you," Katsura

8. Quoted in *Yamagata den,* III, 501–502.
9. Quoted in *ibid.,* III, 502.

wrote, "on the unanimity which was achieved among the elder statesmen in regard to this important matter relating to the future of the nation." [10] To further show his appreciation, Katsura arranged to have Yamagata receive the prized decoration, the Grand Order of the Chrysanthemum.

Itō's Entry into the Privy Council

Katsura's efforts to befriend the Diet parties and his growing prestige as a result of the successful conclusion of the Anglo-Japanese Alliance created an atmosphere in which his policies prospered. Late in 1902 as the Diet met, however, trouble appeared when the government announced a marked increase in the proposed budget and an increase in the land tax. Katsura requested that the five-year limit placed upon the tax increase passed during Yamagata's second ministry be lifted and that the rate be raised. The proposed increase in the budget was a consequence of plans to enlarge substantially the Japanese navy, fulfilling British expectations expressed in the negotiations leading to the alliance that Japanese naval power in the Far East would exceed that of any power other than Britain. As in former attempts to raise taxes, the parties were united in opposition, but this time a new factor was added. Itō as head of the Seiyūkai was in the vanguard of the attack on the government, demanding administrative economies. For Yamagata, this was a deeply disturbing development. It represented defection within the inner stronghold of a bureaucracy conceived as part of a system of defense. Itō, first as a participant in the councils of the defense and then as the leader of the party challenging the government's plans for paying for that defense, occupied a dual position which presented a difficult and unfamiliar problem.

During 1902 and 1903 Katsura often sought the advice of Yamagata. Frequent letters were exchanged on all phases of policy, and other Cabinet members also solicited his counsel. Before the Diet opened, Itō had visited Murinan in Kyoto to explain the Seiyūkai's position favoring government economies and a reduction of nonessential undertakings. His reception had been cool, filled with chilly comments on the impropriety of outside interference in the Cabinet's policy and the difficulty that he, Yamagata, felt in restraining himself from intervening when it came to military affairs. Yamagata's advice at this juncture was for the government to proceed undaunted and force the appropriation bills through the Diet. His position now corresponded in many ways to Kat-

10. Letter of Dec. 7, 1901, reprinted in *ibid.*, III, 510.

sura's position. At the beginning of Yamagata's own second Cabinet, it will be recalled, Katsura had suggested a policy and line of action to be followed by Yamagata. He had been the operations officer proposing various courses for the consideration of the general. The situation had now been reversed, and the general was planning the broad strategic lines to be put into effect by his subordinates. In a letter to that subordinate on the opening day of the seventeenth Diet, Yamagata, phrasing his instructions in military terms, advised Katsura to "assault the center," the same phrase which Katsura had first used in 1898: "At this time it would be most desirable for our nation if a strongly united cabinet would face the opposition squarely and openly engage it in hostilities. I suggest you prepare plans not only to 'assault the center' but take two or three decisive actions preparatory to a head-on attack. Gradually advance by encouraging the fighting courage of the cabinet ministers and strive to realize the nation's plans with unbending spirit . . . In this way problems will be avoided, and with three years of continuity the nation's feelings will become united and tranquility will be restored." [11]

With Yamagata's backing, Katsura submitted his new plan to the Diet but met a solid wall of opposition. Itō joined hands with Ōkuma and his party and prevented any action favorable to the government. Katsura first tried mediation. When that failed he resorted to unscrupulous methods and attempted to buy support, but this also proved to be of no avail. On December 28, as a last resort, he dissolved the Diet. "Assaulting the center" had proved fruitless and compromise with Itō appeared to be the only solution.

Katsura consulted with Yamagata, and the latter attempted to mediate and to dissuade Itō from his opposition. Itō finally agreed to the naval expansion program but refused to alter his stand against increasing land taxes as a source of revenue. Yamagata explained Itō's position to Katsura in a letter dated January 26, 1903. "If, after the government changed its policy, abolished the land tax and instituted other economies, it still was short of funds, it would be necessary to use other sources of revenue for the increased military expenditures." [12]

Two days later Yamagata and Katsura in a meeting at Hirata's home agreed to compromise with Itō,[13] and Yamagata called on Itō to inform

11. Original of letter to Katsura is to be found in the Katsura Tarō monjo in the National Diet Library. The mention of "two or three decisive actions" undoubtedly refers to dissolving the Diet two or three times. This was the same advice Katsura had given Yamagata in 1898.

12. Jan. 13, 1903, letter to Katsura, in *ibid.*

13. Takekoshi, *Prince Saionji*, p. 198.

him that the government was prepared to withdraw the land tax increase and resort to a policy of retrenchment in order to achieve military expansion. Itō was satisfied, and in the special Diet session which lasted from May 8 to June 5 the budget was passed and the government was authorized to issue bonds to raise the revenue. Itō had gained a major victory in recouping his political power when Yamagata and Katsura were forced to bow to the opposition which he led. This defeat was not taken lightly. With the budget passed, the time had come for counter-measures.

For many months Katsura had been troubled and annoyed by the dual nature of Itō's influence. On the one hand, as a distinguished elder statesman he shared with Yamagata the most intimate confidence of the emperor and proffered his advice on all questions confronting the nation. On the other hand, as head of the Seiyūkai and leader of the majority party in the Diet he freely criticized and opposed the government's policy. Thus he combined the authority of the ruling level of the bureaucracy and the power of the party. This placed Katsura in a dilemma. He freely admitted his responsibility to heed the views of the elder statesmen, he was prepared to sit at their feet in carrying out national policy, but he refused to be bound by the leader of the party opposing his policies.

On June 24, Katsura requested Itō to drop one of his two roles.[14] When Itō refused, Katsura made it plain that he would be forced to submit his resignation. He did so on July 1. Yamagata was troubled by this action, particularly in view of the serious situation confronting the nation in its relations with Russia. He felt that unity among the genrō was urgently required and concluded that the only method of accomplishing this was to detach Itō from the Seiyūkai by making him president of the Privy Council. This would bring Itō back within the fold of the higher bureaucracy; it would also weaken the major party obstructing the government's policies. For this line of action he secured the approval of Ōyama, Matsukata, and Inoue.

Inoue had his own reasons for approving Yamagata's plan. Both Inoue (considered to be close to Itō's views) and, in particular, Itō Miyoji, a follower of Itō Hirobumi, had become convinced that continued leadership of a political party would only damage Itō's long and distinguished career.[15] With the cooperation of the other elder statesmen closest to Itō, and with the encouragement of members of the court and prominent

14. *Ibid.*, p. 203.
15. Watanabe Ikujirō, *Meiji Tennō to hohitsu no hitobito*, p. 281.

associates of Itō, Yamagata took the next step. That only an imperial order would dislodge Itō from his position had been made clear by Itō himself when he declared that he would withdraw from the party only at the request of the emperor. Consequently, Yamagata prevailed upon Itō Miyoji to draft a request to the emperor. Yamagata rewrote the draft and prepared to submit it as his own. When, following Katsura's resignation as prime minister, Yamagata was summoned by the emperor for advice on a successor, he presented the document suggesting Itō's withdrawal from party politics: "The present situation does not require a change in the cabinet but a strong united nation to solve our problems with Russia. Itō however, as president of the Seiyūkai, frequently obstructs the cabinet's action, unfortunately impeding the nation's progress. Therefore, nothing would be of greater benefit to the country than Itō's resignation as president of the Seiyūkai and his assumption of the presidency of the Privy Council." [16]

As the historian Watanabe Ikujirō reconstructs this scene, the emperor was not favorably moved by the request that Itō be ordered to enter the Privy Council. At this, Yamagata, who had at first presented his statement as his personal view, reinforced it by adding, "This is not my view alone. Itō's followers, Itō Miyoji and others, all think alike. Actually this draft was written by Itō." [17] Upon hearing this, the emperor requested to speak to Itō Miyoji at once.

The disclosure of the original author of the statement placed Itō Miyoji in a difficult position. He had been assured that his name would not be brought up in the discussion. To carry his point, however, Yamagata felt forced to inject the names of others who supported his suggestion. Yamagata visited Itō Miyoji to explain his move and inform him that the emperor requested his counsel. Itō Miyoji proceeded to the palace and there explained his position. After hearing the explanation, the emperor was more friendly to the suggestion and finally agreed to request Katsura to remain in office and to ask Itō Hirobumi to head the Privy Council.

Itō Hirobumi was unaware of the machinations being carried on behind the scenes. His surprise is recorded in a letter Yamagata received from the grand chamberlain, Tokudaiji: "At 2:30 today Itō held an audience with the Emperor at which time he was asked to become president of the Privy Council. He requested time to consider it for a few

16. Quoted in *Yamagata den*, III, 552.
17. Watanabe Ikujirō, *Meiji Tennō to hohitsu no hitobito*, p. 282; the story told by Watanabe, who had access to court records, is found on pp. 280–285.

days, and the Emperor agreed. After coming out Itō said to me, 'The Emperor's request placed me in a most difficult position, so I asked for time to consider it.' I told him that the Emperor had informed me that in order to become head of the Privy Council he would have to leave his political party." [18] Two days later Tokudaiji wrote Yamagata again stating that he had visited Itō to deliver the written order the emperor had delivered orally on July 6.[19] He reported that Itō's only concern in carrying out the orders was the risk of the Cabinet's resigning. "I can't accept unless I am assured that the cabinet will not resign again," [20] Itō had told Tokudaiji. Yamagata, of course, knew that the one sure way to prevent Katsura's resignation was for Itō to leave the party.

Itō was in a dilemma. When he called on Yamagata to discuss the problem, he learned for the first time that it was his host who had actually suggested the action to the court. Yamagata frankly admitted that he saw no other course. Itō flew into a rage which only increased when he was told that the other genrō had agreed with the plan. At this point in the conversation Yamagata attempted a careful justification for his actions: "If you remain president of the Seiyūkai, Katsura will be forced to resign. It is not of great significance if Katsura resigns, but if his inability to cope with the present situation causes his resignation, then one of us would have to bear the responsibility of forming a cabinet. A cabinet change would be most undesirable at this critical juncture. The genrō must reach an accord and render assistance to the present cabinet in achieving the ends of our negotiations with Russia. That is why I felt I had to recommend the action to the Emperor." [21]

Basing his case on the pressure of foreign relations, Yamagata was able to allay some of Itō's doubts. This was perhaps the most serious clash between the two leading Meiji statesmen. Unquestionably they were broad-guaged men able to subordinate petty discord to their prime duty to the nation, and it was duty to the nation which Yamagata invoked to justify this action. However that may be, there were still overtones of the personal struggle for influence and power which had been waged since the early 1890's, when Itō, realizing his political power was without the broad foundation enjoyed by Yamagata, advocated leading a political party. For over a decade his efforts were thwarted, but at last he had gained renewed power with the formation of the Seiyūkai. He

18. Reprinted in *Yamagata den*, III, 553.
19. In a letter from Tokudaiji to Yamagata, reprinted in *ibid.*, III, 554.
20. Quoted in *ibid.*, III, 555.
21. Quoted in *ibid.*, III, 556.

had used this power with striking success; in fact, he had used it with such effectiveness that there was no question in the minds of Katsura and Yamagata that he must be dislodged from his new position if the bureaucratic structure was not to be dangerously damaged.

At the end of this conversation, Yamagata attempted further to allay Itō's misgivings. He did so by pledging his cooperation. "If you become president of the Privy Council," he promised, "I would not decline to enter the council and give my best in the service of the nation." [22] Somewhat reassured, Itō accepted this pledge and invited not only Yamagata but Matsukata and Inoue to join him in the Privy Council. Yamagata was not trapped in his own game, as some have interpreted it,[23] when he offered to join Itō. It was a voluntary offer taken to assure the achievement of his objective. Bitterly, Hara Kei, then the secretary general of the Seiyūkai, confided to his diary: "Itō's entry into the Privy Council is a trick of the Yamagata clique cabinet aimed at saving the cabinet and leaving it free to carry out its policies by separating Itō from the Seiyūkai and destroying the party . . . misleading the Emperor and subjecting the state to private and arbitrary power are most regrettable from the point of view of constitutional government." [24]

On July 12, Itō became president of the Privy Council and Yamagata and Matsukata became members. The entry of three elder statesmen into the Privy Council transformed what has been called an "asylum for superannuated officials" [25] into a more important body. Katsura was asked to remain in office and he hesitated only long enough for Itō to say he would not enter the Privy Council if Katsura left office. A few Cabinet changes were made and the administration was warned to be prepared for any emergency which might issue from the negotiations with Russia. The emergency was not long in coming.

The War with Russia

During the closing months of 1903, Russo-Japanese negotiations reached a critical stage. At bottom the issue at stake was the rival interests in Korea, not Manchuria. But the failure of Russian troops to withdraw as scheduled from Manchuria and the increasing Russian ac-

22. Takekoshi, *Prince Saionji*, p. 205.
23. *Ibid.*, p. 205.
24. *Hara nikki*, IIB, 96–97; entry of July 7, 1903.
25. *Japan Weekly Mail*, July 18, 1903, p. 61.

tivity there and in Korea indicated no intention of lessening the pressure on Japan's claimed interests. Japan's interests, although described by some as based on economic necessity,[26] were essentially strategic. Economic factors such as the need for new areas for colonization and sources of food may have been present, but the conflict was fundamentally one of strategic interests and imperialistic ambitions: it centered on the strategic importance of the Korean peninsula and the growing capacity of Russian power to thwart Japan's continental aspirations.

Yamagata had always used the argument of self-preservation and national security in favoring Japan's activities in Korea. To allow a hostile power to overrun the Korean peninsula would be a threat to what he called the "line of advantage." "The sum of our reflections," he stated, "was that, from an historical and geographical point of view, a forward policy must be pursued in Korea, and that Japan must not submit to the control of that sphere by any of the great powers." [27] His constant warning had been the necessity of increasing Japan's military power in order to meet the growing threat of Russia in the Far East and gain for Japan a position of prominence in the Orient.

As the nation's senior military figure, Yamagata in 1903 served as an adviser to the chief active military men. His influence was strong among his followers, former subordinates whom he had appointed to office. He continued to be consulted on all important army appointments. For example, in October 1903 he had turned down General Ōyama's candidate to succeed the assistant chief of staff, who had just died. Instead, he persuaded General Kodama, the home minister in the Katsura Cabinet, to step down from the Cabinet position to assume the office. In a letter to General Terauchi, the army minister, Yamagata wrote, "Present conditions require a wartime policy." When Terauchi showed this to Kodama, the latter is quoted as saying, "This means I should become Assistant Chief of Staff." [28] Katsura, Kodama, and Terauchi, all in positions of importance, were Yamagata's most capable military followers. All were Chōshū men who had made major contributions in the organization and development of Japan's modern army.

In the field of foreign relations also, Yamagata played the part of adviser and consultant. He was closely in touch with the negotiations

26. K. Asakawa, in *The Russo-Japanese Conflict: Its Causes and Issues* (Boston, 1904), advances this argument.

27. Quoted in *Japan Weekly Mail*, Sept. 16, 1905, p. 303.

28. Quoted in *Yamagata den*, III, 590.

with Russia. He participated in the frequent conferences, held jointly by the *genrō*, Cabinet, and top military men, which controlled Japan's actions during the negotiations with Russia. This is a significant fact, for the coordination of a national defense policy with the nation's foreign policy was immeasurably aided by Yamagata's involvement in the planning of both.

In her policy in the Far East, Russia had become involved in a chain of actions which it was difficult for her to break: acquisitions of maritime provinces made a railway desirable, and the need for a railway led to the demand for rights in Manchuria and, in turn, an ice-free port. These developments called for the investment of large funds, and the money required protection. With an aggressive clique determining policy in Moscow and a Japanese leadership determined to challenge Russian expansion, and with none of the other powers disposed to prevent a conflict, war became almost inevitable. Yamagata did not seem anxious to clash with Russia; even as late as December 1903 he showed some hesitation to embark on a war. But he was resolute in his conviction that measures were necessary to halt the spread of Russian influence. "Our determination at the time," Yamagata later admitted, "was that as a matter of self-defense and as a matter of national development Korea must not be abandoned to Russia." [29] On January 12, 1904, at a conference before the emperor, Yamagata is alleged to have declared to Itō, "Although we cannot foretell victory or defeat, we must enter battle confident of victory. If we should by any chance fail, it would be an immeasurable calamity for our future." [30] Within the next few days the final plans regarding military operation were fixed, and on February 8 the Japanese navy attacked Port Arthur, with a declaration of war following two days later.[31]

The Russo-Japanese War has been fittingly called "the classical example of a conflict waged for purely imperialistic motives." [32] It was a resolution of conflicting Russo-Japanese interests which dated back well before 1895 and grew steadily more acute. The clash of Japanese ambitions and Russian plans fit into the pattern of imperialism in the Far East in the last years of the nineteenth century and the first years of the twentieth. All of the powers took aggressive steps against China and

29. Quoted in *Japan Weekly Mail*, Sept. 16, 1905, p. 303.
30. Quoted in *Yamagata den*, III, 601.
31. See Takeuchi, *War and Diplomacy in the Japanese Empire*, Chapter 12, for details of the negotiations.
32. W. L. Langer, "The Origins of the Russo-Japanese War," *Europäische Gespräche* 4.6:279 (June 1926).

other weak Far Eastern nations. The significant fact is that Japan, which less than half a century before was threatened as a victim in this game, now stood abreast of the powers and shared in victimizing the weak.

In both the military and political phases of Japan's astounding achievement in the war, Yamagata was a central figure. As chief of the General Staff, a position he assumed in June 1904, he was the final authority in all military matters. As the dominant *genrō* he was also the leading counsellor to Katsura's Cabinet. After the outbreak of war, Katsura had proposed a *genrō* Cabinet, but Yamagata and the others assured Katsura that they would all give him unqualified support. General Ōyama, who had been serving as chief of staff, was placed in command of the field operation. When he left for Manchuria, Yamagata wrote a verse to him:

> One who always
> went first [to war],
> now, because of the passing years,
> sends others off [to war].[33]

The military phase of the war in its broadest aspect occupied Yamagata's attention. His concern for the capture of Port Arthur was particularly acute. On July 16, he wrote General Nogi, the commanding general of the Japanese forces then laying siege to Port Arthur: "The speedy fall of Port Arthur is the most important element in the victory or defeat of our whole army." [34] The following month he again urged Nogi on. No effort should be spared, he felt, in depriving the Russian fleet of the use of that port. With the Russian Baltic fleet slowly making its way to the Far East, capture of this port was felt to be mandatory. After repeated failures to capture Port Arthur, Yamagata continued to rally Nogi's determination. In November 1904 he sent a verse of encouragement after he had imagined the fall of the port in a dream:

> With bombardments so numerous the heavens are frightened,
> for half a year you have laid siege and suffered countless casualties.
> Now with a spirit stronger than iron
> Port Arthur is captured with one blow.[35]

The surrender of Port Arthur in January 1905, the final land victory in the battle of Mukden in March, and the decisive defeat of Russia's fleet in the Tsushima straits a few weeks later were the main battles which marked Japan's victory. Late in January 1905, talks of peace, which

33. *Yamagata den,* III, 645.
34. Reprinted in *ibid.,* III, 653.
35. *Ibid.,* III, 656.

had been carried on in foreign capitals throughout the war, suddenly increased. Halting the war became the main problem not only of Japan and Russia but of other interested powers.

Not only the military and political aspects but also the economic consequences of the war were problems which concerned Yamagata. At an early stage of the war he was persuaded that the nation would be forced to rely on foreign loans to finance the war and encouraged steps in that direction. From his position as chief of the General Staff he surveyed with care the requirements of the military operations and resources of the nation. His realism in relating the military demands with the economic and manpower requirements of war made his activities more complex than those of the military leaders in the field, who left the logistical support of the military machine for others to solve.

Yamagata favored halting further military action in order to reap the benefits of the victories won and avoid the total exhaustion of the nation's resources. His effort to limit the war was perhaps of greater importance than his part in the conduct of the war. In this effort he appeared as the cold realist and not as the irresponsible expansionist; he was the opportunist who had calculated the odds of further success or failure. He feared that continuation of the war would bring few additional advantages and endanger the gains which had been made. Consequently, soon after the victory at Mukden in March 1905, he submitted this view to the emperor and to Katsura. He argued that there were two possibilities before the army. One was to consolidate a line north of Mukden and prepare for its defense against increasing Russian pressure based in Harbin. The other was to advance under the momentum of successive victories, capture Harbin, and then wheel eastward to take the Vladivostok naval base. "But in either case," he added, "strategic plans must be coordinated with national policy. If these are uncoordinated, victory in war will gain no advantage for the nation." [36]

Having stated the alternative plans, he proceeded to enumerate the difficulties involved in fulfilling either. Either course necessitated preparations for a protracted conflict during which Russia's strength in the Far East could be multiplied several times. To hold a defensive line would require the mobilization of greater numbers of troops and, furthermore, positional warfare would mean sacrificing the momentum of victories already won. On the other hand, mounting a large-scale offensive would also require additional troops and increase the complexity of the

36. *Ibid.*, III, 676; the opinion he submitted is reproduced in *ibid.*, III, 676–680.

supply problem and, furthermore, the capture of Harbin and Vladivostok would only amount to amputating a remote appendage of the enemy. Listing three major problem — shortage of troops as against Russia's huge manpower, a critical shortage of officers owing to battle losses and the problem of their replacement, and serious financial strain on the nation — he suggested that serious thought be given to whether or not a new phase in the war should be opened. Although he did not suggest an armistice in so many words, the logic of his argument led inevitably to that conclusion.

Katsura shared Yamagata's views. On May 31, three days after the naval victory at Tsushima, he wrote Yamagata: "In taking advantage of this victory to gain our objectives we cannot allow a moment's delay, so I have consulted with Foreign Minister Komura with a view to taking direct steps in requesting the good offices of the United States which were offered the other day." [37] Thus four days after the naval victory, the Japanese minister in Washington was instructed to approach President Roosevelt and request his aid in bringing the war to an end. On June 6, Roosevelt offered his services.[38]

With the decision made to enter into negotiations for an armistice, Yamagata made an inspection trip to the front lines in Manchuria. His purpose, not unlike that of his mission to Port Arthur after the Sino-Japanese War, was to persuade the field commanders of the logic of the decision which had been made. On July 25 he met all of the field commanders at Mukden; he explained the difficulties involved in raising six more divisions which would be necessary before a new military phase could be undertaken and the fact that continuation of the war effort would require the floating of domestic and foreign loans amounting to 100 million yen. These factors, he concluded, posed a question of the usefulness of further military effort; the results obtainable would not be proportionate to the sacrifice involved.

Thus peace negotiations were initiated by a Japanese government acutely aware of the risks involved in continuing the war. Various nationalistic organizations and individuals were disappointed by the decision to terminate hostilities. These groups joined by the political parties drew up suggestions of what the minimum demands should be in negotiating with Russia. Their suggestions all included the cession of Sakhalin Island and a war indemnity to cover the cost of the war to Japan, de-

37. Letter printed in *ibid.*, III, 692.
38. Takeuchi, *War and Diplomacy in the Japanese Empire*, pp. 149–150.

mands which were included in Japan's original demands. Russia was prepared to concede Japan's domination of Korea, transfer of the rights to the Liaotung Peninsula, and special privileges in Manchuria, but she stubbornly refused to consider any indemnity payment and the cession of Sakhalin Island. Foreign minister Komura, Japan's representative at the peace conference, pressed hard for an indemnity, while President Roosevelt and others encouraged him to withdraw the demands for fear that the conference would fail. Finally, Russia agreed to the cession of southern Sakhalin but absolutely refused to concede any further. In Japan, the elder statesmen, including Yamagata, met to decide Japan's last stand. Yamagata was firm in his belief that the military situation dictated opposition to any thought of continuing the conflict. All the military authorities were now united on this.[39] The decision was made to withdraw the demand for an indemnity.

On September 5, 1905, the Treaty of Portsmouth was concluded. When the terms were revealed in Japan and disclosed that no indemnity had been obtained, there was a great outburst of violent dissatisfaction. The press was almost unanimous in its condemnation of the agreement and mass meetings in Tokyo led to violence. Martial law was declared in Tokyo and strict censorship was clamped on the press.

There is an inescapable parallel between the charged sentiments of the parties and others following Japan's two victories of 1894–95 and 1904–05. In both instances the demands of popular opinion far exceeded the position taken by the government. The parties which had fought the military at every step in their plans for arming the nation now cried for greater fruits. In this wave of nationalism the government was again accused of being unresponsive to the popular will. From the government's point of view, the parties again evinced their irresponsibility only in a different form. Their excesses were met, as before, by stern measures and the enforcement of official regulations.

We have seen that Yamagata was utterly contemptuous of the demands of the parties during the negotiations at Shimonoseki in 1895. In 1905 he was impatient with the extreme demands of the parties. Attempts were made to explain the position of the government. In one of his rare interviews with the press, Yamagata made a long and candid statement to a correspondent of the *Nichi Nichi,* a leading Tokyo newspaper, on September 15, 1905. He frankly confessed that "on the eve of crossing swords with a power of such renowned strength our estimate of the

39. *Ibid.,* p. 154.

issue was not very confident . . . There was no such certainty of success as a non-expert might suppose." [40] He called it an "egregious mistake" to believe that the army could not have taken Harbin, even though it might have been costly in casualties. But this he contended was only one factor to be considered:

> The cabinet, in deciding to make peace, was influenced by several considerations: by the actual state of the Empire's finances; by the sequence of future national development; by Russia's comparative invulnerability to blows struck in the Far East; by the attitude of the world. Viewing the matter from all these standpoints we saw that to continue the war would have involved heavy sacrifice, and would not have attained results greater than those attainable by making peace now. We shrank therefore from wasting the resources which the country would need for its future enterprises in Korea and in the leased regions of Manchuria. From this decision there was not one dissenting person, nor was there any division into "weak" and "strong." If to make peace was wrong, then we are content to be called "weak," all of us together, the elder Statesmen, the Cabinet Ministers and I who speak. [41]

Yamagata's frank and explicit statement helped to moderate some of the extreme and uncontrolled indignation at the government's actions. "The statement will do much to appease popular discontent," wrote the *Jiji Shimpō*, the newspaper which had most vigorously objected to the peace. [42] The *Japan Weekly Chronicle* editorialized, "Marquis Yamagata is a sturdy conservative, strongly opposed to party government, and with as firm a belief as anyone in the great destinies of Japan. When such a man as this comes to the conclusion that the Government was fully justified in making peace on the terms and conditions of the recent protocol, it ought to form a strong argument with the people." [43] The antitreaty feeling at its height spread rapidly and Yamagata was particularly concerned lest it spread to the armed forces. On September 20, he wrote General Ōyama, who commanded the Japanese army in the field: "There are those who expected an absolute unqualified victory and are dissatisfied with the results of the peace treaty. Various newspapers throughout the nation have been denouncing the government and

40. The text of the interview with the *Nichi Nichi* was translated and quoted in full in *Japan Weekly Mail*, Sept. 16, 1905, p. 303.
41. *Japan Weekly Mail*, Sept. 16, 1905, p. 303.
42. As quoted in *ibid.*, Sept. 16, 1905, p. 301.
43. *Japan Weekly Chronicle*, Sept. 21, 1905, p. 363.

myself. By arousing feelings the extremists agitate for rash actions from the people and cause violent disturbances so that martial law was finally put into effect. This is most regrettable both domestically and internationally . . . As it would be a serious matter if this condition spread to the army at home and overseas, I am conferring with the Minister regarding preventive measures. I would like you to consider measures to avoid the spread of this sentiment to the troops in Manchuria." [44]

Japan had, as a result of the Russio-Japanese War, achieved another step in her growth as a modern power. The test of world power had always been in the effectiveness of military strength. In this, Japan had twice given convincing proof. The victory of a Far Eastern nation over one of the great powers of Europe had a startling effect on Asia and Europe. Other Asian nations, especially China, inspired by Japan's success, looked to her as a model for a successful adjustment to the pressure of the West. European powers could no longer neglect to reckon Japan's influence in international relations.

War had exhibited the ability of the army and navy, and the military leaders in Japan had won renewed confidence in their capabilities. Nevertheless, the restoration of peace had come not too soon for Japan, and Yamagata had done much to harden the realistic opinion which called for an end to hostilities. Matsukata in a letter to Yamagata in October 1905 acknowledged this in these words: "I have heard how hard you worked in connection with the peace treaty. Although various criticisms seem to have arisen, the fact that peace was restored at just the right time was a fortunate thing for the nation. Your convictions on this matter were absolutely right." [45]

On December 20, 1905, Yamagata gave up his position as chief of the General Staff of the army to become the president of the Privy Council. Itō had resigned from that position in November of the same year to become the first governor-general of Korea. At sixty-seven, Yamagata now assumed the political office he was to hold almost continuously[46] for seventeen years until his death in 1922. In September 1907, he gained new honors and prestige when he was raised to the rank of prince and ascended the final step in his climb from his humble beginnings to the nation's highest rank. From this exalted rank and his new official po-

44. Letter reprinted in *Yamagata den*, III, 713.
45. Reprinted in *ibid.*, III, 715.
46. Between June 14 and Nov. 17, 1909, Itō again became president of the Privy Council while Yamagata sat as a member. Upon Itō's death, Yamagata assumed the presidency again.

sition, he gave the major political turns following the war his unflagging attention.

The First Saionji Ministry

"A few years ago," wrote Katsura to Yamagata in January 1906, upon resigning the premiership, "I received orders to form a cabinet and, during the four years and eight months since, I have received your constant patronage (*kōhi*). It is indeed a great blessing that the nation has come safely through this period of the Anglo-Japanese alliance, the unprecedented Russo-Japanese War and various other incidents." [47] Saionji Kimmochi, Itō's successor as president of the Seiyūkai and scion of a court family, was recommended by Katsura as his successor. After the usual round of conferences, the *genrō* approved the recommendation. Yamagata, however, did so reluctantly.

Yamagata's misgivings arose, in part, from Katsura's independent actions. In the final years of his ministry, in contrast to his earlier confrontation with the Diet, Katsura succeeded in establishing a working relationship with the Seiyūkai in the Diet. Both the war against Russia and the unextinguishable party hope for greater influence drew the Seiyūkai closer to the government. A condition of the alliance was Katsura's pledge given to Hara, the Seiyūkai's central figure and secretary general, to support Saionji as the next prime minister provided a pure party Cabinet would not be formed.[48] Katsura told Inoue, Itō, and others of his intentions to transfer power to Saionji before he informed Yamagata. In fact, Yamagata learned of it through Hirata Tōsuke. The implications of disloyalty in not being approached first and also in the recommendation of the president of the majority party to lead the country were exceedingly distasteful to Yamagata. It underlined the tendency of Katsura to draw away from his mentor as he grew in political experience and confidence. From this point on Yamagata became steadily more critical of Katsura.

Unhappy at Saionji's party affiliation, he made it clear that he approved the appointment of Saionji not because he was a party leader but because he was of noble rank. Furthermore, he vowed support of the Saionji administration only on the condition that it follow the policies pursued by the outgoing Katsura Cabinet.

47. In a letter dated Jan. 8, 1906, printed in *Yamagata den*, III, 722–723.
48. *Hara nikki*, IIB, 205–207; entry of Dec. 8, 1904.

233

Saionji was agreeable to continuing the policies of his predecessor and sought to win Yamagata's continued support. Soon after taking office, he published a statement in which he declared his adherence to the policies of the outgoing Katsura administration. Moreover, in the organization of his Cabinet he gave concrete evidence that there would be continuity in the nation's administration. The Cabinet was a coalition of prominent bureaucrats and Seiyūkai leaders. Of the ten Cabinet portfolios, four were filled by Seiyūkai members: Saionji was prime minister and minister of education, Hara Kei was made minister of home affairs, and Matsuda Masahisa was appointed minister of justice. The remaining posts were held by nonparty men, most of whom counted themselves as Yamagata's followers. In contrast, Itō's Cabinet shortly after the formation of his party included only three nonparty members.[49] Through frequent letters from Terauchi, the army minister, Yamagata was kept in touch with proceedings and discussions within the bureaucratic-Seiyūkai Cabinet, which took office in January 1906.

A major task to which Yamagata turned his attention during the Saionji administration was the formulation of a comprehensive plan of national defense. Japan's victory over Russia had altered the political situation in the Far East. A policy was called for which would both protect and exploit her new continental position. The policies which were now devised to serve that end were based squarely on the conviction that Russia might seek revenge for her defeat. Russia, therefore, was regarded as the main target for military preparations. By May 1906, a high-level decision was made to follow two courses in safeguarding the nation's security. One was to prepare a strategy to defeat Russia in case of war and to expand Japanese interests in China. The other was to attempt to reach an understanding with Russia through diplomacy.

The first approach was realized largely by the acceptance of a plan first presented by Yamagata to the emperor on October 16, 1906. Known as the "Plan of National Defense for the Empire" ("Teikoku kokubō kōshin"),[50] it was first drafted by Tanaka Giichi, then a lieutenant-colonel on the General Staff, and later revised by Yamagata. The plan included six points: first, cooperative army-navy offensive action would be taken in case of war; second, Russia was to be regarded as the main enemy;

49. Among Yamagata's associates included in the Cabinet were Matsuoka Yasutaka, who had been vice-minister of agriculture and commerce under Kiyoura in the outgoing Cabinet, Terauchi, the war minister, and Yamagata Isaburō, Yamagata's adopted son who assumed the communications portfolio.

50. The plan is reprinted with accompanying comments by Ōyama Azzusa in *Nihon gaikōshi kenkyū: Nisshin Nichiro sensō* (Tokyo, 1962), pp. 170–177.

third, in case of war, military action would be directed against North Manchuria, with Harbin as a target, and naval action would be aimed at Vladivostok; fourth, in fulfillment of the Anglo-Japanese Alliance, an attack would be launched against Russia in case of an Anglo-Russian clash in Central Asia; fifth, Japan's "efforts to expand our National sovereignty and enhance our interests in China must excel others";[51] sixth, if action against China should be necessary, the army would conquer South China and the navy would control the Formosan straits and harass the southern coastal cities.

It is interesting to note that Tanaka's original draft included military plans in the case of hostilities with the United States ("we should occupy Manila, attack the Philippine Islands and for this the navy should place its major strength near Boshi Channel, south of Formosa") [52] and called for attacks on French Indo-China or Kiaochow Bay in case, respectively, of conflicts with France or Germany. However, in Yamagata's revision the plan was limited to measures directed against Russia and China.

The proposed plan of action for national defense was accompanied by a request for the expansion of the armed forces to carry it out. After Yamagata submitted his report to the emperor, it received the endorsement of the Supreme Military Council. In February 1907, the two service chiefs of staff reviewed it, and finally it was submitted to prime minister Saionji for his approval. In May, Saionji declared the plan entirely appropriate, although he pleaded that the expansion of military forces requested for the plan be carried out in stages as the nation's economy was strengthened. With this qualification, the plan as outlined by Yamagata was adopted as imperial policy in April 1907, and the nation's plan of defense was fixed.

Aside from the identification of Russia as the main target of military preparation, the other significant feature of this plan was its coordination of naval as well as army schemes. Before this time, the army and navy had formulated separate defense plans with little consultation. This had produced serious disagreements during the Russo-Japanese War when cooperation was called for. Yamagata's position at the pinnacle of the military system and his wide influence had made possible the new comprehensive strategy of defense.

The second approach to the nation's security policy — diplomatic reconciliation with Russia — produced encouraging results. In July 1907

51. *Ibid.,* p. 175.
52. *Ibid.,* p. 171.

a Russo-Japanese rapprochement was accomplished in the signing of an agreement. It openly declared respect for China's territorial integrity, but a more important secret clause demarcated a sphere of influence in Manchuria for each nation within which the other nation would not interfere. At the same time, Russia recognized Japan's special position in Korea and Japan acknowledged Russian interest in Mongolia.

With this agreement, Japan and Russia came together to prevent American and other economic advances in Manchuria. In 1910 and again in 1912 this basic understanding was reaffirmed and broadened. The spheres of influences were extended to Mongolia and both nations pledged jointly to resist outside threats to their interests in either of their own spheres. By these agreements the former enemies transmuted their relationship into one in which they became partners in the extension of their influence in specified areas of the Far East.

Several of the domestic problems facing the Cabinet were of particular concern to Yamagata and his clique, most particularly the action of the new home minister. Hara Takashi had been the one with whom Katsura had worked out an understanding ensuring the future of the Seiyūkai. This in itself cast doubts on Hara's ambitions. What was more unsettling to the Yamagata faction was to have a party politician entrenched in the vital office they had all but monopolized. Shrewd and able politician that he was, Hara was sensitive to the many eyes fixed upon his actions. In his two years of tenure he conducted himself with circumspection. He frequently consulted with the elder statesmen; he was careful to get the approval of both Yamagata and Matsukata for his plans to reorganize the Tokyo metropolitan police;[53] and he visited Yamagata to discuss even the most routine transfers of local officials.[54] To public criticism that he bowed too low to the genrō, he answered privately that "in the present political world it is most essential to consult with them." [55] Hara tried hard, and not without some success, to win Yamagata's confidence. Yet there were, inevitably, some conflicts.

Both in his appointment of a governor for southern Sakhalin and in his plan to abolish the district level of the local government system, Hara clashed with Yamagata. In the former case, Yamagata's wish had been to have a military man of his own choice appointed governor-general of the newly acquired area, duplicating the administrative organization

53. *Hara nikki*, IIB, 331; entry of April 14, 1906.
54. *Ibid.*, IIB, 342; entry of May 5, 1906.
55. *Ibid.*, IIB, 331; entry of April 14, 1906

of Formosa. Hara, on the other hand, hoped to establish civilian control through his own appointment. Terauchi represented Yamagata's views in the Cabinet. Hara conceded that the area could be under army management, but he objected that Yamagata had made the decision to have a military figure appointed "without even consulting with me, the responsible person" [56] . . . In the end, there was a compromise worked out whereby Hara was empowered to appoint the commander of the local garrison forces as governor.

Determined resistance of the Yamagata clique defeated Hara's plan to set aside the districts. In 1907 a bill was submitted to the Diet abolishing the districts into which the prefectures had been divided, as well as the offices responsible for administering the middle level of local government. The elimination of a rung in the bureaucratic ladder was opposed by Yamagata whose support was deeply embedded in all levels of the bureaucracy. The bill passed the House of Representatives but was forty-one votes short in the House of Peers.[57] Behind the defeat of this legislation were Yamagata's most dependable allies among the peers who worked vigorously to muster the needed votes. "The activity of the Yamagata clique was indeed considerable and produced this result," [58] Hara confided to his diary. Hirata, Kiyoura, Ōura, and Komatsubara, sharing Yamagata's displeasure with Hara's plan, worked through the Kenkyūkai and other groupings within the House of Peers to halt the scheme. From this point on, fears of the incursion of party strength in the home ministry produced a rising pressure against Hara.

A second major problem during Saionji's administration which absorbed Yamagata was the growing radicalism. The phenomenal industrial growth which produced greater wealth and power among the industrialists produced other significant changes. One of the social and political consequences was socialism. Taking root after the Sino-Japanese War, the socialist movement grew rapidly after the Russo-Japanese War. Originally made up of two or more groups, on June 22, 1908, the two major factions came together in a joint meeting. After the meeting the socialists paraded defiantly through the streets of Tokyo displaying red flags and singing revolutionary songs. The government, which had dissolved the Socialist party in 1907 and suppressed all radical organizations ever since, was alarmed at this defiance. In the riots following the parade, the police took severe

56. *Ibid.*, IIB, 352.
57. *Ibid.*, III, 40; entry of March 21, 1907.
58. *Ibid.*, III, 40.

actions, arrested the leaders, and eventually sentenced them to prison. This "Red Flag Incident" marked a new stage in the government's policy to suppress unremittingly all radical movements.[59]

The higher bureaucracy was horrified by the spread of socialist ideas, and among the bureaucrats Yamagata represented the most uncompromising stand against all radicalism. His attitude was not unlike what it had been twenty years before when he demanded and devised the most severe measures of repression against the popular party leaders. Since then, with the development of the constitution, the parties had been brought within the political framework of the nation and had become less revolutionary. But the democratic socialists, anarcho-syndicalists, Marxists, and others were outside of this framework, and the only weapon the government felt it had at its disposal was suppression.

Through his friends returning from abroad, Yamagata had been informed how Japanese abroad, in particular those in the United States, were instigating radical actions and greatly influencing the movement in Japan.[60] Prior to the "Red Flag Incident" Yamagata had discussed the question of the threat of socialism in Japan with Hara. Alarmed by the spread of radical ideas and by the increasing frequency of insulting and irreverent remarks about the imperial institution, he had submitted a written opinion on the evils of socialism and the need for stern measures. Now he repeated his warning to Hara, but the latter attempted to allay his anxiety by saying, "In all Japan there are merely some seventy who could be called socialists, and their bark is like that of a starved and emaciated dog without the energy to bite a man." [61] Despite this assurance Yamagata was disturbed by what he considered the inadequate steps taken by the Cabinet in this matter.[62]

Hara has recorded how Yamagata called on the emperor immediately following the "Red Flag Incident" to express his profound concern about the inadequacy of the measures which had been taken to eliminate radical outbursts. Hara, reflecting the attitude of the grand chamberlain, was critical of Yamagata not only for unnecessarily arousing the emperor's anxiety but for using the occasion of his visit to the court for other purposes. Hara suspected that Yamagata was prompted not only by his dissatisfaction over the lack of strict measures to suppress socialism but by his growing dissatisfaction with the Saionji ministry. He wrote:

59. Yanaga, *Japan Since Perry*, p. 241.
60. Takekoshi, *Prince Saionji*, p. 237.
61. Quoted in Sugiyama, *Yamagata Gensui*, p. 308.
62. *Yamagata den*, III, 764–767.

"Yamagata's craftiness is no longer surprising; after all he is annoyed that he had not succeeded in running the present cabinet as he wished, so it is not strange that he resorts to such scheming methods. True to his character, when I went to Ōiso yesterday, I rode with him from Shimbashi to Ōiso and we talked constantly, but not a word was exchanged about political matters and of course nothing about the socialist party — his character and conduct are always like that." [63]

Yamagata's conduct had already aroused Hara's concern. Several months earlier he had noted in his diary, "Yamagata's conduct is unlike that of a *genrō,* constantly giving contrary orders." [64] Some historians have found Yamagata's criticism of the Saionji Cabinet on July 4, 1908, difficult to understand.[65] Hara, as we have noted, suspected Yamagata was planning to end the life of the Cabinet. There is little direct evidence that this was the case; nevertheless, there is sufficient indirect evidence to encourage the belief that it was the influence of Yamagata behind the scene, exerted in diverse ways, which caused the downfall of the Cabinet.

A major shortcoming of the Saionji government was its inability to manage the financial affairs of the nation to the satisfaction of the elder statesmen, in particular Matsukata and Inoue. The vastly increased expenditures required for postwar administrative expenses, the development of Korea and Manchuria, and large defense undertakings produced a sizable deficit in the budget. The *genrō* were alarmed at this state of affairs and determined that drastic cuts should be made, industrial development postponed, and taxes increased. Inoue and Matsukata took measures to revise the government's budget. The finance minister gave in to the *genrō,* accepted their suggestions, and curtailed the budget. This, however, alienated the business world and precipitated a split in the Cabinet.

When the budget, trimmed to the new economies, was placed before the Cabinet by the finance minister, Yamagata Isaburō, the adopted son of Yamagata who was serving as minister of communications, objected to the cuts made for his department's expenditures. Hirata Tōsuke organized support for Yamagata Isaburō's stand. With Yamagata's adopted son and his closest political confidant taking a position which, it was obvious to all observers, would precipitate a Cabinet crisis, it was commonly felt that he himself was behind the move.

The resignation of the Cabinet was averted when both the finance

---

63. *Hara nikki,* III, 204; entry of Jan. 23, 1908.
64. *Ibid.,* III, 60; entry of May 23, 1907.
65. Rōyama, *Seiji shi,* p. 381.

minister and Yamagata Isaburō resigned. In their places Saionji appointed two prominent members of the House of Peers. This proved to be no solution and developed a strong current of resistance in the Upper House. The reason for this was that never before had a member of the House of Peers been called to serve in a Cabinet led by a party leader or, for that matter, in any Cabinet, and in the House of Peers there was strong opinion against party Cabinets. With this objection as the point of attack, the conservative groups within the Upper House led by Yamagata's lieutenants planned to end the Saionji government.

Yamagata, at this stage, expressed his growing concern over the political situation. Hara noted at the end of June 1908 that "nowadays Yamagata often visits and expresses his extreme anxiety lest foreign affairs and financial conditions be left as they are today." [66] A few days later Hara recorded that Terauchi had been asked by Yamagata to resign and thereby cause the Cabinet to collapse. In this instance, however, Terauchi refused to bear the responsibility for such a result. "It must be said that Yamagata's craftiness is really extreme," concluded Hara.[67] At court, Yamagata made it plain that the loose nature of the laws regarding lese majesty reflected, in his view, a lack of reverence for the emperor on the part of the Cabinet.[68] Thus, he used the socialist issue to apply pressure against the administration while, at the same time, the pressure of the peers against the Cabinet continued to increase. Under the circumstances Saionji elected to resign. It was July 1908.

The political comments of the day claimed, "Yamagata poisoned the Saionji cabinet," [69] and this accusation was elaborated upon in an editorial of the *Hōchi Shimbun* on July 7:

> Why did the Yamagata clique suddenly and vigorously attack and then cause the downfall of the present cabinet? Because, if the cabinet continues until the winter, they fear that the basis of the influence of the Yamagata group in the House of Peers will be undermined. Although detested by the people, Yamagata still is able to hold his political power because of his entrenched strength in the House of Peers centering about the hundred percent Yamagata factions — the Happiness Club and the Tea Conversation Group — with the Study Group (Kenkyūkai) and the Thursday Group (Moku yō kai) as its left and right wings. They hold a position

66. *Hara nikki*, III, 206; entry of June 29, 1908.
67. *Ibid.*, III, 208; entry of July 2, 1908.
68. *Ibid.*, III, 205; entry of June 27, 1908.
69. Kyōguchi Motokichi, *Taishō seihen zengo* (Toyko, 1940), p. 107.

which prevents Itō's supporters from penetrating no matter how hard they tried . . . In the case of the Study Group, although it would be insulting to most of its members to call it a pure party, its attitude is important on all important measures introduced. With Hotta made a member of the cabinet and enthusiastically leading the Study Group in support of the cabinet, his influence among the counts of the House is such that Ogimachi [one of the leaders of the Study Group] is unable to do anything about it. So the Study Group, which has always based its attitude on the decision of the majority, seems to have separated itself from the Yamagata faction and transferred to the Saionji faction.[70]

Saionji's resignation came as a surprise even to members of his own party,[71] and the public saw no specific reason for the Cabinet's fall. The answer to the riddle lies perhaps in the great pressure brought to bear on the Cabinet by Yamagata, his wing of the bureaucracy, and his supporters in the House of Peers.

Activities During Katsura's Second Ministry

When Saionji resigned, the emperor sent a message to Itō requesting him to nominate a successor. Itō suggested Katsura, and with the approval of the other *genrō* Katsura formed his second Cabinet on July 12, 1908. The Cabinet was composed mainly of conservative bureaucrats, veteran officials who followed Yamagata's philosophy of government. In his relations with the Diet, the new premier received the support of the Seiyūkai as a result of a working argreement between Saionji and Katsura.[72] Despite some objections, Saionji was able to persuade his party to support the bureaucratic cabinet. "When I tendered my resignation," reported Saionji to his party members, "I recommended Marquis Katsura as my successor, believing that he was the fittest person to take office. It is, of course, the prerogative of the Emperor to appoint the Ministers of State . . . I, therefore, wish to aid him, as far as possible, and without prejudice, in the discharge of his duty; and I hope that you will take the same attitude towards his Cabinet." [73]

The phenomenon of the major party supporting the conservative

70. Quoted in Tanaka, *Kindai Nihon kanryō shi,* p. 315.
71. Takekoshi, *Prince Saionji,* p. 238.
72. George Etsujiro Uyehara, *The Political Development of Japan, 1867–1909* (London, 1910), p. 253.
73. Quoted in *ibid.,* p. 253.

bureaucratic government would have been difficult to imagine twenty years before. What caused a once vigorous party, fighting for what it considered to be the rights of the people and against the heavy autocratic hand of the government, to lose its vigor? Perhaps the key to this question lies in Itō's intervention in the political party world. Although his period as a party leader was brief, it might be argued that in that short period he did much to set a new alignment of the forces working in the political life of the nation. He had, in effect, succeeded in drawing one of the main popular political forces into the position of supporting the government. He had organized the Seiyūkai on authoritarian lines with the party leader in control. This in itself had robbed the party of much of its vitality. Periods of war, as we have noted, produced enthusiastic party support and unquestioning backing for all government measures. Nationalism and patriotism called for unstinting support, and party weapons of attack against the Cabinets were dulled. Between the wars, high-handed methods of administration had weakened the financial base of the parties as the cost of the elections sapped their resources. The continuing domination of the bureaucracy was justified in the eyes of many by political corruption in the House of Representatives and by petty wrangling which disgraced the parties and convinced many that the house was a weak and feeble body. The policy of breaking the parties by luring their leaders away from the membership into high office had been another successful tactic of the oligarchs. Still, Itō's organization of one of the two forces of traditional opposition to authoritarian government had the most serious long-range effect. It was the "bureaucratization" of the Seiyūkai which made it possible for Saionji to exhort his followers to support the conservative bureaucratic Katsura government.

With the support of the Seiyūkai, Katsura was able to remain in office for over three years. Yamagata, unhappy about the scandals and stories of corruption in the parties and increasingly troubled by Katsura's friendly relations with party members, nevertheless gave Katsura steady support. The only important exception was Yamagata's persuasion of Ōura Kanetake, minister of agriculture and commerce, to leave office and organize the Central Club (Chūō kurabu) on a solid nationalistic platform. Ostensibly it was to serve as a supporting organization for the government's policy, but as an organized political faction it also gave greater leverage to Yamagata.

For Yamagata, the most important events during Katsura's incumbency were the assassination of Itō and the annexation of Korea. On November 26, 1909, Yamagata received a telephone call. A faulty connection obscured the voice at the other end. At first he thought the message was to inform him of Itō's safe arrival (*anchaku*) at Harbin where it was known he was proceeding on a government mission. The voice persisted, however, until the news of Itō's assassination (*ansatsu*) at Harbin had been communicated. Yamagata at first refused to believe the message and then set out for the Foreign Office and Katsura's residence to verify it.[74] In verse he mourned his loss:

> What will I do
> from this point on
> having lost the one
> with whom I used to talk
> and upon whom I depended? [75]

Itō's death ended the career of one of Japan's greatest statesmen; it also ended the fascinating story of his rivalry with Yamagata. Yamagata was three years older, but they had sat together at the foot of Yoshida Shōin in Hagi and had worked hand in hand for the Restoration. For years they had worked together on the major project of building a strong, respected nation. While Yamagata rose rapidly in the army, Itō shot up in the political world — councillor in 1873, home minister in 1878, the first prime minister in 1885, the first president of the Privy Council in 1888. Yamagata entered the political area later — councillor in 1874, home minister in 1883, prime minister in 1889, president of the Privy Council in 1893 — but he had already secured his position in the army. They had intimate relations, often entertaining each other at geisha parties, frequently writing each other, and sometimes exchanging poems and samples of their calligraphy, for they were both accomplished calligraphers. Yet their personalities were basically different: Itō was gay and open, Yamagata stiff and sober. As we have seen, they differed not over the type of political system desirable for the nation — they both favored strong centralized authority under a constitutional monarchy — but over the actual functioning of that system. Politically, Itō was a more progressive conservative, while Yamagata tended to be increasingly conservative as he grew older. They had joined forces to maintain an all-powerful government, but in their rivalry for power the Yamagata

74. Sugiyama, *Yamagata Gensui*, pp. 303–304.
75. *Yamagata den*, III, p. 743.

faction had captured the bureaucracy, the stronghold of the government, and turned it against Itō and his ideas. Although both had compromised with the parties for tactical purposes, Itō finally went beyond this to form a party himself. Without the permanent base of strength that Yamagata had in the army and in the more conservative bureaucracy, Itō had attempted to organize a wider base for his own political powers. Yamagata, as we have noted, met Itō's challenge to his strength by forcing him to relinquish his party power. During the final years, Itō regained some of his prestige if not his formal authority when he was made the first governor-general of Korea. Significantly, in his new position he was given for the first time the right to command troops. With his governor-general's flag, uniform, and long sword as symbols of his command, he occupied a position somewhat similar to the field marshal — similar, that is, to a position of military command which had been the ultimate source of Yamagata's authority.[76]

After Itō's death, no elder statesman could begin to rival Yamagata's power. As Katō Kōmei, the ambassador to the Court of St. James and with whom Yamagata was to clash bitterly in the years ahead, wrote: "The nation lacks one of its foundation pillars; now only you, venerable Prince, remain." [77]

The second noteworthy event during Katsura's second ministry was the annexation of Korea. For some years Yamagata had felt that the total control of Korea by Japan was a necessary and inevitable development. It was necessary, he felt, for the nation's strategic security in the Far East. Because of this feeling he had opposed the efforts of Inoue, following the Sino-Japanese War, to institute sweeping reforms in Korea, favoring instead a policy of unilateral "aid" to increase Japan's influence and guarantee a strategic frontier.

When Itō resigned as governor-general in Korea in the summer of 1909, Katsura sought Yamagata's advice on a successor. Yamagata felt that the time was opportune to institute measures which would facilitate eventual annexation. With this aim in view, Katsura, with Yamagata's approval, appointed Sone as Itō's successor. Sone was a highly placed bureaucrat in the Yamagata faction, fully sympathetic to the aim of incorporating Korea into the Japanese empire. However, owing to severe and sudden illness, Sone's tenure was cut short and General Terauchi took his place.

76. Osatake Takeshi, *Meiji seiji shi tembyō* (Tokyo, 1938), pp. 30–31.
77. Quoted in *Yamagata den*, III, 743.

Even before Itō's resignation, agreements concluded with the Korean court made the Japanese resident general a virtual regent. And in July 1909 Katsura placed before the Cabinet his policy for the annexation of Korea. Yamagata attended all the important meetings concerned with Korean policy and along with the other *genrō* favored and encouraged the course adopted by the government. No real opposition to annexation existed and the problem confronting the government was one of method and timing. In October 1910, Korea was annexed in accordance with a carefully predetermined policy.

It has been noted that when Katsura formed his second Cabinet he succeeded in drawing Saionji's assurance that the Seiyūkai would support his policy. The closer association of Katsura and Saionji was perhaps the most striking feature of this period and it requires a further word. It seems logical enough that with the older *genrō* gradually withdrawing from the active scene their protégées would regard themselves as junior *genrō*, destined in time to bear the responsibilities of their seniors. This conjecture is substantiated by a note in Hara's diary. Late in 1909 Hara called on Saionji and the latter recounted a conversation he had had with Katsura the previous day. The gist of the conversation as Hara retells it was that Katsura told Saionji that "Itō, whose counsel he had always been able to solicit, was dead; Yamagata, alas, avoids responsibility and cannot be relied upon; Matsukata is senile and Inoue is decrepit after his long illness and doesn't have long to live," and he suggested that they should succeed the *genrō* together. To this Saionji replied, "Why don't you and I take over the burden of the nation's welfare?" To this Katsura, overjoyed, answered that that was what he hoped to achieve.[78]

This revealing scrap of information underlines the gradual shift which was occurring within the ruling circles of the nation. Yamagata was aware of this drift, increasingly suspicious of the growing power and influence of Katsura and anxious about the latter's flirtations with the parties. Through his allies at court, Yamagata was informed in detail about Katsura's requests to the emperor,[79] and was led to suspect that several of Katsura's maneuvers were directed at reducing his own authority. Katsura's dealings with party members aroused the indignation of many bureaucrats who took their stories to Yamagata, providing greater cause for the Yamagata–Katsura rift. The rift widened, when Katsura was raised

78. *Hara nikki*, III, 365; entry of Nov. 9, 1909.
79. Takekoshi, *Prince Saionji*, pp. 249–250.

to the rank of prince at his own request; Yamagata was furious, for both Inoue and Matsukata, members of the original oligarchy, still held the rank of marquis.

The End of the Meiji Reign

Another example of Katsura's growing independence was that when he resigned in 1911 he took his resignation directly to the emperor. Moreover, in his audience Katsura suggested Saionji as his successor, whom he had already persuaded to accept. In all of this he conspicuously ignored the traditional role of the *genrō* in the procedure of selecting a new prime minister. After leaving office, Katsura proceeded on a trip abroad, but upon hearing of the emperor's serious illness he returned. Before his return Yamagata had laid plans for promoting Katsura to a position at court, a step reminiscent of the Yamagata–Katsura move to elevate Itō up and out of the field of political party activities. At any rate, upon Katsura's return he was met by Yamagata, who recommended in the firmest possible manner that Katsura should assume the position of both grand chamberlain and Imperial Household minister. Yamagata's stated reason for selecting Katsura was that he alone had the wide experience and knowledge necessary to act as councillor of the new young Taishō Emperor.

On July 30, 1912, the Meiji Emperor died after a short illness. In expressing his sorrow, Yamagata wrote:

> The heavenly light
> has today gone out
> leaving the world
> in darkness.[80]

From his youthful days as a radical loyalist to his aging years as senior statesman of the nation, Yamagata had always regarded the throne as the focus of his loyalty and service. The symbol and man which to him had always been the central core, the raison d'être, of the nation had now passed on.

To commemorate the spirit of the emperor, Yamagata had a small shrine built in the lower garden of his Odawara villa. The cypress timbers were ordered from Formosa, stone for lanterns was brought from Korea, and the torii were made of pine from Sakhalin. When the shrine was completed, Yamagata received a sword used by the Meiji Emperor,

80. *Yamagata den,* III, 783.

which was placed in the shrine as the spirit of the departed emperor. He then wrote the following poem:

> From this day forth
> as a duty to old age
> I will serve day and night
> the spirit of the Emperor.[81]

In fulfillment of his pledge Yamagata worshipped at the shrine every day, as long as it was physically possible. His gardener has recounted that even when it rained or snowed Yamagata would slowly descend to his lower garden and faithfully worship the spirit of the departed emperor.

81. Irie Kan 'ichi, *Yamagata kō no omokage*, p. 5.

7

Preserving Power

Yamagata outlived by a full decade the emperor he had served so loyally. Indisputably the leading elder statesman, he was now the most influential representative of the continuing power of the Meiji oligarchs. The other remaining *genrō*, Matsukata, Inoue, Ōyama, were far less vigorous and forceful in asserting the authority of their prestigious positions. As president of the Privy Council, as the venerated founder of the modern army, and as the most powerful *genrō*, he represented a bridge between a formal constitutional body, the military establishment within but not effectively controlled by the constitutional system, and the extra-constitutional body of senior statesmen. Most of the leading generals were his grateful appointees, and he had done much to establish the position of the military services independent of effective political control. Similarly, many of the privy councillors owed their membership to him, and he had done much to elevate the Privy Council to a position of greater authority than had originally been intended when it was established. It had become a stronghold of bureaucracy. Finally, as the leading *genrō* he was close to the throne, the source, at least in theory, of all political power. With the ascent of a new, inexperienced emperor, Yamagata's wisdom and counsel were more eagerly sought and more highly valued by the court than ever before.

The Yamagata of his last ten years is the figure most vividly remembered by Japanese today. He has been described as "a frail old man whose inborn tenacity, even as he grew older, showed no sign of diminishing his insatiable will to power," and compared to "the figure of a large statue towering and dominating all sides." [1] Surrounded by his loyal followers and supported by powerful allies, his intervention in any key issue was no less decisive than it had been before. Unquestionably,

1. Oka, "Gaikanteki rikkensei ni okeru seitō," p. 37.

as he neared the end, his voice grew somewhat softer and, as we shall see, his power was challenged more effectively than before. Yet to the very end, his attitude could not be disregarded by the political leaders; he was the captain that every pilot could not neglect.

During his last decade he spent an increasing amount of time away from Tokyo in his beautiful villa at the seaside resort of Odawara, often remaining for months before spending a weekend or more at his Tokyo home. It was in 1907, at the age of seventy and in the same year he had been awarded the rank of prince, that Yamagata built the residence that he came to enjoy more than either his home in Tokyo or Murinan in Kyoto. Appropriately named Kokinan (lit., "seventieth-year retreat"), he devoted time and care to the landscaping of his new villa. The garden of Kokinan included several levels and from the waters of a river in the hills behind an artificial brook was diverted to flow gracefully down the three tiers. At the lowest level was to be found the shrine erected to the spirit of the Meiji Emperor. In 1910, the crown prince, who was soon to occupy the throne, paid Yamagata the signal honor of visiting Kokinan and inspecting the elegant garden.

Although he frequently suffered ill health during his last years, his intellectual vigor and his great energy rarely seemed to fail him. Always sensitive to the need for maintaining and expanding Japan's position in world affairs, he forced himself to keep abreast of all developments affecting the nation. He had a small, foreign-style, hexagonal frame structure built some yards from his Odawara home where he could study and read. He gave particular attention to military matters and only ill health could prevent him from attending the annual army maneuvers. His last private secretary has recounted how, in addition to keeping abreast of national and international developments by constant study, he frequently invited scholars, artists, and prominent persons returning from abroad to discuss current affairs.[2] On these occasions he would rarely lead the conversation but listen attentively with the hope of profiting from their knowledge and observations. More than ever he relied on his friends' experiences in forming his judgment and on his loyal followers to voice his opinions on the passing events.

The Taishō period, which lasted to 1926, four years after Yamagata's death, produced developments of great importance. In the field of foreign affairs, Japan grew in stature as a world power. No nation suffered less and gained more through World War I than did Japan. While Japanese representatives were to sit at Versailles and discuss Europe's new

2. Interview with Yamagata's private secretary, Irie Kan'ichi, April 12, 1952.

boundaries, the primary concern of the government was to improve Japan's position in Asia, to implant her strength on the mainland. Rapid economic growth within Japan was also a striking feature of the period: her manufactured products were in eager demand all over the world, and she became for an interval a creditor nation, lending money to major European powers. The external dangers of the earlier period were replaced by opportunities for expanding influence and this was supported by a maturing economic life in which she realized new capacities. Growing strength at home and greater confidence abroad were accompanied by far-reaching political changes. The forward-marching economy caused social dislocations, liberal tendencies were infused with new life, parties gained more political power than they ever had in the past — these developments produced a period of acute internal strains. In this rapidly changing environment, Yamagata attempted to stay close to the crucial issues in order to influence their outcome. It would be fair to say that during his last ten years he was preoccupied with problems of the preservation of power: internationally, preserving the empire and its special interests on the continent; nationally, preserving the Meiji political synthesis in the face of new challenges; personally, preserving his capacity to impress his views on all important matters of state.

The Taishō Crisis

The extent and the limits of that power and prestige in 1912 are revealed in the political crisis which almost coincided with the advent of the Taishō period.

From the end of November 1912 to February 1913, an important battle was fought in the struggle for political power.[3] Within a period of sixty days the government changed hands twice. What began as a crisis over the government's fiscal policy was transformed into an issue involving interpretations of the constitution and into a controversy over the principles underlying the Japanese political system. Each successive phase of this crisis seemed to absorb a larger number of participants and open up new problems. This crisis has been viewed as an open and successful challenge of the authoritarian methods of the conservative bureaucracy by the popular political parties. Without disputing that general interpretation, I would submit that the crisis takes on much of its significance from the understanding it affords of the changing nature of Japanese

3. A good general account is found in Kyōguchi, *Taishō seihen zengo*.

political life. It permits the measurement of the relative strength of major political forces in the transition from an era of the dominance of a conservative bureaucratic government to an era of contending forces.

The Taishō crisis moved through several definable stages. The first may be dated from the Cabinet meeting of November 22, 1912, at which General Uehara, the war minister, presented a plan for the organization of two new army divisions. The army minister argued, first, that in 1907 the Meiji Emperor had approved the addition of four divisions, of which only two had been organized and, second, that Japan's interests in Manchuria and the maintenance of order in Korea required a larger army.

The plan was unanimously rejected by the Cabinet, for the Seiyūkai, prime minister Saionji's party, had been returned in May with an absolute majority in the House of Representatives pledged to economies in government. Accordingly, Saionji had ordered each government department to reduce its budget by 10 to 15 percent. The army had trimmed 1,950,000 yen from its 80,000,000 yen budget, but now it was insisting that this saving be devoted to the establishment of two new army divisions.[4] In the Cabinet there were vigorous advocates of the policy of government reduction in expenditures. They argued that the navy's earlier request for expansion had been denied and that the army's demands would not only wipe out its own small savings but require additional funds which would undermine the whole plan for administrative economies.

General Uehara's repeated attempts to persuade his colleagues did not soften their attitude. But he persisted, encouraged by the knowledge that he had the firm backing of Yamagata. General Uehara visited Yamagata at his villa in Odawara on several occasions in order to make sure that the army was receiving the support of the leading elder statesman. In fact, while in the foreground the war minister pressed for his objectives, behind the scenes Yamagata maneuvered to win over key figures to the army's point of view. He endeavored first to secure the support of his fellow *genrō* and through them to influence Cabinet members. For example, on the day General Uehara presented his plan to the Cabinet, two of Yamagata's political lieutenants visited Matsukata in Kamakura with the hope of persuading him to support Yamagata's position. Matsukata's response was not entirely negative. "If there is absolutely no way of postponing it [the army's plan for expansion]," Matsukata told his visitors, "one half might be put into effect this year and the other half

4. Shinobu, *Taishō shi*, I, 143.

some other year." But Matsukata added the thought that Yamagata must be held responsible for any problems arising out of the army's demands. "Since there surely will be an explosion soon," he said, "we must think of how it can be handled. At such a time, Yamagata is the only one on whom we can rely, so tell him for the sake of the nation, please keep this in mind." [5]

Yamagata was even less successful in promoting his position with other prominent statesmen. Inoue, the *genrō* closest to big business circles, supported the Cabinet's retrenchment policy. Field Marshall Ōyama encouraged postponement of the plan. Although he later changed his stand, even Katsura initially opposed the plan. Despite this lack of support from among the ranks of the prominent elder statesmen, the army continued to press for its scheme. This in itself would seem to indicate the extraordinary political influence which Yamagata wielded. Prime minister Saionji had known for some months that the army desired new divisions, but in the knowledge that the Meiji Emperor would disapprove he had not feared the army's pressure for expansion.[6] But now the Meiji Emperor was dead and the army, with the backing of Yamagata, felt that it was time to take advantage of that fact.

After the Cabinet meeting of November 29, General Oka, the army vice minister, was sent to Odawara to report to Yamagata. Although it is not known what transpired at Yamagata's villa, a decision was evidently made for Yamagata to move to his residence in the capital the next day. In any event, it was on the next day that the army minister received the Cabinet's last rejection of his plan. Leaving the meeting, he proceeded immediately to Yamagata's Tokyo residence to report the outcome and presumably to receive approval for the next step. On the grounds that the need for new divisions was a question affecting the nation's security, and thereby carried with it the privilege of direct access to the throne guaranteed in the constitution, the war minister proceeded (on December 2) to the palace where he submitted his resignation to the emperor.

Prior to this bold move, and in order to dissuade the army minister from his threat to leave the Cabinet, Saionji had visited Yamagata on several occasions to seek his assistance. In each instance he had received little satisfaction. Once the army minister had resigned, Saionji was equally unsuccessful in gaining Yamagata's assistance in seeking a re-

5. *Yamagata den*, III, 808–809; in letter from Hirata Tōsuke to Yamagata of Nov. 23, 1912.
6. Oka Yoshitake, *Yamagata Aritomo: Meiji Nihon no shōchō* (Tokyo, 1958), p. 123.

placement. Saionji's pleas were answered by strong suggestions that a compromise settlement of the two-division issue be made. Significantly, in one exchange Yamagata remarked, "This is no time for me to interfere. The only way to retain the military is to request a message from the Emperor. But while it was a different matter when the Meiji Emperor was alive, we must avoid worrying the present Emperor about such things because he is still young." [7] Meanwhile, all army officers eligible for the Cabinet post agreed not to serve. In due course, the army's intransigence led to the resignation of the Saionji Cabinet on December 5, 1912.

From newspapers and public platforms came cries against the concept of government which insulated the military from political controls and allowed a service minister to topple a Cabinet in which he was a minority of one. General Uehara was publicly denounced for his rash actions; Yamagata was attacked in the press as the overthrower and destroyer of the Cabinet. In one of his rare press interviews, Yamagata defended himself by asserting that "financial difficulty is responsible for the present cabinet crisis." Yamagata argued that no large additional grants from the national treasury were being asked for and that it was not unreasonable to use the savings effected by a reduction in other army expenditures to accomplish the military expansion which "required immediate attention and could not be delayed for even a day." [8]

It seems fair to suggest that Yamagata's stand provided the real backbone of the army's stance; had he disapproved of the plan it is unlikely that it would have been pushed at that moment. Equally undeniable was the fact that legislation inspired by Yamagata cut short the life of the Saionji Cabinet. But to argue that Yamagata's sole objective was to bring down the Saionji Cabinet is unjustified. The later testimony of Saionji himself, as well as that of his finance minister, absolves Yamagata and indicates he had been prepared to work for a compromise settlement when the Cabinet resigned. Nevertheless any flexibility in his support for the army's demands came too late to stave off the Cabinet's resignation.

The fall of the Saionji ministry shifted attention from the army's demands for two divisions to the question of the military's control of the Cabinet, and the means used to force its views on the Cabinet majority. It was this latter question which became the heart of the political con-

7. Quoted by Kyōguchi, *Taishō seihen zengo*, p. 216, note 1.
8. Interview with *Jiji shimpō*, translated in *Japan Weekly Chronicle*, Dec. 12, 1912, pp. 1075–1076.

flict and set the scene for the second stage in the Taishō crisis. The issue over which it had arisen was overshadowed by broader and more significant questions.

Saionji's resignation was followed by a fortnight of complicated negotiations to find a new prime minister. In quick succession four qualified men declined the nomination. One of them, Admiral Yamamoto Gombei, turned down the offer with a pointed remark, "The Chōshū leaders are responsible for this political chaos; let them be responsible for restoring order." [9] This allusion to Yamagata as a leader of the Chōshū faction disclosed another dimension in this political crisis — conflict between the army-Chōshū faction and the navy-Satsuma faction.

In their role as selectors of the prime minister, the *genrō* met almost every day. A stream of visitors called on Yamagata; he, in turn, sent messengers and went himself to consult prospective candidates. At first Yamagata took the lead in trying to persuade Saionji to remain in office — an act which would seem to lend strength to the conclusion that he had not precipitated the crisis in order to overthrow Saionji. In the search for a new prime minister, Yamagata was placed in a difficult position, a predicament he summarized in the following words:

> Ōyama had no desire to involve himself in the political field and Inoue had long before refused to accept, so there was only Katsura and myself to take charge of a difficult situation. However, I am now accused of having caused the downfall of the Saionji cabinet by people; some would even like me killed. Besides, I am merely a soldier not a politician. If I should take charge of the situation now it would only add confusion. Nevertheless, the continuance of the present situation without anyone to head the government was, for the sake of the late and present Emperors and the nation, intolerable. I was therefore forced, for the sake of the monarchy, to take charge of the perplexing situation with what strength remained with me.[10]

The other *genrō* had come to the agreement that Yamagata should choose between himself and Katsura. At that moment, however, Katsura was in the first months of his service to the young Taishō monarch as both grand chamberlain and lord privy seal. If Katsura were to leave

---

9. Quoted in *Yamagata den,* III, 817–818. Yamamoto reportedly was successful in dissuading Matsukata from considering the office for the same reason.
10. *Ibid.,* III, 818–820. This analysis comes from Yamagata's own "Taishō seihen ki" ("Notes on the Taishō crisis"), which is frequently quoted in Tokutomi's biography.

that position and form a new government, he was bound to generate fierce political opposition.

With misgivings, Yamagata recommended to the emperor that Katsura be requested to form the next government.[11] The announcement on December 17 that Katsura would form a new government was greeted by widespread opposition. Katsura's descent into the political arena from a position at court had the appearance of a court official receiving imperial sanction for instructions drafted by himself. Popular indignation was thus aroused by the unfair protection from criticism Katsura's appointment implied. His willingness to invoke the emperor's power in organizing his Cabinet confirmed the opposition in its attack.[12] Political parties joined in denouncing Yamagata for having selected Katsura and organized a movement to defeat the new ministry.

The excitement aroused violent public attacks on Yamagata for his alleged role in overthrowing Saionji and now for his part in selecting Katsura. He received several letters threatening his life. Attacks in the press were climaxed by an apparent attempt on his life. On December 24, a young dental student was discovered within the premises of Yamagata's Tokyo residence, bleeding profusely after an attempt to take his own life. He first confessed that he had tried all night to enter Yamagata's mansion and protest the conduct of the *genrō* by killing him. He failed to gain entrance, so as dawn approached he decided to register his protest by committing suicide. When he was found, he had in his possession newspaper accounts of anti-Yamagata speeches by Seiyūkai party members delivered at the Kabuki Theatre.[13] Later reports discounted the alleged assassination plan but indicated that the young man's despair at not finding employment had led him to suicide which he incidently used to protest against the *genrō*.[14]

Despite mounting protests, Katsura added fuel to the flames by the manner in which he organized his Cabinet. The navy, resentful of the army's behavior in November, refused to cooperate with Katsura. Ad-

11. Many of Yamagata's closest political friends had warned him against favoring Katsura. See *Yamagata den*, III, 821–822.

12. The navy, resentful of the army's behavior in November, refused to cooperate in the formation of the Cabinet. Admiral Saitō, Katsura's choice for navy minister, declined to serve unless he was given assurances that the navy's construction program would be fulfilled. When Admiral Saitō refused to accept even a compromise proposal, Katsura secured an imperial order forcing the navy to join the government. Matsushita and Izu, *Nihon gunji hattatsu shi*, 356–357

13. *Japan Weekly Mail*, Dec. 12, 1912, p. 770.

14. *Japan Weekly Chronicle*, Jan. 2, 1913, p. 1.

miral Saitō, Katsura's choice for navy minister, refused to serve unless he was given assurances that the navy's construction program could be fulfilled. Admiral Saitō refused to accept even a compromise proposal, so with the consent of the *genrō* Katsura secured an imperial order forcing the navy to join the government. But even after this, Saitō, taking a leaf out of the army's book, threatened to resign unless the navy's requirements were met.[15]

As Katsura completed the formation of his Cabinet, which included Yamagata's political vassal Ōura as the home minister, the opposition was gaining direction with a formal organization pledged to protect the constitution. The growth of the opposition and Katsura's countermeasures and efforts to muster forces of his own carried the crisis to a new stage.

In the second stage, Yamagata had clearly exerted his great influence. It is true that in selecting Katsura he had the support of Saionji and the acquiescence of the other *genrō,* but it was primarily his responsibility. He undoubtedly could have prevented Katsura's return to political office. He chose not to; and developments in the next stage perhaps caused him to regret that decision. But for the moment he felt his decision justified. At the end of the year he wrote a verse:

> Though I have taken
> an unpopular stand
> I feel no shame
> at the close of this year.[16]

In the third stage of the crisis, Katsura took audacious steps to strengthen his position in his confrontation with the leaders of the opposition. The Diet session opened late in December just as prominent members from both its major parties, the Seiyūkai and the Kokumintō, had formed the Society for the Protection of the Constitution. Dedicated to the defeat of the oligarchy, to the primacy of political parties, and to the safeguarding of the constitution, this organization mustered support through newspaper and magazine articles, public meetings, and demonstrations. Spokesmen of the society stirred large meetings with shouts of "Government by bureaucracy is like government by eunuchs in China. The Japanese people . . . and the bureaucrats belong to two different races, the one destined to abide by constitutional government and the other to destroy it." The aroused listeners were exhorted to engage in a

---

15. Matsushita and Izu, *Nihon gunji hattatsu shi,* pp. 356–357.
16. *Yamagata den,* III, 823.

"war of political independence" and told that "the farmer should forsake his spade, the merchant his abacus, to join the army of independence." [17] In mid-January representatives from all areas of Japan gathered at the Imperial Hotel in Tokyo, passed resolutions and strengthened their determination to force a showdown with the Katsura government. Party leaders such as Ozaki Yukio of the Seiyūkai and Inukai Tsuyoshi, head of the Kokumintō, sensed a unique opportunity to reduce the power of the bureaucracy.

As the antigovernment campaign of the parties gained momentum, it received aid from within the bureaucracy itself. Resentful of the way Katsura had tied their hands by invoking imperial orders, prominent navy leaders encouraged the opposition. Count Kabayama, the senior Satsuma naval leader, criticized Katsura's leadership and defined the political crisis in such a way as to give comfort to the party politicians. "The struggle now going on in the government and the opposition," he asserted, "is a struggle between Chōshū and the Nation." [18] Admiral Yamamoto, the strongest figure of the navy, also gave encouragement to the political opposition. Indeed, he was to play a decisive role in the downfall of the Katsura ministry; but first Katsura made strenuous efforts to counter the growing pressure.

Katsura's strategy in counteracting the opposition took two forms. One method was to attempt to separate himself from the influence of the genrō by persuading others that he was not dependent upon Yamagata. His decision to demonstrate his independence was really an attempt to deprive his opponents of a major weapon of attack by declaring himself a free agent. In December, Katsura called on Yamagata and told him, "Now that I am responsible for the cabinet there should be no reason for troubling you for advice on political problems. Please feel free to rest at your villa and observe the scene." [19] In an interview with a reporter in mid-January, Katsura tried to counteract the heavy criticism of his conduct by explaining, first, that he had not sought the offices of grand chamberlain and lord privy seal; and, second, that his position at the palace and its separation from government affairs had prevented him from contributing to the solution of the crisis at the time of Saionji's resignation. He told the reporter that he now felt this situation was altered and, as he said, "the genrō will have nothing to say about my future proceeding, nor am I bound to any of the present political parties by any

17. Quoted in the *Japan Weekly Mail*, Jan. 4, 1913, p. 5.
18. Quoted in *ibid.*, Feb. 8, 1913, p. 165.
19. Quoted in *Yamagata den*, III, 827.

ties. I am now on a footing of absolute independence." [20] Remarks such as these encouraged the belief that Katsura was either drifting away from or attempting to place himself beyond Yamagata's influence. In point of fact, the relationship between Yamagata and Katsura was not as it once had been. Katsura's generous opinion of himself, his annoyance at having been elevated to the position of grand chamberlain and lord privy seal at the instigation of Yamagata, and one or two other incidents had produced a change in their relations. Katsura's declaration of "absolute independence" further strained relations, but his next tactic almost severed them entirely.

Katsura's second method of building up his political strength was to form a political party. But he proceeded in a devious manner. On the one hand he led Yamagata to believe that he could cope with the opposition in the Diet. Reassured, Yamagata responded in a letter to the prime minister: "Under present conditions, the attack on the oligarchy under the guise of protecting the Constitution continues . . . so that the strategy of forcing the government's downfall through popular pressure grows more menacing. The only policy which will save the country is, as you say, an 'assault on the center.' Hearing of your determination, I have no fears for the nation." [21] The expression "assault on the center" referred to the device of proroguing or even dissolving the House of Representatives, or of commanding a majority vote by less scrupulous means in order to defeat the opposition in the Diet. Yet at the same time that Katsura tried to reassure Yamagata, he demonstrated his lack of confidence in handling the parties in the House of Representatives by actively planning the formation of a new party. For this move he gained neither Yamagata's sympathy nor his support; indeed the close associates of Yamagata, many of whom occupied seats in the House of Peers, resisted Katsura's invitation to join his party.

Despite such difficulties, Katsura announced his plans to form a party. With the excuse that the budget was not yet printed, he succeeded in getting a fifteen-day extension of the Diet's recess, putting off the opening of its session from January 21 to February 5. In this interval, as president of the newly named Dōshikai, Katsura gathered together a group of bureaucrats, dissenters from one of the two leading parties, and independent conservatives from the Lower House to form his party. The

20. Interview with *Jiji shimpō*, translated in *Japan Weekly Mail*, Jan. 15, 1913, pp. 54–55.

21. Yamagata to Katsura, Jan. 14, 1913, in *Yamagata den*, III, 883.

formal inauguration of the Dōshikai did not take place until February 7, after the opening of the Diet session.

Yamagata grew increasingly uneasy about Katsura's attitude and actions. Disturbed by reports that the influence of the *genrō* was to be reduced and distressed at Katsura's excessive self-confidence, he was further dismayed by what he heard of his scheme for handling the Diet. He was informed that Katsura planned to prorogue or dissolve the House of Representatives if an impeachment petition was forwarded to the emperor, and if a no-confidence motion was introduced he would allow it to pass and have the Cabinet resign. In the latter case, he calculated that the *genrō*, now including Saionji, would be forced to request him to remain in office, for it was Saionji who had encouraged him to leave the palace and reenter political life. Upon hearing this scheme, Yamagata demanded to know who was behind it. Katsura denied he was seriously proposing such a course and reaffirmed his loyalty; but Yamagata's doubts were reinforced, and he must have agreed with the words in a letter from a conservative colleague: "The present political crisis must disturb you in many ways and it must be a disappointment to see Prince Katsura form a new political party. While Prince Katsura grows apart from you and listens more to Gotō and others, their plans will not keep his policy from failing. Then he will try to shift the blame to you." [22]

The meeting of the Diet on February 5 was the beginning of the fourth and climactic stage in the Taishō crisis. While Katsura's lieutenants were busily trying to swell the ranks of the Dōshikai, the antigovernment leaders continued to develop their strategy for defeating Katsura by gaining the support of an aroused populace through meetings in Tokyo. A major trial of strength seemed inevitable. "That political changes such as have not yet been witnessed in the country are pending, no Japanese publicist doubts" were the opening words of an editorial, which then went on to speculate, "the fight between the holders of power and the competitors for it is waxing warmer every week. It looks now as if no quarter would be given or taken, as if the nation had grown weary of resorting to compromises as the easiest way of solving a difficult situation and as though it were bent on the final overthrow of oligarchy and the establishment of genuine representative government." [23] The presence of over a thou-

---

22. Letter from Takasaki Chikai, governor of Osaka prefecture and member of the House of Peers, dated Jan. 18, 1913; reprinted in *ibid.*, III, 840–841.

23. *Japan Weekly Mail*, Feb. 8, 1913, p. 172, quoting editorial of *Japan Daily Mail* of Feb. 3, 1913.

sand police in the vicinity of the Diet building on February 5 indicated that the deliberations were not going to take place in the spirit of harmony and conciliation; the feeling of an inevitable clash had grown stronger on all sides.

The opening speeches of the Diet were strictly routine. The prime minister outlined the administrative and financial policies of the government; no mention was made of the army's demand for two new divisions, the issue that had initially precipitated the crisis. The finance minister indicated that the Cabinet planned to follow the preceding year's budget. There was nothing radical in these speeches, no issues of importance had been raised. But policies and plans were no longer the opposition's point of attack. There were now the larger issues of political philosophy and on these the battle was joined.

A spokesman of the Seiyūkai rose not to question the ministers but to inquire why the imperial rescript delaying the opening of the Diet had not been countersigned by either a minister of state or the lord privy seal. Furthermore, why had not previous imperial decrees resorted to by Katsura been countersigned? And who requested the emperor to issue these rescripts? Katsura's explanations did nothing to satisfy the opposition, and a resolution of no-confidence was introduced which read in part: "Prince Katsura Tarō, has, in receiving his appointment, frequently troubled the Sovereign for rescripts . . . abused his official power to raise a private party, suspended the Diet in a wanton manner, just at the point of its opening . . . He is acting against the true principle of the Constitutional Government and putting obstacles in the path of the country's administration." [24]

The opposition had made its move and it was followed by charges and countercharges amid growing disorder and frequent interruptions. Katsura was accused of never having committed a constitutional act and employing the throne as a shield to hide behind. Before the resolution could be put to a vote, Katsura acted. At 3:20 P.M. an imperial order was issued suspending the Diet for five days.

During the interval both sides organized themselves for the next encounter. Katsura formally inaugurated the Dōshikai at an impressive gathering at the Imperial Hotel on February 7. Eighty-one members of the Diet and all of the ministers of state came to hear Katsura make his stand. In his remarks he claimed experience with political parties on the basis of having formed coalitions with parties during his previous ministries. Sound constitutional government, he admitted, required the organi-

24. *Japan Weekly Mail,* Feb. 15, 1913.

zation of parties and the proper moment had arrived to form a new permanent party. Other speakers attacked the conduct of the opposition parties and a Seiyūkai defector chided his ex-colleagues for introducing a no-confidence motion. Meanwhile, mass meetings elsewhere in Tokyo addressed by the opposition leaders in the Diet generated an enthusiasm and an excitement which foretold danger.

On the day Katsura addressed the inaugural meeting of his new party, he sent a message to Odawara. He asked Yamagata, as president of the Privy Council, to mediate the impasse in the House of Representatives. After stiffly replying that "the function of the President of the Privy Council is to respond to the summons of the Emperor and not mix in the political turmoil," [25] Yamagata did admit that his position as an elder statesman required him to assume some responsibility. News reaching him from the capital of the latest developments caused him anxiety, so he offered to go to Tokyo. But in the end Katsura never accepted this offer; he resorted to other means.

Katsura invited Saionji to his residence and appealed to him, both as leader of the Seiyūkai and as an esteemed veteran statesman loyal to the emperor, to have the no-confidence motion withdrawn. In his wily manner, Katsura reminded Saionji of how he had, six months before, joined in urging Katsura to enter the court and how in December he had encouraged him to assume the prime ministership. He went on to speak of precedent for requesting imperial authority to break deadlocks in the Diet. Saionji was clearly placed on the defensive, but in the face of this pressure and the unchanging attitude of his party associates, he declined to recommend that the motion be withdrawn.

Katsura had anticipated the rejection and had prepared his next step. Saionji was now called to the palace, where the emperor told him of his deep concern over the troubles in the House of Representatives while the court was still in mourning for his late father. He asked that Saionji make every effort to settle the dispute and relieve his anxiety. It was made clear that "troubles" referred to the no-confidence motion. Again Katsura had resorted to the ultimate political weapon: the emperor's request placed Saionji in a most difficult position. But if Katsura thought the deadlock was broken, he must have been shocked by the next day's developments.

Katsura's desperate political maneuvers had alienated far too many. His use of imperial authority had aroused violent sentiments favoring an end to arbitrary oligarchy; his frantic efforts to build support through

25. *Yamagata den,* III, 853–854.

a new political party had antagonized conservative bureaucrats; his trickery had angered Yamagata. On the one hand, he had acted more arbitrarily and arrogantly than the senior oligarch; on the other, he had strutted as a political party leader without an effective party. "He has ruined constitutional government," shouted the opposition; "he has surrendered to popular government," cried the bureaucrats. To these opposing opinions was now to be added, in the actions of Admiral Yamamoto, the indignation of the navy-Satsuma faction. As a loyal subject, Saionji believed he had no choice but to accede to the emperor's wishes. But his party followers were not prepared to bend to Katsura's request; they felt that Saionji's resignation was all that was called for and that the no-confidence resolution introduced in the House of Representatives should not be withdrawn. Seiyūkai members were strengthened in their determination by another development.

Early on the morning of February 10, the day the Diet was to reopen, Admiral Yamamoto, en route to the court to discuss the political situation, suddenly changed his mind and went first to Katsura's residence. In a short but explosive meeting, Yamamoto accused Katsura, as well as Yamagata, of bringing about a "national calamity" and then shamefully shifting responsibility to Saionji.[26] Yamamoto thereupon advised Katsura to resign. The latter denied that he had brought disgrace to the nation, and while he acknowledged that he might have made a mistake in applying pressure on Saionji, he protested that he had no great attachment to the prime ministership and would be glad to resign. Having drawn this statement from the prime minister, Yamamoto moved on quickly to call on Saionji. He found Saionji at Seiyūkai headquarters discussing with some 200 Diet members the position their party should take. Saionji had already informed the palace that he was resigning as head of the party, and he was now admonishing his colleagues not to be swayed by momentary feelings and to think carefully of the decision to be made. He explained that he must obey the emperor; he encouraged caution; but he did not demand party withdrawal of the no-confidence motion. When Yamamoto arrived to inform the party men of Katsura's willingness to resign, he immediately strengthened the position of those at the meeting who were determined to have the party adhere to a policy of open opposition. In these circumstances, the decision was taken not to give up or in any way modify the fight to defeat Katsura.

Long before the one o'clock opening, crowds had begun to gather outside the Diet building to shout against the government and demonstrate

26. Shinobu, *Taishō shi*, I, 167.

their support of the opposition. As the crowds swelled and became more boisterous, the police maintained order with some difficulty. When information reached the crowds that Katsura, because he had received no answer from the Seiyūkai to his demand that the no-confidence resolution be withdrawn, had again suspended the house, they became unmanageable. Mass rioting quickly spread from the environs of the Diet building to other parts of Tokyo. Enraged mobs stormed the residences of Cabinet ministers, demolished pro-government newspaper plants, overturned and burned police boxes. After several people had been killed and widespread damage had been caused, military reinforcements were called out to quell the disturbances. Many hundreds were arrested and by midnight the great city was quiet; the eruption had died down but Katsura was doomed.

At the height of the riot Katsura had met with his Cabinet in an extraordinary meeting in the Diet building. He informed his ministers of his desire to resign and his decision to inform the throne. On February 11 the Katsura government fell, ending the shortest ministry in Japan's history. On February 13 when the Diet reconvened, the Seiyūkai leaders, amid cheers and applause, triumphantly voted to suspend the Diet until a new Cabinet had been formed.

With Katsura's resignation, the crisis moved to the end of its last stage. Yamagata had anxiously observed these events from his villa at Odawara inasmuch as Katsura had never called him to the capital for his advice. When he heard the news he remarked, "it was as if Katsura hanged himself in his private chamber." [27] When Yamagata finally arrived in Tokyo it was not to rescue Katsura but to select his successor. Seeing Katsura at the palace, Yamagata expressed his displeasure with the events of the previous days, adding, "I regret that you have been so impetuous." [28]

The finale of the Taishō crisis was the selection of Admiral Yamamoto Gombei as the next prime minister. This was a natural selection since Yamamoto had supported the Seiyūkai in defeating Katsura and was assured that the party would support his ministry. For Yamagata it was not the most desirable choice, but after the startling developments of the previous forty-eight hours and also because the admiral had been favorably considered in December by the elder statesmen before Katsura was ordered to form a government, he was prepared to accept his nomination.

27. Takekoshi, *Prince Saionji*, p. 278.
28. *Yamagata den*, III, 871.

As the political atmosphere, which had been so highly charged for over sixty days, was neutralized and the Taishō crisis passed into history, varying interpretations of its significance were expressed. One contemporary claimed that "one of those crises has been reached in Japan's history which mark the end of a political period." [29] Manifestly all the major components of Japanese political life had become involved in the crisis: the emperor, the genrō, the civil and military bureaucracy and factions within them, the popular political parties, and a large segment of the population of Tokyo. Bureaucratic power, seen first in the army's demand which led to the downfall of the Saionji Cabinet and then in Katsura's brazen use of imperial authority, was successfully challenged by the popular political parties. Public opinion, aroused by party leaders determined "to safeguard the Constitution," had never been so successful in destroying a Cabinet. Katsura was the main target, but resentment was directed against arbitrary bureaucratic control, most frequently associated with Yamagata's political behavior.

So Yamagata was the symbol of the ill which the removal of Katsura was expected to cure. The political parties which had fought to limit the authority of the bureaucracy had reached their greatest strength. The opposition had maintained with success that there were limits to the use of imperial orders under a constitutional monarchy. United action against the forces mustered by Katsura enabled the antigovernment parties to surmount the arbitrary use of bureaucratic power. This success gave the parties new confidence and foreshadowed the day they would control political power independently.

Yet their victory had not been unconditional. It was a Satsuma admiral interested in curbing the political power of the army who became the first minister. Although supported by the Seiyūkai and moderately sympathetic toward it, Yamamoto was by no means an adherent of the principle of party government. Because of this, the unity of the two major parties which helped to defeat the government was destroyed. Ozaki Yukio left the Seiyūkai, accusing the party of having sold out to the Satsuma faction which, hand in hand with Chōshū oligarchs, had long blocked political progress. One newspaper friendly to Ozaki Yukio declared, "Fifty days of shouting and hustling have resulted in a comedy of submission to the bureaucrats." [30] The Taishō crisis, in the last analysis, represented a skirmish rather than a decisive battle in the cam-

29. *Japan Weekly Mail,* Feb. 15, 1913, p. 202.
30. *Ibid.,* Feb. 22, 1913, p. 218, quoting views appearing in the Japanese press.

paign for the inauguration of party Cabinets. Five years were to pass before that campaign would be won.

Yamagata's part in the crisis was an important one from several points of view. He alone among the elder statesmen gave support to the army's demands which led to the collapse of Saionji's Cabinet. He was most responsible for the selection of Katsura, which aroused fierce political hostility. In both developments his influence was patently great; but in the next two stages of the crisis the limits of his authority were equally clear. Yamagata was not able to affect the political maneuvers Katsura chose to make: freeing himself from *genrō* pressure; inaugurating a new party; and invoking imperial power to attempt to defeat the attack of the parties in the House of Representatives. Yamagata disapproved of these tactics but he was unable to modify or halt them.

Through this crisis we can see both the strength and weakness of Yamagata's political influence. The events of early 1913 did represent a stage in the slow course toward responsible party government and, conversely, a weakening in Yamagata's ability to reverse that course. But the claim that Yamagata and other *genrō* had been consigned to oblivion was to prove hollow. In the immediate resolution of the Taishō crisis, the role and the importance of the *genrō* were comparatively unharmed. It was premature to suppose that Yamagata and the elder statesmen had been sidetracked from the main line of political power. Although the nature of the crisis foreshadowed the open and more equal contest between the major political forces in the 1920's, the development of more genuine parliamentary government would again be retarded by Yamagata's declining but still considerable political influence.

Soon after the crisis, Count Ōkuma claimed that the *genrō* "are now in a state of decrepitude and without the physical energy for achieving anything great." [31] If this remark meant that the *genrō* had lost their capacity to influence events, Ōkuma was to live to eat his own words, as we shall see. But to the extent that it indicated that the *genrō* were unable to prevent the modification of some of the principles adhered to by the most prominent among them, his observation was true. This was demonstrated by measures adopted by the Yamamoto Cabinet.

31. In an article in *Jitsugyō no Nihon* (Business world of Japan), quoted in *Japan Weekly Mail*, March 3, 1913, p. 307.

In the Wake of the Taishō Crisis

Although remembered less for its accomplishments than for the naval scandal that ended its life, the ministry of Yamamoto did produce results reflecting the upsurge of feeling against bureaucratic domination. Both the imperial ordinance sponsored by Yamagata in 1900 to insulate the military from party influence and the civil service regulations enacted during Yamagata's second ministry were revised. At the insistence of the Seiyūkai, the phrase "and retired officers" was inserted in the military ordinance to make it possible for admirals and generals not on the active list to become service ministers. The aim of this revision was to prevent a recurrence of the events leading to the resignation of Saionji in 1912. The effect of the change in civil service regulations was to enable party politicians to qualify for high positions in the bureaucracy. Yamagata objected to both of these revisions of rules he had inspired, but his hope of blocking their approval in the Privy Council was thwarted by Yamamoto. The prime minister warned that if the reforms were defeated he would request the dismissal of the privy councillors. This threat issued against the background of the earlier political crisis caused the Privy Council to shrink from opposing the measures.[32]

By March of 1913, Saionji had finally retired from the Seiyūkai and joined the ranks of the *genrō*; in October, Katsura, defeated, ailing, and powerless, died. Katsura's death called attention to the fact that Yamagata, then seventy-six years old, had lost many of his former political allies. Shirane Sen'ichi, Shinagawa Yajirō, and General Kodama had died some years before. Katsura's death moved Yamagata sadly to recall that he had once remarked to Katsura that many of his juniors, who should be burying him, were preceding him in death, and that Katsura had assured him he would care for him. With this in mind, Yamagata observed Katsura's passing with the words:

> Why, when you promised
> to care for my remains,
> did you go before me? [33]

Smarting from the slap administered by the Yamamoto ministry's

---

32. Actually, Yamamoto was forced to work out a compromise and the same restrictions Yamagata had placed on the civil service thirteen years before were retained. This prompted Ōkuma to write, "What the nation desires to see effected is the restoration of the Privy Council to the status it held prior to Prince Yamagata's objectionable extensions of its prerogatives." *Shin Nihon* (New Japan), quoted in *Japan Weekly Mail,* Dec. 7, 1913, supplement I.

33. *Yamagata den,* III, 881.

legislation, Yamagata became discouraged. Twice, in April 1913 and again in October, he submitted his resignation as president of the Privy Council. Both times the emperor denied his request. His poems of this period express his feelings of detachment from the political world. One, entitled "Thoughts on Present Events," reads:

> Growing old
> I am far removed
> from the young,
> but my feelings of loyalty
> are changeless.[34]

In another he alluded to his disagreement with the views of the Yamamoto Cabinet:

> Though different
> ways endure,
> there is but one road
> to loyalty to the Emperor.[35]

Yet Yamagata could still count an impressive number of loyal followers.

It was the faction in the House of Peers respecting his views, led by Hirata Tōsuke,[36] which organized the attack on the Yamamoto Cabinet. Scandal involving high naval officials in the misappropriation of government funds was disclosed to the public early in 1914. A no-confidence vote in the House of Representatives was defeated by the Seiyūkai, but in the House of Peers Yamagata's faction attacked the Cabinet successfully on another front. The 1914 budget introduced to the Diet included a large expansion in naval appropriations. It was passed, after a reduction, in the Lower House, but the peers refused to pass it despite a further reduction.[37] Sullied by scandal and blocked in his efforts to have his budget passed by the Diet, Yamamoto was forced to resign.

In March 1914, the *genrō* assembled in Tokyo to repeat the ritual of selecting a prime minister. On all such occasions the *genrō* automatically moved to the center of the political stage. In this instance Yamagata's candidates were not found acceptable.[38] The answer was provided by

34. *Ibid.*, III, 883.
35. *Ibid.*, III, 883.
36. Hirata was the leader of the Happiness Club, which included Den, Komatsubara, and other Yamagata stalwarts. Shinobu, *Taishō shi*, I, 209.
37. The 160 million yen budget was reduced by 30 millions in the Lower House and the peers cut another 40 million yen before it was put to a vote. *Ibid.*, I, 201.
38. Yamagata first sought Prince Tokugawa, head of the House of Peers, as candidate, but he declined. Kiyoura was nominated next. Kiyoura found it impossible because he felt he could not meet the navy's conditions for its participation — promise

Inoue who, suffering from a partial paralysis, had been unable to attend the *genrō* meetings. In his meetings with Matsukata and Yamagata after he arrived in the capital, Inoue contended that because of the events of the previous year it was inadvisable for a member of either the Satsuma or Chōshū factions to form a government. Furthermore, he felt that the Seiyūkai should be prevented from gaining power because during Yamamoto's incumbency it had served its own rather than the nation's interests. He advocated calling on Ōkuma Shigenobu to form a government. Yamagata grudgingly admired the talents Ōkuma demonstrated in the post-Restoration reconstruction of the nation, but he found him personally uncongenial and looked on his political party activities with disapproval. By every definition, Ōkuma was an elder statesman, one of the leaders of modern Japan, but by birth, by choice, and by force of circumstance he had separated himself from the Chōshū–Satsuma *genrō*. There was, therefore, a natural reluctance on the part of both Yamagata and Matsukata to support Inoue's suggestion. Inoue pressed on and was finally able to secure their agreement when he reported to them the results of a conversation with Ōkuma. Ōkuma had indicated his desire to weaken the Seiyūkai, his willingness to give attention to military preparedness, and his hope for a strong foreign policy.[39] These assurances seemed to have sufficed to get all the *genrō* to approve the selection of Ōkuma.

Ōkuma proved remarkably accommodating to the desires of the *genrō*, as we shall see. He accepted Yamagata's recommendation that Ōura Kanetake serve first as agriculture and commerce minister and then as home minister, and he included in his Cabinet two others closely associated with Yamagata—Ichiki Kitokurō (education minister) and General Oka (army minister). Ōura provided the major link between Yamagata and the Cabinet and he was to play an important, and unscrupulous, part in weakening the Seiyūkai.[40] But not all members of Ōkuma's Cabinet were friendly to the *genrō*.

---

of a much larger budget. In a sense, the navy, unable to get approval for its expansion program, blocked the formation of a Cabinet. Katsura had resorted to an imperial order to overcome a similar situation. The Taishō crisis, for which Katsura's action was one of the causes, prevented a repetition of such a drastic step.

39. A record of this conversation appears in Sakatani Yoshirō, comp., *Segai Inoue kō den* (Tokyo, 1933–1934), V, 351–358. (Hereafter cited as *Inoue den*.) Military preparedness referred to Ōkuma's willingness to consider an increase in the number of army divisions as well as naval expansion.

40. Ōura was guilty of bribery and other means of influencing the election of 1915 which reduced the strength of the Seiyūkai permitting passage of the army expansion bill. The disclosures led to Ōura's resignation.

Baron Katō Kōmei, Ōkuma's foreign minister, hardly bothered to disguise his opposition to the influence traditionally exerted by the *genrō*. An experienced diplomat and the son-in-law of the founder of the Mitsubishi zaibatsu, he had thrice before served as foreign minister. His respect for Itō and his long friendship with Ōkuma, whom he had served earlier as a private secretary, led one observer to claim that he was "composed of three-tenths of Itō and seven-tenths of Ōkuma." [41] He had cooperated with Katsura in the formation of the Dōshikai and after the latter's death inherited the mantle as head of the party. His long tenure as ambassador to the Court of St. James had given him an exceptional knowledge of English, as well as a high regard for England [42] and an independence that he transferred to his ministerial position. He felt no obligation to keep the *genrō* abreast of diplomatic developments, as had been the practice, by sending them copies of secret government documents relating to foreign affairs. Katō's defiance, his circumvention of the elder statesmen on diplomatic issues of importance, produced stern reactions among the *genrō*. Yamagata heartily disliked Katō and led the *genrō* in threats to sever all support of the Cabinet if they were not consulted and if they were denied access to secret Foreign Office documents. A serious collision was avoided only by the decision of Japan to enter World War I, a decision in which the sanction of the *genrō* could not be overlooked.

As we have seen, the domestic crisis of 1912–1913 had weakened the authority of the *genrō* and Yamagata shared in the loss. Katō's attitude and actions vis-à-vis the *genrō* were reminiscent of Katsura's approach to them in his final years. In addition, Katō's attitude was reinforced by the triumph of the parties in 1913, however qualified that victory may have been. In a sense the old struggle was shifted to the area of foreign relations, with Katō and Yamagata the leading protagonists. Almost as if to divert attention to this area in which he hoped to press his influence, Yamagata turned, as we must, to the critical problems of Japan's foreign relations.

Yamagata's World View and the China Problem

The central position held by problems of foreign relations in the minds of the Japanese leaders in 1914 reflected the world situation. The

---

41. See the article on Baron Katō in *Japan Weekly Mail*, Jan. 25, 1913, pp. 98–100.
42. His English leanings led him inadvertently to refer to "Our England" (*waga Eikoku*) in one Diet debate. F. S. G. Piggott, *Broken Thread* (London, 1950), p. 159.

smouldering fires which burst into flame in Europe affected international relations in Asia. On the mainland of China, the Republican Revolution in 1911 had ushered in a period of instability which was to continue for decades. The conjunction of unsettled conditions in China and the outbreak of war in Europe forced Japan to devise actions suitable for the role she hoped to play in world politics: to bring about stability in the Far East by expanding her influence as an international power. Through her China policy, through agreements with Russia, and by participating in the Siberian Expedition, Japan aimed to enhance the nation's position in East Asia. But there were different reasons underlying this single objective.

For several years preceding the outbreak of World War I, Yamagata expressed alarm over the growing number of conflicts arising from racial hatred. In the course of his reading he had been struck not only by the violent anti-Japanese sentiment in California and the German Kaiser's alleged fear of the "Yellow peril," but by the treatment of Hindus in South Africa and the racial causes of European wars. His conversations, letters, and written opinions during the war reflected a fixed belief in the increasing danger of a world-wide racial struggle. In 1914 he wrote:

> Recent international trends indicate that racial rivalry has yearly become more intense. It is a striking fact that the Turkish and Balkan wars of the past and the Austro-Serbian and Russo-German wars of the present all had their origins in racial rivalry and hatred. Furthermore, the exclusion of Japanese in the state of California in the United States, and the discrimination against Indians in British Africa are also manifestations of the racial problem. As a consequence, the possible further intensification of the rivalry between the white and colored peoples leading to an eventual clash cannot be completely ruled out. When the present great war in Europe is over and order restored, politically and economically, nations will again turn to advantages and rights they might gain in the Far East. Then, the rivalry between the white and colored peoples will intensify, and perhaps it will be a time when the white races will all unite to oppose the colored peoples.[43]

The likelihood of a world racial struggle in which preponderant power would be in the hands of the white peoples became one of the assumptions upon which he formulated specific policies.

43. *Yamagata den,* III, 923. The text of this long memorandum he submitted to the government in August 1914 appears in *ibid.,* III, 920–927. A fuller translation of the memorandum appears in William T. de Bary, ed., *Sources of Japanese Tradition* (New York, 1958), pp. 714–716.

Consistently and persistently, Yamagata endeavored to steer Japan on a course that would prevent this disaster. His basic prescription was to improve and strengthen relations with China and avoid isolation from the Western powers by supplementing the Anglo-Japanese Alliance with an agreement with Russia. Without satisfactory relations with China, Japan's position in East Asia was threatened; without ties to one or more of the leading Western powers her position as a world power could be threatened by their united action. Stable relations with the United States were desirable, but in his thinking America played a less significant role. These policies, he thought, should not be directed against any particular nation but should be developed to prepare Japan for the racial struggle he foresaw. Still, he believed that the nation's security was most likely to be endangered in the future by Occidental countries joining to subjugate the world of the colored peoples.

In the area of foreign relations, two problems concerned Yamagata, one of which was shared by all Japanese leaders. The common problem was the difficulty encountered in establishing friendly relations with China. Adjusting to a rapidly changing continental scene was a prodigious task. Against a background of aggressive action on the continent and a deteriorating situation in China, Japan was inclined to use crude measures to advance her position. Sustaining diplomatic rapport with the major Western powers proved less demanding and more successful than the interminable search to establish satisfactory relations with China.

The second problem for Yamagata was how to exert his influence and persuade others. There is little evidence that he was successful in convincing others of the inevitability of a racial struggle, but there is evidence that the specific measures he conceived or supported were to be reasonably successful. The first requisite in influencing foreign relations, he felt, was to impress his opinion on the Foreign Office. This, however, proved to be a major problem in itself. The collision between his persevering efforts and the resolution of foreign minister Katō to restrain the hands of the old statesman eventually called forth a written agreement defining the rights of the *genrō* to influence foreign policy.

The way in which Yamagata proposed to improve Sino-Japanese relations depended upon his interpretation of the China situation. In a 1910 interview with a representative of the press, he called attention to the growing rivalry between the Western powers in China and urged that Japan not default her position in the competition. He cautioned against arousing misunderstandings of the nation's intentions, but at the same time he argued, "Japan could not remain quietly and look on with folded arms. Neither could Great Britain, France, or Germany, which all had close interests in China, remain disinterested onlookers. The Powers of the world regarded China as an inexhaustible source of wealth, and the Japanese people must harmoniously, earnestly, and sincerely join in the peaceful warfare, and be careful not to sustain defeat." [44] The advocacy of a firm, moderate course — characteristic of Yamagata's approach to foreign affairs — was expressed in somewhat similar terms: "The crux of the matter is that China must be induced by hints and suggestions, and only gradually, before we can realize our plans in the future." [45] But what were Yamagata's plans?

In view of the sentiments Yamagata expressed in 1910, it is not surprising to find that the "disinterested-onlooker" policy adopted by the Saionji government during the Republican Revolution of 1911 in China was not to his liking. Many Japanese had actively assisted Sun Yat-sen in bringing about the revolution, and in general the attitude of the Japanese people was sympathetic toward the revolutionists. But the official policy was one of noninterference.[46] Yamagata felt that revolutionary changes in China were of great importance to Japan and, if allowed to go too far, would be to Japan's disadvantage. As the Ch'ing dynasty was falling in 1911, he explained to Saionji: "Unlike our nation with its single unchanging polity, China's polity has undergone frequent changes; yet under the Ch'ing Empire the nation has continued for over 200 years. Consequently, the key to the peace of the Far East must be an alliance between our nation and a politically reconstructed China, which, in step with world progress, realizes a constitutional monarchy. Even if the Ch'ing dynasty falls and a republic is formed, there is some doubt as to whether or not the objective of uniting China can be achieved. China's revolution has profound consequences for our policy." [47]

Yamagata was dismayed to observe that many officials of the Manchu government did not rise to die for the dynasty but turned against it and helped to bring an end to the old monarchy. However, he was heartened by the triumph of Yuan Shih-kai, an ex-Ch'ing bureaucrat, in the struggle following the revolution of 1911. He harbored doubts that Sun Yat-sen

44. Interview with representative of Tokyo News Agency, reproduced in *Japan Weekly Chronicle,* June 9, 1910, p. 998.
45. *Yamagata den,* III, 927.
46. This attitude of the government as well as certain Japanese groups has been covered by Marius B. Jansen, *The Japanese and Sun Yat-sen* (Cambridge, Mass., 1954).
47. Quoted in *Yamagata den,* III, 779.

would be a reliable ally of Japan and condemned the pro-Sun sentiment in Japan among journalists and writers, blaming it on the government's refusal to take restraining action; later when Sun was forced to flee from China, he scolded the government for allowing him to take refuge in Japan. Any action favoring the opponents of Yuan Shih-kai, he felt, lessened the possibility of establishing good relations with China.

With little success, Yamagata continued to press the government to gain China's trust and confidence through positive measures. The onset of World War I provided a new opportunity to submit his views on the proper conduct of relations with China, on how to overcome the absence of a "settled China policy" and correct the policy which "has been both negligent and wrong, deplorably shaking Chinese confidence in our Empire."[48] In August of 1914, prior to Japan's entry into the war but after an ultimatum had been sent to Germany making her involvement most likely, Yamagata submitted a document of over 4,200 characters to several ministers of the Ōkuma Cabinet.[49] He conceived of the war as an opportunity to improve relations with China in order to strengthen Japan's international position for the difficult conditions he foresaw following the end of the war. He criticized the lack of an overall foreign policy to guide Japan and prescribed a course of action:

> The advantages of Japan enjoyed in Manchuria and Mongolia are of the greatest importance, acquired at the sacrifice of some 200,000 lives and the expenditure of almost two billions. But to make these advantages secure and develop them further it is necessary both to maintain friendly relations with Russia and harmonize our relations with China by eliminating areas of conflict . . . At present all the so-called first line powers are involved in the European war. With its extension into the Far East they will not be able to give thought to their interests in China . . . Now is the opportune time for the Empire to settle on a policy toward China, correct the mistakes and omissions of the past and plan a complete revision.[50]

Elsewhere in this important document Yamagata states unequivocally, "Our present plan should aim primarily at improving Sino-Japanese relations and inspiring in China a feeling of abiding trust in us."

Failure to move in this direction had consequences he could already detect: "suspicious of the real motives of our Empire, China turns in-

48. *Ibid.*, III, 920–927. The quotations following are taken from this memorandum.
49. It was sent to prime minister Ōkuma, foreign minister Katō, and finance minister Wakatsuki; see covering letter in *ibid.*, III, 919–920.
50. *Ibid.*, III, 922–923.

creasingly to America to restrict the activities of the Empire. Should we fail to dispel China's previous doubts . . . she will turn away from us and more to America, and America will take advantage of this and multiply her influence in China." Despite the regrettable immigration problem in California, he felt that Japan's relations with the United States were fundamentally sound, and that "The maintenance of future peace in the Far East and the promotion of China's independence require first and foremost frank and open discussions with America." But relations with the United States were subordinate to those with China.

Behind Yamagata's recommendation for cultivating friendly relations with China lay his conviction that the world would some day be gripped by a life-and-death racial struggle.

> For some time I have felt that in order that Yuan Shih-kai's distrust of us might be dispelled and replaced by confidence, he must be persuaded of the general trend toward a racial struggle and that the most suitable way to preserve the past and independence of the Chinese people would be to place confidence in us. Furthermore, we could offer effective material aid . . .

> Now among the colored people of the Orient, only Japan and China possess independent states. India compares with China in its large territory and large population, but it long ago lost its status as a nation and there seem no prospects for recovering it. Thus, if the colored peoples of the Orient hope to compete with the so-called culturally advanced white peoples and preserve their heritage and retain their independence while maintaining equal and friendly relations with them, China and Japan, culturally and racially so alike, must be friendly and promote each other's interests. Because China has in the past been invaded and subjugated by other races, in the rivalry with the white peoples, she is understandably not as deeply sensitive in this respect as Japan. Nevertheless, the Chinese must know well that in four thousand years the white man has never controlled her. Consequently, if approached with reason it is not unreasonable to feel that this attitude can be changed and engender in her confidence in our Empire . . .

> Although I have explained above the trend toward racial problems and my premonitions of a bitter conflict between white and colored peoples in the future, I consider it wiser, in the case of the Chinese government, not to raise the question of a league of colored peoples. Japan is now in alliance with England; it has agreements with Russia and France; and we are endeavoring mutually to promote the peace of the Far East and the independence of China. Moreover,

we must realize the need to negotiate with America. All politicians must be firmly admonished against raising the race issue which would injure the feelings of other countries and impair their friendship for our Empire. The nub of the matter is that we must gradually draw closer to China, by careful cultivation, and quietly realize our future plans.[51]

To "draw closer to China" Yamagata did not favor coercive measures. "Some people," he wrote, "place too much faith in the armed might of our Empire and believe that against China the use of force alone will gain our ends, forgetting that the problems of life are not solved merely by the use of force." This was not a prescription for controlling China, not a blueprint for the domination of the mainland, but rather a plan for increasing Japan's influence in China through diplomatic consultations and mutual aid. Undeniably he hoped to gain economic and political advantages for Japan while the Western powers, who had dominated China, were preoccupied with the war in Europe. Specifically, he called for financial assistance to China at a time when the war was cutting off European sources of loans. Mutual advantages would flow from financial aid for, as he said, "China is at present already our best market for trade and in the future this will increase still more so that mutual dependence will grow."

As always, Yamagata's primary concern was with the security and welfare of Japan's future. He wanted a cooperative partnership with China, with Japan's greater development the basis of aid and assistance. Looking back on history from our vantage point, one can read into Yamagata's proposals a plan for establishing Japanese hegemony over China. But this would be a distortion of history. In 1914, Yamagata was convinced, and remained convinced in subsequent developments we shall examine, that a strong, friendly China would be to Japan's greatest advantage. It was with the above analysis of the world situation and this prescription for a line of action that Yamagata participated in Japan's decision to enter World War I.

Preserving the Power of the *Genrō*

Yamagata's opinion defining the situation Japan faced was written during the busy August days, which were filled with important meetings with his fellow *genrō* and the Cabinet, and joint meetings before the emperor. Between meetings there were constant exchanges of views

51. *Ibid.*, III, 925–927.

between the *genrō* and Cabinet ministers. No decision as far reaching as a determination to go to war could be made without the blessings of the elder statesmen. Furthermore, as the emperor's ranking military officer and president of the Privy Council which had to pass on war decisions, Yamagata was in the middle of the discussions during those hectic days.

Japan's decision to enter the war was initiated in the Cabinet and based on the spirit if not the letter of the Anglo-Japanese Alliance.[52] The Cabinet reached its decision on August 7, 1914, only thirty-six hours after receiving a British request to use her fleet to "hunt and destroy the armed German cruisers who are attacking our commerce . . . This, of course, means an act of war against Germany, but this is, in our opinion, unavoidable." [53] One day later the Cabinet met with the *genrō* — Matsukata, Ōyama, and Yamagata — to seek their approval. During this meeting one *genrō* cautioned that there was a possibility of German victory which should be weighed before committing the nation.[54] Since Yamagata placed confidence in German military might, it is quite probable it was he who entered this word of caution. He sensed that the only risk to which Japan was exposing herself was an overwhelming German victory. His respect for German power notwithstanding, he favored carrying out Japan's treaty obligations and the Cabinet decision was endorsed by the *genrō*. When Japan informed England of her decision and plans to take action against German ships, as requested, and, in addition, to seize the German naval base at Kiaochow Bay in China, England became alarmed. Second thoughts prompted England to attempt to limit the scope of Japanese operations. This moment of awkwardness displeased foreign minister Sir Edward Grey — "To explain to an ally that her help will be welcome, but that you hope it will not be made inconvenient, it is a proceeding that is neither agreeable nor gracious." [55] British pleas for moderation caused delay but no modification of the Japanese position.[56] Several more meetings of the Cabinet and the *genrō* were required before the final decision was made. The army and navy concluded their plans,[57] and the Foreign Office carried on exchanges

52. Takeuchi, *War and Diplomacy in the Japanese Empire*, p. 170.

53. English text of the British note quoted in Itō Masanori, *Katō Kōmei* (Tokyo, 1929), II, 78.

54. *Ibid.*, II, 80–81.

55. Sir Edward Grey, *Twenty-Five Years, 1892–1916* (New York, 1925), II, 104.

56. Nelson C. Spinks, "Japan's Entry into World War I," *Pacific Historical Review* 5.4:297–311 (December 1936).

57. Army minister Oka visited Yamagata on August 11 presumably to acquaint him with army plans. See Takeuchi, *War and Diplomacy*, p. 172n. On August 23 Yamagata formally joined the supreme Military Council for the years 1914–1915.

with England. On August 14, the *genrō*, excluding the ailing Inoue, met with the Cabinet, and on the next day the Cabinet formally met with the emperor with the three *genrō* in attendance. On the latter occasion, the plan of sending an ultimatum to Germany demanding that her possessions in China be turned over to Japan for eventual restoration to China received imperial sanction. Late the next day, the seven-day ultimatum was sent to Germany. The emperor then called a meeting of the Privy Council to discuss the measures taken by the government. Yamagata sat as president of the Privy Council and after some discussion the council gave its approval. When the ultimatum ran out, on August 23, Japan declared war on Germany.

The formal approval of the *genrō* and the Privy Council of the steps taken by the Foreign Office leading to Japan's entry into the war disguised the growing dissatisfaction of the *genrō* with foreign minister Katō. It did not alter the course of action in August, but it led to a major clash in September. Although Inoue's health would not permit him to attend many of these meetings, through his private secretary, Mochizuki Kotarō, he expressed his opinions to Ōkuma. Inoue was anxious for Japan to extend its alliance with England to include Russia and France, and he encouraged a careful formulation of a long-range policy toward China at this juncture. On August 10, Mochizuki visited Ōkuma and then Yamagata to present Inoue's position for their consideration. Ōkuma agreed in general but said it would be difficult to carry out the proposals.

Yamagata carefully studied the proposals and then remarked to Mochizuki, "I approve wholeheartedly. In particular, the formation of a united group with England, France, Russia, and ourselves, and the importation of capital from France are most urgently required." [58] Yamagata went on to explain his attitude toward the situation:

> Since during the present war our country's future welfare will be affected by the consideration we must give to our China policy, a fundamental policy must be established. Yet the foreign minister seeks only to settle the unresolved issues now pending. Such a short-sighted foreign policy causes concern for the nation's future.
>
> The present war in Europe that began as a Balkan problem had its origin in a Slavic-German racial struggle that spread to include the racial rivalry between the Anglo-Saxon and Latin peoples. Already Indians with British citizenship cannot land in Canada. In short, the

58. Quoted in *Inoue den,* V, 370.

racial attitudes of Europeans and Americans toward Asians will become frightening in the future. Accordingly, the future of Asia and the basis of policy toward China must be carefully considered in the present situation.[59]

This conversation preceded the drafting of the opinion Yamagata submitted to the Cabinet leaders which we have already analyzed; the specter of racial conflict was clearly a major factor in his thinking about Japan's position in international affairs. He agreed with Inoue that the time had arrived to work for closer collaboration with other European nations and to develop a broader policy toward China. In part, the objections of Inoue and Yamagata to Japan's current foreign policy were based on their distrust of Katō. This became evident when they objected to the nature of the ultimatum to Germany. "It is useless," declared Yamagata to Mochizuki when he visited him a week later with another message from Inoue, "our foreign relations have been wrecked. Using the least desirable means, the ultimatum has been announced." [60]

Mochizuki paid a third visit to Ōkuma and to Yamagata on August 20, three days before the declaration of war. Through him Inoue continued to urge a closer alignment with Russia and France. Ōkuma seemed to be in agreement and suggested drawing up plans along those lines. While Inoue undertook to draw up specific proposals for a four-power alliance in which Japan would be responsible for the Far East,[61] the Foreign Office refused to give the idea any serious thought. The extent to which the *genrō* could shape foreign policy at what was generally regarded as a turning point in international relations was dependent upon the influence they could exert on those charged with its formulation. Katō's attitude was proving to be a major obstacle in the attempt of the *genrō* to contribute to the formulation of policy.

Foreign minister Katō studiedly refrained from consulting the *genrō* in the formation of policy. He failed to respond in a satisfactory manner to the proposals suggested by both Inoue and Yamagata regarding a new approach to Japan's foreign relations. Insult was heaped on injury when the Foreign Office, on grounds of security during wartime, severely limited the publication of state papers and, as a consequence, prevented the *genrō* from reading diplomatic correspondence.[62] Deprived of vital

59. Quoted in *ibid.*, V, 370.
60. *Ibid.*, V, 375.
61. *Ibid.*, V, 380–384.
62. This was the consequence of an ordinance issued by the Foreign Office on Sept. 16, 1914. Takeuchi, *War and Diplomacy*, pp. 178–179n. Ōkuma later repealed this ordinance.

information regarding foreign relations and slighted by the foreign minister, the *genrō* decided to take action.

In September, Inoue rose from his sickbed at his villa south of the capital and hurried to Tokyo. Having suggested the selection of Ōkuma as prime minister, his voice was expected to carry convincing weight. To Ōkuma he spoke sharply against Katō's stubborn narrowness and suggested he be dropped from the Cabinet. But Ōkuma was reluctant to reorganize his Cabinet so soon after Japan had entered a major war. Yamagata was equally outraged at Katō's conduct and wrote his *genrō* colleagues: "If offering advice and counsel to the Ōkuma cabinet on national problems is considered political interference, we have no choice but to sever relations with the present cabinet; if showing us diplomatic notes relating to our foreign relations is regarded as compromising secrets, what possible reason is there for us to consult with the present cabinet? [63]

This was a threat to end the life of the government. Ōkuma himself did not necessarily share Katō's views that the *genrō* were meddling in the government's business, and he was embarrassed by the implication that the *genrō* might leak state secrets. He was anxious to quiet their wrath and prepared to make concessions. Ōura, Yamagata's friend and the agriculture and commerce minister, acted as the go-between in bringing together the *genrō* and the prime minister in a most extraordinary meeting, the results of which prevented a major political crisis.

On September 24, at Inoue's Tokyo residence, Ōkuma came together with the *genrō*, Yamagata, Inoue, Matsukata, and Ōyama, to negotiate an agreement regarding the conduct of foreign relations. The report of this meeting, based on the notes of Inoue's secretary, indicates clearly the difficulties the *genrō* faced and the agreed solutions of those problems. A summary of the discussions and the conclusions reached was printed and circulated among Ōkuma and the *genrō* to avoid misunderstanding.

> 1. Since the death of the late Emperor and the advent of the present Emperor the prestige of Japan among the powers has declined. Even the London *Times* of our allied nation disclosed in an article an uneasy feeling about Japan's future . . . The Ōkuma cabinet has not been able to realize its desire for a second Restoration. Yet the present offers an immense and unique opportunity for improving Japan through domestic and foreign policies. With the aim of developing long-range goals for the nation, men of talent from all over the country should be brought together and a unified nation

63. Quoted in *Yamagata den*, III, 910.

should be immediately brought about, the prime minister and each *genrō* should be completely open and candid, conferring closely and exchanging ideas. This is the way we must come together to attain the great objective of the nation's development.

2. The foreign minister, Baron Katō, will faithfully carry out the unanimous foreign policy opinion agreed upon between the prime minister and the *genrō*.

3. The prime minister will determine major foreign policies and have the foreign minister execute them faithfully.

4. Since August 7, when Britain requested that German cruisers in the Far East be attacked, neither incoming telegrams, outgoing telegrams nor correspondence relating to important foreign relations have been shown to the *genrō*. Henceforth all diplomatic correspondence, both originals and translations, will be shown the *genrō* and prior consultations shall be conducted on any important negotiations relating to relations with foreign nations. This will bring about real unity.

5. Prime Minister Ōkuma vigorously defended Baron Katō against widespread criticism but acknowledged the overly bureaucratic conduct of Baron Katō. That there has been no real understanding between Baron Katō and the *genrō* was frankly recognized as a failure on the part of the prime minister. Henceforth, the ill feeling of the past will be forgotten and an exchange of views will be continued that the nation might develop in harmony.[64]

This was the understanding arrived at between the elder statesmen and Ōkuma. Later Katō himself revised the second paragraph, eliminating his own name and substituting the phrase "those in authority" for the term "foreign minister" as well as for the term "prime minister."[65] This made it a more generally applicable agreement, but it did not alter the fact that the immediate purpose was to force Katō to have greater respect for the *genrō*.

This was indeed a remarkable meeting. That the prestigious elder statesmen were called upon to compel the prime minister to recognize their influence was a new development. To be sure it was caused by the independent attitude of Katō, who felt no obligation to filter each decision through the elderly and often ill-informed *genrō*. But that the *genrō* felt forced to negotiate for what had been accepted practice was a measure of their loss of power. On the other hand, the strength of their

64. Reprinted in *ibid.*, III, 912–913. Mochizuki took notes on the conversation which were later corrected by Inoue.
65. *Ibid.*, III, 914, for Katō's revision.

position was acknowledged by the nature of the agreement. In principle, then, their power was reaffirmed, their influence was to be preserved.

The test of this agreement remained to be measured against the actual developments in the field of foreign relations. A yardstick was conveniently presented, for the four *genrō* submitted at this time a signed policy memorandum to the prime minister covering recommendations in five areas of Japan's foreign policy.

A. Basic policy toward China.

1. The major objective should be to dispel the distrust and doubts harbored toward Japan by the Chinese, beginning with Yuan Shih-kai, and demonstrate our sincerity.

2. For special problems send special emissaries who enjoy Yuan's confidence and respect.

3. Hold a conference to examine the condition for the return of Kiaochow Bay for the exchange of rights.

4. Conclude an agreement with Yuan regarding political and economic problems that might interfere with the principle of equal opportunity on the railways, in the mines, etc.

B. Problems with Russia.

Sound out British intentions but, without relying on England alone, conclude an alliance with Russia now and build up the foundations for a future Japanese-English-Russian-French alliance.

C. Problems with France.

Attract capital from France and invest the money in China in the name of a Franco-Japanese Bank.

D. Problems with America.

In order to prevent China from turning to America and to dissolve American doubts about us, place faith in America and examine the most suitable way of furthering friendly Japanese-American relations.

E. On the matter of sending able diplomats to Europe and America.

Send well-known diplomats or semi-official persons with talent to consider the most appropriate policy for the present situation.[66]

It will be noted that many of these recommendations were included in the long memorandum Yamagata had submitted more than a month before. The new elements, the stress on drawing closer to France and

66. *Ibid.*, III, 915–916.

Russia and the luring of French capital, emerged from Inoue's thinking. These recommendations emphasized the desire of the *genrō* to lay down broad policies for the development of Japan's international position.

Two points were paramount: improving relations with China and approaching Russia immediately for an alliance. In a secret letter sent by the *genrō* to the prime minister, some of these recommendations were made even more specific.[67] For example, an alliance with Russia was urged before the latter might emerge as a victor in World War I; China's distrust of Japan could be weakened by disapproving of the Chinese revolutionists in Japan; American activity in China, particularly its effort to interfere in Sino-Japanese problems, should be carefully studied.

These recommendations, following the understanding reached by the prime minister and the *genrō*, served as a guage with which the elder statesmen could judge their real influence. In each of the areas in which suggestions were made important developments were to take place. In two particular instances — the twenty-one demands on China in 1915 and the secret alliance concluded with Russia in 1916 — it is possible to trace the influence of the *genrō*. In both instances the attitude of the government and the policy advocated by the *genrō* were to vary. As the most powerful *genrō*, Yamagata was, in both cases, to bring about some modifications in Japan's foreign policy.

A Test of *Genrō* Influence: The 1915 Demands on China

Japan's declaration of war was followed by military action in China. Japanese troops landed south of the German base in Kiaochow Bay with token British assistance. Desultory fighting continued for a month before the surrender of German forces on October 7, 1914. In the months following the elimination of the German naval base in China, Japanese naval forces in the South Pacific occupied without serious incident German island possessions. Convoying British empire troops through the Indian Ocean and participation in the antisubmarine naval action in the Mediterranean later in the war completed Japan's military activities during World War I.

Japan had not entered the war out of desperation. It was a calculated move to protect and improve her position in East Asia. Viewed from China, this meant aggressive action against the continent. "Japan is

67. See *ibid.*, III, 916–917, for the text of these specific suggestions.

going to take advantage of this war to get control of China," [68] concluded Paul S. Reinsch, the American minister to China. And after the war, Britain's foreign secretary Grey echoed the sentiment that Japan would use the war "to strengthen their position with China in East Asia," adding that "the opportunity for Japan was immense and unique." [69] Grey further added the observation that, given such an opportunity, Japan used it with restraint, a view Mr. Reinsch would not have been inclined to accept. Curiously, even in Japan the conflict over the policy toward China arose in part over the degree of restraint, or boldness, that should be shown. The *genrō* were determined to moderate the actions advocated by the Foreign Office.

A clash between the *genrō* and the Cabinet developed over the appropriate steps to be taken, but the ends were held in common. The aim shared by all the leaders was to safeguard the Far East and to improve Japan's position. The urgency expressed by the *genrō* in their approach to Japan's foreign relations as well as by Katō's policy was owing to the opportunity created by the withdrawal of European power from the Far East because of the battle in Europe. Katō, viewing Japan's participation in the war as a means to larger ends, wished to place a price on the return of the captured German base that would be high enough to buy an advantageous settlement of Japan's position in Manchuria.

That problems regarding Manchuria's future were at the heart of Japan's relations with China is clearly seen in the negotiations during 1915 for the "twenty-one demands." The critical factor was that when Japan acquired Russian rights in Southern Manchuria in 1905 she also inherited the time limits placed upon the possession of these areas. The twenty-five year lease of the Kwantung territory (including Port Arthur and Dairen) was due to expire in 1923; the promise to sell back to China the Antung Railway was scheduled for fulfillment in 1923, and the resale of the South Manchurian Railway to be completed by 1940.[70] A continuing objective after the Russo-Japanese War was to lift these conditions and acquire the rights in perpetuity.

Foreign minister Katō had expressed Japan's concern regarding her rights in Manchuria to foreign secretary Grey before he gave up his position as ambassador to London. Grey was sympathetic to the Japanese

68. Paul S. Reinsch, *An American Diplomat in China* (Garden City, N.Y., 1922), p. 129.

69. Grey, *Twenty-Five Years*, II, 104–105.

70. Kiyosawa, *Nihon gaikō shi*, II, 365.

desire to extend the lease but was noncommittal on the railway question. Katō's own notes of these conversations in London, on January 3 and 10, 1913, indicate that in reply to the query of when Japan intended to enter into negotiations with China, Katō replied, "When the psychological moment arrives." [71] Katō, and through him the Japanese government, was led to believe that he had the sympathetic understanding of Britain in the solution of Japan's relations with China. And Katō made his conversations well known to the leaders in government.

Yamagata also believed in the importance of Manchuria for Japan. "Manchuria is Japan's life line," he told a friend, "so we must secure for our nationals assurance that they may settle there and pursue their occupations peacefully." [72] He was even prepared, as a last resort, to achieve this by force, but he saw no need for such action if China were approached properly. He was of the opinion that victory over Russia a decade earlier had secured certain guarantees for Japanese interests in Manchuria, and that Japan's expanding population required an outlet. Again, however, his stand on issues of foreign policy was related to future racial struggles which loomed so large in his mind. Declaring that the solution to Japan's problems must be based on the concept of "Asia for the Asians," he explained that "China may object to the Japanese setting foot in Manchuria, but if Japan had not fought and repelled the encroachment of Russia in Manchuria, isn't it logical to suggest that even Peking might not be in Chinese territory today? The spread of Japan into Manchuria is for the advantage of our nation and our people, but isn't it also necessary for realizing the principle of the self-protection of Asians as well as for the co-existence and co-prosperity of China and Japan?" [73]

But what was the "psychological moment" for gaining this widely shared objective? Katō felt that participation in the European war, on the basis of friendship for England, presented the opportunity he sought. Even before the war was declared, he instructed Hioki, Japan's minister to China, to approach President Yuan Shih-kai on questions of mutual interest. After the capitulation of the Germans at Tsingtao, minister Hioki returned to Tokyo where he received instructions to attempt an overall settlement with China. The details had been worked out; Hioki was now only to await the appropriate hour. The moment arrived when, in January 1915, the Chinese first announced the abolition of the war

71. Record of the conversation is given in Itō Masanori, *Katō Kōmei*, II, 133–140.
72. Takahashi, *San kō iretsu*, p. 97.
73. *Ibid.*, pp. 98–99.

zone in Shantung which had been established when the Japanese invaded Shantung, and then requested all foreign troops to withdraw from China. Within a few days Japan's demands were presented to China. Through diplomatic channels, Katō informed Britain, France, and the United States that Japan was about to negotiate with China. But he did not disclose the far-reaching demands he was to make.

Originally arranged in five groups and numbering twenty-one articles, these demands were worked out by the foreign ministry. On reading the demands,[74] the Chinese must have felt that they were, as Chiang Kaishek was later to characterize them, "nothing more than the grand culmination of all the unequal treaties . . . intended to transfer the special privileges separately enjoyed by the powers to the exclusive control of the Japanese." [75] But for the Japanese the requests did not seem entirely out of line with the immense advantages gained by the Western powers in the previous half-century. The document demanded exclusive and expanded privileges for Japan in Shantung; extension of leases in Manchuria to ninety-nine years plus rights of land ownership; rights to mining and railway enterprises in South Manchuria and eastern Inner Mongolia; joint ownership of the Hanyehping Iron Company on the Yangtze with exclusive rights to operate the iron deposits near Hankow; and prohibition against the Chinese ceding any harbor or island along her coast. The fifth and last group of seven articles provided for exclusive rights within China — appointment of Japanese advisers, joint administration of the police force, the right for Japanese churches and schools to own land and for missionaries to propagate their faith, the granting of specific railway-construction rights, and China's pledge to purchase at least half of her munitions from Japan and employ Japanese technicians.

Both the extent of the demands and the manner in which they were presented and negotiated came under attack abroad and at home. There ensued a long period of intensive negotiation, as China and the other powers maneuvered, sought clarification, made proposals, and responded to counterproposals. Twenty-four conferences were held in Peking between February 5 and April 17. China, disregarding the request of the Japanese, kept foreign diplomats in Peking informed of the negotiations. As a consequence, pressure was exerted on Japan by both the

74. James W. Morley suggests that the military attaché in Peking had made recommendations which became the basis of the demands. See *The Japanese Thrust into Siberia* (New York, 1957), p. 13, footnote 7.
75. Chiang Kai-shek, *China's Destiny* (New York, 1947), p. 74.

United States and England to have the demands revised. Some concessions were made and a revised draft of the demands was presented to Peking on April 27. The far-reaching demands of the fifth group were rewritten and one article — the demand for a joint police force — was withdrawn, but the changes were not satisfactory to the Chinese.[76]

Thus far the foreign powers had joined China in objecting to some of the demands and some modification had resulted. But Katō pressed on; new tactics were employed. The plan to send troops to support the negotiations was dropped, but Katō agreed to the sending of troops to relieve garrisons in Manchuria and North China; however, the troops to be relieved, the Chinese were told, would not be withdrawn until negotiations had been completed. This form of pressure was not sufficient to get the Chinese to accept the revised demands. Finally Katō decided to resort to a forty-eight-hour ultimatum. On May 4 the Cabinet approved his plan and later the same day the Cabinet met with the genrō. It is doubtful that Katō realized what an obstacle he was to face.

It is impossible to say how closely informed Yamagata and the other genrō were kept. Despite the agreement reached with Ōkuma in September, Katō continued to remain aloof from the genrō. He did, however, get their general agreement for settling issues with China. The genrō's memorandum of September 1 agreed that the first aim should be to strengthen Japan's relations with China. So Katō would have had no difficulty in receiving their encouragement so long as the details were not discussed. In November he visited each of the genrō, and he saw Yamagata again in December. He received general approval for his plans, but he neglected to keep the genrō abreast of developments once negotiations began. In February Matsukata wrote Yamagata, "I still have no authoritative information on the negotiations with China . . . I would like occasionally to hear about a matter of such importance . . . That even you have received no reports is truly shocking." [77] Two days later, with pointed sarcasm, Yamagata wrote Ōkuma, "Since the negotiations with China began, I have come across references here and there in the newspapers. While I am not familiar with progress in foreign negotiations, it must be absorbing much of your energy and time." [78] In reply to this letter, Ōkuma said, in part, "In our problem with China there

76. The original, revised, and final forms of the demands are conveniently listed in parallel columns in Kiyosawa, *Nihon gaikō shi*, II, 367–376.

77. The full letter, dated Feb. 18, 1915, is reprinted in Tokutomi Ichirō, *Kōshaku Matsukata Masayoshi den* (Tokyo, 1935), II, 916–917.

78. Original of this letter is in the Katsura Tarō monjo, in the National Diet Library.

has been some misunderstanding with England and America but I am sure this will soon be overcome and we shall have their agreement. As you know, we haven't made the progress we hoped for in China; this is most regrettable and for it I beg your understanding." [79] This was hardly detailed information. In April, in a letter to Inoue, Yamagata repeated his complaint: "Since the beginning of negotiations with China, we have requested the foreign minister to keep us informed from time to time but we have received no reports, nor any direct word from him." [80]

Yamagata was angered not only by the failure to receive detailed information of the progress of negotiations but also by the cool reception accorded his advice. He told his friend Takahashi: "I have given various suggestions to the foreign office regarding Japanese-Chinese negotiations, but unfortunately they have received little attention. Ōkuma operates that way, so even the foreign minister will not speak to me about diplomatic secrets, perhaps because not a few times developments have indeed moved as I warned. Perhaps a man of my age shouldn't give advice but in matters of importance to the nation I feel I must express my thoughts." [81]

Yamagata was annoyed that he was not better informed and irritated by the rebuff his views received, but there were still other reasons for predicting that the May meeting of the Cabinet and genrō would not go smoothly. The genrō were, as we have seen, anxious to establish friendly relations with Yuan Shih-kai in order to win China's confidence. They were convinced that the fifth group of demands prejudiced that objective. Yuan, informed of their attitude, attempted to work through informal channels to have the Japanese government withdraw some of its demands. In February 1915, Ariga Nagao, a noted Japanese scholar of international law who was then in Peking, was called by Yuan for an interview. "In my interview with Yuan," Ariga later reported, "he said that in the negotiations it would be most difficult to consent to any conditions which would compromise China's sovereignty or territorial integrity. He requested that after returning to Japan I convey the sentiment that any such concessions would weaken the position he had built after much difficulty." [82] Ariga returned to Japan and talked to Yamagata, Inoue, and then Katō of the disadvantages of pressing China too

---

79. Letter, dated Feb. 24, 1915, reprinted in *Yamagata den,* III, 949–950.
80. Letter dated April 29, 1915, appears in Matsumoto Tadao, *Kinsei Nihon gaikō shi kenkyū* (Tokyo, 1942), p. 288. (Cited hereafter as *Gaikō kenkyū.*)
81. Takahashi, *San kō iretsu,* p. 96.
82. Matsumoto Tadao, *Gaikō kenkyū,* p. 280.

far. He found a sympathetic response among the *genrō* who already feared the consequences of the fifth group of the demands.

The anxiety of the *genrō* was increased in the days immediately before the May meeting. For one thing, Yamagata had heard of the plans to issue an ultimatum to China. "Weighing all things," Yamagata wrote Inoue five days before the *genrō* met with the Cabinet, "I was afraid there was a chance that the government might use coercive measures. Therefore, to ascertain the real state of affairs, I sent my private secretary to see the Home Minister." [83] For Yamagata, home minister Ōura was always a source of information about developments within the Cabinet. It is not known what he learned from Ōura at this time, but perhaps he was alerted to the decision for the ultimatum Katō and the Cabinet were soon to issue.

Personal disapproval of Katō for slighting them and fear of crippling Japan's chances for friendly relations with Yuan were two reasons for the *genrō*'s opposition to Katō's approach to China. A third objection was the fear that Katō was arousing the hostility and suspicion of all the major powers. Adverse reaction on the part of England and other nations, they felt, would weaken the chances of fulfilling the long-range objectives of Japan's foreign policy. Inoue, in particular, was insistent on reaching an understanding with England, Russia, and the United States.

On the afternoon of May 4, 1915, the Cabinet met with all the *genrō* except Inoue. Katō opened the meeting explaining why he thought an ultimatum was unavoidable. Yamagata was the first *genrō* to speak and asserted his disapproval of thrusting an ultimatum at China for demands as reckless as those included in the fifth group. On the conduct of the negotiations, he spoke of the necessity of giving[84] "an impression of extreme fairness . . . and not disgracing us in the eyes of the great powers." Turning to Katō he said, "This impasse is your responsibility. And if you admit this responsibility is it not your duty to proceed to China as a special ambassador and attempt a final settlement?" [85] Matsukata added that a break in relations with China would place a heavy financial burden on the nation for which it was not prepared. Yamagata also presented some of Inoue's views that he had received by telephone. Later that day, Yamagata reported to Inoue on the meeting: "Present circumstances allowed no time to consult with the powers and no time for the foreign

83. Letter of April 29, 1915, in *ibid.,* p. 288.
84. Yamagata's remarks in this meeting are quoted in *ibid.,* p. 268.
85. Quoted in *Yamagata den,* III, 930.

minister to go himself. Instead, they [the prime minister and the foreign minister] argued, our country has not only used all its resources but also the newspapers have produced a situation no longer permitting any delay. One after another, the prime minister and the foreign minister disagreed with me. My opinion was not heeded so, with further argument useless, I withdrew." [86]

The conference became difficult and various tactics were used to mollify the *genrō*. Katō, for example, shouldered full responsibility for the course of the negotiations and offered to resign. He continued to believe, however, that the point at which his personal negotiations in Peking would be of any use had already passed. But the *genrō* present continued to insist that great harm was being done in insisting upon demands that Yuan could not accept, and that such demands were, in turn, risking the concessions he seemed prepared to grant.

At 6:00 P.M. the *genrō* withdrew from the meeting before an agreement was reached. But the caution and moderation they had called for had had an effect. The Cabinet continued its meeting and reconsidered the policy it had already approved. Ichiki, the minister of education and a friend of Yamagata, spoke up to suggest that the fifth group of demands be dropped; several others agreed that a logical step was to defer the fifth group for later consideration. The meeting ended without a final decision but with a general agreement that that should be the course. The problem now was how to gain the support of the *genrō*.

Late on May 4, Ōkuma sent a telegram to Ōura calling him back to Tokyo from a business trip to Nara. Ōura, who had been shifted in January to head the home ministry, had been used before to smooth relations between the Ōkuma Cabinet and the *genrō*. He had supported the decision to drop the fifth group of demands, and finally on May 5 the Cabinet took formal action to revise the wording of the ultimatum. Ōura reported the decision to the *genrō* and the following day the *genrō* finally approved the ultimatum. Yamagata agreed to the ultimatum in its revised form, but he still had some misgivings. He was not satisfied with the references to the timing of the retrocession of Kiaochow Bay. "Once the retrocession is declared," he said, "it must be respected. Thus I differ with the foreign minister in the timing of the declaration of restoration. So I regret that it was proposed in the second revised draft." [87]

Ōura, who had played the role of the mediator, described the final settlement as follows: "Katō's plan in general had the tacit understand-

86. Letter of May 4, 1915, reprinted in Matsumoto, *Gaikō kenkyū,* p. 287.
87. Quoted in *ibid.,* p. 278.

ing of England and the other powers, but the fifth group, our "desirable demands," had not been disclosed to our ally. It would be most unfortunate if we should wreck negotiations because of the fifth group of requests, so shortly they were withdrawn to be held in reserve for another year. In this way the *genrō*'s agreement was achieved and the other terms were placed before China and the China problem was resolved." [88]

A few days after China had accepted the ultimatum, Yamagata gave his friend Takahashi Yoshio the following account:

> A nation must resort to arms when it is imperiled, but, as demanded in the recent fifth group, if such trifling things as the acceptance of Japanese advisers, purchase of Japanese arms, and rights for Japanese missionaries were gained by military power, it would disgrace the honor of Japan which stands for justice in the world. That is why I felt I had to use every means to halt these negotiations. As might have been expected, just as the ultimatum was to be sent, a note was received from British Foreign Minister Grey stating that such extreme demands on China as the employment of Japanese advisers and the purchase of arms which would give Japan preponderant rights were contrary to the spirit of the Anglo-Japanese alliance . . . even without Grey's objections I would have found it difficult to approve of the mistaken plan of sending an ultimatum carrying a threat of military force on the questions involved. So eventually the fifth group was withdrawn in the final ultimatum. [89]

By May a treaty was signed with China which gained most of Japan's demands; on January 7, 1916, with Yamagata sitting as its president, the Privy Council ratified the agreement. In this important foreign relations development, Yamagata's role had been to lead the *genrō* in modifying both the extent of the demands and the method of conducting the negotiations. Most of the demands fell within Yamagata's proposed plan for strengthening Japan's position, but ill-advised and arrogant diplomacy had threatened to disrupt what he considered the foundation for building up that position — conciliating China through persuasive diplomacy. In this instance, the influence of the *genrō* had been successfully exerted in the direction of more conciliatory means to strengthen Japan's security in the Far East.

88. Quoted in *Yamagata den,* III, 932.
89. Takahashi, *San kō iretsu,* pp. 97–98.

The Test of *Genrō* Influence:
The Russo-Japanese Alliance of 1916

If the *genrō* gained limited success in influencing the Cabinet to take a more conciliatory approach toward China, the nation's gains in China's acquiescence to the final demands were enjoyed as much by them as by any other segment of the leadership of Japan. Yamagata had spoken and written of the need to induce rather than coerce China to understand Japan's aims and to draw the two nations together against a threat of a racial struggle in the future. Yamagata's specific objectives had included the preservation and expansion of Japan's position in Manchuria and East Mongolia.[90] A strong foothold in this area had indeed been achieved in the negotiations with China in 1915.

Yamagata outlined his own prescription for developing Japan's advantages: "It is necessary, on the one hand, to maintain friendly relations with Russia and, on the other, harmonize our relations with China and eliminate areas of conflict." [91] It would be difficult to grant that the demands of 1915 had achieved the latter. The method employed had been criticized severely by Yamagata and his colleagues, and harm had been done even though wide concessions had been achieved. But what of the other problems? What of the relations with Russia necessary for strengthening Japan's position?

The negotiations leading to a secret alliance with Russia form a second main strand in Japan's wartime diplomacy. In this the *genrō* played a more important role than they had in the negotiations with China. Led by Yamagata, they were to initiate, expedite, and push to a conclusion an alliance. But both strands were interwoven, for while negotiations were being conducted in Peking, Yamagata was applying pressure on the Foreign Office to hasten negotiations with Russia. In February 1915, Yamagata drew up a long memorandum for the prime minister, urging that "now is the time to conclude an alliance with Russia." [92] His reasoning for this demand flowed from the conviction that the world war would disrupt prewar power relations and quite likely accentuate the tendency toward a racial struggle. To prepare for this eventuality, he argued that gaining China's confidence was a first step; another step was to avoid the isolation of Japan from Western (white) allies. He was satisfied that the alliance with England aided this purpose, but it was not enough, particularly because the strength of Britain after the war was

90. *Ibid.,* p. 99.
91. *Yamagata den,* III, 922.
92. *Ibid.,* III, 945.

uncertain. "So the policy of relying solely on the Anglo-Japanese alliance to maintain continued peace in East Asia may be inadequate. The most urgent task for Japan, therefore, is to have, in addition to the Anglo-Japanese alliance, an alliance with Russia which would provide us with adequate means to gain our objectives." [93]

Yamagata's first step in advancing his proposal for the immediate negotiation of an alliance was to gain the support of his fellow *genrō*. This was done by sending for their approval copies of the memorandum he proposed to submit to the prime minister. In his letter to Ōyama, he repeated his statements in the memorandum concerning the disturbing effect the European war would undoubtedly have on the balance of power. With the outcome of the war still in doubt, he felt that "we have an opportunity for strengthening our policy for the future maintenance of peace in the Far East by extending one step further the agreements with our northern neighbor Russia . . . If you should agree with this memorandum after reading it, I would appreciate your signing it." [94]

Because of Inoue's previous encouragement, Yamagata was assured of his support. In fact, a letter to Inoue indicates that Yamagata had made some revisions of his statement on the basis of Inoue's suggestion.[95] Next, both Ōyama and Matsukata endorsed the plan enthusiastically and added their signatures to the statement.[96] With these signatures, the next step was to forward the memorandum to the prime minister. In a covering letter, Yamagata repeated some of the phrases he had used in letters to the other *genrō*. He first mentioned how he was not well informed about negotiations with China, and then he wrote:

> The present war among the powers of Europe, already seven months old and without decisive action, continues unabated with its outcome difficult to predict. But even if the allied armies are victorious we must expect a shift in the position of the powers as a consequence of this war.
>
> As I am convinced that we are faced with a great opportunity for improving our policy of maintaining peace in the Far East by extending one step further the agreements with our northern neighbor, Russia, I have discussed it with the other *genrō* and have received their unanimous support.

93. *Ibid.*, III, 944.
94. Letter, dated Feb. 18, appears in full in *ibid.*, III, 947.
95. The original of this letter to Inoue, dated Feb. 20, 1915, is in the Yamagata Aritomo monjo (Papers of Yamagata Aritomo) in the National Diet Library.
96. See Ōyama's Feb. 18 letter to Yamagata in *Yamagata den*, III, 947; Matsukata's reply of the same date appears in Tokutomi, *Matsukata den*, II, 916–917.

Under separate cover, I am sending the main outline [of the policy] for your examination. For the sake of the nation I hope you will, in harmony with your estimate of the domestic and foreign situations, give it your immediate attention.[97]

Yamagata was not optimistic about the result he would achieve. Advocacy of an alliance in the past had borne no fruit. "Despite our urging on the question of a Russo-Japanese alliance," he wrote Inoue, ". . . I fear the matter has been ignored." [98] Ōkuma's reply was courteous but noncommittal.[99] He promised to have the foreign minister visit Yamagata and bring along background studies of the agreements that had previously been made. But the tone of Ōkuma's response gave Yamagata no encouragement, and a few days later he wrote Inoue, "I doubt if the matter gets any immediate attention." [100]

The truth was that negotiations with China at this time preoccupied the Foreign Office almost to the exclusion of any other matters. The *genrō* themselves, as we have seen, were drawn into the same problems so that interest in a Russian alliance subsided for some time. But Yamagata did not allow the question to die; when the problems associated with reaching an agreement with China were solved, he again directed attention to the need for an alliance. On May 27, two days after the treaties with China had been signed, Yamagata queried Katō: "What consideration has been given the memorandum advocating a Russo-Japanese Alliance which I signed jointly with Matsukata, Inoue, and Ōyama and sent you some time ago? Not only do East-West relations make it more important than ever, but Marquis Inoue and the other *genrō* frequently make inquiries. Please inform me of its status." [101] Whatever Katō's reply was to this query, it did not satisfy Yamagata and it produced another flurry of activity among the *genrō* in support of negotiations with Russia.

This new activity was imbued with emotion as well as reason. The angry clashes with Katō over the China policy prompted the *genrō* to take the initiative and even to force Katō out of office if they could. Responding to Yamagata's urging, Inoue went to Tokyo from his seaside residence and conferred with Matsukata, Ōkuma, and several times with Yamagata. On June 23 the *genrō* met together for four hours, and two

97. Original of memorandum to Ōkuma, dated Feb. 20, 1915, is in the Yamagata Aritomo monjo.
98. Letter dated Feb. 20, 1915, in the Yamagata Aritomo monjo.
99. Ōkuma's letter to Yamagata of Feb. 24, 1915, is in *Yamagata den*, III, 949–950.
100. Yamagata to Inoue, Feb. 25, 1915, reprinted in Watanabe Ikujirō, *Monjo yori mitaru Ōkuma Shigenobu kō*, p. 212.
101. Quoted in Shinobu, *Taishō shi*, I, 257.

days later the prime minister joined them in a conference. What were all these meetings for? At the time their purpose was not too well known. Hara Kei recorded that it was "probably about foreign affairs problems." [102] After a few days it became known that serious thought was being given by the *genrō* not only to the question of a new Russian policy but to the question of the tenure of the foreign minister and the whole Cabinet.[103] Inoue, in particular, appeared determined to force the withdrawal of Katō. It was decided, however, that any reorganization of the Cabinet should await the conclusion of the emperor's coronation ceremonies scheduled for November. But activity on behalf of an agreement with Russia was not curtailed.

On July 7, Yamagata confronted Katō and Ōkuma directly. In the reconstruction of this conversation a year later, Yamagata recollected that he discussed first the general conditions in Europe and found Katō in wide agreement with his analysis. Regarding his specific proposals he had said:

> In the European war, both sides have enjoyed victories and suffered defeats, but Germany is not able to conquer the allied powers and the latter are unable to defeat Germany. So both sides have advantages as well as disadvantages for conditions of peace. Since each nation promotes its own interests, it would be unwise to jeopardize the Japanese Empire by carelessly arousing unthinkingly German resentment. Doubtless it will be necessary to explain to Germany that Japan took belligerent action in fulfillment of the Anglo-Japanese alliance. But what is most urgent today is to conclude a treaty with Russia without any delay. Since the Russo-Japanese war there have been frequent expressions in Russia of anger and revenge and, as Katō of course knows, there is a pro-German faction strong enough so that it could form a cabinet. Therefore now is the time to demonstrate sufficient good will toward Russia to reduce her ill feelings.[104]

Katō's argument in reply was that such an alliance would dilute and weaken the existing alliance with England. It would be, he said, like "adding too much water to whisky." [105] Furthermore, Katō had an unshakable confidence in England and her allies to succeed in the war, so there was less incentive for him to rush into a new agreement with Russia

---

102. *Hara nikki*, VI, 267; entry of June 22, 1915.
103. *Ibid.*, VI, 277.
104. Quoted by Takahashi, *San kō iretsu*, pp. 116–117, from a conversation he had with Yamagata on July 10, 1916.
105. Quoted in Itō, *Katō Kōmei*, II, 49.

for fear of the extension of German power into the East. The conversation ended satisfactorily, Katō agreeing to explore the idea of a Japanese-Russian-English agreement and Yamagata feeling that there had been an acceptance in principle of his proposal.

But Inoue was far from conciliated. For six weeks he had remained in the capital to press for negotiations and a change at the Foreign Office. Losing all patience, he finally gave Ōkuma an ultimatum: "Choose between changing the foreign minister and severing all connections with me." [106] The barb in this remark was sharp for it had been Inoue who originally suggested that Ōkuma be invited to form a Cabinet the previous year. Put on the spot, Ōkuma tried to avoid the choice and hedged enough to cause Inoue to remark, "In that case, hereafter let us discuss matters concerning the cabinet through Home Minister Ōura; but I will have nothing whatsoever to do with foreign relations." [107]

Matsukata was equally displeased. "Under the circumstances," he maintained, "it would be safest to have the whole cabinet change." [108] Yamagata too felt that Katō should go, but he persuaded his colleagues not to move precipitately. Behind the apparent caution was the fact that adequate preparations had not been made to find a satisfactory replacement for Ōkuma should the Cabinet resign. At any rate, Yamagata successfully argued: "The outlook for this cabinet is dim and it shows clear signs of falling itself very shortly. So it would not be the best policy for the *genrō* to be responsible for defeating the cabinet before the coronation." [109]

The coronation ceremonies delayed the fall of the Cabinet, but Katō's position was most precarious. The flurry of meetings and conferences in June had produced so much adverse criticism of his actions that Katō merely awaited the first opportunity to resign from the Cabinet. An accumulation of grievances had built up solid *genrō* opposition to the plans and the conduct of his policy. He had defiantly tried to remove their influence in the conduct of foreign affairs. He would have to pay the price they demanded, and another Cabinet crisis over a domestic issue gave him his opportunity.

Late in July 1915 it was revealed that home minister Ōura had flagrantly violated the election laws and through the generous use of bribes had contributed to the defeat of the Seiyūkai party in the March elec-

106. Quoted in Shinobu, *Taishō shi*, I, 259.
107. *Ibid.*, p. 259.
108. *Ibid.*, p. 259.
109. *Ibid.*, p. 259.

tions. The Seiyūkai was deprived of its absolute majority in the elections and the direct interference of officials under Ōura's orders had, it was claimed, been the direct reason. Ōura, friend of Yamagata and long experienced in the police work of the home ministry, had received the cooperation of many governors in influencing the outcome of the election. When his responsibility was made clear, Ōura resigned. At the same time, Katō, pleading that he was also responsible for difficulties encountered by the Cabinet, finally resigned.

What the *genrō* had hoped to avoid until after the coronation of the emperor had occurred. As a group, the *genrō* asked Ōkuma to reconsider the Cabinet's resignation, to reorganize the Cabinet excluding Katō and the finance minister Wakatsuki, and to remain in office.[110] Yamagata would have preferred a national unity Cabinet at this point, but preparations had not been completed so he pledged his support to Ōkuma.

The reorganization of Ōkuma's Cabinet at first had little effect on Yamagata's interest in an alliance with Russia. The coronation in Kyoto, in which Yamagata played an honored part, the early days of the new Cabinet, and his determination not to interfere unduly with Katō's successor at the Foreign Office resulted in a lull in approaching the Russian question. The new foreign minister, Ishii Kikujirō, was more sympathetic than Katō to the idea of a new agreement with Russia. Overtures were made both in Petrograd and in Tokyo, but negotiations were carried on in a desultory fashion. By the end of the year Yamagata became restive; he was anxious to see some progress made. The event which finally catalyzed action was the visit of Russian royalty.

In January 1916, Grand Duke Georgi, uncle of Tsar Nicholas II of Russia, paid a state visit to Japan. His arrival presented Yamagata with an opportunity to further his objectives. As he explained it:

> When I heard of the Russian Grand Duke's visit, I felt it was an opportunity that could not be missed. Confiding my aim to Terauchi [then governor-general of Korea], I expressed the feeling that this was the time to warm up Russian-Japanese negotiations and arranged the reception with great care. But a great mistake was made. When the Russian Grand Duke's suite made inquiries regarding the meaning of the proposed Russo-Japanese treaty, Ishii's reply

110. Inoue sent word to Yamagata by his secretary that he would encourage Ōkuma to stay in office but "did not approve of Katō and Wakatsuki remaining in office." *Inoue den*, V, 423. The *genrō* meeting of August 3 was Inoue's last act; he died three weeks later.

was curt and discourteous; doubts were thus raised about our government's sincerity toward friendly Russian-Japanese relations. I was astonished beyond words when I heard about it. First I had Terauchi, who speaks French well, explain to them that Japan's real intentions should not be judged by this cold reception. When I criticized Ishii's impudence, he and Ōkuma justified their indifference as a way of ascertaining the sincerity of the Russians. However, I said it was inexcusable behavior for them to take lightly the memorandum that he [Grand Duke Georgi] presented in good faith. Ishii then presented a second plan advocating Russian-Japanese friendship more or less along the lines I favored.[111]

These recollections, if taken at face value, show in general the changes brought about at the insistence of Yamagata. And the details of his maneuvering are instructive about the way in which Yamagata tried to exert his considerable authority in the formation of foreign policy. Even before the arrival of the Russian delegation, Yamagata arranged through the Imperial Household minister to have General Terauchi called from Korea to serve on the welcoming committee. In this way he enlisted the aid of a staunch and loyal supporter who, in addition, spoke Russian. Throughout their stay, Terauchi was to act as liaison between Yamagata and the Russians.

The Russians knew well the value of Yamagata's support and acted accordingly. Knowing the old *genrō*'s attitude, the grand duke visited Yamagata one day after his arrival in Tokyo, making it his first call after an imperial audience. In a short, dignified ceremony the seventy-eight-year old Yamagata was presented with a medal of the Order of Saint Alexander Nevsky as an expression of the tsar's appreciation for his work in promoting friendly relations. During the visit Yamagata's understanding and aid were solicited and he was quite happy to reassure his guests that he would use his influence to consummate a mutually satisfactory alliance.

The precise way in which Yamagata's influence was brought to bear cannot be completely reconstructed from the available documents. It is known that several more conversations regarding an alliance were held between the Russians and Yamagata. Similar conversations were held with Foreign Office officials but with less satisfactory results. It was when Yamagata was apprised of the Foreign Office's negative response to the

111. Takahashi, *San kō iretsu*, p. 118.

Russian overtures that he applied his influence with vigor and with striking success.[112]

The policy of the government on January 20 was to delay negotiations. Foreign minister Ishii's reply to the Russians pointed out that no disputes had arisen lately over Manchuria and Mongolia, so an agreement regarding these areas was uncalled for. He also intimated that Japan was in no position to offer arms and ammunition. But three weeks later the policy of the government was reversed and negotiations leading to an alliance were sanctioned. On the day the Cabinet made this decision, Yamagata sent General Tanaka to inform the Russian ambassador secretly that instructions were being sent to the Japanese ambassador in Petrograd ordering him to begin negotiations.[113] The logic of the situation and all available information compel the conclusion that the shift in policy was the consequence of Yamagata's stand. In his diary, Hara records that he was reliably told that both Katō and Ishii had opposed an alliance but that Yamagata's dissatisfaction with their position led to a change in policy.[114] When negotiations were well along, army minister Ōshima wrote Yamagata, "As a result of your unfaltering efforts, the offensive-defensive Russo-Japanese Treaty has been concluded. Yesterday the Privy Council endorsed it unanimously." [115]

At the time of the grand duke's departure, three genrō (Yamagata, Matsukata, and Ōyama) met with Ōkuma and Ishii to agree on an alliance and the transfer of war materials to Russia. The foreign minister suggested that in exchange for arms and ammunition the Russians should hand over the ownership of part of the Chinese Eastern Railway. But this was dropped when Yamagata argued that it was quite unreasonable.[116] Negotiations for an alliance were carried on in Petrograd for several months; on July 3, 1916, the treaty was signed. During the negotiations Yamagata was kept closely in touch; he commented on early drafts of the treaty. When it was signed, he could claim that it was "the realization of a long-cherished desire of mine, so I am overjoyed." [117]

The public articles of the treaty dealt with the defense of the special

112. The most thorough examination of this episode in Japan's foreign relations is that by Peter Berton, "The Secret Russo-Japanese Alliance of 1916" (unpublished Ph.D. dissertation, Columbia University, 1956).
113. *Ibid.*, p. 177.
114. *Hara nikki*, VI, 396.
115. Letter dated June 30, 1914 (sic), printed in *Yamagata den*, III, 951. By both the date of the treaty and the fact that Ōshima was war minister in March 1916 — which title he uses to sign his letter — the date given must be in error.
116. Shinobu, *Taishō shi*, I, 276.
117. Takahashi, *San kō iretsu*, p. 114.

interests of the two countries in the whole Far East; both parties pledged not to join any combination of nations directed against the other. The more important secret clauses provided for the loaning of arms and, in addition, for joint efforts to prevent China from falling under the domination of a third power. This was an allusion to Germany. The alliance would remain in effect as long as the Anglo-Japanese Alliance continued.[118]

The secret agreements of the treaty suggest that in 1916 Yamagata anticipated a German victory. Earlier in the year he had expressed to visitors that inasmuch as Britain and Russia were weakening and France was barely holding her own a German victory appeared likely. At the time, this view prevailed in the Japanese army.[119] It was felt that a German victory and the presence of a strong pro-German group within Russia pointed to the possibility of a German-Russian alliance which would place Japan at a great disadvantage. Yamagata did not share the fear of some at the Foreign Office that a treaty with Russia would weaken the Anglo-Japanese Alliance. It was his position that it would complement it and protect the nation against a powerful alliance that might be formed to threaten Japan.

These were some of Yamagata's reasons for engineering an agreement with Russia. But there was still another motive for insisting on the alliance. The isolation of Japan, he argued, which would probably result from an "all-white" alliance, would fatally weaken Japan's position in a future racial struggle. Both his advocacy of a policy which would draw Japan and China closer and his demands for an alliance with Russia derived from his conviction of an unavoidable racial struggle which would follow the war.

This episode in foreign relations illustrated how Yamagata's acknowledged authority in the government assured him more than a courteous hearing of his views. With Inoue, he had initiated the idea of an alliance with Russia. But so long as Katō was foreign minister with his fixed pro-British[120] views and his preoccupation with China affairs, the idea languished. Persistence, however, was a trait keenly developed in Yamagata. After the removal of Katō, it was possible to impress his views with greater success, even to guide the development of foreign policy to meet his own objectives. That the Soviet revolution supervened to render the

118. The text of treaty is available as an Appendix to Berton's study of the alliance.
119. Conversation with Hara; *Hara nikki,* VI, 371–373.
120. Katō had opposed it because he was persuaded that an alliance with Russia would weaken the Anglo-Japanese Alliance, which he regarded as the main pillar of Japan's foreign relations.

alliance meaningless and set a new stage in East Asia does not alter the conclusion that Yamagata, in his seventy-eighth year, had demonstrated that under certain circumstances his authority was as impressive and decisive as it had ever been. And up to the end of his life his authority in domestic and foreign affairs, while not unrivaled, could never be discounted.

8

The Final Years

In his final years, Yamagata spent most of his time at his villa in Odawara, traveling to Tokyo only on special occasions. He spent his days in a simple routine: rising early, paying his respects to the spirit of the Meiji Emperor, walking about his gardens with a thin cane, enjoying the visits of his friends. He never tired of listening to issues of importance discussed by recognized authorities who would be invited to Kokinan. He continued to read widely and study the documents which the government delivered for his information. He continued to carry on a lively correspondence. Above all, he acted as the guardian of the nation's welfare; he represented the heroic rise of Japan from the Meiji Restoration; possessed the experience and the wisdom accumulated through years of service close to the heart of the nation's problems. His vigor, his resilience, and the political authority he enjoyed as a veteran statesman and leader of the military and civil bureaucracy kept him close to the center of the major decisions faced by the government. He rarely attended meetings of the Privy Council of which he was president, but an endless procession of official and unofficial visitors traveled back and forth from the capital to Odawara to learn of his opinion on issues confronting the national government and not infrequetly carried out the policies he favored. Yamagata's enduring influence in these years is best seen in a series of important episodes which this chapter will examine — the appointment of prime ministers, the intervention in and withdrawal from Siberia, and the affair of the royal engagement.

In the process of selecting prime ministers in Japan, the relative strength of political forces was often revealed. It was an event which received Yamagata's most careful attention. To be sure, the *genrō* had the formal function of recommending a candidate to the emperor, but the recommendation could be made only after consideration had been given to the various factors which would contribute to stable government under a given candidate's ministry. The evolution of constitutional government, the growing strength of the political parties, and the generally diminishing power of the aging oligarchs made the selection of a prime minister after World War I a trial of strength. By following in some detail the maneuvers preceding the final selection of a new prime minister in 1916, we can observe the contending forces and Yamagata's position.

Although Ōkuma was long sympathetic and even affiliated with the party movement, his Cabinet was still a step removed from a party Cabinet in which the prime minister was the leader of the elected majority party. Nevertheless, Ōkuma believed in moving in that direction just as Yamagata believed in moving away from it. The contradictory views of Ōkuma and Yamagata resulted in a long, bitter struggle over the selection of Ōkuma's successor. Both supported rival candidates with equal determination; the tactics Ōkuma employed were a challenge to the traditional *genrō* authority in selecting the first minister; the efforts of Yamagata were aimed at maintaining that authority and lifting the Cabinet above the control of political parties.

The Selection of General Terauchi

The life of the Ōkuma Cabinet was prolonged by the exclusion of Katō, who had alienated the *genrō,* the coronation ceremonies, and the absence of a suitable successor in 1915. But at the end of 1915, when the Diet convened, criticism of Ōkuma increased; many conservatives were opposed to the policy of the Cabinet and joined forces to weaken its precarious hold.[1] The attack was aimed at Ōkuma's legislative program and in particular his financial policy. The opposition centered in the House of Peers[2] where there was strong dissatisfaction with Ōkuma's conduct. As the pressure mounted, Ōkuma expressed to Yamagata his desire to resign, but first he requested aid in getting his legislation accepted.[3] He received a favorable response and Den Kenjirō, a sympa-

1. In September 1915, Gotō Shimpei, who was interested in defeating the Cabinet, visited Terauchi in Korea with the aim of sounding him out as a prospective prime minister. Tokyo newspapers in October spoke openly of preparations for a national unity Cabinet. On the occasion of the coronation in November, Gotō met with conservative politicians in Kyoto who agreed on Terauchi as a suitable successor to Ōkuma. The choice was supported by Yamagata. Shinobu, *Taishō shi,* II, 263.

2. Many peers objected to Ōkuma's plan to use amortization funds for railway development instead of raising loans.

3. Conversation quoted in Shinobu, *Taishō shi,* II, 265–267.

thetic friend of Yamagata and a leader in the House of Peers against Ōkuma, was persuaded to work for a compromise with the prime minister when he was told that Ōkuma wished to retire at the close of the Diet session.

Yamagata's intercession was apparently successful; most of the controversial money bills were passed by both houses. Furthermore, the condition of success had been Ōkuma's pledge to resign, and Yamagata's successful mediation placed him in an advantageous position in the selection of the next ministry. Had Ōkuma gracefully resigned and left to others the appointment of a successor, all would have been well. However, Ōkuma had his own plans; he was prepared to challenge the authority of Yamagata by continuing in office in order to have a candidate of his own choice succeed him.

Ōkuma let it be widely known that he favored as his successor Katō Kōmei, the former prime minister and at the time head of the Dōshikai party. When he first spoke to Yamagata about resigning, Ōkuma had asked the latter to give some thought to a successor. In March, at Odawara, Ōkuma first mentioned to Yamagata the possibility of Katō as the next prime minister.[4] Yamagata thought it strange that he should first be asked to think of a replacement and then be told who the replacement should be, so he evaded this feeler and suggested that it be discussed in April when he planned a trip to Tokyo. Illness prevented the scheduled visit to the capital so Yamagata communicated his reaction in a letter, dated April 13, 1916. After speaking of the need to take into account the attitude of the parties and to show every care in selecting a prime minister, he broadened the basis for his conclusion:

> Today the world is witnessing a great war whose end cannot be predicted but whose outcome will affect our country's future. Moreover, we cannot tell whether disturbances in China will grow; but the fate of the Far East will doubtless be determined by the development of the two important events. In such circumstances, our nation's welfare needs to be adjusted to conditions altered by these momentous developments.

> If we wish to preserve peace and order in the Far East we must first preserve unity and tranquility within the nation by consolidating our strength and presenting a united front to the world through the combined efforts of all. Under these circumstances, even if sufficient strength were available for decisive control through a majority in one House, and the leader of one party appointed to manage the

4. Interview at Kokinan, summarized in *Yamagata den*, III, 954.

political situation, how, in view of recent political developments, can we hope for unified cooperation in Japan? If domestic quarrels persist and we lack the strength of national unity, how, in these difficult times, can we further the nation's interests and preserve law and order in the Far East?

In selecting the next government, I believe we must choose someone who will regard these as paramount objectives. I am sorry but that is the reason I cannot agree with your proposal.[5]

Confronted by a rejection of his proposal, Ōkuma worked for a compromise. In an audience with the emperor on June 28, he expressed his desire to withdraw because of poor health and his hope that Katō and Terauchi would be asked to form a coalition government. This direct approach to the emperor on the question of his successor was unprecedented, and it represented a challenge to the government-appointing role of the *genrō*. Had he resigned, the whole question would have been readily solved by Yamagata, who, with the assured support of Matsukata and Ōyama, would have proposed Terauchi to the court. But Ōkuma remained in office while he maneuvered.

Early in July, at the urging of General Tanaka, Terauchi returned to Japan.[6] At a meeting at Ōkuma's private residence at Waseda University he was invited to participate in a coalition government. Terauchi's reply was stiff and formal; he insisted that such invitations were not properly discussed without permission since it was the emperor's prerogative to appoint the leader of the government. "That is not my private view," protested Ōkuma, "I have already conferred with the Throne and I should like you to consider it."[7] Ōkuma argued that the next Cabinet could not be successful unless it formed a coalition with the party which presently supported the Cabinet. Therefore, he reasoned, Terauchi and Katō should jointly form a Cabinet. Terauchi's prescription for a successful Cabinet was quite different, and it showed how closely in step he was with Yamagata's unchanging attitude: "At this time of momentous world events, whoever is entrusted with this responsibility will surely fail in his policy if he takes sides with one faction or another, antagonizes other groups and fosters political warfare for no good purpose. What is

5. *Ibid.*, III, 955–957.
6. Watanabe in *Meiji shi kenkyū*, pp. 244–245, stresses the active part taken by General Tanaka. It was he who sent the telegram to Terauchi urging him to return. Whether he did this on his own initiative or at the suggestion of Yamagata is not known.
7. Kuroda Kōshirō, ed., *Gensui Terauchi hakushaku den* (Tokyo, 1920), p. 814. (Cited hereafter as *Terauchi den.*) The interview took place on July 6, 1916.

needed is the formation of a national unity cabinet bringing together the leaders of every faction in the Diet. Under present circumstances it would never be suitable for the next cabinet to continue present policies. For that reason I cannot make you any promise." [8] The conference had settled nothing and both Terauchi and Ōkuma turned to Yamagata. In his visit to Odawara, Terauchi reported on his meeting with Ōkuma and in writing outlined in greater detail his reasons for turning down Ōkuma's suggestion.[9] A second meeting between Ōkuma and Terauchi proved fruitless. Tanaka reported this to Yamagata and also that Ōkuma expected to visit Odawara. He added that Yamagata should feel free to remain at Kokinan[10] and let Ōkuma bear the full responsibility for the delay in appointing his successor.

Yamagata was fully briefed and prepared when Ōkuma visited Odawara a few days later (July 22). But since Terauchi's views coincided with his own, little progress was made. Yamagata did agree, however, to encourage Terauchi to meet again with Ōkuma. The next day Yamagata wrote Ōkuma, "I have had a conversation with Terauchi giving him the substance of our conversation. In a few days . . . he plans to meet with you." [11]

The impasse in the negotiations brought forth others who attempted to mediate.[12] But the days stretched into more than a week before anything of importance happened. Public criticism was aroused, newspapers condemned the paralysis of the government, there were demands from every quarter that the issue be settled. Still Terauchi and Ōkuma held stubbornly to their views; it was still a coalition versus a nonparty, national unity Cabinet. A third meeting between Ōkuma and Terauchi, on August 8, failed to break the deadlock.

In August two developments occurred that affected the protracted search for a new prime minister. Katō Kōmei was actively engaged in bringing together three political groups — his own Dōshikai and two smaller parties, the Chūseikai and the Seiyū Club — to form the Kenseikai. The prospective of a large party under Katō's leadership strength-

8. Quoted in *Yamagata den*, III, 959.
9. In a memorandum to Yamagata, Terauchi objected to: forming a coalition with the Dōshikai; holding private conversations with Katō before imperial orders had been issued; jointly forming a Cabinet with Katō; continuing the policies of the Ōkuma Cabinet. Memorandum reprinted in *ibid.*, III, 960.
10. Tanaka's letter is dated July 12, 1916, and is reprinted in *ibid.*, III, 961–962.
11. Yamagata's letter to Ōkuma, dated July 23, 1916, is in Watanabe, *Meiji shi kenkyū*, pp. 245–246.
12. At this juncture Sugiyama Shigemaru, a close friend of Yamagata's but well known also to Ōkuma, tried his hand at mediating. See his letter to Ōkuma in Watanabe Ikujirō, *Meiji shi kenkyū*, p. 246.

ened Ōkuma's view that Katō should be in the government — leading the Cabinet or at least participating in a coalition. The second development was the sharp accentuation of the criticism over the inordinate delay. The prolonged, ineffective conversations to determine a successor were severely attacked in many quarters. Conservatives were angered by Ōkuma's challenge of *genrō* power by insisting on arranging for his successor before resigning. Party members, on the other hand, accused Yamagata of blocking orderly procedures by refusing to accept Katō as a prime minister.

At the end of September, Ōkuma prepared to play his last card. He informed Ōyama, both a *genrō* and at the time the lord keeper of the privy seal, that he had decided to nominate Katō. After eight months of profitless bargaining during which to placate Yamagata he had urged a coalition government rather than his first choice of a Cabinet under Katō, he returned to his original plan. On October 3, Ōkuma invited Katō to his private residence and told him of his intention to nominate him. Katō replied, "I know that this is something many do not wish for, but I am not opposed . . . It may even aid in demonstrating that there is such a thing as party politics." [13] To his Cabinet Ōkuma announced his decision to nominate Katō, reportedly saying, "he has achieved much in the field of finance and diplomacy and he, furthermore, has the support of the majority in the Diet." [14] On October 4, Ōkuma submitted his resignation to the emperor and, by-passing the *genrō* in an unprecedented manner, included in his written resignation the statement, "Katō Kōmei is a man of great competence and skill . . . so I should like to select Katō as my successor." [15]

This bold stroke did not catch the *genrō* unprepared. For over a week Ōyama, to whom Ōkuma had confided his decision, had scurried about to bring the *genrō* together. Yamagata arrived in Tokyo from Kokinan on October 1; Matsukata came from Kamakura and Saionji from Oiso. Yamagata called on Ōkuma to emphasize again his opposition. Ōkuma was adamant, so the *genrō* prepared their countermeasures. On the day of Ōkuma's resignation, the *genrō*, outraged at his conduct, quickly met before the emperor and had their choice for the next prime minister approved, thereby blocking any consideration of Ōkuma's recommendation. Terauchi was speedily designated to form the next government.

13. Quoted by Shinobu, *Taishō shi*, I, 284.
14. Quoted in *Yamagata den*, III, 967.
15. Shinobu, *Taishō shi*, I, 284.

In the end, Yamagata and his colleagues had defeated Ōkuma. All the delay and maneuvers employed by Ōkuma had not prevented the selection of Terauchi. Ōkuma had chosen tactics that, as they were expressed to Yamagata, "most inconveniently placed responsibility on the Emperor . . . That a prime minister should carry on that way is most outrageous." [16] Yamagata was also aware that the outcome of the contest to select the prime minister would be used by the parties and a section of the public press to attack the *genrō*. That would hardly place them in an unaccustomed position. And the return to a Yamagata-style Cabinet was a source of confidence for him and, as he saw it, a healthy development for the nation. Ōkuma had tested the strength of the *genrō* and especially the influence of Yamagata and found them vigorous.

Terauchi's Problems at Home and Abroad

The Terauchi government, formed on October 9, 1916, was composed of conservative statesmen who subscribed to the prime minister's view, which he expressed soon after his inauguration, that "The policy embracing our nation's destiny must come from the strength of national unity. Regarding the different political opinions in the various party factions, be completely impartial and open-minded to avoid taking the wrong course . . . This is what I believe the people wish." [17]

But aloofness from political parties caused major difficulties in meeting the critical domestic and foreign problems of the government. How does a Cabinet professing to transcend political parties bargain with them in order to get support for its proposed legislation? The question was complicated by the fact that the newly formed Kenseikai, the majority party in the House of Representatives under Katō,[18] declared its intention of opposing the Cabinet. Past experiences of nonparty Cabinets showed that the government's best hope was to adjust its views to realism and seek the cooperation of the rival Seiyūkai party.

This was attempted but met with only limited success. Hirata Tōsuke undertook to organize Seiyūkai support for the Cabinet's program. With

16. In a letter from Kiyoura in *Yamagata den*, III, 973, dated Oct. 10, 1916.
17. Kuroda, ed., *Terauchi den*, p. 821. The text of the speech, given on Oct. 28, 1916, appears on pp. 821–825. The use of the phrase *heikō jihei* ("strictly impartial") led the press to dub his Cabinet the "strictly impartial cabinet." Rōyama, *Seiji shi*, p. 415.
18. Katō formed the Kenseikai on Oct. 10, 1916, one day after Terauchi was installed in office. It was a fusion of the old Dōshikai and two smaller groups, and it increased the plurality that the Dōshikai had enjoyed from 150 to 197 votes.

the aid of Den Kenjirō, minister of communications, and Gotō Shimpei, house minister, he appealed to the Seiyūkai for cooperation. The Seiyūkai, which had lost its majority in the election of 1915, was anxious to regain its strength and received the overtures positively. Hara, the Seiyūkai president, was persuaded that gaining Yamagata's favor was an indispensable requisite for grasping political power. Cooperation with the Terauchi Cabinet, Hirata argued, would lead to that objective as well as improve the party's position in the event of a general election. Thus, while publicly proclaiming an independent policy, the party agreed privately to support the government.

Hirata had begun his work well. But still the opposition, both in its size and in its determination, was too strong. When the Diet opened in December, little business could be accomplished because of bitter denunciations of the antiparliamentary character of the Cabinet. When the Diet reconvened late in January, after the customary holiday recess, a no-confidence motion received 231 votes out of the total membership of 381.

No more convincing evidence could have been presented to the Cabinet that compromises or splitting the opposition by fair means or foul stood little chance of succeeding. The only hope seemed to be to dissolve the Diet and call for a general election that might result in a more favorable alignment. Before taking this step Terauchi sought Yamagata's support. Predictably, Yamagata gave his support to action that he had so often favored before. The Diet was dissolved on January 25 because, as Hirata reported to Yamagata, "the situation in the Diet has been one of increasing hostility on the part of the Kenseikai after its arrangement with the Kokumintō [a smaller party cooperating with the major opposition party] and has led to passage of a no-confidence motion and, finally, dissolution . . . What the outlook is for the general election only time will tell." [19]

Yamagata was keenly interested in the future of the Cabinet. He spent hours discussing with his friends the most suitable tactics for the election. He aided in raising campaign funds by approaching Masuda Takashi, a top Mitsui company official, who was a friend and an Odawara neighbor.[20] However, his low opinion of the two major parties led him to encourage the formation of a third party, loyal to the government, which would hold the balance between the two.[21]

19. Reprinted in *Yamagata den,* III, 980.
20. Den, in his letter to Yamagata of Feb. 10, quoted below, reported a satisfactory interview with Masuda Takashi. *Ibid.,* III, 981.
21. Yamagata was reiterating a concept he had held consistently. On Feb. 18, 1917,

While his Cabinet colleagues prepared for the April elections, Terauchi justified his political philosophy in words reminiscent of early declarations by his mentor, Yamagata. In a speech to the prefectural governors he stressed, with greater emphasis on the position of the House of Peers, the political doctrines of the conservative bureaucracy.

> The Imperial Diet is formed by both the House of Representatives and the House of Peers, and it is a mistake to feel that only one House reflects public opinion . . . The judgments of the House of Representatives express only the attitude of one House . . . so it is presumptuous to say that if the majority party does not form the government it is not based on the Imperial Diet . . . The appointment and dismissal of state ministers are decided by sovereign authority and outside interference must never be tolerated . . .

> In England, party cabinets must be based on the majority party of the House of Commons, but in our imperial constitutional system the Imperial Diet is formed by both the House of Representatives and the House of Peers, with no relative difference in their importance. Thus the formation of a cabinet simply on the basis of representatives of the majority party of the House of Representatives is not only interference with the Emperor's sovereignty but neglect of the two House system.[22]

The elections favored the Seiyūkai which increased its seats from 111 to 158 while the Kenseikai was reduced from 200 to 119 seats. But the latter votes if combined with those of the smaller Kokumintō, which increased its representation from 28 to 36, were only three short of the Seiyūkai plurality. This precarious edge meant that unaffiliated independents held the balance. In order to carry out its policies, the government would be required to play a skillful game indeed. To secure help for the government's foreign policy, Terauchi decided to invite the leaders of the parties to meet with him and selected members of the Cabinet in an advisory council to pass on crucial issues.

The Advisory Council on Foreign Relations was officially formed on June 5. Several important figures outside of the government had helped

---

in a conversation with his companion Takahashi Yoshio, he repeated again his belief in building a small third party which could "stand between the parties that exist" and thereby serve as a brake on party excesses. See Takahashi, *San kō iretsu*, pp. 139–141.

22. The speech, printed in Kuroda, ed., *Terauchi den*, pp. 855–866, echoed in substance and spirit the instructions Yamagata gave to local officials twenty-eight years before. Cf. McLaren, ed., *Documents*, pp. 419–422.

in its formation and Yamagata had given it his blessings.[23] Of the three party leaders, Hara and Inukai agreed to join, but Katō refused. But the reduction of Katō's party in the election no longer made his cooperation indispensable. The organization of the Advisory Council succeeded in bringing together the government and two cooperating parties whose combined votes represented an absolute majority in the House of Representatives. The redistribution of the power of the main parties and the formation of the council facilitated the task of passing the government's legislative program. But the council's major impact was on the foreign policy issues facing the nation.

The event that precipitated a series of foreign policy decisions was the Soviet revolution of November 1917. The alliance with Russia, so long advocated, encouraged, and engineered by Yamagata and designed to prevent the spread of German power into the Far East, was now a shambles. The peace concluded by the Soviet government disrupted the diplomacy of the allies, and the unsettled conditions in Soviet Asia in the wake of the revolution profoundly influenced the situation in the Far East. This new factor in the situation led Japan first to sign a military agreement with China and then to participate in the inter-allied expedition to Siberia.[24] Long months of meetings, consultations, and negotiations preceded the final decisions. Yamagata, moving into his eightieth year yet remarkably vigorous and alert, was still influential in shaping the course of the nation's foreign policy.

From December 1917 when General Foch first requested Japanese intervention in Russian Asia to the final decision committing the nation to an expedition in August 1918, the "Siberian debate" moved through three phases. In each Yamagata's influence was of great importance. The first of these periods occurred in mid-March 1918 when Yamagata submitted to the government his opinion on the question of an expedition. To the earliest requests of France that Japan consider sending troops to the European front, Yamagata had not responded with favor. He had favored supplying arms to the European allies, advocated naval assistance, and supported military action against Germany's holdings in China. But he had consistently rejected all suggestions of military intervention in Europe. The Bolshevik Revolution placed problems in a new context, and both in the Foreign Office and in the Japanese army there were many advocates of intervention on the continent. Several plans for action were

23. Miura Goro and Itō Miyoji drafted the ordinance for establishing the council and secured Yamagata's approval. Morley, *The Japanese Thrust into Siberia*, p. 25.
24. See Chihiro Hosoya, "Origin of the Siberian Intervention, 1917–1918," *Annals of the Hitotsubashi Academy* 9.1:96–98 (October 1958).

drawn up early in 1918 by its proponents. The ambitions of the army General Staff and the designs of foreign minister Motono were the twin forces pushing for intervention. In March, Yamagata addressed himself to the problem which he had discussed at length with a good number of visitors to Odawara. In a reassured, restrained memorandum to prime minister Terauchi, foreign minister Motono, and home minister Gotō he set forth his views.

> It is entirely premature to think of immediately sending our troops out of fear of the spread of German power in the Far East following the separate peace between the Bolshevik government and Germany. To invade her territory before Russia has requested aid may be a good idea but it would constitute interference with her authority. Not only is there no justification for it but it would arouse England and more particularly America, so that it would prevent requesting later aid as well as run the risk of stirring up many future problems that could concern us. Therefore in order to determine the Empire's policy toward Russia, we must first ascertain the Russian policies of England, France and America. If without discovering their attitude Japan proceeds to take independent military action with the aim of preventing the spread of German power to the East, even if we tried to convince them that we do not regard them as our enemy how could the Russian people feel secure and passively observe our soldiers enter their country and occupy their territory?
>
> Of course Germany will employ various means of getting Russian support. Furthermore, since at present important leaders in Russia have already come under German domination and have skillfully been brought in line to support them, we could do little more than give support to a small group in Russia lacking both military and financial power. Consequently we would find ourselves at war with Germany and most of Russia.
>
> In addition, if we should find ourselves in such a position and German power were to conquer the Far East, we could raise enough troops for the army and navy but unfortunately we would have to get assistance from England and America for military supplies and funds. We would find ourselves in great peril in the future if we did not get clear the attitudes of the Powers and fix our policy with reference to them. Therefore, in our policy toward Russia we must at all times heed the plans of England and America.[25]

25. Memorandum appears in *Yamagata den*, III, 987–989. Morley suggests that Yamagata may have opposed action before an agreement with China was reached. Morley, *The Japanese Thrust into Siberia*, p. 140.

Yamagata's opinion favoring a cautious approach, reminiscent of his position prior to Japan's participation in the allied effort to defeat the Boxer Rebellion in 1900, carried sufficient weight so that when it was added to the reluctance of some of the members of the Advisory Council to support action, the plan's proponents were blocked. At the Advisory Council meeting of March 17, foreign minister Motono's arguments favoring military measures on the continent were not accepted. Not enough felt that there was any clear threat to Japan's security or that independent action would assure allied and particularly American support. With this the problem was postponed, not eliminated.

The negative decision did not dissuade Motono from giving up plans for armed intervention, and through diplomatic channels the possibility was continually explored. The course of developments in Siberia seemed to favor the interventionists. For one thing, in response both to the local situation and to its own designs, the Japanese army acted on its own initiative. The army in Manchuria was attempting to give support to anti-Bolshevik factions along the Russian-Manchurian border and line up a major force friendly to Japan. These developments were complicated by events farther afield. Czechoslovakian troops captured in European Russia by tsarist forces were granted permission by the Soviet government to leave Russia via the Trans-Siberian Railroad.

A second stage in the "Siberian debate" was reached in April when the murder of several Japanese in Vladivostok resulted in the landing of Japanese and British marines. For Motono and army planners in the General Staff this was an opportunity to set in motion plans for dispatching Japanese troops into Russian Siberia. With naval troops already in Vladivostok, Motono urged an expedition. Terauchi was at this time a sick man. With the news of the landing and troubled by the persistence of his foreign minister, he was unable to face the situation and tried desperately to withdraw from office. In a scene reminiscent of medieval tales in which the gallant samurai pleads in vain to be released from duty to his lord, Terauchi's pleas were rejected.[26] Instead, Yamagata instructed Terauchi not only to remain in office until the Siberian issue was settled but immediately to take measures restraining the navy in its actions at Vladivostok. The navy was restrained and a few days later Yamagata, in response to Motono's request for a final decision, led the *genrō*[27] in

26. For a description of Terauchi's abortive effort to resign, see *ibid.*, pp. 152–153.
27. Ōyama died in December 1916 leaving only Matsukata and Yamagata of the original *genrō*.

a formal rejection of any plans for action in Siberia. "If we are to send troops," he wrote Terauchi, "we must ask the views of each country; they must be unanimous and we must be truly justified." [28] Twice defeated by Yamagata, Motono resigned and home minister Gotō Shimpei shifted to head the foreign ministry.

Preparations for military operations were furthered in May 1918 by the conclusion of a secret military defense agreement with China.[29] The Chinese had resisted the agreement, which in effect gave Japan freedom to resist "enemy influence" in the Chinese area of the Amur Basin, until warned that failure to sign would result in the loss of financial and military aid to the Peking government. China and Japan agreed to work together "against the common enemy." [30] This agreement completed military preparations for Japanese action in Siberia, but the political obstacles still remained.

The early days of July immediately preceding the final decision constitute the third stage of the "Siberian debate" in which Yamagata's influence had a telling effect. The uncertain plight of the Czech troops in Siberia where they became enmeshed in the Russian civil war became a factor of overriding importance. The United States became more interested in measures to rescue the Czechs, and the Allied Supreme War Council urgently requested Japan to accept an invitation for a joint expedition to Siberia. Japan elected at first to await the agreement of the United States to participate. When, on July 5, the United States invited Japan to join in an operation to rescue the Czechs, thereby signifying their approval, one of Yamagata's basic conditions for participating was met.

Foreign minister Gotō favored the acceptance of the American invitation. His first step in winning support for his position was to gain Yamagata's endorsement. Although many people conferred with Yamagata on the issue of Japan's participation, Gotō, as foreign minister, was in a preferred position to lay out before him the new conditions

28. This was an excerpt from a letter Terauchi received from Yamagata that he showed Hara Takashi. *Hara nikki*, VII, 389; entry of April 22, 1918.

29. This was the period when the Chinese government in Peking was relying upon the Nishihara loans. For a discussion of the aims and problems relating to the loans, see Frank C. Langdon, "Japan's Failure to Establish Friendly Relations with China in 1917–1918," *Pacific Historical Review*, 27:245–258 (August 1957).

30. Morley, in *The Japanese Thrust into Siberia*, describes the negotiations (pp. 161–165, 188–189) and includes the text of the agreement as Appendix N, pp. 363–365. In a letter of May 24, 1918, war minister Oshima requested Yamagata to have the Privy Council, of which he was president, consider the agreement favorably. *Yamagata den*, III, 994. The Privy Council approved it on May 28.

that prevailed.[31] With America's acceptance it appears that Yamagata's disapproval of an expedition disappeared. He is quoted as explaining, in connection with his previous opposition to a military venture on the continent, that "The handle is not grasped to draw a sword until one first knows it can be sheathed."[32] One reason he had been against an expedition was his concern with how Japan would withdraw from Siberia, once the commitment was made. Participation in a joint allied expedition including the United States provided the answer; the sword could now be drawn.

The prospect for the acceptance of the expedition was greatly improved by Yamagata's endorsement. The Cabinet quickly approved the decision. Yamagata then joined Cabinet members in persuading other leading figures to approve the government's decision. Yamagata talked to Saionji[33] and Hara in an attempt to win over their support for a decision he had just accepted himself. In his conversation with Hara, he emphasized both the opportunity and the need to send troops in a joint expedition. Hara expressed his approval of joining the United States in giving assistance to the Czech forces, but he opposed a large-scale expedition into Siberia as contemplated by the government. He believed any such expedition would prejudice good relations with the United States and Britain. Hara, unmoved by arguments in favor of a major expedition, concluded, "In any case, since the aim of the American proposal is straightforward there should be no great difficulty in replying to it. Nevertheless, the consequences that might hereafter flow from it are unlimited so it must be given adequate consideration."[34]

Before the scheduled meeting of the Advisory Council on July 16, Yamagata was anxious to gain as much support in favor of the decision as possible. He had not persudaed Hara to go along, and in a meeting of the *genrō* on July 15, attended also by Gotō and Terauchi,[35] he made little headway. Matsukata and Saionji were not fully in accord with the Cabinet's concept of the expedition but agreed to go along with the government's plans if the Advisory Council gave its approval.

Yamagata's failure to convince Hara and his inability to make the

31. Morley, *The Japanese Thrust into Siberia*, p. 266. In a footnote Morley quotes Ozaki Yukio as saying that it was probably Tanaka Giichi who won over Yamagata.

32. Mochizuki Kotarō, Inoue's last private secretary, told this to Ozaki Yukio. Ozaki, *Nihon kensei shi okataru*, II, 234.

33. Shinobu, *Taishō shi*, II, 517.

34. *Hara nikki*, VII, 436–437; entry of July 14, 1918.

35. Ōkuma was invited to attend this meeting but declined. Shinobu, *Taishō shi*, II, 518.

Cabinet's case convincing to Matsukata and Saionji were uncharacteristic developments. The split within the *genrō* was not to alter the final decision along the lines favored by Yamagata, but rarely had he met such limited success among the *genrō*. It was perhaps a sign of the changing character of the *genrō*[36] and at the same time an indication that Yamagata now spoke in a softer voice.

In the Advisory Council meetings Hara spoke in favor of "sending troops only within the limits set by the American note," [37] while the government proposed to tell the United States that, with her vital interests threatened, Japan could not agree to limit beforehand either the number of troops or the area of operation. The disagreement, therefore, was over the extent of Japan's intervention. As the issue was debated, a larger area of agreement was formed,[38] but Hara remained doubtful of the effects of full-scale intervention.

Hara's doubts were justified. Washington, claiming that Japan was really introducing a new proposal, informed Tokyo that unless changes were made the United States would withdraw from the proposed expedition. The Cabinet was not prepared to limit Japan's activity, as the United States demanded, to the Vladivostok area. At the same time there was little sentiment favoring the alienation of the United States. In the end the disagreement was resolved through the flexible language of diplomacy. Yamagata, who had been kept carefully informed of the negotiations, favored the interpretation that the United States had not rejected in principle the stated plans of Japan, and that all could be clarified when a private understanding was reached.[39] An exchange of carefully worded notes resolved the disagreement.

On August 2, 1918, Japan publicly declared its intentions of sending an expedition to Siberia. The Cabinet and the Advisory Council had agreed to limit Japan's operations and execute changes only within the allied concept of the expedition and after consultations. On the surface this would appear to have been a victory for the moderates — Saionji, Hara, and others — who favored a clearly limited action. In the end, however, those advocating a less restricted operation, one covering the

36. This is Shinobu's argument, *ibid.*, II, 518–519.
37. Quoted in Tsurumi Yūsuke, *Gotō Shimpei den* (Tokyo, 1944), VIII, 319.
38. Morley gives a vivid description of the debate in *The Japanese Thrust into Siberia*, pp. 274–275.
39. Itō Miyoji is credited with resolving the issue in this fashion. See *ibid.*, pp. 301–302. Both Gotō and Itō discussed the question with Yamagata. *Hara nikki*, VII, 463; entry of July 30, 1918.

whole Amur Basin area and even extending to the island of Sakhalin, got their way. Once the expedition was launched, moderating political influences in Tokyo were unsuccessful in preventing the army from extending the scope of its operations. Each extension would be justified as a necessary response to local circumstances. The Japanese army did not withdraw from Siberia until after Yamagata's death.

Yamagata's attitude had been a factor of considerable importance in the decision to send an expedition to Siberia. He approached the issue from the broad base of Japan's future in East Asia. He had refused to support the idea until assured that it would not arouse the doubts and open opposition of the allied powers. Twice he had firmly rejected the plans for extensive operations in the Amur Basin. When his conditions had been met and he had been converted, he was unable to carry other important figures with him, but his shift was critical in strengthening the hands of the less moderate advocates of an ambitious operation on the continent. His opposition had checked an earlier expedition; his approval was not unqualified but it was indispensable for Japan's participation. In his eightieth year, on issues affecting the future of the nation's foreign relations, Yamagata's influence, if he chose to exert it, remained second to none.

The Appointment of Hara Kei

Japan's decision to participate in the Siberian expedition preceded by only one day the first of several serious riots that plagued the government in the last quarter of 1918. There is no connection implied between these two events. The riots were a direct result of the spiraling inflation which squeezed the people economically; the cost of living had risen by 130 percent between 1914 and 1918.[40] Emergency government measures to check the rocketing prices failed, and when those who suffered most discovered rice hoarding, riots broke out. The rice riots began in a fishing village in Toyama prefecture on the north coast of the main island, and from there they spread to other parts of Japan.[41] As they spread other discontents were stirred, radical political agitation was stimulated, and a rash of labor problems broke out. The govern-

40. Shinobu, *Taishō shi*, II, 541.
41. The rice riots have received considerable attention in recent scholarship, and great, indeed excessive, significance has been attached to them. Shinobu concludes that they were the severest disturbances in Japan after the 1870's, and were of great importance because they cut across class lines and date the rise of a new popular Japan. *Ibid.*, II, 672–673.

ment, fearing the riots and acting with its normal reflexes, suppressed the outbreaks with a firm hand.

The violence caused by the economic crisis added to the burdensome problems of foreign relations was an oppressive weight for Terauchi to hold up. He continued to suffer ill health and found it impossible to maintain his leadership of the government. The acts of the Cabinet in controlling the riots aroused considerable opposition. It was perhaps only Yamagata's insistence that he set aside thoughts of resignation until the Siberian question was solved that had kept Terauchi in office. Despite his Cabinet colleagues' pleas that resignation would only satisfy the public demands for a change in government, he refused to give up his plans to retire. In the press Ōkuma urged Yamagata to advise his resignation. "Since the Terauchi ministry has fallen into public disfavor, and all hopes of recovering its lost prestige are gone," wrote Ōkuma, "it is manifestly the duty of Prince Yamagata, who is not only the patron of the present ministry but an Elder Statesman of recognized ability, to save the Government from the difficulties it is faced with." [42] Although it was by no means a response to the demands of Ōkuma, which he never heeded if he could possibly help it, Yamagata was not inclined to block Terauchi's decision to resign.

As a consequence, August and September 1918 were busy days for Yamagata as he labored in the selection of a new prime minister. For most of this time he remained in Odawara where a steady procession of visitors arrived to meet with him, trying to influence him or relaying messages from him to others involved in the complex procedure of selecting the next first minister. Many who visited him have left accounts of their conversations, but the fullest account of the selection procedure is found in the pages of the diary of Hara Kei.

Before going to the capital in mid-September to begin a final series of conversations leading to the selection of a prime minister, Yamagata had been asked by several visitors his attitude toward Hara, the president of the Seiyūkai, as a prospective candidate. "I have no particular objections to Hara," he said, "except that he believes that an absolute majority is necessary, while I consider it an evil." [43] By this he meant that Hara might be considered for the position so long as nonparty members of the House of Representatives and perhaps some from the

42. Ōkuma writing in *Taikwan*, September 1918, quoted in *The Japan Chronicle*, Sept. 12, 1918, p. 388.
43. Interview with Yokota Sennosuke, a leader in the Seiyūkai. *Hara nikki*, VII, 749; entry of August 19, 1918.

House of Peers were included in the Cabinet. To other visitors he disclosed that he opposed a party Cabinet and hoped Saionji could be persuaded to form a government. Sensing the inevitable, however, Yamagata sought more information about the state of the Seiyūkai from its secretary general and inquired about what type of Cabinet Hara might form if he were designated.[44]

Hara was acutely aware of his possibilities. Saionji assured him that he could not be persuaded to form a Cabinet and pointedly added, "Itō's line of descent is through myself and Hara." [45] But Hara was doubtful of Yamagata's intentions, and his confusion was compounded when he heard that Saionji had been called to the palace not to suggest a candidate but to receive a request that he consider forming a Cabinet. Yamagata had been working through his allies at the court. Little wonder that Hara confided to his diary, "Today the maker of cabinets is Yamagata. It is senseless to try to guess what Yamagata's intentions are; so it is well at this time to be patient." [46]

Yamagata pressed Saionji to accept the invitation to form a Cabinet, even if for only two or three months,[47] in order to avoid designating Hara as the next prime minister. Saionji resisted the pressure on the grounds of poor health and expressed his resentment at Yamagata's tactics. Yamagata, still undefeated, made one last effort by enlisting Hara's aid. This tactic did not succeed either. Recording in his diary the report of this meeting to Saionji, Hara wrote: "Yamagata is distressed that there may be no way of preventing a political party from assuming power. Persuading Saionji to stand even temporarily would assist him; in short Yamagata is consulting his own interest. Furthermore, should Saionji decline those motives will probably be revealed in any move he makes. Even if Saionji should assume office in response to Yamagata's words, from then on the latter would oppose him." [48]

Yamagata's capitulation came in a conference with Saionji on September 24.[49] As reported to Hara, Yamagata finally abandoned his efforts to force Saionji and turned to consider the serious alternatives. He also

44. *Ibid.,* VIII, 15.
45. *Ibid.,* VIII, 14.
46. *Ibid.,* VIII, 17.
47. Saionji disclosed this to Hara who recorded it in his diary. Saionji said the bitter remarks he addressed to Yamagata for being called to the palace were laughed off by Yamagata. *Ibid.,* VIII, 24, 18–21.
48. *Ibid.,* VIII, 24; entry of Sept. 23, 1918.
49. For the reconstruction of this conversation we are dependent upon Hara's recording of Saionji's recollections. *Ibid.,* VIII, 26–27; entry of Sept. 25, 1918.

shifted the main responsibility of selecting a successor to Saionji. Several possible candidates were discussed and dismissed and Saionji finally asked, "What about Hara? At the present I believe Hara would be good." Yamagata conceded the possibility and then asked two questions: Would Hara accept? What does he think of me? Saionji answered that although he had not asked Hara, he was sure he would accept. If a Cabinet were formed quickly, Saionji felt there was no reason to fear an alliance with the Kenseikai. To the last question Saionji replied, "Hara has no reservations about you; if he forms a cabinet he would always accept instructions from you and solicit your advice from time to time." [50] Yamagata was reassured by these words and repeated what he had often said before: "Hara and I have no differences of opinion except that Hara, despite his talk of improving the party, will lead a party with a large majority and to this I am opposed. With this one exception we have no differences." [51]

In defeat Yamagata refused to handle the surrender flag. He agreed to explain the situation to Matsukata,[52] but he requested that Saionji make the recommendation to the emperor. Before doing that, according to Hara's account, Saionji saw Yamagata again and, as if to console him in his defeat, explained: "If the Kenseikai with Ōkuma's aid formed a government and failed, and then if Hara should lead the Seiyūkai and also fail, it would provide another opportunity for a transcendent cabinet (chōzen naikaku). But if the parties are disappointed today they will join forces, disrupt the political situation and destroy the chances for another transcendent cabinet. Katō would follow Hara and someone else would follow Katō and finally the parties would take over." [53]

Whether such arguments consoled Yamagata or not, he had been forced to agree to the selection of Hara. On September 27, 1918, Hara organized a Cabinet made up of Seiyūkai party stalwarts with the exception of the foreign minister and the two service ministers. Fulfilling his pledge to "seek the good will of Yamagata as much as possible," [54] he sought assistance in appointing the army minister. In a visit to Yamagata he

---

50. *Ibid.*, VIII, 27.
51. *Ibid.*, VIII, 27.
52. *Yamagata den*, III, 1,000. Matsukata seemed to prefer the nomination of Masuda Takahashi but, as so often before, he was willing to go along with Yamagata's decision.
53. *Hara nikki*, VIII, 29; entry of Sept. 25, 1918. To this Hara adds, parenthetically, "These words of Saionji were to appease Yamagata but no matter how long Yamagata remains on the scene, political affairs will have to proceed this way."
54. *Ibid.*, VIII, 29.

presented three possible candidates and asked which would be most suitable. "On this occasion," Yamagata responded, "I was intending to refrain from expressing myself on the selections, but since you put it that way how about Tanaka Giichi?" [55] Hara was quite agreeable for as long as Yamagata's loyal follower would go long with cabinet policies, he was anxious to maintain through him good relations with Yamagata's faction.[56]

The inauguration of the Hara Cabinet has often been used to mark off a new era in Japan's history, a period in which political parties were to assume major responsibility for national policy. For Yamagata it was a development against which he had worked sedulously. His name and the bureaucratic faction looking to him stood for nonparty Cabinets removed from the swirl of party squabbles, impartially executing national policy in behalf of the emperor. Of course, Yamagata, as had every other prime minister, had worked out an arrangement with opposition representatives. But Yamagata had never believed it in the interests of the nation to have a Cabinet directed by the leader of the majority party; he despised narrow partisanship; he was convinced that once given power the parties would divide and ruin the country. Ironically, even Hara believed Yamagata had the power to prevent what eventuated; he thought it futile, as he said in 1906, "to hope for the fulfillment of constitutional government during Yamagata's lifetime." [57] If Yamagata did not want a party Cabinet and if, as Hara said, he was the "maker of cabinets," why did he permit Hara's appointment?

It was indeed, as one author has said, "one of the most extraordinary facts in Yamagata's history." [58] He had reacted violently to the short-lived Ōkuma–Itagaki cabinet in 1898, he had opposed Itō's party activities, he had vigorously rejected Katō as Ōkuma's successor in 1916. Why the change in 1918? There are several possible explanations, none of which is entirely satisfactory. These reasons do not include the fact that as an old man he was not capable of conducting difficult political battles. That was, of course, true to some extent, but in other issues it had not appreciably reduced the strength of his position.

In the first place, he had come to respect Hara, to recognize the wide

55. *Ibid.*, VIII, 32.

56. Hara's biographer says, "Hara felt that as long as Tanaka Giichi would go along with the cabinet's policy, he wished to maintain harmony with the Yamagata military faction." Maeda Renzan, *Hara Kei den* (Tokyo, 1943), II, 361.

57. *Hara nikki*, III, 212; entry of July 16, 1906.

58. Tokutomi, *Yamagata den*, III, 1,992.

area of their agreement, and to place confidence in his judgment. Through the many conversations they had on a broad range of subjects, mutual respect had grown into genuine esteem. This was possible because Hara's general outlook was conservative; although he was a party man and, by choice, untitled[59] — both of which irritated Yamagata — his attitude on most subjects was not far removed from Yamagata's. To this must be added Hara's assurance that Yamagata would not be cast aside, that he would be consulted and given an opportunity to influence decisions.

In the second place, Hara's Seiyūkai had cooperated with the Terauchi Cabinet. In that cooperation Hara had been most effective, not without some anticipation of what might follow. It was logical then that the Seiyūkai would profit from its cooperation with the bureaucratic Cabinet of Terauchi, that resistance among the conservative bureaucracy would not grow to oppose its authority. In the third place, some believe that the growing pressure for a party Cabinet was a natural by-product of the leftism accompanying the rice riots.[60] It would be an exaggeration to claim an irresistable public demand for a "commoner" prime minister, yet ever since the Taishō crisis the parties had felt confident that their time would arrive — it appeared to be an unmistakable trend. In this light, Saionji's suggestion that failure to approve of Hara might invite an alliance of the parties with far more disastrous results must have scored a point with Yamagata. To the extent that this was a reason for Hara's selection, popular opinion may be counted a reason for Yamagata's concession.

Lastly, it may be argued that there was no suitable alternative.[61] The Seiyūkai had a large majority and its president, after a period of cooperation with the government, enjoyed authority rivaled by only a few prominent bureaucrats. And Hara, generally respected for his compe-

59. It is interesting to note that, with the exception of Saionji, Hara came from a higher social status than any preceding prime minister. He was an uncommon commoner; he got his title "commoner" mostly because he repeatedly resisted the offer of titles which his prominence had earned him. See Hattori Shisō and Irimajiri Yoshinaga, *Kindai Nihon jimbutsu seiji shi* (Tokyo, 1955–1956), II, 66.

60. Maeda Renzan, a biographer of Hara, once asked him if Yamagata had not been asleep to allow a party Cabinet. Hara replied, "It was the rice riots. If at the time our party had carried on an agitation (*sendō*) it would have been a most serious thing. Even Yamagata comprehended the powerlessness of a bureaucratic cabinet." Maeda, *Hara Kei den*, II, 366.

61. Inukai told a reporter at the time that "a scarcity of suitable men among the bureaucrats who came forward to assume power has compelled them to turn to Mr. Hara." Quoted by Robert A. Scalapino, *Democracy and the Party Movement in Prewar Japan* (Berkeley and Los Angeles, 1953), p. 214.

tence, appeared far more capable of coping with the political problems of the postwar years. Furthermore, his willingness to listen to Yamagata and the fact that Yamagata's close associate Tanaka Giichi was to be in the Cabinet made the decision more acceptable. It was force of circumstances, not a change in his attitude toward party government, that led to Yamagata's acquiescence.

Hara and Yamagata

The last three years of Yamagata's eventful life roughly coincided with Hara's party administration. It forms a strange epilogue to a remarkable story. Despite the continuity with the past that his policies were to manifest, Hara's ministry did represent a break in the political life of the nation. Unlike previous prime ministers, Hara had reached power through a new avenue; he thought of himself first and foremost as a party politician, he was wedded to the belief that political parties must be the base of power in the state, and he remained loyal to the aim of a party performing the task of running the country.[62] His twenty-one years as a party politician outweighed in importance his fifteen years as a bureaucrat. But his difference with those who had served as prime ministers before him was one of political style rather than substance.

It is probable that Yamagata lived out his last years satisfied that his acquiescence in Hara's appointment was not an error. Hara's political faith did not vary significantly from that of his predecessors; his policies did not radically alter an order dominated by the principle of an all-powerful government. When out of power the political parties were prepared to utilize every convenient issue to reduce the authority of the oligarchs and the domineering bureaucracy, and they expressed programs essentially at odds with the ideals set forth by Yamagata. Once in office differences faded.

The attitude toward social change discernible in the policies and actions of the Hara government varied little from the conservatism of the oligarchs. Toward social unrest, radical ideas, labor strikes, and other rumblings of social discontent, Hara's attitude was one of paternalism not unlike the principle of bureaucratic guidance implicit in the term "transcendent" Cabinets. In introducing educational changes, Hara spoke of "perfecting national morality" and "Japan's unique civilization."

62. On this point I am following Lawrence A. Olson, Jr., in his study, "Hara Kei: A Political Biography" (unpublished Ph.D. dissertation, Harvard University, 1954), Chapter 15.

New education statutes stressed the patriotic functions of education, in many ways restating the "Imperial Rescript on Education" passed during Yamagata's first ministry and thereafter serving as an ideological bulwark of conservatism. Hara was as alarmed as Yamagata at the outcropping of socialist thought and "subversive tendencies." [63] To counter such tendencies, he resorted, in the name of domestic tranquility, to police pressure and rigid censorship.

Hara faced troubled times. Tides of change manifested in riots and labor violence were built upon the shifting economic floor of inflation followed by depression. Unrest, the growing unpopularity of the army's activities in Siberia which cost much and produced few favorable results, social growing pains following a period of rapid industrial growth and urban expansion — these conditions established the climate within which Hara carried out what he called his "positive policy." In the carrying out of the party's four platforms of educational improvement, encouragement of production, development of communications, and the fulfillment of national defense, no major departures from the past were visible. Minor administrative changes placed more party members in positions of importance, such as governors of prefectures, and civilians replaced generals as governors-general of Korea and Formosa, but most policies were strikingly unchanged from those of previous ministries.

Yamagata's agreement with Hara on most policies was a measure of the continuity with the past. Most issues of importance facing the Cabinet were discussed together at length. According to Hara's diary, during his thirty-seven months in office he met with Yamagata a total of some thirty-eight times. Spaced fairly evenly over the three years, these conversations at Odawara lasted several hours. Each of these is recounted at length in the diary. In addition to these personal encounters, there were many who reported to Hara the old general's views on this or that matter. These reports were duly noted in his diary, which includes more hearsay than firsthand information about Yamagata. Rarely did Hara talk with war minister Tanaka when Yamagata's name did not enter the conversation. Thus there was a steady flow of information between the two directly and even more often indirectly. Thus, it seems fair to conclude that Hara maintained a remarkably close relationship with the aging *genrō* throughout his term of office.

The substance of these conversations, as recounted by Hara, reveal that the range of views exchanged left out no subject of importance, and thus they serve as an excellent source for determining Yamagata's

63. *Hara nikki,* VIII, 460; entry of Jan. 16, 1920.

attitude toward the major issues of the day. Hara clearly kept the elder statesman informed and lived up to his pledge to seek his advice. He frequently sought approval for administrative reforms, and he discussed appointments to government offices, the changing economic conditions, and the nation's foreign relations. On each subject Yamagata would voice his opinions. The interest and the knowledge he had, and the fact that he did not hesitate to express his judgment, attest to Yamagata's remarkable vigor and alertness up to the end of his life. More than that, Hara's deference and his willingness (or his political acumen) to consult Yamagata, his desire to be in touch with his attitudes, suggest Yamagata's importance. A dozen years before, Hara had remarked about the *genrō,* "in today's political world it is imperative to confer with them." [64] In 1918 and after, he held the same view except that the name "Yamagata" was substituted for "the *genrō.*"

The economic problem confronting Hara's government was one they frequently discussed. Yamagata was disturbed by the high price of rice and other commodities and the riots that had resulted. On several occasions he goaded the Cabinet into countermeasures.[65] At intervals throughout 1918 he would reiterate his apprehensions to Hara and to the finance minister Takahashi.[66] The press carried rumors that it was Yamagata's urgings that prompted the government to give more attention to alleviating conditions. One newspaper reported, "While the Government continued to turn a deaf ear to the loud cries of the people for lower prices for a long time, a piece of advice given it by a *genrō* had an instantaneous effect." [67] The effectiveness of his advice is questionable because in 1921 Yamagata was still bringing up the question of high prices.[68]

The wave of labor unrest created by radical political activists also troubled Yamagata. 1919 was a year of strikes in mines, in factories, and on several transportation systems. The 1921 strike of the Kawasaki shipyard workers in Kobe accompanied by mass demonstrations was a highwater mark for labor activity. During this strike Hara met with Yamagata to discuss the unrest of labor and pleased him with the promise that "The government has decided to take firm measures in handling

64. *Ibid.,* IIB, 331; entry of April 4, 1906.
65. On Dec. 18, 1918, Hara tried to allay Yamagata's anxiety by outlining a plan to import rice. *Ibid.,* VIII, 124.
66. On Dec. 6, 1919, finance minister Takahashi visited Yamagata to get his views on the problem. *Ibid.,* VIII, 418.
67. *Japan Weekly Chronicle,* Oct. 30, 1919, p. 679.
68. See *Hara nikki,* IX, 477; entry of Oct. 21, 1921.

labor problems." They both agreed that "the laws regarding extremism [Bolshevism] are inadequate." [69] Restrictive legislation and stern police measures, the methods Yamagata had used in attempting to control the early stirrings of the party movement in the 1880's, were the approach they agreed upon.[70]

The spread of radical political ideas, often tinged with anti-imperial sentiments, greatly distressed Yamagata. We have already seen how after the Russo-Japanese War, when Hara was serving as home minister in Saionji's Cabinet, Yamagata was agitated by radical political thoughts and shocked by threats against the imperial institution. A month after Hara organized his Cabinet, Yamagata spoke to him about his fear of the spread of socialism and was relieved by Hara's statement that "whenever the people are infected by the climate outside of Japan and internal conditions affected by instigators, the instigators should be handled firmly." [71] On later occasions Hara assured him that he would take any measures necessary to prevent internal disturbances.[72]

A celebrated instance of "firm handling" was the arrest and conviction of Professor Morita Tatsuo of Tokyo Imperial University for an article he wrote on the anarchist Peter Kropotkin. Although this was a specialized essay that appeared in a scholarly journal, the ideas of communism and anarchism that it presented were judged to be seditious. The journal was withdrawn from circulation and the professor was fined, sentenced to two months in prison, and dismissed from the university. Hara recorded his approval of these drastic steps in his diary: "With the advantage of their reputations, university professors have lately, quite senselessly, produced extreme and dangerous writings which surely are not good for the nation. I believe they must be handled severely." [73] Yamagata shared this attitude and more than once he spoke of the harm being done by subversive scholars.[74]

Agreement on the need for resolute action to counter leftism was

69. *Ibid.*, IX, 387; entry of July 31, 1921.

70. Only two weeks before his assassination Hara told Yamagata, "Wages of labor have not fallen at all, yet there are boisterous actions demanding increases. Even when we try to control it some important capitalists meet the demands to get temporary relief. We can do nothing. We would like to put into effect some good plan but there are no good ideas. We are distressed." Yamagata added that he was troubled too, but offered no suggestions. *Ibid.*, IX, 477–478; entry of Oct. 21, 1921.

71. *Ibid.*, IX, 75; entry of Nov. 3, 1921.

72. *Ibid.*, VIII, 254; entry of July 19, 1919.

73. *Ibid.*, VIII, 453; entry of Jan. 9, 1920.

74. *Ibid.*, VIII, 443; entry of Dec. 18, 1919. See also entry of Jan. 16, 1920; *ibid.*, VIII, 460.

often coupled with discussions of educational reform.[75] Yamagata was firmly of the opinion that the proper educational measures were the best means of preventing the inroads of radicalism. Greater stress, he felt, should be placed on "national morality" and the principles of the 1890 rescript on education.[76] In the educational bill passed by the government for the improvement of higher education, the duty of indoctrinating proper attitudes was emphasized.

One of the major domestic issues faced by the Hara administration was caused by the demand of the opposition Kenseikai for universal manhood suffrage. Yamagata was pleased that Hara resisted the demand and gave him every encouragement. Hara did pass reforms reducing the tax requirement for voters and altered electoral areas, but he had no intention of moving beyond that point. Hara argued that universal manhood suffrage would destroy the class system and endanger the state's foundation; Yamagata applauded and added that "universal suffrage would destroy the country." [77] "We already have universal military conscription," argued Yamagata, "and even though universal suffrage may eventually occur it should not be enacted now, therefore I support the present cabinet's view." [78] When agitation in the House of Representatives for universal manhood suffrage could not be calmed in February 1920, Hara took the extreme step of dissolving the Diet.[79] Yamagata judged that circumstances called for dissolving the Diet, but his approval was mixed with fears that in the election the Seiyūkai might become too strong and, as a consequence, arbitrary and irresponsible.[80] A newspaper comment that "even in these days of the general cry . . . for universal suffrage Prince Yamagata is a force to be reckoned with," [81] was not in error.

75. See entry of Dec. 8, 1920; *ibid.,* IX, 150.
76. On Jan. 17, 1920, Hara recorded that he received a memorandum from Yamagata on the subject of education and distributed copies of it to his Cabinet colleagues. *Ibid.,* VIII, 460.
77. *Ibid.,* IX, 110; entry of Oct. 21, 1920. Yamagata repeated the statement in a conversation on Nov. 12, 1920; *ibid.,* IX, 131.
78. *Ibid.,* IX, 65; entry of Sept. 13, 1920.
79. *Ibid.,* VIII, 498; entry of Feb. 28, 1920. Two days before, on the date the Diet was dissolved, Hara recorded that he telegraphed the information to Yamagata and then wrote him why he had taken the action. *Ibid.,* VIII, 497.
80. Yamagata judged that circumstances called for dissolving the Diet, but his approval was mixed with fears that in the election the Seiyūkai might become too strong and, as a result, arbitrary and irresponsible. Hearing from Tanaka that Yamagata had opposed the idea of dissolution, Hara speculated that it was either "because he fears that the Seiyūkai would increase its strength to get a majority or is hinting that the time is ripe for raising doubts about me." *Ibid.,* IX, 391–392.
81. *Japan Weekly Chronicle,* April 1, 1920, p. 381.

Despite their wide agreement on the issues confronting the Cabinet, despite Hara's deference to the opinions of the old *genrō*, it should not be thought that Yamagata ever relinquished his skepticism toward the rule of a political party. The Seiyūkai made inroads into the bureaucracy by appointing an increasing number of governors from the ranks of party members. A reform of the colonial administration called for the substitution of civilians for military governors-general in Korea and Formosa. Yamagata at first opposed these developments but then approved when acceptably conservative men were appointed governors and when the first civilian governors-general of Korea and Formosa respectively were his adopted son Isaburō[82] and his staunch political ally Den Kenjirō. These appointments overcame his initial objections,[83] but his misgivings were not entirely dispelled.

His doubts were reinforced by the results of the election in May 1920. The Seiyūkai was able to convert its plurality in the House of Representatives into a healthy absolute majority by capturing 279 out of the 464 seats.[84] This was not comforting to Yamagata; it raised in his mind the spectre of irresponsible party government. By August, Hara came to feel that Yamagata was interested in ending his ministry; he suspected that the hostility of certain peers and even Tanaka's inclination to resign, while nominally attributed to other reasons, were part of Yamagata's plot.[85] Such observations in his diary as "While Yamagata's words are extremely friendly on the surface, the real meaning is difficult to know," [86] and "no matter what Yamagata says directly, behind the scenes he will contradict it," [87] became more common. As Yamagata's attitude toward the Cabinet became less favorable, Hara's suspicions of Yamagata's intentions increased. The area of agreement on domestic issues had been, as we have seen, impressive, and, as we shall see, their conflicts on foreign policy were not great. Nevertheless, as time went on, Hara was more inclined to believe those who accused Yamagata of wanting to meddle in everything.[88] Only three months before his death in

82. In 1920 Yamagata Isaburō became governor-general of Kwantung.
83. *Hara nikki*, VIII, 113; entry of Dec. 17, 1918. In June 1919, Tanaka reported to the Cabinet that Yamagata agreed with the administrative reform. *Ibid.*, VIII, 241; entry of June 10, 1919.
84. The electoral law passed by the Diet had increased the electoral districts and the total seats in the Lower House from 381 to 464.
85. See entries for August 8 and August 9, 1920; *ibid.*, IX, 27–28, 34.
86. *Ibid.*, VIII, 391–392; entry of Nov. 18, 1918.
87. *Ibid.*, IX, 76; entry of Sept. 22, 1920.
88. Record of Muira's conversation with Hara on April 12, 1920; *ibid.*, VIII, 526.

1921 Hara wrote in his diary, "Yamagata even now hasn't given up the thought of checking the political parties." [89]

The Disengagement from Siberia

Yamagata's unflagging interest in all domestic developments was equaled by his concern for Japan's foreign relations. He faithfully read the "red telegrams," [90] the diplomatic reports filed from all over the world, and solicited answers to anything he did not understand. Just as he invited experts to Odawara to discuss economic problems with him and studied to teach himself the cause of the nation's economic ills, he entertained authorities on international relations from whose knowledge he could profit. As we have seen, Yamagata approached the problems of foreign affairs with deliberation and discretion. Unlike his self-assured and steady, even implacable, approach to the state's internal affairs, his road to foreign policy was traveled with caution and moderation.

On foreign issues he had no major disagreements with Hara. The three years began and ended with important international meetings, but Yamagata's involvement was limited to suggesting or approving delegates for the Versailles and Washington conferences.[91] Hara favored a "positive policy" in foreign affairs which, translated into diplomacy, called for the progressive disengagement from Siberia and the development of Japanese interests in China in order "to help China herself." He believed in Japan's mission "to assume the responsibility of safeguarding peace in Eastern Asia" [92] and called for equal opportunity for Japan in the political and economic life of the world.

The question of the withdrawal from Siberia was one of the most troubling foreign questions facing the government. Hara inherited a policy he had worked against; the termination of hostilities in Europe and the growing strength of the Bolsheviks in Russia made an unwanted situation more complicated. The other allied powers decided to withdraw; the United States informed Tokyo of its intentions in January 1920. The de-

89. *Ibid.*, IX, 391; entry of August 3, 1921.
90. This was a term used to refer to diplomatic dispatches because of the color of the sheets on which the messages were taken down.
91. In November 1918, Hara visited Kokinan to discuss the selection of representatives to participate in the Versailles Conference. At the time Yamagata had no special nominees, but later he pushed to have Saionji go and approved the choice of Makino Nobuaki. *Ibid.*, VIII, 84, 95.
92. Hara Takashi, "Reflections on Lasting Peace," *The Living Age* (Jan. 7, 1922), p. 11. Hara hoped to increase Japanese influence in both Manchuria and Mongolia through the support of Chang Tso-lin, the warlord of Manchuria. See entries of May 17 and 18, 1921, in *Hara nikki*, IX, 310–311.

cision now forced upon Japan revealed a division of opinion between the Cabinet and the army's General Staff. Yamagata was concerned, as he said, with "sheathing the sword" and expressed his opinion favoring withdrawal to several Cabinet ministers.[93]

The Cabinet's decision to withdraw from Siberia was delayed for two reasons: the massacre of Japanese troops and civilians at Nikolaevsk and the opposition of the army chief of staff. Japan occupied the northern half of Sakhalin and strengthened her troops in Siberia in retaliation for the massacre. An outraged public demanded a reappraisal of the decision to withdraw. Yamagata approved these military moves, but he still insisted that "unless withdrawal is quickly carried out [from western Siberia] serious incidents may occur in the future." [94] The second obstacle was the chief of staff's objection to the Cabinet's decision. In this conflict General Uehara, the chief of staff, openly clashed with General Tanaka who supported the Cabinet's decision. The army General Staff felt the need to counter the spread of Bolshevik power in East Asia. General Uehara was backed by opinions expressed by commanders in the field,[95] and, furthermore, he was angered by the Cabinet's failure to consult him. Hara, on the other hand, declared he would not tolerate military disobedience[96] and raised the question of altering the relationship between the military staff and the civilian segment of the government. Tanaka was indignant at Uehara's arbitrary attitude. He spoke to Hara of "moving into the sphere of the General Staff Headquarters," [97] he declared that "The Siberian affair is not a war and therefore subject to the decision of the government [i.e., the cabinet]," [98] and to strengthen his stand he threatened to resign. Yamagata worked to prevent an open break; with Hara he dissuaded Tanaka from resigning[99] and at the same time was able to mollify General Uehara. A compromise was reached.

93. On December 13, Gotō Shimpei reported to Hara that Yamagata did not oppose the idea of a withdrawal. *Ibid.,* VIII, 436. Shortly after the United States government notified Tokyo of its withdrawal in January 1920, Yamagata told Tanaka he approved Japan's withdrawal. *Ibid.,* VIII, 468. He repeated this to Hara later. *Ibid.,* VIII, 513; entry of March 26, 1920.

94. Yamagata told Hara that he had "explained to the army vice-chief of staff the disadvantage of leaving troops there." *Ibid.,* VIII, 562; entry of June 12, 1920.

95. See a speech by a General Suzuki, quoted by Shinobu, *Taishō shi,* III, 1,001–1,002.

96. *Hara nikki,* VIII, 558; entry of June 8, 1920.

97. *Ibid.,* VIII, 578; entry of June 28, 1920.

98. *Ibid.,* IX, 36; entry of August 10, 1920.

99. Hara discussed Yamagata's middle role in his diary entry of August 5, 1920; *ibid.,* IX, 27. Tanaka also agreed that his resignation might be interpreted to mean he was in some way connected with the Nikolaevsk affair. He had already stoutly denied charges of government responsibility in the Diet. *Ibid.,* IX, 37.

In July the Cabinet announced that Japan would continue to occupy several points in northern Sakhalin and retain troops in the east Siberian cities of Khabarovsk and Vladivostok until the Nikolaevsk affair was settled, but would withdraw from the Baikal region of Siberia. In the process of arriving at the decision, the larger problem of the relationship between military and civil authorities had been revealed. Hara, reacting in part to criticism of Japan's militarism widely expressed abroad, gave attention himself to the need for army reforms. Interestingly, Tanaka seemed to agree that the General Staff needed reforming and that postwar sentiment unfavorable to the army called for a reexamination of the relationship between the army minister and the chief of staff.[100] But Hara doubted Yamagata's support for such reforms. He confided to his diary: "While Tanaka seems concerned about this matter, the General Staff, backed by Yamagata, doesn't realize present conditions. Since the present is totally unlike the past it would be harmful for the future to have the rights of supreme command resorted to arbitrarily. I believe that the aim of constitutional government is to have the government assume complete responsibility to avoid burdening the Emperor with problems and act on his behalf. The Emperor has no direct relations with politics . . . but the soldiers of the General Staff do not understand that point." [101] Hara's contention was supported in September when the Cabinet decided to withdraw troops from Khabarovsk and cancel the secret Sino-Japanese agreement which had given Japan freedom to send troops into the Amur Basin area. When the chief of staff opposed the decision of the Cabinet, Tanaka resolved to use the disagreement to bring about military reforms.[102] He said to Hara that "The General Staff flaunts its right of imperial command and tries to control the Army Ministry. Moreover the General Staff, taking all matters to him immediately, always gets Yamagata's support, making it completely impossible to carry out policies." [103] With the hope of precipitating action, Tanaka submitted his resignation, believing that "Yamagata fears most the collapse of the cabinet which my resignation might prompt. Since he will try to placate me and urge my continuance it would be an opportunity to get a firm pledge for a future reform." [104] It was not like Tanaka to go against what he believed to be Yamagata's position, but he

100. The navy minister pointed out to Hara that Tanaka, as vice-chief of the staff during the last Cabinet, had acted toward the war minister in a manner he now disapproved. *Ibid.,* IX, 48; entry of August 23, 1920.

101. *Ibid.,* IX, 52; entry of Sept. 2, 1920.

102. *Ibid.,* IX, 56; entry of Sept. 7, 1920.

103. *Ibid.,* IX, 60; entry of Sept. 10, 1920.

104. *Ibid.,* IX, 60.

was embittered by Uehara's conduct and convinced that something should be done.

The scheme had its effect. When Hara, with Tanaka's resignation in hand, visited Yamagata at Odawara, he intimated that Tanaka's withdrawal might cause the Cabinet to fall. Yamagata had consistently urged withdrawal from Siberia, but he was also sympathetic to the attitude of General Uehara, believing that the Cabinet's jurisdiction over military divisions should be limited. Above all, however, he feared the collapse of the Hara Cabinet because it could lead to the rise of Katō, the opposition leader, the prospect of which was less than comforting.[105] Alarmed at the possible consequences, he said to Hara, "If things have come to this we must put a stop to it." [106]

Yamagata's mediation was successful. Tanaka's resignation was not accepted, and he reported to Hara, "Chief of Staff Uehara's attitude seems to have changed completely recently." [107] The breach was healed, but the reforms which Tanaka's gesture were designed to further were postponed. The question was raised again a little later, however, and in a far more drastic form. Finance minister Takahashi proposed in October that the General Staff be abolished. It was not seriously considered by the Cabinet, but Uehara and Yamagata both got wind of the proposal and reacted sharply. Tanaka was thrown off guard and, while assuring his Cabinet colleagues that he could control the General Staff, he hastened to assure his army colleagues that no such drastic measures were being contemplated.[108] Yamagata believed that the scare might well serve as a warning against the abuse of military power, but it would be safe to assume that he would never have agreed to any reorganization that jeopardized the army's independence from political control. Hara was assuredly convinced of it when he wrote in his diary, "Naturally, should Yamagata die, there would be a chance of abolishing the General Staff as well as the world's misunderstanding of [our] militarism." [109]

The procedure of the chief of staff opposing the Cabinet's decision to withdraw from Siberia thereby causing the army minister to threaten or attempt to resign, and then the appeasing of both sides to prevent the

105. Yamagata feared that Katō would pass radical legislation, such as universal manhood suffrage. Katō did in fact do this, but not until 1925.
106. It was Yamagata's plan that Tanaka's resignation be forwarded to the emperor, and, without accepting it, the grand chamberlain could send it back. He added, "I shall memorialize to have the petition returned." *Ibid.*, IX, 64; entry of Sept. 13, 1920.
107. *Ibid.*, IX, 68; entry of Sept. 14, 1920.
108. *Ibid.*, IX, 114; entry of Oct. 25, 1920.
109. *Ibid.*, IX, 113; entry of Oct. 25, 1920.

Cabinet's fall, was to be repeated a third time. Late in 1920, pressure outside and within the government built up to complete the withdrawal of troops from Siberia, which in effect meant Vladivostok, the only area still occupied. The expedition had served to gain no advantage, and in the climate of opinion following a war presumably fought for democracy it became a vulnerable target for antigovernment forces. Sensitive, if not responsive, to pressures of this sort, Yamagata told Hara that while protection for Japanese residents was needed in both Sakhalin and Vladivostok, "sooner or later it will be necessary [to withdraw] so it would be well to do it. I haven't spoken to Tanaka about this yet. What do you think?" [110] Hara believed the question should be raised, particularly since many nations were considering the recognition of the Soviet government.

For months the question was debated. When the decision favoring withdrawal was arrived at in May 1921, the chief of staff opposed it. Again Tanaka and Uehara clashed, and again Tanaka, this time with poor health as an additional reason, offered his resignation.[111] In the withdrawal decision Hara received Yamagata's support and, much to his surprise, listened to Yamagata criticize the army's conduct in such words as "It is utterly useless to consult military men." He is reported to have also said, "recently the Vladivostok commander Tachibana visited me and fearing what might follow the withdrawal argued against it . . . Regardless of the opposition of the military, there is no other policy." [112] Many delays in plans were encountered before the troops were completely withdrawn from Vladivostok, but the Cabinet decision was not reversed.

In three instances the opposition of the chief of staff was overcome. But Tanaka's resignation on June 7, 1921, did not result in any reforms of the military organization; the chief of staff's position of independent strength remained unchanged, and it was to grow much stronger. It did, however, make General Uehara's position as chief of staff untenable and his resignation became a foregone conclusion. But it was delayed at Yamagata's insistence because of urgent questions concerning the court, most notably the problem of a regency.

Looking back, Hara could claim to have weathered many domestic storms and to have passed through troubled waters in Japan's foreign relations. But during three uncertain years he had received the steady support of Yamagata. He was never deluded that Yamagata accepted the

110. *Ibid.,* IX, 151; entry of Dec. 8, 1920.
111. *Ibid.,* IX, 318; entry of May 25, 1921. Tanaka's resignation is reprinted under this date in Hara's diary.
112. *Ibid.,* IX, 324; entry of May 31, 1921. Final withdrawal came in June 1922, after both Hara and Yamagata were dead.

notion that parties should thereafter manage the nation's affairs, for he knew at firsthand Yamagata's deep well of suspicion when it came to party politicians. In the autumn of 1921 he told Yamagata that he was weary of the unending problems. After returning from a tour of Japan with the crown prince, he revealed his plan to resign from office. Yamagata would not hear of it. "Since the Crown Prince is about to assume sovereign rights as a Regent, you must delay it at such a critical moment and assist the Emperor." [113] Hara did postpone his plans, and early in November at Tokyo station he was fatally stabbed by a nineteen-year-old rightist railway employee who hated party politicians. Yamagata had seen Hara only five days before, but he was sick in bed when he heard of the assassination. Profoundly shocked, he said in grief, "I killed Hara. If I had granted his request to resign this disaster would never have occurred." [114]

The Sad Affair

The chief of Staff's delayed resignation because of a problem at the court highlights another area of Yamagata's activities in the last years of his life. In most of the thirty-eight extended conversations he had with Hara, matters relating to the emperor and his family were included. Hara's diary entries of 1920 and 1921 frequently contain references to Yamagata and the problems of the court. Hara's hope was to have the *genrō* assume responsibility for questions relating to the imperial family so that the government could concentrate on political affairs.[115] Yamagata seems to have accepted this; Hara quotes his opinion that "politics are the government's responsibility and the Court is the *genrō's*." [116] This arrangement was facilitated by the fact that after the death of General Ōyama in December 1916, Matsukata replaced him as lord keeper of the privy seal. Furthermore, Yamagata had powerful allies at the court; Hirata Tōsuke, for example, had been appointed an imperial court official in 1919, and his friend Nakamura Yajirō was the Imperial Household minister.

Three issues of importance engaged the attention of the advisers to the throne. The first, which had postponed Uehara's resignation, was brought about by the continuing deterioration of the health of the Taishō Emperor. Although this is a subject on which no great detail has ever been

113. Quoted in *Yamagata den*, III, 1,010.
114. Quoted in *ibid.*, III, 1,010.
115. *Hara nikki*, IX, 150; entry of Dec. 10, 1920.
116. *Ibid.*, IX, 77; entry of Sept. 22, 1920. It is interesting that on occasion Yamagata warned Hara not to make too frequent visits to the palace. See *ibid.*, IX, 64; entry of Oct. 13, 1920.

disclosed, it was made clear in the autumn of 1919 that his illness was serious. After the annual army maneuvers were concluded that year, the the emperor was treated as an invalid. He failed both in body and mind, and it was reported that his speech and memory were both affected. For some months hopes were held out for a recovery, but they never materialized. Hara's diary entries indicate that the possibility of a regency under the crown prince was in the minds of court advisers during 1920 and 1921. Yamagata discussed the question with many highly placed officials who visited Kokinan. Delayed as long as possible, a regency was finally declared on November 25, 1921, soon after Hara's successor had been appointed.

A second problem relating to the imperial family was whether or not the crown prince should travel abroad. The question was related to the emperor's illness for some argued that, under the prevailing conditions, permitting the heir apparent to travel abroad involved too great a risk. The empress was not enthusiastic,[117] and her disapproval was encouraged by a faction at court led by Sugiura Jūgo, a prominent classical scholar and instructor of the crown prince. Against those favoring a postponement of such plans both Yamagata and Matsukata encouraged the court to plan a tour abroad for the prince without delay.[118] In October 1920, Yamagata heard from Nakamura Jajirō that the empress still hesitated to grant permission. For Yamagata there was nothing but profit to be gained from experience abroad. All of the Meiji leaders had achieved benefits from wide travel; so Yamagata anxiously urged the same advantages for the crown prince. As lord keeper of the privy seal, Matsukata was in some ways in a better position than Yamagata to influence the decision, but the latter lost no opportunity to encourage directly and indirectly a favorable decision. In January 1921, permission was finally secured and Yamagata expressed his gratitude to Matsukata for his efforts and ventured that "in the future when the Crown Prince takes up his political task . . . he will be most enlightened and the nation will be pleased." [119] The favorable results of the prince's tour of Europe, which lasted from March to September, cheered the genrō in his final year. Two months following his return, the crown prince was made the regent of the realm.

But there was another court problem that was not resolved to Yamagata's liking. The issue was related to the marriage of the crown prince, not of momentous consequences, but since it turned out against his wishes

117. Itoko Koyama, *Nagako: Empress of Japan* (New York, 1958), p. 36.
118. In August, Yamagata said to Hara that he hoped the crown prince could go in the autumn. *Hara nikki*, IX, 35; entry of August 9, 1920.
119. Yamagata's letter to Matsukata, Jan. 16, 1921, in *Yamagata den*, III, 1,019.

Yamagata's final year was deeply saddened. He felt so pained and displeased at the outcome that he requested that his official offices, his rank, his honors, and his privileges all be withdrawn. Neither Yamagata's petition nor a similar one submitted by Matsukata was accepted, but at least two prominent court officials resigned as a result of this "grave incident."

Late in 1920 whispers reached the Tokyo press of a serious disagreement among the advisers to the throne. The cause of the trouble was obscured as details were not permitted to be divulged. Newspapers spoke guardedly of the "grave court affair" and carefully indicated that it was a tussle between a few dozen influential men at the palace and in the high bureaucracy. The "sordid struggle on the steps of the Throne" [120] hardly touched the nation at all. For those involved, however, and most of all for Yamagata, it was a matter of first importance.[121] From Hara's diary and other sources it is possible to reconstruct the event.

Soon after the eldest son of the Taishō Emperor was formally installed as crown prince in 1916, the search began for a suitable wife. By 1918 the eldest daughter of Prince Kuni had been selected from among many candidates. Prince Kuni was the head of a branch of the imperial family;[122] he had been trained as a military man, and he had several wives and a total of eighteen children. The mother of Nagako, the crown prince's bride-to-be, was from the Shimazu family, the ex-daimyo of Satsuma.[123] In January 1918, the emperor gave his approval to the selection, Prince Kuni accepted, and the Imperial Household ministry began the necessary arrangements. Nagako, then fifteen years old, was withdrawn from the peers' school and placed under private tutors. Seven years of careful training lay ahead of her before the marriage was to take place.[124]

Preparations were suddenly disrupted in 1920 by the disclosure that there was hereditary color blindness in the Shimazu family. Yamagata had been so informed by his physician, and he passed the information on to the minister of the Imperial Household, Nakamura Yajirō. When color blindness was confirmed by five eminent medical professors of the Im-

120. A. Morgan Young, *Japan under Taisho Tenno* (London, 1920), p. 227.
121. In a popular pictorial history of Yamagata, Yoshida Sadoko, his common-law wife, claimed that the most important event to Yamagata in his last years at Kokinan was this "grave affair." See *Kokusai Shashin Jōhō* (International graphic) 30.10:6 (October 1956). Its importance is also indicated by the numerous references made to it in Hara's diary in late 1920 and the first quarter of 1921.
122. Princess Nagako's grandfather had been involved in a plot at the time of the Restoration; pardoned in 1875, he was given the name of Kuni, and in 1883 the family was declared a branch of the imperial family. See E. Papinot, *Historical and Geographical Dictionary of Japan* (Ann Arbor, 1945), p. 324.
123. Koyama Itoko, *Nagako*, p. 19.
124. *Ibid.*, p. 20.

perial University,[125] the advisability of continuing the marriage plans was raised. The *genrō*, Hara, Nakamura, Hirata, and others assumed that disclosure would make it necessary to change plans.[126] Without imperial sanction they proceeded to alter plans. Prince Kuni was approached to withdraw his daughter as the crown prince's prospective bride. Yamagata wrote him a letter to that effect and Saionji visited him in Kyoto to persuade him.

However, Prince Kuni refused to be rushed into canceling plans, and he found support in an influential group at court. His major ally was Sugiura Jūgo, tutor in ethics to both the crown prince and Princess Nagako, a scholar of conservative convictions well known for his writing on ethics and the spirit of Japan. Sugiura reportedly first discovered the problem in a visit he made to Odawara to report on the crown prince's progress and display a sample of his writing.[127] As he was departing, Yamagata remarked that Prince Kuni was being very difficult. As Sugiura was not yet familiar with the color blindness issue, the remark perplexed him. Prince Kuni not only clarified the remark for him but expressed his displeasure over the fact that he was being asked to retract his decision. He had accepted the emperor's word as final; now he wondered whether a reversal was really sanctioned by the imperial family. Sugiura satisfied himself that there were insufficient grounds for canceling the engagement and accused Yamagata and others of interfering with imperial orders and undermining the principles of loyalty he was at that very moment teaching the future monarch. He declared that it was a disgrace to the virtue of the court and prepared to oppose any change in plans.

Fortified by this support, Prince Kuni refused to bow to the pressure. In a letter to the empress he asked to be given imperial advice. If the empress was persuaded that the marriage would weaken the imperial line, he was prepared to cancel the engagement immediately.[128] Prince Kuni did not receive an immediate reply, but he stood firm against the continuing prodding of Yamagata and others[129] and received considerable support for his position.[130]

125. *Hara nikki*, IX, 201.
126. See conversation between Hara and Saionji of Dec. 7, 1920, in *ibid.*, IX, 147.
127. This is recounted by Kojima Kazuo, a Seiyūkai leader and a former student of Sugiura, in his *Ichi rōseijika no kaisō* (Tokyo, 1951), p. 183.
128. Yamagata reported this to Hara on Dec. 8, 1920, and added that General Kurita, attached to Prince Kuni, had visited him to say that Prince Kuni wished to proceed with the original plans. *Hara nikki*, IX, 150. See letter of Prince Kuni to the empress in Koyama Itoko, *Nagako*, pp. 30–31.
129. Part of Yamagata's letter to Prince Kuni urging him to reconsider and give weight to the family medical history is quoted in Koyama Itoko, *Nagako*, pp. 31–32.
130. Prince Kuni was encouraged in his position when the court physicians pointed

Charges and countercharges swirled around the court and the highest levels of the government. And a wide variety of explanations were offered for the cause of the conflict. One view held that Yamagata was determined to prevent an alliance between the court and the Satsuma family.[131] This was hardly likely since Matsukata, the senior Satsuma statesman and lord keeper of the privy seal, supported the decision to alter the plans. Another explanation offered was that scheming people in the household of Prince Koya, whose daughter was not selected to be the bride of the crown prince, out of spite had influenced Yamagata's physician to bring the question of color blindness to his attention.[132] Still another view was that it was a consequence of the rivalry among scholars hoping to be selected to tutor Nagako. It was said that one well-known woman scholar was rejected by the supervisor of the Kuni's household affairs and sought revenge by opposing the marriage. Other explanations were rumored about, but none satisfactorily answered the question of why the issue was raised when it was. The answer seems to be that it was purely accidental; that a physician in the course of some research stumbled across the information and it reached Yamagata's ears through his doctor. Once discovered it was not strange that a "pure blood argument" developed in favor of halting the marriage plans. Once cancellation was proposed, however, it fed latent rivalries and jealousies at the court to produce an embarrassing situation.

Those who opposed any change in plans for the crown prince's marriage argued from moral principles. Sugiura insisted that imperial decisions must not be tampered with. He began to doubt Yamagata's loyalty and resigned his position as tutor in order to gather support to block Yamagata. He solicited the aid of former pupils in influencing the Imperial Household ministry and persuading people in key positions.[133] Tōyama Mitsuru, the head of a well-known ultra-nationalist clique with fabled power to influence through threats and violence, was one of his staunch backers. The dispute was intensified when the question of the crown prince's travel abroad was injected. Sugiura and his supporters opposed the trip as a violation of filial piety when the emperor was ill; Yama-

out that "color weakness" rather than "color blindness" was the more accurate term. *Hara nikki*, IX, 158; entry of Dec. 11, 1920.

131. Hara claims Yamamoto Gombei expressed this view. *Ibid.*, IX, 215; entry of Feb. 9, 1921.

132. Kojima, *Ichi rōseijika no kaisō*, p. 182.

133. Kojima's main activity in this connection was to prevent questions from being brought up in public through questions in the Diet. In this he was successful. *Ibid.*, pp. 187–191.

gata was even accused of desiring the trip to help him win his argument against the marriage. But the *genrō* did, as we have seen, win that argument.

The marriage problem absorbed the attention of an increasing number of people. Newspapers reported scraps of information which caused consternation at the palace, and all future references to the "grave court affair" were forbidden. Yamagata could not be moved and, as a consequence, his motives were brought into question and his loyalty impugned by those who opposed him. Owing to fears that Yamagata might be physically attacked by the henchmen of Tōyama Mitsuru,[134] police guards were placed around Kokinan in Odawara. Rumors persisted about Yamagata's dark plots despite the efforts of many to point out that both Yamagata and Sugiura were acting from the highest motives.

Pressure mounted for the Imperial Household minister to resolve the conflict. General Tanaka and Hirata Tōsuke, supporting Yamagata, suggested he suspend the engagement on his own responsibility.[135] On the other hand, he received many callers and letters demanding that no changes should be made. He thought of submitting the question to the Privy Council, but then decided that he could not delay an announcement any longer. He knew that the imperial family was not anxious to reverse their decision, and at the same time he received information that a mass demonstration by rightists was being planned for February 11, the great annual Founding Day holiday. On February 10 the government finally issued a cryptic announcement that there were no changes contemplated in the choice of the crown prince's bride-to-be. At the same time Nakamura's resignation was announced. Writing Yamagata later that day, he explained: "I returned to the capital tonight and discovered various movements afoot and disturbed conditions prevailing . . . As I said to you yesterday, I have decided to be resolute, announcing that there would be no change and, at the same time, feeling a heavy responsibility, offer my resignation today. Not realizing that such pressure would be placed upon me . . . I wanted to see you again, but I proceeded with the decision because of the situation. I hope you will understand." [136]

Yamagata understood only too well. He had been affected by the widespread rumors and criticism of his part in the affair; his loyalty had been doubted, his motives discredited, and his life threatened. He was accused of abusing his power and interfering in a family matter. At last, he came

134. There are several references to these reports in Hara's diary. *Hara nikki*, IX, 179 (Dec. 28, 1920), 193 (Jan. 15, 1921), 206 (Feb. 2, 1921).
135. *Ibid.*, IX, 211 and 214.
136. Letter of Feb. 10, 1921, reprinted in *Yamagata den*, III, 1,911.

to the realization that the emperor and empress were not anxious to cancel the engagement. The *genrō* had been rebuffed and Yamagata had failed. When the *genrō* met at Kokinan on February 14, they were chagrined and saddened by the trouble they had caused. They had come together to select a successor to Nakamura, but they talked more of the possibility of resigning themselves. Never before had the unanimous opinion of the *genrō* been rejected.

Yamagata was genuinely grieved at what had happened. He felt a heavy responsibility and prepared to resign his position. At intervals over the previous few years, he had asked the throne to allow him to relinquish his official duties as president of the Privy Council and adviser to the emperor; each time the request had been turned down. Now there were sad, new reasons for resigning. The newspapers were blaming him for an incident they dimly understood; his old foe, Ōkuma, was quoted as saying: "The Minister of the Imperial Household was nothing but a cat's paw in the matter, though of course he must assume his share of responsibility for the part that he acted. Marquis Matsukata will also have to resign his post. As for Prince Yamagata, it is incumbent upon him to resign all the public offices he holds, to say nothing of renouncing his treatment as a *Genrō*, so as to apologize to the Emperor and to the nation. Otherwise it would be impossible to placate the nation, which feels high resentment against his attitude." [137]

Yamagata was not accustomed to placating the nation; and he had never paid much heed to the clamor of the newspapers. But he was profoundly distressed by the intimation of disloyalty and deeply injured to have been, as the final outcome proved him to be, in error. For him it was indeed a sad affair.

On February 21, 1921, he addressed a letter to the throne in sedate and humble language. He apologized for neglecting his duties, entreated to be allowed to reaffirm his loyalty and honor. He began his letter with the familiar phrase he had used at the beginning of his political career—"I am merely a soldier." [138] He then begged to be released from all his official positions, and he asked permission to be allowed to give up his court rank and his princedom, and all his decorations and honors. He was moved to write an acquaintance, "The major principle of my life has been to serve the Emperor first, last and always. If I am fortunate enough

137. Quoted in *Japan Weekly Chronicle*, Feb. 24, 1921, p. 261.
138. Accompanying the resignation was a document explaining why he had taken his stand against the marriage plans. Both are reprinted in *Hara nikki*, IX, 227–230, under the entry of Feb. 22, 1921. The date of March 21 given in *Yamagata den*, III, 1,011, appears to be an error.

to have my wish granted, I am determined to die for my Emperor and my country as plain Yamagata Kyōsuke." [139]

Matsukata had joined Yamagata in this unprecedented step. In the following weeks Hara, Makino, the newly appointed Imperial Household minister, and others pleaded with the older *genrō* to withdraw their resignations. Hara said to Kiyoura, Yamagata's loyal friend, "He has spoken out of true loyalty and there is no reason for the Emperor to allow the resignation of one who serves as adviser at the behest of the late Emperor." [140] But Yamagata would not reconsider. April passed and May was entered and still there was no acceptance of Yamagata's resignation. Finally on May 15, Makino traveled to Odawara and formally delivered an imperial message refusing the request.[141]

Three days later Yamagata donned his military uniform. It no longer fit him properly because recurrent illness had made him thin and wan; the cap was too large and the visor rested too low over his eyes. But with unmistakable courage and head erect, he traveled to Numazu where the emperor was then residing. In a formal audience with the Taishō Emperor he was handed another message rejecting his resignation. His part in the whole sad affair was excused, his positions and honors as well as his implacable loyalty were confirmed. A similar message was delivered to Matsukata.[142] The issue of color blindness remained a subject of conversation for months, but for Yamagata the emperor's message had ended the episode.

Speculation turned to the question of how the affair might affect Yamagata's influence. It would exclude him from the political world, said some. Some tried to claim that "Yamagata's actual power in the political field was wiped out. At that point the era of the oligarchs ended completely." [143] Yet it might well be argued that his authority, while not unchanging, was not of the character that could be dissipated so easily. The roots of his power were deep in the bureaucracy of Japan and the branches spread in all directions. During Hara's tenure, Yamagata's influence had not been as vigorously asserted as in his younger days, but his prestige had not waned, his friends had not faded nor been ejected from countless positions of importance. Until the end,

139. Quoted in *Yamagata den,* III, 1,913. Kyōsuke was the name he had used before adopting Aritomo.
140. Kiyoura repeated Hara's remark in a letter to Yamagata on April 28, 1921. Reprinted in *ibid.,* III, 1,013–1,014. Kiyoura also reported that Makino shared Hara's feelings and that they were not likely to agree to his resignation.
141. Letter reprinted in *Hara nikki,* IX, 303.
142. *Japan Weekly Chronicle,* May 26, 1921, p. 726.
143. Maeda, *Hara Kei den,* II, 404.

little of importance was done without his assent; his was a voice which had to be heard.[144] Hara knew this and, as we have seen, up to the time of his assassination he continued to see and consult the old *genrō*. In a rare letter to a foreigner in October 1921, Yamagata wrote, "I have long since retired from active politics and am no longer identified with affairs of state." However, the editor of the newspaper in which this letter appeared was moved to remind readers that "it remains true that no important decision is come to in Japan without his approval and sanction." [145]

As winter closed in on the year 1921, dusk descended on the old warrior's life. He was struck by an illness from which he was never to recover. In 1922, Yamagata approached his eighty-fourth year; the vigor of his mind remained remarkably unimpaired but his body failed him. He could no longer leave his bed to walk about his beloved gardens, or descend the garden steps to bow before the shrine he built to the Meiji Emperor. He remained in bed, wrote, read or was read to, received special visitors. Matsukata, Tanaka, Kiyoura, and others conversed with him on a variety of topics as he lay sick in bed.[146] When an imperial messenger arrived with greetings from the emperor, Yamagata insisted, against the orders of his doctor, that he be changed into formal attire. Flowers arrived from many sources and his closest relatives gathered at Kokinan for the last days. It rained in Odawara on January 31, and Yamagata remarked to his doctor that it was probably a bad sign. He died at 1:00 P.M. on February 1, 1922.

On February 9, a funeral service was performed in Hibiya Park in Tokyo with all the solemnity befitting the passing of a great man. His body, resting in a coffin, was placed on a gun carriage and, escorted by many dignitaries, was drawn slowly through streets lined by troops and thronged by large crowds. In the distance could be heard a nineteen-gun salute. The funeral procession moved quietly to the park where a brief

144. After Hara's assassination, Yamagata tried again to persuade Saionji to lead the government. Saionji refused and Yamagata consented to the calling of Takahashi, Hara's finance minister. Earlier, Yamagata had been instrumental in blocking the appointment of Yamamoto Gombei as lord privy seal when Matsukata resigned. *Hara nikki*, IX, 233; entry of Feb. 25, 1921. Hara's diary is sprinkled with the suggestions, rejections, and consent of Yamagata on names for public offices.

145. Letter to Mr. Poultney Bigelow, an American newspaperman, in *Japan Weekly Chronicle*, Oct. 27, 1921, p. 592.

146. Tanaka recounted how, four days before his death, Yamagata called him to his bedside for a conversation. What Tanaka most remembered was the old warrior telling him, "As people grow older they neglect general trends . . . and as your position rises you have less opportunity for thinking about things . . . so endeavor to stay abreast of general affairs." Quoted in *Yamagata den*, III, 1,096.

ceremony was held in a temporary funeral hall. Prayers were repeated by Shinto priests, and invited guests and dignitaries were allowed to worship briefly before the coffin. The coffin was again placed on the gun carriage and taken to the cemetery of the Gokokuji temple, where Yamagata was buried not far from the grave of Ōkuma, who had died a month before him.

As Yamagata Aritomo was laid to rest, his name was showered with accolades, his life was praised, his career saluted. He was celebrated as a great reformer, hero of the army, major architect of new Japan — the greatest man of the modern era. But, as when he was still living, there was no accord in these judgments. Even as his body was being moved slowly through the streets of Tokyo in an elaborate state funeral, a voice in the Diet bitterly opposed the use of public funds to bury "an enemy of mankind and suppressor of democratic institutions." [147]

He remains today a figure of controversy. As with most great but disputed figures, the interpretations of his career and character have varied according to the current fashions in political greatness, goodness, or wickedness. As Japan plunged into a suicidal war in Asia, he was identified as the "key figure in Japanese reaction and aggression." [148] "If there is any one Japanese more responsible than any other for the present Pacific war," wrote a Western observer in 1943, "the man is Yamagata, dead twenty-one years." [149] This verdict has often been repeated by Japanese authors since the end of the war. He has been designated as the ringleader in the antidemocratic movement and chief war criminal.[150] "If you asked who led Japan to defeat and ruin, it was Yamagata who was the arch-villain." [151] Others would contend that had he lived longer he would have saved the nation from the extremities of violence that lay ahead, that he would have blocked the reckless military ventures that led to ultimate defeat. But whatever the differences in the political and moral judgment of his life, there is at least no doubt that he occupied a position of great importance. No contemporary list of the outstanding figures of Japan's modern century ever excludes his name.[152] Even his

147. London *Times,* Feb. 7, 1922, p. 9.
148. E. Herbert Norman, "Feudal Background of Japanese Politics" (mimeographed, New York, 1945), p. 80.
149. Gustav Eckstein, *In Peace Japan Breeds War* (New York, 1943), p. 228.
150. Abe Shinnosuke, "Yamagata Aritomo," p. 227.
151. Nomura Hideo, "Gumbatsu Yamagata Aritomo no zaiaku," p. 55.
152. *Chūō kōron* in August 1965 carried an article entitled "One Hundred Who Built Modern Japan."

most irreconcilable enemies have never been given to belittling his ability and power.

By any measure, Yamagata Aritomo had an extraordinary career. From insignificant beginnings he rose to become both the most important military and the most influential political figure of modern Japan. The principal landmarks in his career come quickly to mind: a revolutionary opening phase; two chapters of mounting influence and prestige, first in the military bureaucracy and then in the civil; subsequent phases in which he gained new stature through the political triumphs which he grasped; and finally an epilogue in which his senior rank as statesman gave him limitless opportunity to impress his attitude on the major decisions of state. For over half a century he served in official capacities — as chief of the army and minister of war, as minister of home affairs, as minister of justice, twice as prime minister, long as privy councillor and *genrō*. From a fixed military center, his authority and influence spread ineluctably, as an ever-widening circle, into the civil administration and the court.

Political leadership in Japan has tended to rest in a ruling group, not in an individual, and Japan was guided into the modern world by an outstanding group of men dedicated to the same goal who were remarkably successful in fashioning the means to achieve it. This makes it difficult to penetrate the surface of political life to locate the exact center of power. Furthermore, within the leadership a careful balance was maintained between the representatives of the western han of Chōshū and Satsuma. Nevertheless within the oligarchy there were those who, while bearing significant responsibility, had less influence than others in determining the course of state affairs. Among them would be included Saigō Tsugumichi, Ōyama Iwao, and to a lesser extent Inoue Kaoru and Matsukata Masayoshi—each accomplished in a given field but none a masterful political figure. Similarly there were a few, such as Itagaki Taisuke and Ōkuma Shigenobu, who, while important in certain aspects of the development of modern Japan, were excluded from sustained political power because they were not from Chōshū or Satsuma. After the death of Ōkubo Toshimici, Itō Hirobumi and Yamagata became the prime shapers of the destiny of their country. By the turn of the century Yamagata's power overshadowed even that of Itō; after Itō's assassination in 1909 and until his own death in 1922 Yamagata was unrivaled.

During his life Yamagata played the triple role of general, bureaucrat, and Chōshū clansman. As the oligarch joining the top of the civil and military bureaucracies, he was the key figure in executing national policy. The extension of his influence was purchased by means which insured that its impact would be more than superficial. It is not fair, nor the intention of this study, to credit him personally with all the accomplishments of the government — he contributed little to the amazing economic growth of Japan and even in practical political affairs he claimed he was "merely a soldier." Yet on the whole he deserves to rank first both for the importance of his achievement and the force of his character in the shaping of modern Japan. It was because of his key position, his long active career, and his wide following that no other statesman could equal the sustained impact he brought to bear on the modern development of the nation.

It is the direction, not the extent, of his influence which has been disputed. Yet the judgment of any man's career will often vary from one period to another. During his lifetime Yamagata represented many things at many times — revolutionary, innovator, conservative — as times and circumstances changed and as he grew older.

In early manhood he was a revolutionary. As one of the many young activist samurai of western Japan whose "martial spirit" had been stimulated both by the external crisis and by the teachings of such men as Yoshida Shōin, he spent a decade in conspiratorial activity in the intra-han and national struggles to destroy the Tokugawa government and restore the emperor to power. Antiforeign sentiment expressed in the form of traditional vendettas proved futile and led to military action against the bakufu in the name of loyalty to the han and the emperor. Traditional feelings of local loyalty were transmuted into national patriotism and combined with a revolutionary "spirit of innovation" to provide the impetus for transforming the nation.

In maturity, after the restoration of imperial rule, his role was that of an innovator; an architect of the new order. The immediate objective after the Restoration was to develop sufficient strength for the new regime to assure its internal security and through unified power to resist the encroachment of Western power. Both objectives called for the progressive development of a national military force. Through the innovation of universal conscription, Yamagata set the pattern in the efficient organization of the military; the new-style army succeeded in consolidating the new central government's authority, in stabilizing internal affairs, and in deterring the advance of foreign powers. Thus it is hardly surprising that the army had a preponderant role in the development of modern Japan, for military power was decisive in gaining security at home and, eventually, equality abroad. Nor, because of his key role in military reforms, is it surprising that Yamagata's political power always rested squarely on his unquestioned position as the first soldier of the land.

By contributing to the creation of new political institutions — local government, the police, the home ministry — he expanded his base of political power to major sectors of the civil bureaucracy. By developing a large following of personal associates whom he could influence or manipulate, he was able to sustain his political power in both the civil and the military bureaucracy. His capacity to attract and hold the loyalty of others was, in the last analysis, more striking than his ability to innovate and administer.

The form of the new government responded to national realities but also to the character of the architects of the new nation. Brought to the realization that Japan had been left behind in the march of civilization and consequently endangered by those who were turning advantages to means of exploitation, Yamagata and his colleagues followed one general prescription. This was deliberately to introduce those aspects of Western civilization which would help create a new type of strength for Japan. Through travel, study, and the use of foreign experts, the Meiji architects learned the nature of Western political, economic, and military institutions. Yamagata knew no foreign language, but through translated works he avidly sought knowledge of the West and especially Prussia, whose accomplishments he knew also through firsthand experience. In this he revealed an amazing capacity to learn and adopt rapidly many of the technological and institutional features of the Western world.

Yet in each development of the new political system, Yamagata showed himself to be conservative. He recognized the need for reforms and contributed to change, but he retained grave reservations about the ethical and moral principles which undergirded many Western institutions. He favored borrowing the prescription to revive the health and robustness of Japanese civilization, but he was convinced that the nation could best be ruled through the strong centralized authority of an all-powerful bureaucracy. In the face of growing demands for a more liberal political order, he became increasingly conservative. In his view the government should rightfully act as the instrument for maintaining imperial authority and for furthering the nation's welfare; and in this he represented a main current in Japanese political sentiment. This

345

conviction caused him to advocate a military organization independent of political control and a civil bureaucracy, consolidated by the home ministry as the heart of internal administration, separated from the political parties. To him the political freedom and power of the people expressed through elected representatives should be limited and subservient to the overriding goals of the nation. In sum, his political outlook was that of an autocrat who, while reluctantly acknowledging the validity of political parties in a constitutional system, turned to the sanction of imperial rule to justify the prevention of parties from infiltrating the bureaucracy, forming cabinets, or holding executive power. He believed that the nation should be led firmly by the civil and military bureaucracy acting as a responsible servant of the emperor not as the servant of the people.

The extent of his power may seem surprising in view of the fact that Yamagata did not have the qualities of a popular hero. His lean figure and his finely chiseled face — high cheekbones, thin lips, bright eyes, and cropped, grizzled mustache — reflected a stern and austere personality. He was robbed of physical robustness during much of his life by recurrent stomach ailments. His manner was stiff and rigid, and the world looked on him as a cold, disciplined militarist. He found it difficult to adjust to the political life of the modern statesman. He was not an able speaker, disliked publicity of any kind, and never sought and never depended upon public support. In contrast to the magnetism of Itō and Ōkuma, Yamagata had qualities of leadership which stemmed from other traits.

In many respects he was an idealized version of the ancient warrior. His frugality, discipline, strong sense of self-denial, unbending will, and devoted loyalty were the traditional virtues associated with the samurai class. In his private life he reflected traditional values and more than any other Meiji leader he had the refined tastes of an aristocrat. This is most clearly seen in his love of poetry. He was a prolific correspondent, with a graceful style and a classical flavor to his phrasing, but poetry was his most gratifying means of expression. His intellect was direct and analytical, rarely clouded by sentiment, yet frequently, and even in the heat of battle, he would capture his emotions by composing poems. Many of these have received national recognition for their beauty. He was also a master of landscape gardening. His residences were not sumptuous by the standards of the time, but he always planned his own gardens and in their beauty effectively showed the great genius of Japanese art for the glorification of the singular and specific. He enjoyed the company of *geisha,* their dancing and singing, but he enjoyed even more the traditional tea ceremony and the quiet company of a few close friends.

In his relations with others he was stern and strict. All who met him were struck by his erect, spare figure, his simplicity and directness. His granddaughter and his mistress retain vivid memories of his dignified and austere presence.[153] Both admit to having been tense and frightened in his presence.

Yamagata always gave the impression of great strength; there was great dignity in his manner. He was sensitive and warm toward his few intimate friends, and a wider circle of friends was impressed by his self-discipline, his resoluteness, and his unswerving devotion to the emperor and the nation's welfare. An unprepossessing exterior concealed a strength of will and persistence that won over men of many temperaments. By his quiet ability, perserverance, and steadfastness he inspired the loyalty of his following, carefully chosen admirers and beneficiaries whom he admitted to the court of his confidence. As he grew older he would more frequently act through the hands and speak through the lips of those upon whom he had bestowed his friendship.

This then was the character of Yamagata — a man in whom the values traditional to Japan continued with vigor, a man with the sensitivity of the refined aristocrat and the austere exterior of the model samurai. It is not surprising to find that the principles which guided his political thought and actions did not stem from a modern political philosophy. They were formed, rather, by a conception of politics which flowed from the authoritarian tradition of the past.

Brought up in an era of authoritarian feudal rule and imbued with a belief in strong government, he tended to perpetuate the traditional idea of bureaucratic omnipotence. He was implacable and uncompromising in the preservation of the power of the state at home. This led him to manipulate men and institutions, often from behind the scene, to where many saw him as the quintessence of bureaucratic conservatism. Undeniably the firmness of his leadership and the dominance of the bureaucracy set the pattern in the government's relations with the people, and obstructed the growth of constitutional government and democratic tendencies. The independent power he achieved for the military and the dominance of the bureaucracy in the political life of

153. His granddaughter has recounted that when she visited Yamagata at his residence, perhaps three-quarters of a mile from her home, he would greet her by inquiring if she had walked the distance. Rather than face his disapproval she would lie and not disclose that she always took the trolley.

the nation were at the expense of these tendencies, so that traditional authoritarianism was continued in a new form. Yet his political beliefs, shared for the most part by the other Meiji leaders, helped to give Japan a steady course in a difficult period of transition. Strong leadership was perhaps necessary for rapid and successful modernization. In the end, this authoritarianism constituted an anachronism which led, in the 1940's, to disaster.

However, it would be misleading to think of Yamagata as a prototype of the militarists who forced Japan into a suicidal war. Yamagata, in common with his colleagues, was obsessed with national security, he desired the growth of Japan as a great power, and his strategic concept of security necessitated the constant military strength and preparedness which he incessantly demanded. Yet his determination to enhance the position of the nation was fused with caution in the expansion of Japan abroad. Time and again he advocated settling disputes through compromises, by negotiations or a system of alliances. Yamagata grew up with the institutions of new Japan; some of them he helped to create, and in the process he acquired power. In the 1930's when the balance and restraint he represented as both a civil and military leader were removed, the militarists competed to gain a monopoly of power. In that competition, it must be granted, the army had the advantages which Yamagata had developed in an earlier time. Once in power, however, they lacked the responsibility felt by Yamagata and the oligarchs who had developed with the new nation. Without this responsibility and tempted by what they interpreted as favorable world conditions, they pursued recklessly the goal of hegemony of all East Asia. But historical events after his death should not becloud our judgment of Yamagata who must be seen against the background of his time and his objectives.

For what he set out to do, Yamagata was spectacularly successful. He brought to his work remarkable energy and vitality and the ability to act decisively; if he originated few ideas, when he was convinced an idea was good he firmly and unflinchingly adhered to it. What he lacked in profound and imaginative thought he made up by methodical thinking and planning. He achieved power by constant, assiduous effort; his patience and concentration enabled him to bend events and men to his own fixed pattern. He was not the type of statesman who was a natural political being sensitive to the perpetually altering contours of events and capable of subtly adjusting a nation's course to harmonize with those changes. His life affords the study of a contrasting type of statesman, equally compelling. Essentially he was a man of a single principle, with few doubts about his own vision and by concentration of will power able to ignore a great deal that went on about him. The secret of his personal success was his stubborn self-absorption in the objectives to be attained. This included the maintenance of his own political power and the exertion of his influence in building and perpetuating a strong nation under unchallenged central authority in order, as he expressed it, "to establish the independence of our country and increase the nation's strength in facing the Western powers" [154] and "to preserve the nation's rights and advantages among the powers to keep it from lagging behind in general progress." [155]

Yet he was more than the sum of these qualities. Great as these may have been, the greatness of Yamagata was to a large extent the product of times which called for greatness. For this reason, his career not only illustrates in microcosm the phenomenal transformation of Japan into a modern nation, it is inseparable from it. The central position he held for so long in that heroic story gives him a greatness which transcends his personal merits or limitations. In a very real sense the biography of Yamagata is more than a story of a gifted individual, it is the history of modern Japan.

154. This phrase appears in a memorial submitted by Yamagata in October 1893 urging military expansion. Memorial reprinted in *Yamagata den,* III, 108.
155. *Ibid.,* III, 108.

Bibliography

Glossary

Index

Bibliography

The starting point, and still the richest source of primary materials for the study of Yamagata's career, is the three-volume *Kōshaku Yamagata Aritomo den* (Biography of Prince Yamagata Aritomo) by the journalist-historian Tokutomi Iichirō. Published eleven years after Yamagata's death, each volume of over a thousand pages includes many of the 1,800 letters and documents from Yamagata's collection that survived the fire following the great earthquake of 1923. It contains relevant letters from the collections of other important Meiji figures and information supplied by Yamagata's friends and associates who were living in 1933 when the biography was compiled. Tokutomi also used Yamagata's own account of his activities during the decade before the Restoration, dictated to a friend and privately published in 1898; Yamagata's brief diary and poems recording his experiences in Kyoto in 1867, first published in 1892; and other poems in the possession of the Yamagata family. In short, the biography compiled by Tokutomi constitutes the extended editing of much of the primary material available on Yamagata's life. Additional letters and documents on his career are to be found in the Yamagata Aritomo monjo (Papers of Yamagata Aritomo) in the National Diet Library. A second major source is a compilation of eighty-two documents with accompanying analysis published in 1966 by Ōyama Azusa under the title *Yamagata Aritomo ikensho* (The written opinions of Yamagata Aritomo). These include memorials, policy proposals, public statements, and private opinions, some of them previously unpublished, dating from 1871 to 1919.

Most of the half-dozen prewar biographies of Yamagata appeared shortly after his death and were written by friends prompted by the instinct to adulate his accomplishments. They help to flesh out the narrative of his history, but for the most part they do not provide a critical analysis of his career. Of the three short postwar biographies, the study by Oka Yoshitake is distinguished by its balanced and perceptive analysis. In addition to full-scale biographies, there are numerous articles on his career which have appeared over the past seventy years, frequently in conjunction with essays on other Meiji leaders or in studies of the history of the military in modern Japan.

A fourth source on which this study has relied includes general histories, monographic studies, journal articles, and popular accounts. I have also been able to include information gained from a few Japanese who knew Yamagata personally, especially his last private secretary Irie Kan'ichi and his granddaughter.

Abe Shinnosuke 阿部眞之助. "Yamagata Aritomo" 山県有朋, *Bungei shunjū* 文芸春秋 (Literary annals), 30.1:224–235 (January 1952).

―――― *Kindai seijika hyōden* 近代政治家評伝 (Critical biographies of modern politicians). Tokyo, 1953.

Adachi Isamu 足立勇. "Itō to Yamagata" 伊藤と山県 (Itō and Yamagata), *Rekishi kōron* 歴史公論 (Historical review), 2.1:196–206 (1933).

Adachi Kinnosuke. "Japan's Elder Statesman and the Peace," *Review of Reviews*, 32.189:430–432 (October 1905).

Akita, George. "The Meiji Constitution in Practice: The First Diet," *Journal of Asian Studies*, 22.1:31–46 (November 1962).

―――― *Foundations of Constitutional Government in Modrrn Japan, 1868–1900*. Cambridge, Mass., 1967.

Allen, George C. *Japan, the Hungry Guest*. New York, 1938.

Araki Sadao 荒木貞夫, comp. *Gensui Uehara Yūsaku den* 元師上原勇作伝 (Biography of Field Marshal Uehara Yūsaku). 2 vols. Tokyo, 1937.

Asahina Chisen 朝比奈知泉. *Meiji kōshinroku* 明治功臣録 (Distinguished Japanese of the Meiji period). Tokyo, 1924.

Asakawa, K. *The Russo-Japanese Conflict: Its Causes and Issues*. Boston, 1904.

Baelz, Toku, ed. *Awakening Japan: The Diary of a German Doctor, Erwin Baelz*. Translated from the German by Eden and Cedar Paul. New York, 1932.

Balet, J. C. *Military Japan*. Yokohama, 1910.

Beckmann, George M. *The Making of the Meiji Constitution*. Lawrence, Kansas, 1957.

Berton, Peter, "The Secret Russo-Japanese Alliance of 1916." Unpublished Ph. D. dissertation, Columbia University, 1956.

Borton, Hugh. "Peasant Uprisings in Japan of the Tokugawa Period," *Transactions of the Asiatic Society of Japan*, 2nd ser., 16:1–219 (May 1938).

Brown, Sidney D. "Kido Takayoshi and the Meiji Restoration: A Political Biography." Ph. D. dissertation, University of Wisconsin, 1952.

―――― "Ōkubo Toshimichi: His Political and Economic Policies in Early Meiji Japan," *Journal of Asian Studies*, 21.2:183–197 (February 1962).

British Sessional Papers, House of Commons. *Accounts and Papers*. 1864–1866.

―――― Government Publications. *British and Foreign State Papers, 1872–1873*. Vol. 63.

Causton, E. E. N. *Militarism and Foreign Policy in Japan*. London, 1936.

Chamberlain. Basil H. *Things Japanese*. 6th ed. London, 1939.

Chiang Kai-shek. *China's Destiny*. New York, 1947.

Clement, Ernest W. "The Saga and Satsuma Rebellions," *Transactions of the Asiatic Society of Japan*, 50:14–58 (December 1922).

―――― and Uyehara Etsujirō. "Fifty Sessions of the Japanese Imperial Diet," *Transactions of the Asiatic Society of Japan*, 2nd ser., 2:5–35 (December 1925).

Colegrove, Kenneth. "The Japanese Privy Council," *American Political Science Review*, 31.6:1027–1049 (December 1927).

―――― "The Japanese Constitution," *American Political Science Review*, 25.3:589–614 (August 1931) and 25.4:881–905 (November 1931).

―――― "The Japanese Cabinet," *American Political Science Review*, 30.5:903–923 (October 1936).

―――― *Militarism in Japan*. Boston, 1936.

Coleman, Horace, tr. "The Life of Yoshida Shōin," *Transactions of the Asiatic Society of Japan*, 45:117–188 (September 1917).

Collum, Chute. "Prince Katsura," *The Contemporary Review,* 575:656–662 (November 1913).

Conroy, Hilary. *The Japanese Seizure of Korea, 1868–1910.* Philadelphia, 1960.

Craig, Albert M. "The Restoration Movement in Chōshū," *Journal of Asian Studies,* 18.2:187–197 (February 1959).

———— *Chōshū in the Meiji Restoration.* Cambridge, Mass.: Harvard University Press, 1961.

Dai jimmei jiten 大人名事典 (The great biographical dictionary). Tokyo, 1953–1955.

Dai Nihon Yūben Kōdansha 大日本雄弁講談社, pub. *Yoshida Shōin* 吉田松陰. Tokyo, 1941.

de Bary, William T., ed. *Sources of Japanese Tradition.* New York, 1958.

Den Kenjirō denki hensankai, 田健治郎伝記編纂会, ed. *Den Kenjirō den* 田健治郎伝 (Biography of Den). Tokyo, 1922.

Dull, Paul S. "Count Katō Kōmei and the Twenty-one Demands," *Pacific Historical Review,* 19.2:151–161 (May 1950).

Earl, David. *Emperor and Nation in Japan.* Seattle, 1964.

Eckstein, Gustav. *In Peace Japan Breeds War.* New York, 1943.

The Far East. 1870–1873.

Ford, Guy S. *Stein and the Era of Reform in Prussia.* Princeton, 1922.

Fujimura Michio 藤村道生. *Yamagata Aritomo* 山県有朋. Tokyo, 1931.

Fujita Takeo 藤田武夫. "Meiji shi ni okeru chihō jichi seido no igi" 明治史に於ける地方自治制度の意義 (The significance of the local government system in Meiji history), *Meiji Bunka shi ronshū* 明治文化史論集 (Essays in Meiji cultural history), Tokyo, 1952.

Fujita Tsuguo 藤田嗣雄. *Meiji kempō ron* 明治憲法論 (Essays on the Meiji Constitution). Tokyo, 1948.

Fujiwara Akira 藤原彰. *Gunji shi* 軍事史 (Military history). Tokyo, 1961.

Fukaya Hiroji 深谷博治. *Shoki gikai: jōyaku kaisei* 初期議会：條約改正 (The first Diets: Treaty revision). Tokyo, 1940.

———— "Taishō seihen no rekishiteki igi—Nihonteki seiji seikaku no shūchūteki hyōgen" 大正政変の歴史的意義—日本的政治性格の集中的表現 (The historical significance of the Taishō crisis—A manifestation of centralization characteristics of Japan), *Nihon rekishi* 日本歴史 (Japanese history), 24.5:21–25 (May 1950).

Fukuchi Shigetaka 福地重孝. *Shizoku to Shizoku ishiki* 士族と士族意識 (Shizoku and the samurai spirit). Tokyo, 1956.

———— *Gunkoku Nihon no keisei* 軍国日本の形成 (Formation of military Japan). Tokyo, 1959.

Gaimusho 外務省 (Foreign Ministry), *Dai Nihon gaiko bunsho* 大日本外交文書 (Documents on Japan's Foreign Policy). Tokyo, 1936—.

Gansetsu Yamagata kō ikō 含雪山県公遺稿 (Posthumous works of Prince Yamagata). Tokyo, 1926.

Grey, Sir Edward. *Twenty-Five Years, 1892–1916.* 2 vols. New York, 1925.

Griffis, William E. "The Elder Statesmen of Japan: The Power behind the Portsmouth Treaty," *North American Review,* 182.2:215–227 (February 1906).

———— *The Mikado's Empire.* New York, 1913.

Gubbins, J. H. *The Making of Modern Japan.* London, 1922.

Hackett, Roger F. "Nishi Amane: A Tokugawa–Meiji Bureaucrat," *Journal of Asian Studies,* 18.2:213–225 (February 1959).

―――― "Yamagata and the Taishō Crisis, 1912–1913," in Sidney D. Brown, ed. *Studies on Asia*. Lincoln, Nebraska, 1962.

―――― "The Meiji Leaders and Modernization: The Case of Yamagata Aritomo," in Marius B. Jansen, ed., *Changing Japanese Attitudes Toward Modernization*. Princeton, 1965.

―――― "Political Modernization and the Meiji Genrō," in Robert Ward, ed., *Political Development in Modern Japan*. Princeton, 1968.

Hall, Josef W. *Eminent Asians: Six Great Personalities of the New East*. New York, 1929.

Hall, Robert K. *Kokutai no Hongi*. Cambridge, Mass., 1949.

Hamada Kenji. *Prince Itō*. Tokyo, 1936.

Hara Kei nikki 原敬日記 (Diary of Hara Kei). 10 vols. Tokyo, 1950–1952.

Hara Takshi [Kei]. "Reflections on Lasting Peace," *The Living Age*, 312.4044:7–11 (Jan. 7, 1922).

Hattori Shisō 服部之總. *Meiji no seijikatachi* 明治の政治家達 (Politicians of Meiji). 2 vols. Tokyo, 1950, 1954.

Hattori Shisō and Irimajiri Yoshinaga 入交好脩. *Kindai Nihon jimbutsu seiji shi* 近代日本人物政治史 (Outstanding figures in recent Japanese political history). 2 vols. Tokyo, 1955–1956.

Hayashi Shigeru 林茂. "Rikkensei no bōei: dai ni gikai no kaisan o megutte" 立憲制の防衛: 第二議会の解散をめぐって (The defense of constitutionalism: Concerning the dissolution of the second Diet), *Kokka gakkai zasshi* 国家学会雑誌 (Journal of the Association of Political and Social Sciences), 58:486–508 (April 1944).

―――― "Dai san gikai to dai ichiji Matsukata naikaku no gakai" 第三議会と第一次松方内閣の瓦解 (The third Diet and the collapse of the first Matsukata Cabinet), *Kokka gakkai zasshi*, 62:14–37, 23–34, 23–39, 31–51 (April, May, October, November 1948) and 63:79–95 (March 1949).

Hirata Tomotarō 平田友太郎, comp. *Ōkuma monjo* 大隈文書 (Papers of Ōkuma). 5 vols. Tokyo, 1958.

Holtom, Daniel C. *Modern Japan and Shinto Nationalism*. Chicago, 1947.

Honjo Eijirō. *The Social and Economic History of Japan*. Kyoto, 1935.

Horie Hideichi. "Revolution and Reform in Meiji Restoration," *Kyoto University Economic Review*, 22.1:23–34 (April 1952).

Horie Yasuzō 堀江保藏 "Yamaguchi han ni okeru bakumatsu no yōshiki kōgyō" 山口藩に於ける幕末の洋式工業 (Western-style industries in the Yamaguchi han at the end of the Tokugawa period), *Keizai ronsō* 経済論叢 (Economic review), 40:153–165 (January 1935).

Hosokawa Ryūgen 細川隆元. *Tanaka Giichi* 田中義一. Tokyo, 1958.

Hosoya Chihiro. "Origin of the Siberian Intervention, 1917–1918," *Annals of the Hitotsubashi Academy*, 9.1:91–108 (October 1958).

House, Edward H. *The Japanese Expedition to Formosa*. Tokyo, 1875.

Idditti, Smimasa. *The Life of Marquis Shigenobu Ōkuma: A Maker of Modern Japan*. Tokyo, 1940.

Ienaga Saburō 家永三郎. "Kindai" 近代 (The present), *Nihon rekishi*, 29.10:56–62 (October 1950).

Iizuka Kōji 飯塚浩二. *Nihon no guntai* 日本の軍隊 (The military of Japan). Tokyo, 1950.

Ike Nobutaka. "The Truimph of the Peace Party in Japan in 1873," *Far Eastern Quarterly*, 2.3:286–295 (May 1943).

―――― *The Beginnings of Political Democracy in Japan*. Baltimore, 1950.

Imai Seiichi 今井清一. "Yamagata Aritomo to kanryō shihai" 山県有朋と官僚支配 (Yamagata Aritomo and control of the bureaucracy), *Chūō kōron* 中央公論 (Central review), 80.1:380–386 (January 1965).

Inoue Kaoru Kō denki hensankai 井上馨候伝記編纂会, ed. *Segai Inoue Kō den* 世外井上公伝 (Biography of Inoue). 5 vols. Tokyo, 1934.

Inoue Kiyoshi 井上清. *Nihon no gunkokushugi* 日本の軍国主義 (Japan's militarism). 2 vols. Tokyo, 1953.

―――― *Tennō sei* 天皇制 (The emperor system). Tokyo, 1953.

Irie Kan'ichi 入江貫一. *Yamagata kō no omokage* 山県公のおもかげ (Biographical sketches of Prince Yamagata). Tokyo, 1930.

Ishin shiryō hensan jimukyoku 維新史料編纂事務局, comp. *Ishinshi* 維新史 (History of the Restoration). 6 vols. Tokyo, 1939–1941.

Itō Isao 伊藤勲. "Meiji jidai ni okeru genrō, gumbatsu, seitō" 明治時代に於ける元老, 軍閥, 政党 (The *genrō*, military clique, and political parties in the Meiji period), *Hōgaku shimpō* 法学新報 (New law review), 74.2–3:73–125 (March 1967).

Itō Jintarō 伊藤仁太郎. *Meiji rimenshi* 明治裏面史 (The inner history of Meiji). Tokyo, 1927.

Itō Masanori 伊藤正徳. *Katō Kōmei* 加藤高明. 2 vols. Tokyo, 1929.

―――― *Kokubō shi* 国防史 (History of national defense). Tokyo, 1941.

Itō Takashi 伊藤隆. "Taishō shoki Yamagata Aritomo danwa hikki" 大正初期山県有朋談話筆記 (Record of Yamagata Aritomo's conversations in early Taishō), *Shigaku zasshi* 史学雑誌 (Journal of history), 75.10:68–86 (October 1966); 76.3:63–78 (March 1967); 76.9:62–81 (September 1967); 77.2:65–79 (February 1968); 77.7:63–83 (July 1968).

Iwasaki Uichi. *The Working Forces in Japanese Politics, 1867–1920*. New York, 1921.

Iwata Masakazu. *Ōkubo Toshimichi: The Bismarck of Japan*. Berkeley and Los Angeles, 1964.

Jansen, Marius B. "Opportunists in South China during the Boxer Rebellion," *Pacific Historical Review*, 20.3:241–250 (August 1951).

―――― *The Japanese and Sun Yat-sen*. Cambridge, Mass., 1954.

―――― *Sakamoto Ryōma and the Meiji Restoration*. Princeton, 1961.

――――, ed. *Changing Japanese Attitudes Toward Modernization*. Princeton, 1965.

The Japanese Chronicle (before 1918 called *The Kobe Chronicle*), Sept. 12, 1918.

Japan Times and Mail. 1921, 1922.

Japan Weekly Chronicle. 1905, 1910, 1912, 1913, 1919, 1920, 1921.

Japan Weekly Mail. 1889, 1890, 1891, 1898, 1899, 1903, 1905, 1913, 1917.

Kajima Morinosuke 鹿島守之助. *Nihon gaikō seisaku no shiteki kōsatsu* 日本外交政策の史的考察 (Historical study of Japan's foreign policy). Tokyo, 1951.

Kano Masanao 鹿野政直. "Nihon guntai no seiritsu" 日本軍隊の成立 (Establishment of Japan's army), *Rekishi hyōron* 歴史評論, 46:37–56 (June 1953).

Katsura Tarō monjo 桂太郎文書 (Katsura Tarō papers). In National Diet Library, Tokyo.

Kennedy, Malcolm D. *The Military Side of Japanese Life*. London, 1924.

Kimura Toshio 木村敏雄. *Yoshida Shōin* 吉田松陰. Tokyo, 1938.

Kiyosawa Kiyoshi 清沢洌. *Nihon gaikō shi* 日本外交史 (History of Japan's foreign relations). 2 vols. Tokyo, 1942.

The Kobe Chronicle. 1898, 1913.

Koizumi Shinzō 小泉信三. "Yamagata Aritomo to Mori Ōgai" 山県有朋と森鷗外 (Yamagata Aritomo and Mori Ōgai), *Bungei shunjū,* 44.8:83–96 (August 1966).

Kojima Kazuo 古島一雄. *Ichi rōseijika no kaisō* 一老政治家の回想 (Recollection of a politician). Tokyo, 1951.

Komatsu Midori 小松緑. *Itō kō to Yamagata kō* 伊藤公と山県公 (Prince Itō and Prince Yamagata). Tokyo, 1936.

—— *Itō Hirobumi den* 伊藤博文伝 (Biography of Itō Hirobumi). 3 vols. Tokyo, 1940.

Koyama Hirotake 小山弘健. *Nihon gunji kōgyō hattatsu shi* 日本軍事工業発達史 (History of the development of Japan's military industry). Tokyo, 1943.

—— *Kindai Nihon gunji shi gaisetsu* 近代日本軍事史概説 (A survey military history of modern Japan). Tokyo, 1944.

Koyama Itoko. *Nagako: Empress of Japan.* New York, 1958.

Kramer, Irving. "Tycoon Yamagata and Nationalism," *Contemporary Japan,* 20.4: 184–222 (April–June 1951).

Kublin, H. "The 'Modern' Army of Early Meiji Japan," *Far Eastern Quarterly,* 9.1: 20–41 (November 1949).

Kuroda Kōshirō 黒田甲子郎, ed. *Gensui Terauchi hakushaku den* 元師寺内伯爵伝 (Biography of Field Marshal Count Terauchi). Tokyo, 1920.

Kyōguchi Motokichi 京口元吉. *Taishō seihen zengo* 大正政変前後 (The Taishō political crisis). Tokyo, 1940.

—— *Dai ichiji sekai taisen zengo* 第一次世界大戦前後 (The First World War). Tokyo, 1944.

Langdon, Frank C. "Japan's Failure to Establish Friendly Relations with China in 1917–1918," *Pacific Historical Review,* 26.3:245–258 (August 1957).

Langer, W. L. "The Origins of the Russo-Japanese War," *Europäische Gespräche,* 4.6:279–322 (June 1926). English original available at Widener Library, Cambridge, Mass.

—— *The Diplomacy of Imperialism.* 2 vols. New York, 1935.

Lanman, Charles. *Japan: Its Leading Men, with an Historical Summary of the Empire.* Boston, 1886.

Lebra, Joyce C. "Ōkuma Shigenobu and the 1881 Political Crisis," *Journal of Asian Studies,* 18.4:475–487 (August 1959).

Lory, Hillis. *Japan's Military Masters: The Army in Japanese Life.* New York, 1943.

Maeda Renzan 前田蓮山. *Hara Kei den* 原敬伝 (Biography of Hara Kei). 2 vols. Tokyo, 1943.

Maeda Tamon 前田多門. *Chihō jichi no hanashi* 地方自治の話 (Talks on local self-government). Tokyo, 1930.

Maki, John M. *Japanese Militarism: Its Causes and Cure.* New York, 1945.

Maruyama Masao 丸山眞男. "Meiji kokka no shisō" 明治国家の思想 (Thought of the Meiji state), in *Nihon shakai no shiteki kyūmei* 日本社会の史的究明 (Historical studies of Japanese society). Tokyo, 1949.

Mason, Gregory. "Japan in a Changing World," *The Outlook,* 123.1:15–18 (Sept. 3, 1919).

Matsumoto Tadao 松本忠雄. *Kinsei Nihon gaikō shi kenkyū* 近世日本外交史研究 (Studies in the history of the foreign relations of modern Japan). Tokyo, 1942.

Matsumoto Tadashige. *Stories of Fifty Japanese Heroes*. Tokyo, 1929.

Matsushita Takeo 松下竹雄. *Kindai Nihon kyōiku shi* 近代日本教育史 (History of education in modern Japan). Tokyo, 1949.

Matsushita Yoshio 松下芳男. "Samban no goshimpei to haihan chiken" 三藩の御親兵と廃藩置県 (The imperial bodyguards of the three han and the absolution of the han), *Rekishi kōron*, 3.10:34–42 (October 1934).

—— *Wadai no rikukaigunshi* 話題の陸海軍史 (Topics in army and navy history). Tokyo, 1937.

—— *Meiji gunsei shi ronshū* 明治軍制史論集 (Essays on the military system in Meiji Japan). Tokyo, 1938.

—— *Nihon gunji hattatsu shi* 日本軍事発達史 (History of the development of Japan's military forces). Tokyo, 1938.

—— *Nisshin sensō zengo* 日清戦争前後 (The Sino-Japanese War). Tokyo, 1939.

—— *Kindai Nihon gunji shi* 近代日本軍事史 (Military history of modern Japan). Tokyo, 1941.

—— *Chōheirei seitei shi* 徴兵令制定史 (History of the establishment of the conscription system). Tokyo, 1943.

—— and Izu Kunio 伊豆公夫. *Nihon gunji hattatsu shi* 日本軍事発達史 *(History of Japan's Military Development)*. Tokyo, 1938.

—— *Meiji gunsei shiron* 明治軍制史論 (Historical essays on the Meiji military system). 2 vols. Tokyo, 1956.

—— *Nihon gunsei to seiji* 日本軍制と政治 (Japan's military system and politics). Tokyo, 1960.

—— *Nogi Maresuke* 乃木希典. Tokyo, 1960.

—— *Meiji no guntai* 明治の軍隊 (The Meiji military system). Tokyo, 1963.

Mayahara Jirō 馬屋原二郎. *Bōchō jūgonen shi* 防長十五年史 (Fifteen-year history of Chōshū). Tokyo, 1915.

Mayo, Marlene. "The Iwakura Mission to the United States and Europe, 1871–1873." Master's thesis, Columbia University, 1957.

McLaren, Walter W. *A Political History of Japan During the Meiji Era, 1867–1912*. New York, 1916.

——, ed. "Japanese Government Documents," *Transactions of the Asiatic Society of Japan*, 42.1:1–681 (May 1914).

Meiji bunka zenshū 明治文化全集 (Collected works of Meiji culture). Comp. Yoshino Sakuzō 吉野作造. 24 vols. Tokyo, 1927–1928.

Mitarai Tatsuo 御手洗辰雄. *Yamagata Aritomo* 山県有朋. Tokyo, 1958.

Miyake Setsurei 三宅雪嶺. "Yamagata Kō Ichidai no seijiteki kōka" 山県公一代の政治的功過 (The political pros and cons of Prince Yamagata's career), *Chūō kōron*, 37.3:65–69 (March 1922).

—— *Dōjidai shi* 同時代史 (Contemporary history). 6 vols. Tokyo, 1950.

Mizuno Rentarō 水野錬太郎. "Chihō seido no kako narabi ni genzai ni okeru sho mondai ni tsuite" 地方制度の過去現在に於ける諸問題について (Concerning the local government systems of the past and various problems of the present), *Kokka gakkai zasshi*, 51.10 (October 1938).

"The Moltke of Japan," *The Outlook*, 130.7:244–245 (Feb. 12, 1922).

Morley, James W. *The Japanese Thrust into Siberia*. New York, 1957.

Morris, J. *Makers of Japan*. London, 1906.

Mounsey, Augustus H. *The Satsuma Rebellion: An Episode of Modern Japanese History*. London, 1879.

Murata Minejirō 村田峰次郎. *Ōmura Masujirō sensei jiseki* 大村益次郎先生事蹟 (The legacy of Ōmura Masujirō). Tokyo, 1919.

Murdoch, James. *A History of Japan*. 3 vols. London, 1903–1916.

Mushakoji Saneatsu. *Great Saigo*. Tokyo, 1942.

Nagahama Masahisa 長濱政壽. *Chihō jichi* 地方自治 (Local self-government). Tokyo, 1952.

Nagaoka Shinjirō 長岡新治郎. "Yamagata Aritomo no rokoku haken to Nichi-Ro kyōtei" 山県有朋の露国派遣と日露協定 (Yamagata Aritomo as envoy to Russia and the Russo-Japanese convention), *Nihon rekishi*, 59.4:16–18 (April 1953).

Naikaku shokikanshitsu kiroku ka 内閣書記官室 記録課 (Record Office of the Cabinet Secretariat). *Nihon genkō kitei hyō* 日本原稿規定表 (Summary of Important Current Japanese Laws). Tokyo, 1906.

Najita Tetsuo. *Hara Kei in the Politics of Compromise, 1905–1915*. Cambridge, Mass., 1967.

Nakano Tomio 中野登美雄. *The Ordinance Power of the Japanese Emperor*. Baltimore, 1923.

———— *Tōsui ken no dokuritsu* 統帥権の独立 (The independence of the right of supreme command). Tokyo, 1934.

Nakayama Yasumasa 中山泰昌, comp. *Shimbun shūsei Meiji hennen shi* 新聞集成明治編年史 (A documentary history of Meiji compiled from newspapers). 15 vols. Tokyo, 1935.

Naramoto Tatsuya 奈良本辰也. *Yoshida Shōin* 吉田松陰. Tokyo, 1951.

Nation. Feb. 16, 1888, July 3, 10, 1890.

New York Daily Tribune. April 11–14, 1896.

Nihon gaikō shi kenkyū: Meiji jidai 日本外交史研究：明治時代 (Studies in the history of Japan's foreign relations: Meiji period). Tokyo, 1957.

Nish, Ian H. *The Anglo-Japanese Alliance and the Diplomacy of Two Island Empires*. London, 1966.

———— "Japan's Indecision during the Boxer Rebellion," *Journal of Asian Studies*, 20.4:449–461 (Aug. 1961).

Nishimura Fuminori 西村文則. *Genrō Yamagata* 元老山県. Tokyo, 1922.

Nitobe Inazō. *Western Influences in Modern Japan*. Chicago, 1931.

Nivisen, David S., and Arthur F. Wright, eds. *Confucianism in Action*. Stanford: Stanford University Press, 1959.

Nomura Hideo 野村秀雄. "Gumbatsu Yamagata Aritomo no zaiaku" 軍閥山県有朋の罪悪 (The crime of the militarist Yamagata Aritomo), *Bungei shunjū*, 34.2: 54–59 (February 1956).

————, comp. *Meiji Taishō shi* 明治大正史 (History of Meiji and Taishō). 6 vols. Tokyo, 1931.

Norman, E. Herbert. *Japan's Emergence as a Modern State: Political and Economic Problems of the Meiji Period*. New York, 1940.

———— *Soldier and Peasant in Japan: The Origin of Conscription*. New York, 1943.

———— "Feudal Background of Japanese Politics" (mimeographed). New York, 1945.

Ogawa Gotarō. *The Conscription System in Japan.* New York, 1921.

Ōishi Shinzaburō 大石慎三郎. "Chōheisei to ie" 徴兵制と家 (The conscription system and the household), *Rekishigaku kenkyūkai* 歴史学研究会 (The Historical Science Study Society), 194:1–12 (April 1956).

Oka Yoshitake 岡義武. "Teikoku gikai no kaisetsu" 帝国議会の開設 (The opening of the Imperial Diet), *Kokka gakkai zasshi,* 58.1:40–77 (January 1944).

———— "Dai ichi gikai ni kansuru jakkan no kōsatsu" 第一議会に関する若干の考察 (Some thoughts on the first Diet), *Kokka gakkai zasshi,* 60.2:63–78 (February 1946).

———— *Kindai Nihon no keisei* 近代日本の形成 (The formation of modern Japan). Tokyo, 1947.

———— "Gaikanteki rikkensei ni okeru seitō" 外観的立憲政に於ける政党 (The political parties in the so-called constitutional system), *Shisō* 思想 (Thought), 333.3:36–39 (March 1952).

———— *Yamagata Aritomo: Meiji Nihon no shōchō* 山県有朋: 明治日本の象徴 (Yamagata Aritomo: Symbol of Meiji Japan). Tokyo, 1958.

Ōkuma Shigenobu, ed. *Fifty Years of New Japan.* 2 vols. London, 1909.

Okutani Matsuji 奥谷松治. *Shinagawa Yajirō den* 品川彌二郎伝 (Biography of Shinagawa Yajirō). Tokyo, 1940.

Olson, Lawrence A., Jr. "Hara Kei: A Political Biography." Ph. D. dissertation, Harvard University, 1954.

Osatake Takeshi 尾佐竹猛. *Meiji Keisatsu saiban shi* 明治警察裁判史 (History of Meiji police and justice). Tokyo, 1926.

———— *Meiji Bunka Sōsetsu* 明治文化叢説 (Collected essays on Meiji culture). Tokyo, 1934.

———— *Meiji seiji shi tembyō* 明治政治史點描 (Sketches in Meiji political history). Tokyo, 1938.

———— *Nihon kensei shi taikō* 日本憲政史大綱 (An outline of Japanese constitutional history). 2 vols. Tokyo, 1938–1939.

———— *Meiji ishin* 明治維新 (Meiji Restoration). Tokyo, 1942–1949.

————, ed. *Gendai Nihon shi kenkyū* 現代日本史研究 (Studies on modern Japanese history). Tokyo, 1938.

————, ed. *Meiji Bunka no shin kenkyū* 明治文化の新研究 (New studies on Meiji culture). Tokyo, 1944.

Ōtsu Jun'ichirō 大津淳一郎. *Dai Nihon kensei shi* 大日本憲政史 (Constitutional history of Japan). 10 vols. Tokyo, 1927–1928.

Ōyama Azusa 大山梓. *Nihon gaikōshi kenkyū: Nisshin Nichiro sensō* 日本外交史研究: 日清日露戦争 (Studies in the history of Japan's foreign relations: The Sino-Japanese and Russo-Japanese wars). Tokyo, 1962.

————, comp. *Yamagata Aritomo ikensho* 山県有朋意見書 (Written opinions of Yamagata Aritomo). Tokyo, 1966.

Ozaki Yukio 尾崎行雄. *Nihon kensei shi o kataru* 日本憲政史を語る (Talks on the constitutional history of Japan). 2 vols. Tokyo, 1938.

Papinot, E. *Historical and Geographical Dictionary of Japan.* Ann Arbor, 1945.

Piggot, F. S. G. *Broken Thread: An Autobiography.* London, 1950.

Pittau, Joseph. *Political Thought in Early Meiji Japan, 1868–1889*. Cambridge, Mass.: Harvard University Press, 1967.

Pooley, A. M. *The Secret Memoirs of Count Tadasu Hayashi*. New York, 1915.

―――― *Japan at the Cross Roads*. London, 1917.

―――― *Japan's Foreign Policies*. New York, 1920.

"Prince Yamagata," *America-Japan*, 11.2:16–20 (February 1922).

Quigley, Harold S. *Japanese Government and Politics*. New York, 1933.

Reinsch, Paul S. *An American Diplomat in China*. Garden City, N.Y., 1922.

Reischauer, Robert K. *Japan Government Politics*. New York, 1939.

Ross, Frank. "The American Naval Attack on Shimonoseki in 1863," *Chinese Social and Political Science Review*, 18.1:146–155 (April 1934).

Rōyama Masamichi 蠟山政道. *Seiji shi* 政治史 (Political history). Tokyo, 1942.

Saegusa Kōtarō 三枝光太郎. "Yamagata kō to Rai Sanyō" 山県公と頼山陽 (Prince Yamagata and Rai Sanyō), *Rekishi chiri* 歴史地理 (Historical geography), 39.4:315–318 (April 1922).

Saito Man. "Yamagata: Life and Death," *Japan Times and Mail*, Feb. 11, 1922, p. 134.

Sakamoto Tatsunosuke 坂本辰之助. *Gensui kōshaku Yamagata Aritomo* 元師公爵山県有朋 (Prince Field Marshal Yamagata Aritomo). Tokyo, 1922.

Sakata Yoshio 坂田吉雄. "Meiji dōtoku shi" 明治道徳史 (History of Meiji morals), in *Meiji bunka shi* 明治文化史 (History of Meiji culture). Tokyo, 1956.

―――― *Meiji ishin shi* 明治維新史 (History of the Meiji Restoration). Tokyo, 1960.

――――, comp. *Meiji zen hanki no Nationalism* 明治前半期のナショナリズム (Nationalism of the first half of Meiji). Tokyo, 1958.

Sakatani Yoshirō, comp., 阪谷芳郎. *Segai Inoue ko den* 世外井上公伝 (*The Life of Marquis Inoue Kaoru*). 5 vols. Tokyo, 1933–1934.

Sams, Stanhope. "Last Bulwark of Feudal Japan: The Passing of Prince Yamagata," *The Independent*, 108:157–158 (Feb. 8, 1922).

Sansom, George B. *The Western World and Japan*. New York, 1950.

―――― *Japan in World History*. New York, 1951.

Satow, Ernest M. *A Diplomat in Japan*. London, 1921.

Sawada Hideo 沢田英雄. *Nihon chimei daijiten* 日本地名大辞典 (Geographical Dictionary of Japan). Tokyo, 1935.

Scalapino, Robert A. *Democracy and the Party Movement in Pre-War Japan*. Berkeley and Los Angeles, 1953.

Scherer, James. *Three Meiji Leaders: Ito, Togo, Nogi*. Tokyo, 1936.

Seeley, J. R. *Life and Times of Stein*. 3 vols. Boston, 1879.

Shinobu Seizaburō 信夫清三郎. *Mutsu Munemitsu* 陸奥宗光. Tokyo, 1935.

―――― *Kindai Nihon gaikō shi* 近代日本外交史 (History of the foreign relations of modern Japan). Tokyo, 1948.

―――― *Meiji seiji shi* 明治政治史 (Political history of the Meiji). Tokyo, 1950.

―――― *Taishō seiji shi* 大正政治史 (A political history of the Taishō period). 4 vols. Tokyo, 1951–1954.

Shively, Donald H. "Motoda Eifu: Confucian Lectures to the Meiji Emperor," in David S. Nivisen and Arthur F. Wright, eds., *Confucianism in Action*. Stanford: Stanford University Press, 1959.

Silberman, Bernard S., and Harry D. Harootunian, eds. *Modern Japanese Leadership: Transition and Change*. Tucson, Arizona, 1966.

Smith, Thomas C. "The Introduction of Western Industry to Japan During the Last Years of the Tokugawa Period," *Harvard Journal of Asiatic Studies*, 11.1:130–152 (June 1948).

———— *Political Changes and Industrial Development in Japan: Government Enterprise, 1868–1890*. Stanford, 1955.

Spinks, Nelson C., "Japan's Entry into World War I," *Pacific Historical Review*, 5.4: 297–311 (Dec. 1936).

Stead, Alfred. *Japan To-Day*. London, 1902.

————, ed. *Japan by the Japanese*. London, 1904.

Suematsu Kenchō 末松謙澄. *Bōchō kaiten shi* 防長回天史 (A history of Chōshū during the Restoration period). 7 vols. Tokyo, 1921.

Sugiyama Shigemaru 杉山茂丸. *Yamagata Gensui* 山県元帥 (Field Marshal Yamagata). Tokyo, 1925.

Suzuki Yasuzō 鈴木安蔵. *Jiyū minken: kempō happu* 自由民権：憲法発布 (Democratic movement: Promulgation of the constitution). Tokyo, 1939.

————*Nihon seiji no kijun* 日本政治の基準 (The Basis of Japanese Politics). Tokyo, 1941.

———— *Meiji ishin seiji shi* 明治維新政治史 (Political history of the Meiji Restoration). Tokyo, 1942.

Tabohashi Kiyoshi 田保橋潔. *Nisshin senyaku gaikō shi no kenkyū* 日清戦役外交史の研究 (A diplomatic history of the Sino-Japanese War). Tokyo, 1951.

Takahashi Yoshio 高橋義雄. *San kō iretsu* 山公遺烈 (The distinguished deeds of Prince Yamagata). Tokyo, 1925.

———— *Hōki no Ato* 箒のあと (After the broom). Tokyo, 1933.

Takekoshi Yosaburō. *Prince Saionji*. Kyoto, 1933.

Takeuchi, Sterling Tatsuji. "The Japanese Civil Service," in Leonard D. White, ed., *The Civil Service in the Modern State*. Chicago, 1930.

———— *War and Diplomacy in the Japanese Empire*. New York, 1935.

Tanaka Sōgorō 田中惣五郎. "The Military's Role in Japanese Politics," *Contemporary Japan*, 3.4:663–667 (March 1935).

———— *Seikan ron: seinan sensō* 征韓論：西南戦争 (Debate on the subjugation of Korea: Satsuma rebellion). Tokyo, 1939.

———— *Kindai Nihon kanryō shi* 近代日本官僚史 (History of the modern Japanese bureaucracy). Tokyo, 1941.

Teters, Barbara J. "The Conservative Opposition in Japanese Politics, 1877–1894." Ph. D. dissertation, University of Washington, 1955.

Tokutomi Iichirō 徳富猪一郎. *Kōshaku Katsura Tarō den* 公爵桂太郎伝 (Biography of Prince Katsura Tarō). 2 vols. Tokyo, 1917.

———— *Kōshaku Yamagata Aritomo den* 公爵山県有朋伝 (Biography of Prince Yamagata Aritomo). 3 vols. Tokyo, 1933.

———— *Hakushaku Kiyoura Keigo den* 伯爵清浦奎吾伝 (Biography of Count Kiyoura Keigo). 2 vols. Tokyo, 1935.

———— *Kōshaku Matsukata Masayoshi den* 公爵松方正義伝 (Biography of Prince Matsukata Masayoshi). 3 vols. Tokyo, 1935.

———— *Rikugun taishō Kawakami Sōroku* 陸軍大將川上操六 (Army General Kawakami Sōroku). Tokyo, 1942.

———— *Sohō kanmeiroku* 蘇峯感銘録 (Recollections of Sohō). Tokyo, 1944.

Tokyo Shisei Chōsakai 東京市制調査会. *Jichi gojū nen shi* 自治五十年史 (The history of fifty years of self-government). Tokyo, 1929.

Toyabe Shuntei 鳥谷部春汀. *Shuntei zenshū* 春汀全集 (The complete works of Shuntei). Tokyo, 1909.

Tōyama Shigeki 遠山茂樹. "Tennō sei guntai no seiritsu" 天皇制 軍隊の成立 (Formation of the emperor system's military forces). *Chisei* 知性 (Intellect), 11.6:2–14 (June 1949).

—— *Meiji ishin* 明治維新 (The Meiji Restoration). Tokyo, 1951.

Treat, Payson J. "China and Korea, 1885–1894," *Political Science Quarterly*, 49.4: 506–543 (December 1934).

Tsiang, T. F. "Sino-Japanese Relations, 1870–1894," *Chinese Social and Political Science Review*, 17.1:1–106 (April 1933).

Tsurumi Yūsuke 鶴見祐輔. *Gotō Shimpei den* 後藤新平伝 (Biography of Gotō Shimpei). 4 vols. Tokyo, 1937–1938.

Uchida Roan 内田魯庵. "Yamagata no shi to seitō, gumbatsu, kanryō" 山県の死と 政党, 軍閥, 官僚 (Yamagata's death and the parties, army, and bureaucracy), *Kaizō* 改造 (Reconstruction), 4.3:213–225 (March 1922).

Umetani Noboru 梅溪昇. *Meiji zenki seiji shi no kenkyū* 明治前期政治史の研究 (Studies in early Meiji political history). Tokyo, 1963.

—— "Meiji ishin shi ni okeru kiheitai no mondai" 明治維新史における奇兵隊の 問題 (The Problem of the Kiheitai in the Meiji Restoration), *Jimbun gakuhō* 人文学報 (Humanistic Studies), 3:27–36 (Mar. 1953).

Uyehara, George Etsujiro. *The Political Development of Japan, 1867–1909.* London, 1910.

Van Straelen, Henri. *Yoshida Shōin, Forerunner of the Meiji Restoration: A Biographical Study.* Leiden, 1952.

Veblen, Thorstein. "The Opportunity of Japan," *Journal of Race Development*, 6.1:23– 38 (July 1915).

Watanabe Ikujirō 渡辺幾治郎. *Monjo yori mitaru Ōkuma Shigenobu kō* 文書より見たる 大隈重信公 (A documentary biography of Count Ōkuma Shigenobu). Tokyo, 1932.

—— *Meiji shi kenkyū* 明治史研究 (A study of Meiji history). Tokyo, 1934.

—— *Jimbutsu: Kindai Nihon gunji shi* 人物: 近代日本軍事史 (Biographical history of the modern army of Japan). Tokyo, 1937.

—— *Meiji Tennō to gunji* 明治天皇と軍事 (Emperor Meiji and military affairs). Tokyo, 1938.

—— *Meiji Tennō to hohitsu no hitobito* 明治天皇と輔弼の人々 (Emperor Meiji and his advisors). Tokyo, 1938.

—— *Nihon kinsei gaikō shi* 日本近世外交史 (A history of the foreign relations of modern Japan). Tokyo, 1938.

—— *Meiji Tennō no seitoku: kyōiku* 明治天皇の聖徳: 教育 (The virtues of Emperor Meiji: Education). Tokyo, 1941.

Watanabe Shūjirō 渡辺修二郎. *Yamagata Aritomo* 山県有朋. Tokyo, 1896.

Watanabe Yōsuke 渡辺洋助. "Ishin no henkaku to Chōshū han" 維新の変革と長 州藩 (The Chōshū han and the Restoration), in *Meiji ishinshi kenkyū* 明治維新史 研究 (A study of the Meiji Restoration). Published by *Shigakkai* 史学会. Tokyo, 1929.

Wheeler, Post. *Dragon in the Dust.* Hollywood, New York, 1946.

Wilson, Robert. *Genesis of the Meiji Government in Japan, 1868–1871.* Berkeley and Los Angeles, 1957.

Yamagata Aritomo. "The Army," in Alfred Stead, ed., *Japan by the Japanese.* London, 1905.

——— "The Japanese Army," in Ōkuma Shigenobu, ed., *Fifty Years of New Japan.* Vol. 1. London, 1909.

——— "Chōhei seido oyobi jichi seido kakuritsu no enkaku" 徴兵制度及び自治制度の沿革 (History of the establishment of the conscription and local government systems), in *Meiji kensei keizai shiron* 明治憲政経済史論 (Historical essays on the constitutional government and economy of Meiji). Tokyo, 1919.

———, comp. *Rikugunshō enkaku shi* 陸軍省沿革史 (History of the development of the army ministry). New ed. Tokyo, 1942.

Yamagata Aritomo monjo 山県有朋文書 (Papers of Yamagata). In National Diet Library. Tokyo.

"Yamagata kō no shōgai to kōgyō" 山県公の生涯と功業 (The life and achievements of Prince Yamagata), *Taiyō* 太陽 (The sun), March 1922, pp. 1–92. Special issue devoted to Yamagata.

Yanaga Chitoshi. *Japan Since Perry.* New York, 1949.

Yoshikawa Suejirō 吉川末次郎. "Yamagata Aritomo to chihō jichi" 山県有朋と地方自治 (Yamagata Aritomo and local self-government), *Toshi mondai kenkyū* 都市問題研究 (Studies in city problems), 15:58–69; 16:77–82; 18:77–78 (1951).

Yoshino Sakuzō 吉野作造. *Nisshi kōshō ron* 日支交渉論 (Essays on the Sino-Japanese negotiations). Tokyo, 1915.

——— *Nijū seifu to iaku jōsō* 二重政府と帷幄上奏 (Dual government and direct access to the emperor). Tokyo, 1922.

——— "Rekishigan ni eizuru Yamagata kō" 歴史眼に映ずる山県公 (Prince Yamagata as seen through the eyes of history), *Chūō kōron*, 37.3:70–76 (March 1922).

——— "Fascism in Japan," *Contemporary Japan*, 1.2:185–197 (September 1942).

Young, A. Morgan. *Japan in Recent Times, 1912–1926.* London, 1929.

——— *Japan Under the ·Taisho Tenno.* London, 1921.

Glossary

Abu 阿武
Aizu 會津
Aki 安藝
Aoki Shūzō 青木周藏
Arisugawa Taruhito 有栖川熾仁
ashigaru 足輕

bakufu 幕府
Bizen 備前
Bunkan bungen rei 文官分限令
Bunkan chōkai rei 文官懲戒令
Bunkan nin'yō rei 文官任用令

chō 町
Chōshū 長州
chōzen shugi 超然主義
chūgen 中間
Chūō kurabu 中央倶樂部
Chūō tokkan no saku 中央突貫の策
Chūshi ha 中止派

Daidō kurabu 大同倶樂部
Dajōkan 太政官
Danko ha 斷乎派
Dannoura 檀浦
Dattai sōdō 脱退騒動
donchō naikaku 緞帳内閣
Dōshikai 同志会

Echigo 越後
Edo 江戸
Edō-Ōta 繪堂―太田
Enomoto Takeaki 榎本武揚
Etō Shimpei 江藤新平

Fujita Denzaburō 藤田伝三郎
Fuken kaigi 府県会議
fukoku kyōhei 富国強兵
Fukuchi Gen'ichirō 福地源一郎
Fushimi 伏見

genkun 元勲
genkun naikaku 元勲内閣
genkun yūgū no i 元勲優遇の意
genrō 元老
Genrō-in 元老院
genrō kaigi 元老会議
Genyōsha 玄洋社
Goshimpei 御親兵
Gotō Shōjirō 後藤象二郎
Gozen kaigi 御前会議
Gunjin kunkai 軍人訓戒
gunjiteki kanryō naikaku 軍事的官僚内閣

Hagi 萩
Hagiwara 萩原
hambatsu 藩閥
han 藩
Hara Kei (Satoshi) 原敬
Hayashi Tadasu 林董
Hayashi Yūzō 林有造
heimin 平民
Hirata Tōsuke 平田東助
Hiroshima 広島
Hizen 肥前
Hoshi Tōru 星享
Hyōbushō 兵部省
Hyōbushōyū 兵部少輔

Hyōbutaiyū 兵部大輔

Ii Naosuke 井伊直弼
Inoue Kaoru 井上馨
Inoue Kowashi 井上毅
Irie Kyūichi 入江九一
Itagaki Taisuke 板垣退助
Itō Hirobumi 伊藤博文
Itō Miyoji 伊東巳代治
Iwakura Tomomi 岩倉具視

jiyū minken undō 自由民権運動
Jiyūtō 自由党

Kagoshima 鹿児島
Kaishintō 改進党
kamme 貫目
Kaneko Kentarō 金子堅太郎
karō 家老
Kataoka Ken'ichi 片岡健一
Katō Takaaki (Kōmei) 加藤高明
Katō Tomosaburō 加藤友三郎
Katō Hiroyuki 加藤弘之
Katsu Awa 勝安芳
Katsura Tarō 桂太郎
Kawakami Sōroku 川上操六
Kenkyūkai 研究会
kenrisen 権利線
Kenseihontō 憲政本党
Kenseikai 憲政会
Kenseitō 憲政党
Kido Takayoshi (Kōin) 木戸孝允
Kiheitai 奇兵隊
Kinnōtō 勤王党
Kiyoura Keigo 清浦奎吾
Kōbe 神戸
kōbu gattai 公武合体
Kodama Gentarō 児玉源太郎
kōhi 高庇
Kokin'an 古稀菴
koku 石
Kokumin kyōkai 国民協会
Kokura 小倉
Komatsubara Eitarō 小松原英太郎
Komuro Shinobu 小室信夫
Kōno Hironaka 河野広中
Konoetai 近衛隊
Kōtoku Shūsui 幸徳秋水

kozō naikaku 小僧内閣
kuge 公卿
Kumamoto 熊本
Kuroda Kiyotaka 黒田清隆
kuromaku naikaku 黒幕内閣
Kusaka Genzui 久坂元瑞
Kyūshū 九州

Maebara Issei 前原一誠
Maeda 前田
Matsuda Masahisa 松田正久
Matsukata Masayoshi 松方正義
Meiji 明治
Meirinkan 明倫館
Mino 美濃
Mintō 民党
Mishima Tsūyō (Tsunemichi) 三島通庸
Mitajiri 三田尻
Mito 水戸
Miura Gorō 三浦梧樓
Mori Arinori 森有禮
Mōri Takachika 毛利敬親
Mōri Terumoto 毛利輝元
Motoda Eifu 元田永孚
Murata Seifū 村田清風
Murin'an 無隣菴
Mutsu Munemitsu 陸奥宗光

Nagai Uta 長井雅樂
Nagasaki 長崎
Nakaoka Shintarō 中岡慎太郎
Naniwa (Ōsaka) 難波 (大坂)
Nishi Amane 西周
Nogi Maresuke 乃木希典
Nomura Yasushi 野村靖

Odawara 小田原
Ōgosho 大御所
Ōiso 大磯
Ōkubo Toshimichi 大久保利道
Ōkuma Shigenobu 大隈重信
Ōmura Masujirō 大村益次郎
Ōyama Iwao 大山巌

ri 里
riekisen 利益線
rittō 立党
rōnin 浪人

367

ryō 兩
ryōkan 獵官

Saigō Takamori 西郷隆盛
Saigō Tsugumichi 西郷従道
Saionji Kimmochi 西園寺公望
Sakamoto Ryōma 坂本龍馬
Sakuma Shōzan 佐久間象山
sambun teiritsu 三分鼎立
samurai 侍
Sanjō Sanetomi 三條實美
Sankin kōtai 參觀交代
sanyo 參與
Sasa Tomofusa 佐々友房
Satsuma 薩摩
Seigitō 正義党
seiheitai 精兵隊
Seikantō 征韓党
Seiyūkai 政友会
Shimazu Hisamitsu 島津久光
Shimonoseki 下関
Shimpotō 進歩党
Shinagawa Yajirō 品川弥二郎
Shirane Sen'ichi 白根専一
shizoku 士族
shogun 將軍
Shōka sonjuku 松下村塾
shotai 諸隊
shōya 庄屋
Shūkai jōrei 集会條例
shukensen 主権線
Soga Yūjun 曽我祐準
Sone Arasuke 曽禰荒助
sonnō jōi 尊王攘夷
Suematsu Kenchō 末松謙澄

tairō 大老

Takasugi Shinsaku 高杉晋作
Takehashi sōdō 竹橋騒動
Tanaka Giichi 田中義一
Tanaka Kōkan 田中光顯
Tani Kanjō 谷干城
Teikokutō 帝国党
Teiseitō 帝政党
Terauchi Hisaichi 寺内壽一
Terauchi Masatake 寺内正毅
Tokudaiji Sanenori 徳大寺實則
Tokugawa Ieyasu 徳川家康
Torio Koyata 鳥尾小弥太
Tosa 土佐
Toshi mondai kenkyū 都市問題研究
Tōyō dōmei ron 東洋同盟論
Toyotomi Hideyoshi 豊臣秀吉

Umeda Umpin 梅田雲濱

Wakamatsu 若松

Yamada Akiyoshi 山田顯義
Yamaga Sokō 山鹿素行
Yamagata Arinori 山縣有禮
Yamagata Aritomo 山縣有朋
Yamagata Isaburō 山縣伊三郎
Yamaguchi 山口
Yamamoto Gonnohyōe 山本権兵衛
Yanagawa Seigan 梁川星巖
yo wa ikkai no buben 余は一介の武辨
Yoshida Shōin 吉田松陰
Yoshikawa Kensei 芳川顯正
Yuda 湯田
Yūhōsha 有朋者

zokurontō 俗論党

Index

Harvard East Asian Series